A
COMMUNITY
IN
SPITE
OF **ITSELF**

SMITHSONIAN SERIES IN ETHNOGRAPHIC INQUIRY
William L. Merrill and Ivan Karp, Series Editors

Ethnography as fieldwork, analysis, and literary form is the distinguishing feature of modern anthropology. Guided by the assumption that anthropological theory and ethnography are inextricably linked, this series is devoted to exploring the ethnographic enterprise.

A
COMMUNITY
IN
SPITE OF ITSELF

SOVIET JEWISH ÉMIGRÉS
IN NEW YORK

FRAN MARKOWITZ

SMITHSONIAN INSTITUTION PRESS

WASHINGTON AND LONDON

Editor: Jill Mason
Production Editor: Jack Kirshbaum
Designer: Linda McKnight

Library of Congress Cataloging-in-Publication Data

Markowitz, Fran.
    A community in spite of itself : Soviet Jewish émigrés in New York
/ Fran Markowitz.
        p.   cm.
    Includes bibliographical reference and index.
    ISBN 1-56098-200-4 (cloth).—ISBN 1-56098-225-X (pbk.)
    1. Jews, Soviet—New York (N.Y.)—Social conditions.   2. Jews—New
York (N.Y.)—Social conditions.   3. Immigrants—New York (N.Y.) –
Social conditions.   4. New York (N.Y.)—Social conditions.   5. New
F128.9.J5M27   1993
305.892′407471—dc20   92-31989

British Library Cataloging-in-Publication data available

Manufactured in the United States of America
96   95   94   93   5   4   3   2   1

⊗The paper used in this publication meets the
minimum requirements of the American National
Standard for Permanence of Paper for Printed
Library Materials Z39.48-1984.

For Zhenya, Sasha, Lina, Marina, and Misha
with gratitude and love

CONTENTS

A NOTE ON TRANSLITERATION

Choosing a system of transliteration from Russian to English invariably leads to problems. Weighing the desire to appeal to a wide English-speaking audience with the need to respond to the accuracy demanded by Slavicists, I have decided to follow the precedent set by S. Frederick Starr in his inspiring book *Red and Hot: The Fate of Jazz in the Soviet Union* (New York: Oxford University Press, 1983). Starr's decision to use conventional English spelling (omitting, for the most part, soft signs and double vowels) for words in the body of the text, while using the Library of Congress style to present bibliographical references, works well to solve the dilemma of satisfying both generalists and specialists.

PREFACE

This book presents an ethnographic study of Soviet Jewish émigrés in New York City, conducted five to seven years after the 1978–80 peak of immigration. It documents a short time span in the process of Soviet Jews' confrontations with and adjustment to a new society and illustrates the directions that culture change takes within this immigrant group. In particular, it investigates the reworking of émigrés' knowledge and sentiments, or, the constitution of their community.

I lived in Brighton Beach in Brooklyn, New York, from January 1984, through September 1985, the last years of the pre-*glasnost* era, during which time virtually no new immigration from the USSR occurred. My major research interest was to study the interrelated processes of individual and cultural change among immigrants who had arrived four to ten years earlier. Dissatisfied with theories of cultural determinism yet skeptical of notions of boundless individualism, I wished to observe and understand how the individual shapes his or her social world, while also studying the impact of social structure in shaping the individual. My goal was to immerse myself among not-so-new Soviet Jewish immigrants in order to learn from them what kinds of new lives they have made for themselves, and into what kinds of new lives they have fallen, and how they make sense of these changes. In the process of living among them, it became apparent to me that as they were individually experimenting with and carrying out their new lives, these tens of thousands of émigrés from various parts of the USSR had also, though quite unwittingly, formed a community.

This community differs from "urban villages" or "institutionally complete" ethnic neighborhoods, because it is based neither on an attempt to replicate the Old Country nor on any kind of formal organizations. In fact, many Soviet immigrants, communal service workers, resettlement professionals, journalists, and perhaps even you, the reader, may argue that while Soviet Jewish immigrants have certainly established new lives, they have not created a community. I do not think that this is so, and what follows is, in effect, my proof.

This book begins with a three-part introductory chapter, which first offers some novel approaches toward the definition of community and then considers the problem of cross-cultural adaptation in the late twentieth century. The second and third parts of this chapter situate Soviet Jewish émigrés within the "third wave" of post-1965 immigration to the USA and then describe, in brief, my research strategies and methodology.

Chapter 2 may also be considered an introductory chapter, because it provides historical background on Soviet Jews and their emigration. While much of the material included here has been gleaned from secondary sources, Soviet Jewish history is presented in the words of émigrés as it moves ever closer to the present.

Chapters 3 through 6 may be considered the "meat" of the study. They describe Soviet Jewish immigrants' knowledge, sentiments, and patterns of sociability, demonstrating how these strands of social and symbolic life intertwine old and new ways of being and doing, to create a fabric of mutual understanding—a subculture, or community—that unites former Soviet Jews.

Chapter 7 examines the sociosymbolic community from the perspective of on-the-ground social forms. One of the purposes of this chapter is to show, first and foremost, that Soviet Jewish émigrés do have tangible channels of mutual assistance and group expression, but, because these derive directly from a key value that deplores bureaucratic institutionalization, that may be imperceptible to outsiders. Second, I wish to demonstrate the means by which this community is manifested, showing that "ethnic" demonstrations occur continuously, although individuals themselves participate sporadically. Indeed, the goal of this chapter is to show that instead of visible, formal organizations that provide the foundation of many an ethnic community, Soviet Jewish émigrés have devised quasi-institutions. While they are barely perceptible, they do exist as focal points, and this existence, I contend, gives substance to an otherwise amorphous idea of community.

The two-part concluding chapter deals with the power of social interaction, particularly that of talk, in creating and maintaining the Soviet émigré community. I argue that this community differs in form from the traditional community, but nevertheless serves the same purposes of group identity, expression, and ballast as those *Gemein-schaftn* delineated earlier by Toennies (1957). In closing the study on the eve of the dissolution of the USSR, I probably raise more questions than provide answers about the nature of community in this, our postmodern world.

Two appendices are provided to guide the reader through the text. Appendix A outlines the emigration-immigration procedures that virtually all Soviet emigrants (1970 through 1989) endured. Appendix B provides brief portraits of fifteen men and women who arrived in New York between 1975 and 1983; as "key informants," they are quoted throughout the book.

In writing, rewriting, and reediting this book, I have tried as much as possible to allow explanations and generalizations to derive from conversations and interactions with my "field partners" and with my predecessors and contemporaries in anthropological and sociological endeavors rather than to force my findings into a tidy theoretical framework. Thus, as a perceptive reviewer chided me, you will find, "*Communitas* here, Schneider on kinship there, Wirth on urbanism, and Berger and Luckmann on knowledge elsewhere." In trying to explicate the elusive phenomenon of post-migration adaptation and community formation, I was not talented, or perhaps brash, enough to develop one overarching explanatory model that would do justice to the tremendously complex social life, often contradictory cultural patterns, and powerful personalities I encountered. As Stephen A. Tyler (1986, 132) remarks, "We confirm in our ethnographies our consciousness of the fragmentary nature of the post-modern world, for nothing so well defines our world as the absence of a synthesizing allegory, or perhaps it is only a paralysis of choice brought on by our knowledge of the inexhaustible supply of such allegories that makes us refuse the moment of aesthetic totalization, the story of stories, the hypostatized whole."

What I have tried to do is tap the well of anthropological and sociological knowledge to help me decode the conversations and stories of former Soviet Jews as a way toward comprehending the meanings and motivations in these new immigrants' lives and to shed some light on the variety of social processes that intertwine to form their community. I leave it to you, the reader, to judge my success in these endeavors.

ACKNOWLEDGMENTS

In the 1970s, when Soviet Jews began to arrive in the United States, I had no knowledge of Russian and little understanding of Soviet-Russian culture. I did know, however, that this migration was intrinsically interesting to students of urban life and ethnicity. In the fall of 1980, I came to the Department of Anthropology at the University of Michigan, where I received the education, training, and encouragement I needed to make this study of the Soviet Jewish immigrant community.

The research upon which this study is based was supported by several sources. The National Institute of Mental Health granted me a predoctoral fellowship, which funded much of my fieldwork. In addition, the Center for Russian and East European Studies (CREES) and the Horace G. Rackham School of Graduate Studies, both of the University of Michigan, and the Wenner-Gren Foundation for Anthropological Research awarded me grants for fieldwork and the writing of my doctoral dissertation. I am most grateful to all of these institutions for the faith they have shown in my work.

Several friends and colleagues at the University of Michigan encouraged my efforts and influenced this product. I am indebted to all the members of my doctoral dissertation committee for teaching me with their helpful comments: Professors William G. Lockwood, Zvi Gitelman, Susan Harding, Sergei Kan, and Aram A. Yengoyan. I am also grateful to several members of the anthropology faculty, especially Professors Sherry B. Ortner and Raymond C. Kelly, for their intriguing courses and interest in my work. My sincere gratitude goes to Professor John V. A. Fine, Jr., of the Department of History, who read this entire manuscript and helped to change it from a Ph.D. thesis into a book. Éva Huseby-Darvas, Ken George, Susan Pattie, and Nick James were the best fellow graduate students one could ever wish for. I owe them, and Linda Swift, Kathryn Kozaitis, Olga Supek, Lynne Schepartz, Lynne Robins, and Anna Kertulla, a great debt for their stimulating conversation and friendship.

To my family, who could never quite understand what I was doing hanging out in Brighton Beach "with the Russians," thanks for trying! My uncle, Rabbi Gilbert Shoham, was very helpful in clarifying issues of Jewish law and in providing me with references to answer my questions. Maximillian Blue, and later Maxie and Bluey, provided me with the blind love of their feline companionship both in the field and in the ivory tower.

Steven M. Cohen, Riv-Ellen Prell, and William L. Merrill offered me valuable comments on earlier versions of this manuscript. Jill Mason, my editor, contributed many helpful suggestions that have made this a more readable and coherent book.

Finally, I am most indebted to all the people who made the journey from the USSR to Brighton Beach, Ocean Parkway, Queens, and other exotic locales in New York, who welcomed me into their lives, fed me—oh how they fed me!—and answered my tiresome questions, thereby making this book possible. Knowing the difficulty of establishing friendship, only to have the friend leave, my appreciation is all the more deep. Most names have been changed or simply not used in the text. Here I would like to acknowledge Marina and Vadim, Sasha, Mark and Ida and Nelly and Alex, Lina and Vadim and Dmitri and Misha, Lala and Iya, Irina, Larisa and Ilya, Zhenya and Dima and Aleona (*moya vtoraya semya*), Lillia and Misha, Leonid and Galina, Elvira, Ella and Victor, Tetya Raya and Channa and Naum and Faina and Donny and Elizabeth, Iskra and Misha, Tetya Nessa and Igor, Inna and Igor, Sophy, Misha and Lena, Rita, Tetya Fanya and Helen, Violetta, Rita and Yan and Tetya Maya, Nina and Oleg, Yefim, Dina and Misha, Ella, Luba and Sasha, Igor, Mila and Volodya and Dina, Misha, Polina and Gregory, Marina, Eugene, Aida, Kira, and all my neighbors, friends, friends of friends, and students. *Bolshoye Vam spasibo!*

A
COMMUNITY
IN
SPITE
OF **ITSELF**

1.
THE NATURE OF THE STUDY

Beginning in the late 1960s, the government of the Soviet Union responded to international and internal pressures and allowed over 300,000 Jews to emigrate. Between 1972 and 1984 around 100,000 resettled in the United States, about half of whom chose to live in greater New York City. While a sizable literature describes the conditions under which Jews live in the USSR and traces the development of this emigration movement,[1] the dynamics of their post-migration experiences have received spotty attention. The media periodically report on this "third wave of immigration,"[2] focusing primarily on the exotica of the émigré enclave,[3] and on the peculiar character of former Soviet citizens' encounters with the West.[4] Several Jewish philanthropic organizations have sponsored studies of Soviet émigrés' adjustment to the United States,[5] and a number of authors have focused their attention on specific aspects of Soviet immigrants' lives.[6] With few notable exceptions (e.g., Orleck 1987; Gold 1985; Simon 1985, 1983; Simon and Brooks 1983; Levkov 1984; Gitelman 1984; Jacobs and Paul 1981), and these usually just in passing, analysts have largely ignored the wider question of community among Soviet Jewish émigrés.

Perhaps the reason for this oversight is that a Soviet Jewish community in the traditional sense may not exist. The several thousands of individual émigrés in the United States come from many different parts of the USSR and have settled in scores of American cities. They represent a wide age range and a variety of occupations, educational backgrounds, interests, and aspirations. In the New York City area alone, more than fifty thousand Soviet immigrants are dispersed throughout the boroughs and in neighboring suburbs. Even those areas in Brooklyn and Queens with large numbers of émigrés are not homogeneous ethnic enclaves, and immigrants as a rule interact on a daily basis with other American neighbors and co-workers. Further, Soviet Jewish immigrants have not established a unifying structure of voluntary organizations or religious institutions, nor have they gathered into any one occupational niche. Although they all speak Russian and share the experience of living in and then leaving the USSR, these commonalities alone do not constitute community.

This study is the first major investigation into the question of community among Soviet Jewish émigrés in New York.[7] Since they are residentially dispersed and occupationally diversified, this study is not nor can it be a traditional ethnography of a discrete society located in one specific place. Instead, the study focuses on the emergence and articulation of group consciousness—the recognition and expression on the part of many disparate individuals that they are members of a specific collectivity. While it investigates the influence of their Jewish, professional, and regional identities formed in the USSR and the ways in which ingrained patterns of behavior and value orientations developed in their home country inform daily life, this study is not a discussion of "continuities and discontinuities" of Soviet-Russian-Jewish culture in exile. Rather, it aims to document and explicate the social and symbolic commonalities that emerge as meaningful in constituting a new group identity after immigration. In short, the study is an inquiry into the phenomenon of ethnogenesis, the interlinked processes of individual change and culture creation that result in the appearance of a specific (immigrant, ethnic) group, identifiable both to its members and to those outside the group, where one had previously not existed.

What follows then is a story of life among Soviet Jewish émigrés in New York City and their ongoing endeavors to make sense of and put to use the new realities they encounter there. In its broadest sense, my aim in telling this story is to understand post-migration adjustment as a dynamic between immigrants' prior knowledge, or the symbolic systems by which they have always interpreted the universe, and current practice, their daily goings-on in a sociocultural environment different from, and sometimes threatening to, the one in which they learned to become competent, knowledgeable adults. But this is not merely a documentary of individuals making independent new lives for themselves. Try as I might to understand post-migration adjustment in this way, I am continually struck by the social nature of acculturation and the ironic emergence of community among immigrants who never expected this to happen.

Taking issue with psychological inquiries that show how individuals pass through a predictable series of stages,[8] and analogous sociological approaches,[9] I have not presented post-migration adjustment as a unilinear evolutionary scheme by which immigrants are transformed into ethnic versions of their host society's majority group. Instead, I have sought to show how culture change and community formation derive from immigrants' active experimentation with their knowledge. Adjustment to cross-cultural migration is here presented as an ongoing, creative, sometimes integrative, sometimes fragmentary process. It is a dialectical relationship between old and new knowledge schemes mediated by people's practice and social reflection—a process of change, but not an *ex*change of old for new in a predictable direction.

Two major concepts are central to the theoretical framework of this study. First is the idea of human freedom, the ability for self-reflection, evaluation, and change.[10] The second, in concert with the first, is the premise that human consciousness is shaped by being a member of a society. Reality itself, along with culture and knowledge, is made, molded, and changed by people within the context of a community.

These two premises underlie the study to no small extent and reflect my dissatisfaction with overarching evolutionary theories of culture change. Further, because of their inherent rejection of the idea that people or their cultural systems can resist or direct the process of change, I have difficulty with explanatory schemes that view change solely as the result of dominance, or, in its more subtle version, cultural hegemony.[11] Most important, these theoretical approaches simply do not work in the case of Soviet immigrants.

In contrast, Pierre Bourdieu (1977, 20) looks to human consciousness for an explanation of how social transformations occur. He indicates that when a disconnection takes place between the way people expect things to be and the reality of the way things are, they begin to evaluate their thoughts and actions. It is the practical result of such personal reflections that produces change: "Even if they affect practice within narrow limits, the fact remains that whenever the adjustment between structures and dispositions is broken, the transformation of the generative schemes is doubtless reinforced and accelerated by the dialectic between the schemes immanent in practice and the norms produced by reflection on practices, which impose new meanings on them by reference to alien structures."

Human choice and the ability to effect change are never absolute or total. Nor is freedom. Clifford Geertz (1973a, 52) emphasizes this point in his statement that every individual becomes him- or herself through the internalization and use of a specific symbolic system. "Becoming human is becoming individual, and we become individual under the guidance of cultural patterns, historically created systems of meaning in terms of which we give form, order, point and direction to our lives." These rules of behavior and belief, while they limit the full extent of human choice, make possible individual creativity as they provide people with the security of knowing, and therefore being able to predict a normal course of events in, their physical and social universes. Berger and Luckmann (1967, 52) explain, "The inherent instability of the human organism makes it imperative that man provide a stable environment for his conduct." Lacking this, people face normlessness or anomie, and in losing the capacity to understand and take part in the world around them, they become anxious, insecure, overwhelmed, and not free.[12]

The cultural patterns that provide direction and meaning for humans' lives take shape within the context of a community. Following Marx, through Berger and Luckmann (1967) and Bourdieu (1977), not only is each individual's consciousness determined by one's social being, but reality itself—definitions of the physical universe and the social world—is socially constructed as well. This seemingly objective reality provides each person with a sense of social location, an identity, a point of reference. Gerald Suttles (1972, 264) elaborates this point: "The desire to find a social setting in which one can give rein to an authentic version of oneself and see other people as they really are is not some unanalyzable need but the most fundamental way in which people are reassured of their own reality as well as other people." Community provides individuals with an arena in which they can test, express, and confirm their subjective understandings of the realities they encounter.[13] While such a setting is essential to all people, it takes on added significance for immigrants, whose realities—of self and society—are daily called into question as they confront new situations and new meanings for old situations in the normal course of their lives.

Common knowledge and common values, coupled with consciousness of these commonalities, are the stuff by which people delineate social space and form their communities.[14] René Koenig (1968, 29) envisions community as "a relationship which is characterized . . . by the fact that the people concerned are conscious of the relationship, conscious of its limits, and conscious of its differences from other similar relationships." This acknowledgment of significant boundaries that set people off from each other (Barth 1969) is what makes a community real (see also Cohen 1985; Suttles 1972, 13); it is the recognition on the part of its members (and those outside its boundaries) that they share in or identify with "something" that they do not have in common with others. And by virtue of this common identification, people find that they have something to say to each other.

To say something to each other necessitates having a medium of mutual expression and understanding, a language. Mikhail Bakhtin (1981) describes a linguistic universe of polyphonic languages out of which people (everyday speakers, authors, interest groups) select meaning-imbued, historically informed voices to use with each other so that they can create and demonstrate slices of their identity and place. A unifying language is always in the process of creation through dialogue; it is not a received monolithic entity available to any and all users. "A unitary language," Bakhtin (1981, 270) explains, "is not something given (*dan*) but is always in essence posited (*zadan*)—and at every moment of its linguistic life it is opposed to the realities of heteroglossia." In order that a word, a voice, a language be meaningful to its listeners and speakers (and readers and writers), it must derive from and clarify its meaning through dialogue with other meanings.

Community, like language, emerges from dialogues. Indeed, community is made possible only through conversations among people who assume that they are alike, and with other societies and cultures that are viewed as alien and come to be placed along a continuum of difference. From the multifaceted world of roles, identities, beliefs, and values, we select some, discard others, and attempt to make our choices worthwhile and right by confirming them with people we believe are like us while we also contrast them from those we believe to be foreign. Community then is not a passed-on, unchanging tradition, but rather an ongoing dialogue among people and traditions.

Community is constituted by talk. In the words of John Dewey (1929, 5), "Men live in a community in virtue of the things which they have in common and communication is the way in which they come to possess things in common." Community boundaries are established and solidified (and indeed sometimes changed) through the patterned selection of conversation partners and reinforced as information is exchanged.

Conversation, as Berger and Luckmann (1967, 253) claim, is "the most important vehicle of reality maintenance." But, they continue, "At the same time as the conversational apparatus ongoingly maintains reality, it ongoingly modifies it." Conversation is not solely a repetitive confirmation of what is; it also enables the participants to process and integrate new information and different perspectives.

Community, like conversation, is an interactive process that both confirms shared understandings and contests them via incorporation of new realities encountered and carried back to the community by its individual members. George Herbert Mead (1962, 168) elucidates: "We are not simply bound by the community. We are engaged in a conversation in which what we say is listened to by the community and its response is one which is affected by what we have to say." Community, then, is shaped by its members just as each individual is molded by it. While the community provides meaning and security for its constituents, the knowledge it contains is often susceptible to challenge and alteration through conversations among its members.

The development of community among Soviet Jewish émigrés is treated in this study as one such ongoing dialogue. Their prior knowledge, Jewish "nationality," and native Russian language, brought with them from the USSR, and the discovery of common migration experiences provide initial symbolic material by which the immigrants unify and then differentiate themselves—and are delineated by others—from other Americans. And it lays the groundwork for intensification of intragroup interactions, embellishment of symbolic content, sharing of new experiences, and further conversations.

As they talk, Soviet Jewish immigrants exchange ideas, opinions, evaluations, and judgments, creating an arena in which prior knowledge does battle with competing meaning systems. The community they construct from these confrontations is not and cannot be one consistent, monolithic set of responses. It resembles instead what Lévi-Strauss (1970, 16–17) calls *bricolage*,[15] a compendium of materials, ideas, histories, and designs, which emerges from the ongoing dialectic between the immigrants' polyphonic cultural system and the new meanings they discover through practice in the society they have chosen for their new home. "The triumph of community," Anthony Cohen (1985, 20) notes, "is to contain this variety [so] that its inherent discordance does not subvert the apparent coherence which is expressed by its boundaries." This is a study of the social and symbolic construction of one such community.

WHY SOVIET JEWISH IMMIGRANTS?

The object of this study is to explore how it is that disparate individuals come together after migration to constitute a community. The subjects of the study, however, are individual human beings, émigrés from the USSR who arrived in America between 1974 and 1983. My focus on their particular migration experiences derives from a desire to continue expansion of anthropological inquiry into modern, complex societies and, in so doing, to provide material for the comparative study of urban life, ethnicity, and culture change.

The case of Soviet Jewish immigration to America provides a rich source for documenting three interrelated phenomena. First, Soviet emigrants' migration involves cross-cultural acculturation without urbanization, an ideal situation for examining culture change because of a built-in control for social scale. City-dwellers both in the USSR and in the USA, Soviet Jews employ patterns of adjustment to a new cultural environment that call into question the explanatory force of the *Gemeinschaft-Gesellschaft* split (after Toennies 1957), or the transition from small-scale, traditional societies to complex, urban life, to account for post-migration community formation. Of related interest is the question of how ethnicity—in this case, Jewishness and Russian-ness—is contextually constituted and how individuals respond when the meanings they attach to their ethnic identity conflict with those of others who identify as members of the same group. And finally, since the immigrants use the knowledge and social skills they developed in the USSR to make sense of their new lives in the USA, their experiences and the reflections they make on their two lives provide great insights into the differences and similarities between Soviet society, its values, beliefs, and structure, and American society.

First things first.

Unlike the image of the Russian Jew portrayed in *Fiddler on the Roof,* Jews in the USSR are, as a rule, highly educated cosmopolites who live and work in the center of Soviet life. More than five decades have passed since Jews left their "little communities," the *shtetls,* or Jewish towns, and urban ghettos that kept them separate from the rest of the populace. During the 1920s and 1930s, they flocked into major Russian cities, earned university degrees, and entered the professions. Cutting ties with what they considered to be a parochial and repressive past, most abandoned Yiddish for Russian and the Jewish religion for socialist "internationalism." In the 1970s and 1980s, Soviet Jews were often forward-looking members of the professional elite who identified strongly with their work, "international" or high culture, and the idea of progress.

Throughout the large cities of the Soviet Union, Jews live dispersed among their Russian and Ukrainian (and Georgian, Latvian, etc.) neighbors.[16] With the exception of a tiny, but well-publicized, fraction of the population who participated in Jewish study groups,[17] and underground religious congregations coordinated by, among others, the Lubavitcher Hasidim (see Panish 1981, 84–109), Jews had no specifically Jewish communal organizations and virtually no public religious life to bind them together. With the exception of *Sovetish Heymland,* a Yiddish literary journal that in the 1970s and 1980s attracted a very small readership, and the *Birobidzhaner Shtern,* the Yiddish-language daily of the Jewish Autonomous Province located five thousand miles east of Russia's major Jewish population centers, there are no nationwide or citywide Jewish publications. Nor, for the most part, do Jews want exclusively Jewish forms of information and entertainment; Jewish writers, poets, artists, actors, musicians, and dancers contribute their talents to the cultural mainstream and take great pride in their "international" accomplishments. For all intents and purposes, Soviet Jews have achieved what Gordon (1964, 70) calls "structural assimilation."

Jews in the Soviet Union recognize each other as Jews, and are recognized as Jews by non-Jews, by their physical appearance, last names, and sometimes by mannerisms or a Yiddish-tinged accent. They also carry the nationality designation, *Jew,* in their identity documents. However, while they constitute a juridico-historical category in the Soviet Union, Jews there do not form a community.

This fact alone differentiates the "third wave" of Jewish migration both from rural to urban population movements and from earlier waves of Jewish immigration to the United States. Soviet Jews arrive in New York with no Jewish communal institutions to transfer to their new home, no *landsmanschaftn* (mutual aid societies based on town of origin), no political organizations, burial societies, or religious institutions. They have no "village," urban or otherwise, to transport to the new setting, for they are experienced cosmopolites, accustomed to living in Soviet-Russian society's mainstream. In America, initially at least, they are confronted with a seemingly familiar environment but, due to linguistic barriers, occupational nonequivalence, and simply the newness of the locale, one in which they do not hold a central, known place.

Soviet Jewish immigrants' construction of community is therefore not an attempt to transfer group-specific social institutions from the home country to a different location but represents a creative response to rethinking, upon encountering an unknown environment, who they are. That their mode of making sense of alien surroundings via community formation, while subtle and largely unconscious, resembles, to some extent, strategies of those migrants who experience urbanization as well as cross-cultural encounters may be indicative of a general process of acculturation and culture change.

The movement of Soviet Jews from metropolitan centers in the USSR to New York City presents an ideal case not only for examining how migration impels the construction of community out of a historico-cultural category but also for examining the effect of prior urbanism on post-migration adaptation. An assumption underlying much of the literature on migration states that because urbanites everywhere are accustomed to occupational specialization, dependence on many different kinds of people and institutions for meeting survival needs, and acting in terms of roles rather than as individuals in public situations, people moving from a city in one part of the world will have little difficulty adjusting to city life in another (Daniels 1983; Pisarowicz and

Tosher 1982; Richmond 1974). While a number of studies have challenged Louis Wirth's (1938) classic statement that "urbanism is a way of life,"[18] several investigations of migration point to prior urbanism—no matter what the context—and personality characteristics associated with urban living as key predictors of successful post-migration adjustment. Grubel and Scott (1967) note that highly skilled urbanites' identification with and dedication to their jobs tend to lower the psychic costs of migration. A cosmopolitan attitude, they argue, weakens dependence on the home culture and "makes it easier [for people] to adjust to the environment of the culture to which they migrate" (p. 135).

As far back, however, as 1951, Ralph Beals (p. 7) suggested that "rural-urban acculturation and cross-cultural acculturation differ only in degree and do not represent substantially different processes of change." It would follow then that migration without urbanization is also disruptive, but that this disruption takes a different form from that characterizing rural-urban immigration. Anthony Richmond (1981, 319) points out that "the more highly skilled and professional immigrants must achieve a high level of instrumental acculturation to function effectively at the level for which they have been trained," and contrasts their post-migration decline in status with the position of low-skilled workers who are "able to function with lower levels of linguistic flexibility or cognitive acculturation." These findings indicate that while urban-to-urban migrants do not confront the radical change in lifestyle, that is, the *Gemeinschaft-Gesellschaft* split experienced by urbanizing migrants, they do face a challenge to their image of self and how they fit into the status structure of their new society.

What then are the strategies international urban-to-urban migrants develop in response to confronting a seemingly similar environment in which their training and level of expertise are often not recognized, and where things look the same but have different meanings from those in the home country? How do people adjust to lower social (and initially, at least, economic) levels than those to which they were accustomed and with which they strongly identify?

Eleanor Rogg's (1971) study of Cuban refugees in New Jersey points to the immigrant community as the source of psycho-social satisfaction for individuals who have suffered downward mobility and disconnection between the identity they developed at home and that foisted on them as a result of migration. The community Cubans have created is institutionally strong and socially close-knit. It resembles immigrant enclaves developed by rural-to-urban migrants both in form and in structure. "By providing a comparison referent which does not demean the refugees' self-worth as well as by providing psycho-social strength and satisfaction to its members" (Rogg 1971, 481), the Cuban-American community acts as a bridge between old ways of thinking of self and a new social reality.

Illsoo Kim's (1981) investigation into the Korean immigrant community in New York City addresses these same issues. Noting that immigrants experienced with urban life possess the resources for, and usually achieve, rapid and successful economic adjustment, Kim indicates that their desire for community is just as strong as that of urbanizing immigrants. Koreans, he explains (p. 204), experience a sense of "status alienation" resulting from forfeiture of their professions after migration. As they develop small businesses, they earn more money than ever before but lose the prestige (formerly) attached to their high education and white-collar professions. Their efforts to construct new communities, Kim points out, respond to individuals' desires for social esteem and for reinforcement of occupational and lifestyle choices made after migration.

While the impetus for community formation and the functions the Cuban and Korean communities serve are identical, the Korean community, unlike the Cuban, is not territorially based. Korean immigrants have settled in ethnically heterogeneous neighborhoods throughout New York City. Yet, although they are residentially dispersed and live among Americans, they have separated themselves "both socially and psychologically from the larger American society . . . [and] have attempted to achieve a sense of community among themselves. . . . They identify themselves primarily as Koreans and treat the institutions of the larger society as an alien force that is strange, unmanageable, and frequently hostile" (Kim 1981, 181).

These cases of Cuban and Korean urban migrants in the United States, as they represent two contrasting community forms, provide a comparative backdrop for the present investigation of community among Soviet Jewish immigrants. While Cubans have created commercial-residential enclaves, Koreans have not; but both groups are characterized by communities of affect based on psychological and social preferences for fellow immigrants. Territoriality occupies an intermediate position among Soviet émigrés. Several thousands live in Brighton Beach, a neighborhood with a definite Russian presence, where a wide range of goods and services is offered for a Russian-speaking immigrant clientele. An equal, if not larger, number of Soviet Jewish immigrants, however, have opted for residential dispersal throughout Greater New York City.

Despite the variation in immigrants' commercial-residential patterns, it appears that the needs for self-affirmation, prestige, and belonging impel creation of community, whether localized or scattered, among urban-to-urban migrants. The present study will demonstrate that Soviet Jewish immigrants are no exception by describing the factors that impede or encourage localization of this community. One goal of the research, then, is to discover how cross-cultural urban-to-urban migration differs, if indeed it does, from rural-to-urban migration, in order to make even a small contribution to the building of a general theory of social change.

The post-migration experiences of Soviet Jewish émigrés allow for consideration not only of comparative migration and the contextual nature of urban life but also for observing how ethnicity is shaped and reinterpreted after making a change in sociopolitical context (see Keyes 1981, 27–28). Émigrés from the USSR arrive in the United States not only speaking Russian and accustomed to Soviet rules of public behavior, but also as Jews—according to their parentage, their identity documents, and their own consciousness. Yet upon contact with American Jews, at resettlement agencies and in their new neighborhoods, Soviet émigrés find their Jewishness challenged. Even more disturbing to them is the discovery that they are referred to by fellow Jews, by other Americans, and increasingly among themselves as "Russians," an identity that was inconceivable for them in the USSR. This study aims to illustrate the contrasts between the conception, constitution, and communication of Jewishness in the USSR and in the USA, and to delineate strategies that the émigrés develop and employ in response to finding their own definitions and behaviors ethnically suspect. In broader terms, this is an investigation into the process of ethnic change resulting from encounters among people who identify with the same ethnic label but attach different practices, behaviors, and meanings to it.

Finally, although Jews compose but a minuscule and nonrepresentative portion of the Soviet population, they were raised, educated, and employed within the mainstream of Russo-Soviet life; therefore, émigrés' values, behaviors, and beliefs can certainly provide insights into Soviet "national character."[19] Precisely because they rejected, by leaving, the Soviet system, Russian Jewish emigrants are an ideal population for evaluating the pervasiveness of personality characteristics—such as conformity, obedience, xenophobia, patience, generosity, authoritarianism—reported by analysts of *Homo Sovieticus* (e.g., Mead 1955; Inkeles and Bauer 1959; Mehnert 1961; Miller 1961; Bronfenbrenner 1972; Smith 1976; Shipler 1984). With the dismantling of the Soviet Union and the reshaping of the form and history of its former republics currently under way, these characteristics have come under even sharper scrutiny. In addition to simply describing these psychological tendencies, this study examines their influence upon Soviet immigrants' encounters with America and how they shape the cultural contours of the émigré community.

FIELDWORK AMONG SOVIET JEWISH IMMIGRANTS

From January 1984 through September 1985 I lived in Brighton Beach in Brooklyn, New York, the acknowledged commercial-residential-entertainment hub of the Soviet Jewish émigré community. With the recognition that Russian Jews are a dispersed immigrant population, I decided that my best entry point into their social world would be to live in the ethnic enclave. As Sydel Silverman (1984, 14) explains, "much anthropological study is still rooted in a *place,* where the anthropologist can be a participant observer and witness a wide range of activities in his informants' lives. . . ." I avoided, however, confining my study to the localized community of Brighton Beach, because such research would have created a skewed caricature of Soviet Jewish immigrants in America. Throughout my fieldwork, I strived to meet people from a broad range of living and occupational arrangements, seeking out those who live within and outside of Brighton Beach, as well as those who work in the American mainstream and those whose business or services cater to an immigrant clientele.

My research was facilitated by a number of interrelated phenomena. First, the curious and hospitable nature of my neighbors enabled me to establish good relationships with both "Russian" and "American" residents of Brighton Beach. Being "an American who speaks Russian" (and especially because my command of Russian parallels many immigrants' command of English) made me a sought-after conversationalist, a wonder in a land where Americans speak only English. A few days after arriving in Brighton I went into a card store where a Russian-speaking man was attempting to ask a question of the store's Korean-American clerk. I answered the question in Russian, and the customer's eyes opened wide as he exclaimed, "You are an American and you speak Russian!" He invited me to join him and a friend for a light supper later that evening in one of Brighton Beach's Russian restaurants. This serendipitous meeting led to long and fruitful associations with a number of informants/friends.

Most Americans (really American Jews) in Brighton Beach are elderly, and their children have long ago moved away from the neighborhood. My arrival in Brighton Beach was welcomed by "Americans." "It's so nice to see young Americans moving back to the area."[20] They took this opportunity to complain about the "Russians" taking over, while in the same breath stating that this takeover helped stem the tide of Puerto Ricans moving in. Thus, from the very start of my fieldwork, the question of ethnic boundaries, intra-Jewish or otherwise, became a critical issue.

During much of the time I lived in Brighton Beach I directed a study of Soviet immigrants' Jewish identification and affiliation patterns for the Federation of Jewish Philanthropies of New York. In the process of hiring interviewers and conducting interviews myself, I met many émigrés, most of whom live outside Brighton Beach, and was thereby able to extend the range of my informants. Moreover, I was afforded the opportunity to become well acquainted with the web of Jewish social service and cultural facilities, and their personnel, that serve the immigrant population.

Another strategy I used to make contact with immigrants was teaching an English As a Second Language course two nights a week in Brighton Beach. The classroom provided an ideal context for discussing themes of utmost concern to the immigrants. More so than "how to find a good job," the students wanted to discuss the American criminal justice system, presidential and congressional elections, the meaning of "freedom," religious holiday traditions, and the matter of raising children and grandchildren in their new country. Being a teacher, more than anything else, gave me great visibility and legitimacy among my Russian-speaking neighbors in Brighton Beach.

As to fieldwork techniques, I learned early on that formal interviews, and what seemed from the many ethnographies I read to be the anthropologist's ubiquitous notebook and pencil or tape recorder, were not to be part of my repertoire. At one of my first meetings with an émigré couple in their store on the fashionable east side of Manhattan, as we were discussing artistic circles in Moscow, I was told, "You don't have to write. Put your paper away." Sometimes I would go off to the bathroom and scribble notes, but mainly I relied on what I came to see as an ethnographer's greatest asset: a good memory. Despite the informal nature of my interviews, I advised all my informants of what I was doing and why I was there talking to them, and as a result, most people were quite concerned that I get everything they told me "right." I was frequently asked if everything was clear and then checked to make sure that I understood, not only the language but also the feeling or analysis that was being conveyed. Interviews were usually conversations, and I ended up answering just about as many questions as I asked. Often I was called upon to explain why Americans do this or that, to act as a cultural broker in questions of banking, college loans and scholarships, American cuisine and food products, medical insurance, and school curricula.

My participant-observation, living, shopping, teaching, and "hanging out" in Brighton Beach, became a normal inclusion into the everyday life and special occasions of increasingly close friends. These friends introduced me, often as "our American friend who speaks Russian," to their families and friends, and then I met friends of friends, until by the time I left New York I had established relationships, of greater or lesser magnitude, with more than two hundred individuals. Quotations throughout this text were gathered from many people in several ways: some from informal interviews with people I met with a couple of times; others from ongoing dialogues with "key informants"; and still others from conversations at parties and other gatherings, chance meetings with friends of friends, comments from neighbors, and statements by students in my English As a Second Language classes. A brief profile of fifteen key informants is found in Appendix B to "embody" their quotations and to guide the reader through specific, yet not atypical, individuals' interpretations of their experiences. Names are changed to protect their privacy.

Many of my relationships with these key informants are still intact. I have returned to Brighton Beach seven times since September 1985, most recently in August 1991, to join in celebrations, to update my findings, and simply to visit. In a sense I feel as though I have never left, since the telephone, and much more rarely the U.S. Postal Service, keeps me in contact with the close friends I have made. Yet the stunning developments in the USSR from 1987 to the present have resulted in some major changes in the émigré community, most notably the receipt of scores of thousands of newcomers and a sense that the community has a new divide between the "old wave" immigrants of the 1970s and the post-1987 "new wave." For the most part, however, the ethnographic present of this book occurs in the years 1984–86.

On a final note, I must add that there is a slight bias to my "sample" of informants. First, because I concentrated on Russian and Ukrainian Jewish émigrés (the vast majority of America's Soviet immigrants), the question of non-Jewish Soviet immigrants as well as of other Jewish subgroups (e.g., Georgian and Bukharan Jewish immigrants) is beyond the scope of this study. So, too, are the famous literary, dance, musical, and political figures who have received so much attention from the press. Their stories have been or will be told by others elsewhere. Second, I had no contacts with or even exposure from afar to the so-called Russian Mafia. Rumors, yes, but personal contacts—none. I did not look for them, nor, I suspect, were they eager to tell their stories to me. It might then be said that the information I gleaned is biased toward intelligentsia-technocrats and does not well enough reflect severe problems among the immigrants. I was frequently told by informants that anywhere from 65 to 99 percent of Russian immigrants are *podonki* (dregs, garbage) and that my naivete and good-heartedness prevented me from seeing this obvious fact. The same people told me, often in the same breath, of the great contributions this group of immigrants is making to America because of the education and intellect they bring with them. Perhaps I lean too far to this second interpretation. But then again, perhaps not.

2.

HISTORICAL BACKGROUND

Soviet Jewish immigrants consciously underscore the importance of history in explaining who they are, why they left the USSR, and how they are forging ahead with life in their newly adopted country. People usually recount their individual life histories beginning not with their own births but a generation or two before, with, "My grandfather was a . . ." or "My grandmother's family. . . ." As they tell their life stories, they create a self that is shaped not against, but as part of, a perceived historical process. Reflecting internalization of a Marxist-influenced worldview, their stories show human beings not as atomistic, self-made individuals, but as intimately related to and molded by a larger-than-life historical process. In fact, when discussing reasons for Jewish emigration in the 1970s, some, like Maxim, who emigrated in 1979, have gone so far as to state, "It was like a wave. The additional reasons do not matter as much as the moment in history. Each people, I think, has its purpose, its mission, and the mission of Jews in Russia is over. That's why we left."

Their group's history, coupled with the notion that each individual is intimately involved with the historical process, shapes Soviet émigrés' encounters with each other, America and Americans, and especially with American Jews. This is all the more interesting because by the late 1940s, Jews' specific history and the contributions that Jews had made in shaping the Soviet state were officially eliminated. Nonetheless, in the course of conversations with me, several informants insisted on giving history lessons, explaining, as did Vladimir, "You Americans do not know, do not understand anything about our experience. You think all of Russia is bears and Siberia. People in my building—they would show me how to use an elevator, my wife they would show hot water in the sink and ask if we had electricity [in Russia]. Why do they all expect us to be like Tevye from Sholom Aleichem stories? We're an educated, modern people. I want you to understand this."

The understanding that former Soviet Jews have of their history and the pride they take in the niche that they had carved for themselves in the USSR contrasts with the way they believe they are perceived by Americans. Thus, Russian Jews recount how they, or their parents or their grandparents, welcomed the opportunity to become part of the modern world, to move to cities, to receive university educations, to leave behind the parochialism of Yiddish for Russian, a language of the world, to participate in Russian culture. A practicing physician in America since 1979 states, "My children laugh and make fun of me because I'm from a small town. They say, 'Papa, tell us about life on the farm.' I only smile and make up stories for them because as soon as I finished [secondary] school, I came to Leningrad to the medical institute and stayed." This doctor is not alone; in a recent survey of New York City's Soviet Jewish immigrants, only 22 percent stated that they were born in a small town or village, while a much smaller portion (7 percent) reported that they had lived in one immediately prior to emigration (Federation of Jewish Philanthropies 1985, 11; see also Fain 1984).

Many more report with pride that their families have lived in large Russian cities for generations: Natalya recounts, "We were a wealthy Jewish family in Leningrad. My grandfather and his brother had a butter factory—even after the Revolution"; and Yakov begins his reminiscences with, "My grandmother is from a well-educated family; her father was an engineer from the first guild of engineers who were, during the time of the tsars, allowed to settle in Odessa. They had an apartment in the center of town and lived very well."

In embracing the opportunities to become part of the wide world, Jews, in most cases, abandoned distinctive traditions. Zvi Gitelman (1972, 499–500) points out that the early Socialist state's Jewish schools failed mainly because parents thought of Russian culture as superior to their own and wanted their children to avoid the stigma of speaking Yiddish-accented Russian throughout their lives. Certain passage rites were increasingly rejected to show solidarity with modernity. Yakov explains, "Father had been circumcised at birth and he wanted me to be circumcised, but grandfather [Mother's father] forbade it. In those days they believed it was a barbaric practice, and he forbade it for health reasons."

Despite the watering down of tradition and high rates of intermarriage, especially in the years immediately following the Revolution (Pinkus 1988, 90–91), Jews did not lose sight of their distinctiveness. They became a cosmopolitan people, highly educated professionals, part of the modern world; but they always remained strangers (Simmel 1950a) in their native country. Their history, and their understanding of that history, helps clarify the reasons these Soviet-born Jews decided to leave the land of their birth, their expectations for new lives in America, and how they have adjusted to their new surroundings.

In recounting their history, Soviet Jewish émigrés give voice to their common knowledge, or to a "collective consciousness," thereby laying the foundation for a community (Spicer 1980, 306). As they mull over their past, they carve for themselves a legitimate place in world history and shape their current position vis-à-vis other groups in America. Thus, in the narrative that follows, immigrants' own stories will be used as much as possible to present this historical overview.

JEWS IN RUSSIA: AN OVERVIEW

The history of Jews in Russia has been a long and painful one, marked by religious persecution, denial of civil rights, onerous taxation, and ever-present uncertainty due to threats of expulsion and pogroms. Yet by the end of the nineteenth century almost five million Jews resided within the boundaries of the Russian Empire, where they had succeeded in creating and maintaining self-governing communities, a culture, and a way of life of their own.

Although Russia itself housed no Jews until late in the eighteenth century, Jews have lived in the present-day USSR for thousands of years. Following Greek traders and settlers eastward since before the Common Era, Jews became part of these Greek settlements in the Crimea, where they engaged in trade in port cities on the Black and

Azov seas (Dubnow 1916, 1:14–17; Baron 1964, 2–3). Later, during the Middle Ages, the Jewish rulers of Khazaria reigned between the Black and Caspian seas, bounded by the Volga River to the north, for several centuries. Legends tell that the khagan of the Khazars, around 740, decided to abandon paganism and embraced Judaism after conferring with representatives of Christianity, Islam, and Judaism (Dubnow 1916, 1:21). Khazaria prospered in the eighth and ninth centuries and played an important role in international trade, situated as it was between the caliphate in Baghdad and the Byzantine Empire. Between 965 and 969, however, Khazar territories on the Volga were routed by Slavic tribes under the leadership of the Prince of Kiev, pushing the Khazars back to their small holdings on the Black Sea. The Khazars finally fell to Russian troops in 1016, and the ancient Jewish settlements on the Crimea suddenly received new members.

When Vladimir, Prince of Kiev, decided in 986 to abandon paganism, he, too, according to legend, invited representatives from the three Western religions to woo him. Vladimir embraced Christianity, rejecting Islam because of its prohibitions against alcohol and Judaism because Jews were a dispersed people without an earthly kingdom: "How then dare you teach others when you yourselves are rejected from God and scattered? If God loved you, you would not be dispersed in strange lands. Do you intend to inflict the same misfortunes on me?" (Vladimir, reported in Dubnow 1916, 1:30; also Baron 1964, 4–5).

According to Dubnow (1916, 1:32), Vladimir's choice of religion had dire consequences for the future of Russian Jewry: "The coincidence of the settlement of Jews in Kiev with the conversion of Russia to the Greek Orthodox faith foreshadows the course of history. The very earliest phase of Russian cultural life is stamped by the Byzantine spirit of intolerance in reaction to the Jews" (see also Pinkus 1988, 4).[1] By the beginning of the twelfth century, the Jewish colony in Kiev had been ravaged by its first pogrom.

Jews from the west, especially from Catholic Germanic lands, moved eastward into Poland, Lithuania, Byelorussia, and the Ukraine during the Middle Ages. Although they themselves do not know how or when their ancestors arrived in these Slavic regions, many Russian Jews point to their German last names (e.g., Epshteyn, Rosen, Schvartz, Ortenberg) in discussing their Jewish background and the origins of their families. This migration occurred in two waves, the first during the Crusades, when Jews suffered great persecution, and then in even greater numbers during 1348–1349, the year of the Black Death, when Jews were accused of poisoning the wells of Europe. Jews were welcomed by the Polish king and nobility for their commercial expertise, and many were enlisted into the service of the Polish nobility to serve as estate overseers and tax collectors. Others established inns, liquor distilleries, and small general stores on the estates. Jews became the only visible link between the diverse peasant population (Polish, White Russian, Lithuanian, Ukrainian) and their Polish lords.

The situation was particularly tense in the Ukraine, where Catholic Polish nobility virtually owned the Russian Orthodox serfs. In their bid for independence, organized by Khmelnitzki and his cossack brigades, the Ukrainian peasants directed their hatred at the Jews. Not only were these Jews enforcers of the nobility's taxation policy, but their status as nonbelievers added ideological fervor to the economic issue. Between 100,000 and 500,000 Jews were killed during the ten years (1648–1658) of the peasant-cossack rebellion.[2] Dubnow (1916, 1:44) points to this peasant war as the inauguration of "the era of pogroms, which Southern Russia bequeathed to future generations down to the beginning of the twentieth century."

After the fall of Kiev (1240) to Mongol invaders, Russia remained in a state of conquest for over two centuries. Moscow, unlike Kiev, Chernigov, and other early cities, was not utterly destroyed, and in 1480 Ivan III of Moscow repudiated the Mongol overlordship and refused to pay tribute. Moscow became the capital of Russia, while Ivan expanded and unified his empire.

Under this new regime, the Empire instituted a policy of Jewlessness. Moscow, having experienced a brief Judaizing heresy (1490–1504), expelled its small number of Jews and denied them even temporary residence permits to conduct trade. Even Peter the Great (1682–1725), who opened Russia to Western influences, refused residence to Jews. In an interview with the pro-Jewish mayor of Amsterdam in 1698, Peter claimed that the Russian people were not ready to welcome Jews and felt that Jews, although potentially useful to the economic development of the Empire, would suffer at the hands of his Russian subjects (Baron 1964, 11). Although several Jewish converts found their way into influential positions in Peter's court, they failed to pave the way for the admission of professing Jews, as they did in

Western Europe. The Russian quarantine against Jews lasted well into the eighteenth century.

During the reign of Anna Ivanova (1730–1740), it was discovered that despite prohibitions, numerous Jews were still residing in the Ukraine, working on the estates of Russian landlords as overseers, tax collectors, and innkeepers. The empress issued an expulsion order in 1739, and the following year these 573 Jews (292 males, 281 females) were forced to leave Russia. To summarize this period, Benjamin Pinkus (1988, 10) concludes, "Deep hostility toward the Jews, originat[ed] not only in the general xenophobia prevailing in ruling circles in Moscow, but also in fear and hatred of the Jews because they were judged 'enemies body and soul of Christianity'."

Russia's expulsion of fewer than six hundred Jews stands in ironic contrast to its receipt of millions of them with the partitioning of Poland (1772, 1793, 1795), by which the Empire acquired Byelorussia, the Ukraine, Lithuania, Latvia, and several Polish provinces. After the first partition, a series of measures was passed to contend with the ever-increasing numbers of Jews in the Empire. First, recognizing their fiscal and legislative usefulness, a governmental decree of 1776 sanctioned the continuation of the *kehillas,* Jews' self-governing councils of elders. Under Polish rule these councils not only oversaw Jewish daily life but also collected taxes for the king. This dual function was preserved by the government of the Russian Empire. Then, Empress Catherine II (the Great) instituted a one-ruble-per-capita tax on all Jews and placed restrictions on liquor distilling and selling in cities, occupations in which many Jews were engaged. Most significant of all was her *ukaz* (decree) of 1791 that responded to objections by Moscow's merchant class to the few newly arriving Jewish traders. Catharine stopped the influx of Jews from the western provinces by proclaiming that "the rights [previously] extended to Jews as members of guilds of merchants and burghers related only to territories newly taken over . . ." (Baron 1964, 21). In 1794 an additional decree circumscribed the area of Jewish settlement and established taxation of Jews at double the rate of Christians (Dubnow 1916, 1:318). Thus was laid the foundation of the Jewish Pale of Settlement.

The Pale of Settlement consisted of the Russian Empire's westernmost strip of territory from the Black to the Baltic seas. Jews were permitted residence only in this area and, unless they had special dispensation, were forbidden from its major cities as well as those outside of it. Since tsarist Russia had an internal passport system in which religion and minority status were recorded, free movement from one place to another was all but impossible. The *shtetl,* a Jewish town or nonagricultural village in the midst of peasants, was the typical residential pattern of Jews in the Pale. With few exceptions, it was not until the Russian Revolution that Jews were freed from residential and occupational restrictions.

The nineteenth century brought many changes to the lives of Russian Jews. They experienced an era of "enlightened absolutism" (Dubnow 1916, 1:225) under the reign of Alexander I (1801–1825), whose general policy toward his Jewish subjects was Russification. Toward this end, he granted Jewish children free access to public schools, secondary schools, and universities, where Russian Orthodox religious instruction was a central part of the curriculum.

Alexander I's reign was followed by a period of particularly severe privations during Nicholas I's regime (1825–1855). Nicholas I considered Jews to be "leeches" and an "injurious element" to his country and devised a plan that would use them to his advantage and, in the process, reduce their numbers. In 1827 he decreed that a certain number of eighteen-year-old Jewish men would be drafted each year for twenty-five years of military service. Nicholas did not grant civil rights to Jews when demanding military service of them, as the rulers of Western European countries did. Further, he assigned to the *kehillas* the duty of selecting the conscripts; boys as young as twelve were sometimes drafted to fill the quota when enough eighteen year olds could not be found, which fostered dissent and class antagonism within the Jewish communities.

Alexander II (1855–1881), known for emancipating Russia's serfs, ended Nicholas's repressive measures and extended to Jews civil liberties and other opportunities to participate in the wider world of the Russian Empire. On the heels of these reforms, however, Russia's Jews found themselves again pushed back into the Pale and not only deprived of the liberties they had been granted, but also made the objects of even greater restrictions and violent pogroms.

Although only one Jew, a woman who played a tangential role, was involved in the assassination of Alexander II (March 1, 1881), rumors spread that the Jews were responsible for this deed and that the new tsar wished for vengeance during the upcoming Easter season. The government called the pogroms that spread throughout the

Ukraine a popular reaction to Jewish exploitation. The following year, Alexander III (1881–1894) signed the May Laws prohibiting new settlements outside towns and making it unlawful for Jews to conduct business on Sundays and Christian holidays. Five years later, these "temporary laws" were reviewed and confirmed, and a strict quota system was imposed on Jewish secondary school and university enrollment.

In the course of these wide pendulum swings, Russian Jews expanded their horizons from the parochial, religion-based *shtetls,* in which tradition and rabbinical authority were unquestioned, to the incorporation of *Haskalah* (enlightenment) into their secular and religious lives. Some went even further, looking outward to Russian revolutionary movements aimed at bettering conditions for all. Toward the end of the nineteenth century, demoralized by a series of counter-reforms after a period of liberalization, increasing numbers of Jews came to believe that Russia held no future for them and emigrated to North America and Palestine (see table 1).[3]

Conditions worsened for Jews under the last tsar, Nicholas II (1894–1917). Using the strategy of diverting revolutionary fervor against the regime to hostility against the Jews, official and semiofficial state organs (newspapers, handbills, secret patriotic organizations) encouraged anti-Semitic agitation by calling the Jews aliens responsible for the rebellious movements, which they characterized as foreign to the Russian people. Anti-Jewish pogroms, framed as popular protests against "Jewish revolution," swept the south of Russia at the turn of the century (Dubnow 1920, 3:69–99; Pinkus 1988, 27–30). The pogroms at Kishinev (April 1903) and Gomel (September 1903), followed by more looting and rioting in dozens of other locales in 1904, drove from Russia to America more than 125,000 Jewish emigrants (Dubnow 1920, 3:104). Among those who stayed, many, especially the youth, increased revolutionary activities and, in direct reaction to the massacres, participation in self-defense organizations.

Along with the "popular" anti-Semitic campaign came an executive one. Arbitrarily interpreting residence policies outlined in Alexander III's May Laws of 1882, the tsar's government expelled many Jewish families from their village homes. The already crowded towns and cities of the Pale offered little economic relief for new arrivals. Measures forbidding Jews from buying or renting parcels of land precluded their entry into agriculture. Pauperism increased tremen-

TABLE 1
Jewish Emigration from Russia in the 1880s

Year	Number of Emigrants
1881	8,193
1882	17,497
1883	6,907
1884–1886	15,000–17,000 a year
1887	28,944
1888	31,256
1889	31,889

Source: Dubnow, *The History of the Jews in Russia and Poland from the Earliest Times until the Present Day* (1918), 2:373.

dously. "Between 1894 and 1898 the number of Jews without definite occupations amounted in certain cities to fifty percent and more" (Dubnow 1920, 3:23–24; also see Baron 1964, 113–117).[4] Opportunities for the youth to escape the poverty of the Pale were further constricted by a tightening of quotas on places for Jews in institutions of higher learning.

As a response to rising revolutionary momentum throughout Russia—strikes among workers and university students, as well as proposals and petitions to the tsar—Nicholas accepted the Bulygin Constitution of August 6, 1905, which provided for universal suffrage, including the Jews, and a freely elected assembly (Duma) with consultative privileges.[5] This constitution was followed by a decree on August 27 to permit academic self-government. Rather than quelling the strikes, these half-hearted measures further enraged students and workers, resulting in a general strike in the industrial centers during October 1905. The tsar responded on October 17 by granting all civil liberties and included a provision for a legislative Duma in his decree.

Despite threats of Passover and election-day pogroms if Jews exercised their newly won right to vote, twelve Jews were elected to the Duma. This first elected legislature in Russia was composed primarily of deputies with liberal sympathies, and less than three months after its inauguration on April 27, 1906, it was dissolved by the tsar.

Succeeding attempts at self-government also failed; the second Duma (February–June 1907) was short-lived, and the third, or "Black Duma," was stacked with reactionaries.

In 1911, a year after 1,200 Jewish families were expelled from Kiev, a ritual-murder trial was held there and used to scapegoat the Jews. European Christian courts had brought such charges against Jews at least since the case of William of Norwich in 1144 (Langmuir 1991; Holmes 1991, 101). The number of cases reached a peak during the Middle Ages, but virtually disappeared from court dockets after the Renaissance. Thereafter, the beliefs behind these charges about Jews persisted in "blood libel legends," that recount how "Jews murder an innocent Christian child for the ritual purpose of mixing the victim's blood with their matzah around Easter time" (Dundes 1991, vii). During the nineteenth century, ritual-murder accusations began to be brought against Jews with increasing frequency, first from within the Greek communities in Damascus and Cairo, and then later in Central Europe (Holmes 1991, 103; Rappaport 1991, 309–312).

The facts of the 1911 case were, in short, that the body of a thirteen-year-old Russian boy was discovered near a brick-kiln owned by Mendel Beilis, a Kievan Jew. In July of that year, Beilis was accused of the murder, arrested, and imprisoned for more than two years. In the meantime, the perpetrators, the boy's own relatives, were questioned and released in order to keep negative attention focused on Beilis, and by extension, the Jews. This old tactic of diverting dissent onto the Jews used by the Russian government was particularly timely; in September 1911 Prime Minister Stolypin was assassinated at the theater in Kiev by a man whose father was of Jewish descent. The two events combined to further inflame anti-Jewish sentiments and distract the populace from their rising hostility toward the regime.

Mendel Beilis and the Jews of Russia, however, were fortunate that this ritual-murder case attracted international attention. The English, French, and American press condemned the tsar for medieval anti-Semitism and pogroms. Under international pressure, Nicholas finally dictated that no "popular reprisals" be taken against the Jews, and in October 1913 Beilis was acquitted.

During the First World War, under tsarist decrees, Jews were deported first from border provinces and then from neighboring regions. An elderly woman (born 1905) who came to the United States in the mid-1920s recalls the evacuation of her small town in Lithuania near the Baltic Sea:

> I don't remember exactly how it happened because I was a young girl at that time, but all of a sudden there was an order that all Jews had to pack up and leave. That's how we came to Nizhni Novgorod: today this city is called Gorky. That's where they have the brilliant physicist Sakharov. I don't understand why they keep him there. This was a beautiful city; I remember the *kuptsy* [merchants] had their market stalls at the top of the steps and how, when I was young, I ran up and down those steps to do the marketing. Now I can't tell you exactly when we came to Nizhni Novgorod or who expelled us from our town. I think, I don't know, that the Red Army was on its way, and we were sent out because they were killing Jewish bourgeois. Since we were the rabbi's family, we would have been slaughtered if we stayed.[6]

THE SOVIETIZATION OF JEWISH LIFE

The Early Years

Not surprisingly, the March Revolution of 1917 was joyfully greeted by much of the Jewish populace throughout Russia. Several months later, after almost a century of turbulence culminating in tsarism's most severe repressions and an outpouring of anti-Jewish violence, the Bolshevik government's espousal of brotherhood and equality, expressed in Lenin's Declaration of the Rights of Nationalities after the November Revolution, represented for Russia's Jews the fulfillment of a long-awaited dream: equal rights and the opportunity to live in peace.

Early in the revolutionary struggle, however, Bolshevism had failed to attract many Jewish followers. The leading Bolshevik Jews—Trotsky, Zinoviev, Kamenev, Sverdlov—were, as Gitelman (1972, 108–110) points out, "marginal men," alienated from and often disavowing ties to a specifically Jewish community. Most Jews preferred instead to join their own Socialist or Socialist-Zionist parties or to remain politically uninvolved. During the ensuing years of revolution and counter-revolution (1917–1921), Jews, especially in Ukraine, experienced an exceedingly violent series of pogroms from Ukrainian nationalist and White Army forces. In contrast, "the official attitudes of the Red Army and the relative mildness of Red Army pogroms allowed the Jews to regard that Army as their protector" (Gitelman 1972, 165). As a result, by 1919 the Red Army's role as liberator reaped wider political benefits for the Bolsheviks among Jews, giving to them a near monopoly by 1921.

The Communist party thereby gained new and enthusiastic members from former Jewish political parties. It was in fact many of these Jews who, through their own zeal as political agitators in the *Evsektsiia* (Jewish section) of the party, destroyed traditional Judaism. Their decision to bring Jews into the "wide world" was achieved through show trials of the Jewish religion, its clergy and practices, and resulted in synagogue closings, prohibition of traditional Jewish self-government (*kehillas* and rabbinical courts), dissolution of Zionist organizations, closing of Jewish community-sponsored schools and social welfare institutions, and a ban on Hebrew (see Gilboa 1982).

Consistent with the theme expressed by Lenin (1951, 20) that all national cultures contain within them two competing elements—a bourgeois/clerical, reactionary one, and a workers' culture—Jewish Communists declared Hebrew, the sacred language of religion, and Zionism as diversionary, anti-Socialist elements of Jewish culture. Proletarian Jewish culture was seen as revolving around Yiddish, the "jargon" spoken in everyday life and the language of the Jewish workers' struggle. Use of Yiddish was encouraged by the *Evsektsiia;* it was the language of instruction in its schools for Jewish children and frequently the language used for party agitation. Just as the 1920s and 1930s witnessed the closing of many synagogues and the disgrace of Jewish clergy, this era also gave rise to a florescence of Yiddish-language literature and a large number of Russian-language literary achievements by Jewish authors.

It is difficult to evaluate the accomplishments of the *Evsektsiia*, because analysts of its brief history disagree as to its role in furthering the development of Jewish culture in the USSR. Benjamin Pinkus (1988, 62) views the *Evsektsiia* leaders as well-meaning revolutionaries who attempted to carve a legitimate place for Jews in the new regime by reworking their culture: "The *Evsektsiia* had fought hard against the Zionist-Socialist Parties, against democratic Jewish communities, against the Jewish faith, and against Hebrew culture. It had, however, succeeded in shaping a secular life pattern based on Yiddish as the recognized national language of the Jewish nationality; in fighting for Jewish national survival in the 1920s; and in working in the 1930s to slow down the assimilatory process of the Sovietization of Jewish language and culture." Others, however, believe that the Jewish proletariat substitutes that the *Evsektsiia* established in place of the institutions they destroyed, perhaps because they were hastily conceived and lacked the affect of centuries of tradition, never quite rallied Jewish participation and were therefore short-lived (Gitelman 1972, 270–371; Baron 1964, 229–237; Levin 1988, 85–86). Immigrants themselves, especially those under age forty, generally do not know what the *Evsektsiia* was or what specific contributions it made. Indeed, former Soviet Jews (usually in their late fifties or older) point to the Yiddish-language *Evsektsiia* schools they attended as their Jewish education, although the curriculum of these schools was devoid of religious instruction and Jewish history.

By 1930, when the Communist party of the Soviet Union (CPSU) abolished the *Evsektsiia,* it had already succeeded in changing the face of Russia's Jewish population. *Evsektsiia* members had agitated Jews to leave behind the parochialism of the Pale for participation in the new Soviet state. Gitelman (1972, 114–118, 165–166) notes that Jews were over-represented in the Red Army (more to avenge murdered family members than from commitment to the Socialist cause), in the Cheka (secret police—Lenin trusted Jews not to be counter-revolutionaries), and as managers and officials in the state apparatus. In the last case, the jobs provided sorely needed steady salaries and represented sweet revenge for Jews who had been denied civil service posts under the tsars (see also Pinkus 1988, 79). Furthermore, the new government had a pressing need for literate, urbane personnel, since those who had formerly held administrative positions (the Whites) either refused to cooperate or fled.

During these early years of the new Socialist system, Jews began moving into new enterprises and continued their flight from provincial *shtetls* into large cities and from the old Pale into the Russian interior. Lvavi (1971, 92–94) notes that by 1925 over 100,000 Jews were engaged in agriculture, farming land in Byelorussia and the Ukraine, particularly in the Crimea, that they found vacated due to the wars. Baron (1964, 246–247) points to the remarkable growth of the Jewish population in cities of the interior. He notes that although Odessa still had the greatest number and the largest proportion of

TABLE 2
Jewish Population of Major Cities

City	1897	1926
Odessa	139,267	153,194
Kiev	32,093	140,256
Moscow	8,095	131,244
St. Petersburg/Leningrad	16,944	84,480
Kharkov	11,013	81,138

Source: Baron, *The Russian Jew under Tsars and Soviets* (1964), 247.

Jews, its Jewish population grew by 10 percent while Moscow's increased sixteenfold.

Economic conditions in Russia during the post-revolutionary years were dire, especially in the countryside. "What a Jewish agronomist said at a convention of Jewish farmers in Minsk in January, 1928, about the conditions in the small Jewish communities was doubly valid for the preceding years. He contended that the population of these Jewish hamlets was dying of hunger three times daily, and that its only foodstuff consisted of potatoes" (Baron 1964, 251). Given this terrible situation and the demand that Jews, along with the rest of the population, radically change their economic patterns and occupations, their movement into the large cities is no surprise. The Revolution had brought about widespread unemployment for a significant portion of the Jewish population—for clergy, schoolteachers, and the commercial class. Artisans were not clearly separated from traders and were also condemned as exploiters.[7] In industrial centers, former traders, shopkeepers, and self-employed craftsmen had greater opportunities to become wage-earners by joining the ranks of the proletariat, becoming members of artisans' cooperatives, or finding employment in government service.

Jewish youth flocked to institutes of higher learning, also in the major cities. Whereas in 1897 Jews constituted 9.4 percent of the student body, during the 1926–27 academic year they held 16 percent of the seats (Baron 1964, 273).[8] Jews clustered in a small number of preferred fields: medicine (almost half of all Jewish university students), followed by economics, industry and technology, teaching, and art.

Baron (1964, 268) argues that "the general cultural level among Jews had not declined and that they merely exchanged their traditional Jewish for new Russian cultural values." As Jews increasingly preferred to speak Russian, even with fellow Jews, use of Yiddish lessened. Recognizing that linguistic fluency in Russian was a key to upward mobility, Jewish parents often shunned the Yiddish schools established by the *Evsektsiia*.[9] Gitelman (1972, 499) interprets these assimilatory trends not as substitution of cultures but as a logical derivation from Jewish traditions: "Ironically, Jewish values themselves contributed to Jewish assimilation and the decline of Jewish culture. Since Russian Jews generally considered Russian culture of greater practical value than Jewish culture . . . many Jews applied their traditional love of learning, respect for culture and high achievement motivation to Russian culture."

During the first fifteen years after the Bolshevik Revolution, Jews enjoyed an array of rights and liberties they had never experienced on Russian soil. Led by the zeal of dedicated Socialists, Jews themselves destroyed the traditional community institutions and lifeways that had shaped their Jewish culture during the preceding centuries. As proof that they were at least as modern and committed to socialism as others, Jews mocked their own religion, closed houses of worship, condemned the Hebrew language and Zionism, and blazed the trail for the cultural denuding of Soviet Jewry. The Yiddish secular culture they attempted to introduce in its place, although it produced several prominent writers, journalists, and a number of theatrical troupes, never quite filled the void, and many Jews began to view Russian culture as their own. Ironically, the agitators who did their job of indoctrination and re-orientation so well would be among the first to lose their lives in the great purges of 1936–38.

Nationalities Policy and the Birobidzhan Experiment

The foundations of Soviet nationalities policy, particularly as it affects Jews, derive from a series of debates about the sociopolitical status of Jews that date back to the nineteenth century. Until well into the 1800s, Russian Jews considered themselves a religious entity, adherents of Judaism. The Jewish nation, they claimed, had been destroyed in the Diaspora, and, according to religious teachings, this "nation" would only reemerge with the arrival of the Messiah. In the mid-1840s, however, Karl Marx formulated his materialistically based thoughts on the Jewish question. Responding to Bruno Bauer's inquiries on the same subject,[10] Marx expressed his conviction that Jews and Judaism are inextricably tied to the economic structures of bourgeois society. After the demise of capitalism, when diversionary and divisive social institutions such as religion and nationalism were demystified and the means of production owned by the producers, there would be no future for Jews as a distinct people: "As soon as society can abolish the empirical nature of the Jew, that is usury and its preconditions, being a Jew will become impossible because his conviction will no longer have any object, since the subjective basis of Judaism (practical necessity) will have become humanized and the conflict between man as a sensual individual and as a species will have been abolished" (Marx [1843] 1975, 45). For Marx, too, then, the idea of a Jewish "nation" was inconceivable but for reasons much different from those of Orthodox Jews. Jewry, according to Marx, is a religion that prospers under specific economic conditions, which, once abolished, will produce the self-destruction of the Jewish religion and the elimination of Jews as a distinct people.[11] According to Dubnow (1918, 2:222–223), the secularizing Russian Jews who had joined mid-nineteenth-century revolutionary circles agreed with Marx's prediction: "The fundamental article of faith . . . was cosmopolitanism. . . . Jewry was not believed to be a nation, and as a religious entity it was looked upon as a relic of the past, which was doomed to disappear."

Many "enlightened" Russian Jews who had embraced assimilation only to find that road blocked during the reigns of Alexander III and Nicholas II (1881–1917) came to the realization that Jewry included not merely an archaic religion but a contemporary people as well. During the late nineteenth century, a literary renaissance flourished, and Jewish Socialist movements, some of them (the Poale Zion and the Socialist Zionists) directed at a national return to Palestine, gained numerous adherents. The Bund (General Jewish Workingman's Party of Russia, Poland, and Lithuania), organized in Vilnius in 1897, "denounced Zionism as a reactionary and petit bourgeois movement" (Greenberg 1976, 2:158), and, although conceived as a specifically Jewish party, it worked as part of the overall Socialist struggle for the liberation of Russia. In fact, leaders of the Bund were among the organizers of the 1898 Minsk conference at which the Russian Socialist Democratic Party was formed.[12]

At the second conference of the Russian Socialist Democratic Party, in London (1903), the Bund's platform, which called for party organization along national lines, with Jews being accorded the status of a nationality, was overwhelmingly rejected. The Bund's demand for recognition as the sole representative of the Jewish proletariat was also denied, and the Bundists left the congress and withdrew from the party (see Greenberg 1976, 2:153–154; Gitelman 1972, 38–43).

Although sympathetic to those groups that had been the objects of tsarist oppression, Lenin, whose views on the national question closely follow those of Marx, opposed development of national culture, cultural autonomy, and federalism: "The slogan of the workers' democracy is not 'national culture', but the international culture of democraticism and of the world working class movement" (Lenin [1913] 1951, 12). In a series of articles appearing in *Iskra* during the early 1900s, Lenin "scored the stand of the Bund as reactionary, chauvinistic, and an impediment in the path of assimilation [which he] regarded as the solution to the Jewish problem" (Greenberg 1976, 2:153). Refusing to acknowledge the idea of a Jewish "nation," Lenin regarded Jews rather as a caste whose isolation in Russia resulted from the tsarist government's discriminatory policies. He praised those Jews who "live in a civilized world [where] the Jews are not segregated in a caste. There in the great world—progressive features of Jewish culture have clearly made themselves felt; its internationalism, its responsiveness to the advanced movement of the epoch," and he urged them to "continue the best traditions of the Jews and fight the slogan, 'national culture' " ([1913] 1951, 20–21). Lenin's proposals for the rights of Jews and limitations on their national autonomy in no way distinguished them from other minority groups in the Russian Empire.

Lenin gave to Joseph Stalin the task of further developing the Bolshevik position on the issue of nationalities. Stalin's 1913 essay, "Marxism and the National Question," reflects Lenin in principle but foreshadows a later split. Embarking on an even more ambitious pragmatic application of socialism than his mentor, Stalin not only operationalized the concept of "nation" and put forth a policy of treating the nationalities question, but he outlined a program for implementation of this policy as well.

Stalin began his essay by formulating a definition of nation that rejects Otto Bauer's (1909, 1–2) view that "a nation is an aggregate of people bound into a community of character by a common destiny." Since this definition lacks a material base, Stalin considered it incomplete and misleading. He asserted instead: "A nation is a historically constituted, stable community of people, formed on the basis of a common language, territory, economic life, and psychological make-up manifested in a common culture" ([1913] 1975, 22).

Stalin, following Marx, envisioned a time when capitalism would be destroyed, and, in the context of Socialist society, barriers between peoples would disappear. As a result, so, too, would barriers between nations. Recognizing, however, the strength of lingering nationalist sentiments, Stalin proposed as an interim measure the right of national self-determination for "nations": "A nation has the right freely to determine its own destiny. It has the right to arrange its life as it sees fit, without, of course, trampling on the rights of other nations" ([1913] 1975, 38).[13] He proposed ([1913] 1975, 88) complete democratization as the basis for the solution of the national question. Regional autonomy, or blending of peoples into (majority) territorially based nations, was his immediate goal: to unify "the workers of all nationalities of Russia into *single, integral* collective bodies, to unite these collective bodies into a *single* collective party—such is the task" ([1913] 1975, 93, emphasis in the original). To further the short-term goal of proletariat consciousness-raising, leading to regional amalgamation, dispersed minorities were to use their own languages, have their own schools, and be granted full liberties in the new Socialist state.

Simply put, Stalin reiterated that Jews do not constitute a nation, do not qualify for the program of self-determination, and should therefore work toward immediate amalgamation with the peoples of the regions in which they live. Those who urged national-cultural autonomy were reactionaries, harmful to the Socialist struggle. Since Jews had already begun assimilating, they should continue that trend, "and thus make possible the direct union of the Jewish workers with the workers of the other nationalities of Russia" ([1913] 1975, 96).

Yet even before the Jewish section (*Evsektsiia*) of the Communist party was dissolved in March 1930, it had become increasingly apparent that "assimilation and national identification were the two poles around which nationality policy revolved" (Gitelman 1972, 507) and that a middle course would not be tolerated, at least as regards the Jews. During the first fifteen years of the USSR, assimilation was indeed an option for Russian Jews. With the elimination of internal passports and residence permits, Jews were free to move out of *shtetls* and into cities and from the old Pale of Settlement into the interior. Intermarriage, especially in the Russian Republic, was occurring at high rates, of about 25–30 percent (Nove and Newth 1972, 134–135), and Jews increasingly abandoned their Yiddish mother tongue for Russian. Jews were able to assume new identities by changing their names and "blending" in with their neighbors. One might then interpret the liquidation of the *Evsektsiia* as the party's recognition that assimilation was proceeding as expected and that a specifically Jewish section was no longer necessary.

The creation of a Jewish Autonomous Province, however, contradicts the notion that both Jews and the party were satisfied with the assimilatory course. In 1926 a decision was made in the *Evsektsiia,* with the strong backing of the Soviet Presidium President Kalinin, allowing Jews to settle on the land to further the goals of economic modernization, employment for déclassé elements, and national consolidation. Despite strong arguments for colonization projects in Byelorussia and in the Crimea, where Jewish farming enterprises had already begun to reap results, by the beginning of 1928 the Presidium of the Central Executive Committee of the USSR made public its decision to assign the area of Birobidzhan, a region in the Russian Far East, to the Jews. With the establishment of a Jewish region, there was now "a possibility of 'creating the objective conditions' which would force a redefinition of the Jewish people, as the super-structure would have to accommodate itself to the all-determining base" (Gitelman 1972, 410).

Although the creation of a Jewish Autonomous Province seems to run counter to Stalin's increasingly centrist policy, it solved, in principle at least, the pressing problems of national security, that is, the increase of Chinese migrants into Birobidzhan and Japan's invasion of Manchuria. By providing homes and employment for dislocated, unskilled *shtetl* Jews, this insecure border could be solidified and the national integrity of the Soviet Union could be protected.

Needless to say, the choice of Birobidzhan as the site for a Jewish province was not the product of Jewish initiative (Abramsky 1972); its location thousands of miles from centers of Russian Jewry and its living conditions (virgin forests and undeveloped swamp lands)—more primitive than the most miserable villages in the Pale—doomed this project from the start. Goldberg (1961, 181) observed after his first visit to Birobidzhan in 1934, "None of the people I met there found the place better than they had expected. Most found it worse. . . . A frequent complaint was that [although] they had not expected to find a Garden of Eden, they had not expected such a hell, either."

This disappointment is reflected in migration statistics. Between 1928 and 1933, 19,635 Jews came to Birobidzhan; during the same five years, 11,550 left (Gilbert 1976, 37). Most new arrivals came from the Ukraine, where economic conditions were very bad, but the majority were trained and skilled workers rather than the destitute and homeless the Jewish Autonomous Province was designed to attract (Schwarz 1972, 181). Propaganda efforts in 1934–36 appealed to nationalistic sentiments, and the idea of a Jewish nation resulted in larger numbers of new immigrants (nine thousand in 1935 and seven thousand in 1936, according to Schwarz 1972, 177). When in 1937 Birobidzhan's entire leadership was purged, immigration came to a virtual halt and did not revive until after the Second World War.

During the mid-1930s, Jewish efforts to achieve both ideals of Soviet nationalities policy were thwarted. The establishment of a territorially based Jewish "nation" was destined to fail by its placement in the remote Far East.[14] Of far greater consequence was the reintroduction of the hated internal passport in 1933. Although *Evsektsiia* activists had virtually eliminated religious Jewish culture and Jews themselves were rapidly heading toward the goal of "blending" into the Russian nation, the government decided that persons born of Jewish parents would be designated as Jews on their identity documents. After 1933 it became increasingly difficult to change one's name,[15] and by virtue of the label, "Jew," assimilation, at least in one's own generation, was blocked.[16] The Jew now became: "not someone who chooses to identify himself as such; he is a juridically defined person who inescapably is a part of the Jewish nationality" (Korey 1968, 317).

World War II and the Black Years

The purges of the late 1930s (1936–38), in which most Jewish Communist leaders, many Jewish "economic criminals,"[17] and ideological iconoclasts (for example, the poet Osip Mandelshtam) were executed, were a general "cleansing" of rivals to Stalin's increasingly centralist regime. A woman in her fifties, who emigrated in the mid-1970s from Leningrad with her elderly mother, her husband, and their children and grandchildren reminisces with anger:

> My father was such a big Communist that he named me Iskra. Iskra means spark, but that's not why he named me this—he named me for Lenin's newspaper that spread the word about socialism. . . . We were Jewish. You know, many, many Jews took part in the 1917 Revolution, and many were active in the diplomatic corps, in high positions, in the army. My father was a big Communist—he was an economist and struggled alongside Lenin to bring about the Revolution. After the Revolution, in the 20s, my father sided with Trotsky, and when that paranoid-monster and sick little man, Stalin, got power, my father was sent to a camp.

These purges were not specifically anti-Jewish; hundreds of thousands of Ukrainians, Russians, and members of other nationalities were executed as well. As Stalin's idea of a strong, centrally planned, and controlled state took form, land-owning peasants (*kulaks*) and NEP (New Economic Plan) businessmen were killed, as well as most of the old Bolshevik leadership and a considerable portion of the Red Army's commanding officers (see Conquest 1968 for the most thorough documentation of the Great Terror). After this period, Trotsky, Zinoviev, and other great Jewish leaders of the Revolution disappeared from Soviet history books altogether, or, if they were mentioned, were called leftist deviationists.

The rise of fascism in Germany occurred while Stalin was in the throes of power consolidation. Although rhetoric and press accounts during this period condemned fascism, in August 1939, a week before Germany invaded Poland, the USSR signed a nonaggression pact with the Third Reich. While undoubtedly few Soviet citizens wanted war, especially those in the border areas, this abrupt turn-about was difficult to understand. The very word, *Fascist,* disappeared from newspapers, "and everything we had been taught to abhor as hostile, evil and menacing from our *Komsomol* [Communist Youth League]—nay, Pioneer—days, suddenly became, as it were, neutral" (Ainsztein 1972, 270, quoting Mark Gallai's article, "Pervy boi my vyigrali" [The first battle we have won], *Novy Mir,* Moscow, September 1966). Needless to say, no mention was made of the Third Reich's anti-Jewish measures and the tremendous sufferings they brought to the Jews of Poland and Germany.

The Soviet Union was unprepared for Germany's invasion twenty-two months later (June 22, 1941), and Soviet Jews were unaware of the "special treatment" the SS had in store for them. When the Germans arrived in larger towns and cities, they herded Jews into ghettos, confiscated their belongings, and marked them off from the rest of the population. In smaller towns and hamlets, it was not unusual for shock troops to gather all Jews onto the main square and systematically shoot them. In a steady monotone, Yakov recounts his father's wartime horror:

> My father was very little then, and as he was running to join his family, one of his aunts motioned for him not to come, so he climbed a tree and saw the Germans pluck out his father's beard and then machine-gun down everyone he knew.

Those who were brought into ghettos believed at first that if they simply performed the tasks they were assigned they would be left alone. These ghettos, however, were densely packed, unsanitary, and the scanty rations allotted to their residents were not evenly distributed. Workers were sent out early in the morning to toil until evening in defense factories or at more dangerous jobs. The ghettos thus provided an alternative to mass shootings and concentration camps; in Minsk alone, in the course of ten weeks, only 6,000 of the original 100,000 Jews brought into the ghettos were still alive (Goldstein 1969, 99).

Survivors of the ghettos rarely talked of their experiences in later years but maintained close bonds with other inmates. At the 1985 Brooklyn funeral of an eighty-three-year-old Odessa ghetto survivor, one elderly woman cried and sobbed throughout the service and the burial. The deceased's daughter-in-law, Lera, explained:

> This woman was a neighbor of his, all their lives in Odessa. She and he knew each other before the war, and after the war—when they were in the ghetto together—she came back cold, naked and hungry like all, and he gave her a room in his apartment. After some time she moved into the apartment next door, and they lived together always. Of course she is very grateful to him for helping her so much. Then when Shura

came to marry him, she helped in making all the arrangements and in helping her set up her home. They lived almost as one family, very, very close. And then they came to America and also lived as neighbors. That is why she is crying, "How can I go on without you!"

Estimates of Jewish civilian deaths, either in the ghettos or in mass graves, including those in the newly annexed Baltic republics, the West Ukraine and western Byelorussia, range from 750,000 to one and a half million people.[18] The Soviet government has published no official statistics delineating the particular ordeal Jews underwent.

Thousands of women and children, sometimes accompanied by elderly parents and grandparents, like Grigory from Kiev, Irina from Kharkov, and Anna, also from Kiev, escaped the torment of the ghetto or death in mass executions by fleeing into the interior.

Grigory:

> Then came the war—the Second World War—when everyone who could left Kiev. We went to the Urals then, my mother, my brother, and I. My father went to the front. When I was fourteen my family and I returned to Kiev, but my father did not come back.

Irina:

> I was born in the Ural Mountains. You have heard of *evakuatsiia?* Everyone who could, when they found out about the German invasion, moved to the Urals. My father died at the front when I was eight months old. I never knew him.

Anna:

> I am from Moscow, but I was born in Irkutsk, in Siberia, during *evakuatsiia.* My parents are from Kiev. After my father completed medical institute he was sent for duty to Irkutsk. He stayed there forever because there he found peace, no anti-Semitism, beautiful forests, a calm way of life. This he had never before dreamed of in his life.

The evacuations, with the exceptions of the rescue of Jewish agricultural workers from Crimean *kolkhozy* (collective farms) and the thousands of Polish Jews who fled eastward into Russia in September 1939 and were assigned quarters in the interior (Baron 1964, 279), were not state-supervised rescue missions of Soviet Jews. Evacuation was left to individual initiative.

Others hid in forests or at the homes of non-Jewish sympathizers, or joined the partisans. Vladimir, a fifty-year-old former Odessan, proudly asks:

> Did you know that there are underground catacombs in Odessa? They are from ancient Greek and Roman days. They were used for centuries for storage and as hide-outs for thieves and pirates. During the war partisans hid there. I know them like the back of my hand. I was a little boy then and ran messages and brought in food. They never suspected me.

Ainsztein (1972, 281) estimates that of the 86,000 Soviet partisans, 20,000 were Jews.

Over 500,000 Jews served in the Soviet military, earning distinguished battle records and gaining recognition by the state for their heroism. One hundred twenty-one Jews were awarded the highest military decoration, Hero of the Soviet Union (Ainsztein 1972, 274–275; Baron 1964, 303). These accomplishments also are downplayed, if not ignored, in official accounts of the war, which stress instead the overall effort of the Soviet peoples.

On August 24, 1941, in Moscow, which was never occupied by German troops, a gathering of prominent Jews—ranging from Yiddish authors and actors to a Red Army officer and the Russified writer Ilya Ehrenburg—formed the Jewish Anti-Fascist Committee. Their task at home was to appeal to Jewish pride to increase enlistment in the Red Army. Abroad, they collected millions of dollars from Americans and the British to help the war effort. "The very existence of the Jewish Anti-Fascist Committee was the most important concession made by the Kremlin to Soviet Jewry. For here was a body that represented all Soviet Jews, irrespective of their political and religious beliefs" (Ainsztein 1972, 253).

Just after the war, throughout the Jewish communities of the USSR, a short-lived cultural renaissance and nationalistic reawakening occurred. Ilya Ehrenburg spoke for many Soviet Jews when he stated, "I grew up in Moscow. My native tongue is Russian. I do not know the Yiddish language. I am a Russian, a Soviet citizen, a man who cherishes the culture of Europe. But now I feel bound to the Jews because of the great misery of my Jewish people" (quoted in Baron 1964, 312).[19] Jewish national self-consciousness, tacitly encouraged during the war, was given another boost by the creation of the state of Israel on May 14, 1948, and Foreign Minister Andrei Gromyko's moving endorsement of it. Golda Meir's visit to the Moscow synagogue in October of that year was celebrated with joyful Jewish demonstrations.

Post-war reconstruction, however, brought many disappointments to Soviet Jews. First, many Jewish evacuees, veterans, and ghetto/camp inmates returned (especially in the Ukraine) to find their homes and jobs occupied, and the new occupants often refused to vacate (Baron 1964, 310). Following the trend of the previous decade, many more Jews moved to the large cities of the interior to make a fresh start. Migration to Birobidzhan increased for a short time; from the second half of 1946 to July 1948, nine organized parties of Jewish settlers plus spontaneous, unorganized groups of migrants arrived there to begin life anew (Schwarz 1972, 186).

But then, toward the end of 1948, the entire leadership of the Jewish Autonomous Province (Birobidzhan) was liquidated. The Jewish Anti-Fascist Committee, which at the time was reuniting war-torn families, was disbanded, and its leader, the actor Solomon Mikhoels, was killed.[20] Yiddish newspapers, printing presses, and libraries were shut down, the last Jewish schools and theaters were closed, and many Jewish Communists, writers, and other cultural figures were arrested, some to be shot, others to be interred in camps (Aronson 1969, 195). Stalin's own anti-Jewish suspicions, strengthened by the anomaly of the Jewish Anti-Fascist Committee (one voice for a scattered people that is not a nation), coupled with displays of Jewish pride and Zionistic sympathies, led to these brutal purges of Jewish leaders and artists. In 1949, Soviet newspapers began listing the transgressions of "cosmopolitan" intelligentsia, placing strong emphasis on their Jewish last names and patronymics. This paranoid anti-Semitism culminated in early 1953 with Stalin's accusation of a Jewish Doctors' Plot aimed at poisoning all Soviet leaders and ending socialism in the USSR. Arrests of Jewish doctors spread from Moscow across the country to the Ukraine and Lithuania. This last rampage of anti-Semitism ended in March 1953 with Stalin's death.

Many former Soviet citizens remember the day of Stalin's death with mixed emotions. Natalya, from Leningrad, recalls that her patriotism and idealism were shattered on that day:

> When did I first begin to doubt that system? I remember it very well. I was in school when our teacher announced that our dear, beloved Comrade Stalin, guardian of world peace, had died. I, like everyone in my class, burst into tears. I was so scared that now we would have war again since Stalin who was guarding the peace was now gone. When I got home my father asked me why I was crying. "Because," I told him, "now we are going to have war. Our dear, beloved Comrade Stalin has died." My father hissed, "Thank God the dirty dog is dead."

A former Odessan's bitterness and anger emerge in his recollections:

> I remember very well the day Stalin died. I was eight years old and in Odessa. All the teachers came around and took all us Jewish kids to the toilet. We stayed in there all day until they received their directives about what to do with the Jews. Oh yes, I remember that and all the other ways my Soviet comrades always reminded me that I am a Jew.

The Thaw

After charges of attempted poisonings and espionage were dropped against the doctors, thousands of Stalin's surviving "enemies" were quietly rehabilitated, that is, released from prison camps and sent home. In February 1956, Khrushchev's speech to the Twentieth Congress of the Communist Party publicly condemned that which many had already known—the deviationist course of Stalin's cult of personality. To return to the proper Socialist path of development, several fallacious "Socialist" schemes were abandoned,[21] restrictions on literature and art were somewhat relaxed, and scientific research in the defense industry and in agriculture was greatly encouraged. The postwar Soviet labor shortage, coupled with this policy of rationalized modernization, provided many opportunities for people in "scientific (professional, technical) work." Jewish parents urged their children to develop their talents through education, particularly in the relatively ideology-free fields of mathematics, physics, and engineering. As one father told his son, "In earlier days Jews had to rely on money to make their way. Now our capital is knowledge."

During Khrushchev's regime, although Jews had disappeared

from high-level government positions and party posts, they remained over-represented in institutes of higher education and universities and in the professions. Countering international charges of anti-Semitic discrimination, after the 1959 census the Soviet government released statistics revealing that Jews, a mere 1.1 percent of the total population, constituted 14.7 percent of the nation's medical doctors, 10.4 percent of its lawyers and judges, 10 percent of the scientists, 8.5 percent of journalists and writers, 7 percent of workers in graphic and theater arts, 19 percent of all doctors of science (Ph.D.), and 3.1 percent of the country's university students (Baron 1964, 375).

Western observers of Soviet Jewry (e.g., Baron 1964, 331, 336; Smolar 1971, 63–70; Wiesel 1966), however, consider far more important the lack of Jewish cultural facilities and failure to mention specifically Jewish achievements or tragedies in the encyclopedias, media, or monuments throughout the USSR.[22] They decry the fact that Jews have become nothing more than a juridically defined minority group with no opportunities for cultural or religious expression, and condemn the Kremlin for thwarting the maintenance of communal links among Jews, thereby undermining their very peoplehood.

Soviet Jews do not always share Western Jews' impressions that they are a disconnected or people-less people. Émigrés reiterate time and again that they always knew they were Jewish—and not only from their passports. They stress that in the USSR they had devised ways to maintain positive identification with a wider Jewish group and to sustain an accompanying sense of pride. Iskra speaks about this:

> We knew, and how I cannot tell you exactly—but we knew every leading actor, actress, writer, artist—anyone who too was Jewish, and in this we took great pride. As an example, you know the cosmonauts who went up into space? When we found out that the mother of one of them was Jewish—although he himself has a Russian last name and claims himself as Russian—we became very proud.

In some cases, this sense of pride becomes overblown, and not infrequently Soviet Jews express the belief that Jews are smarter than everyone else. In their search for fellow Jews, sometimes Jewish identity is attributed to entertainment figures and political leaders (e.g., Charlie Chaplin and Abraham Lincoln) who are not Jewish. A graduate student, originally from the academic town of Novosibirsk, asserts:

Yes, Jewish [there] is a *political* category—for me there is no religion, no tradition of religion in my family. . . . But being Jewish does make me different—Jews were the intelligentsia of Russia. Lenin's mother was Jewish—don't argue with me on this! Jews are more intelligent than other people, that's all there is to it!

Soviet Jews devoted themselves to their work and their studies, deriving satisfaction from their achievements and the contributions they were making to rebuild Soviet society. This sense of satisfaction was increased with personal discoveries that a number of people making great accomplishments were also Jews and by believing that, to a large extent, Jews compose Russia's intelligentsia. The more the government failed to take positive note of Jewish nationality, the more, it seems, Jews noted it themselves.

Several immigrants were somewhat surprised to learn that in the West Soviet Jews are regarded as a "shadow people" (Ben Ami 1967, 24), devoid of any distinctive Jewish heritage. Many Soviet Jews simply do not see themselves in this way. Although synagogue closings increased and formal education in the Jewish religion all but ceased, many Jews had at least a superficial knowledge of Jewish history and continued to mark Jewish holidays in their homes as a natural part of their otherwise Russo-Soviet lives (Fain 1984, 70–81). Boris, a former musician from Odessa, recalls:

Of course my family went to synagogue, and they celebrated all the holidays. As for me, I simply didn't care about this at all. I went to synagogue a few times in my life, but I didn't like it. As you Americans say, it wasn't for me. I just wasn't interested. In my circle of friends, and as you would see in most circles of artists and intellectuals, we were a mixture of all nationalities—Russian, Ukrainian, Jewish. Our interests were music and other things, not religion. I always knew I was Jewish, but I didn't think about it one way or the other. . . . It never hurt me in school, at the institute, or in my profession.

During "the thaw," the Soviet Union and Israel maintained diplomatic relations, and Israeli delegations were always greeted with enthusiasm by public demonstrations of Jewish citizens during their tours (Baron 1964, 337; Schechtman 1969, 43). Jews showed pride in their heritage throughout Khrushchev's regime, for despite condemnations of religion, "many thousands of Jews openly attended prayer meetings in Moscow, Leningrad, Kiev and so on. In 1962, 10,000 people gathered round the principal Moscow synagogue on Yom Kippur. In 1963 their numbers went as high as 15,000" (Shapiro 1969, 464).

While the Khrushchev years brought anti-religious measures, continued closings of remaining Jewish cultural institutions, prosecution of economic criminals among whom Jews figured prominently, publication of *Judaism Without Embellishment,* and silence regarding Jewish war heroes and Nazi exterminations, Jews did not face overt discrimination.[23] More important, during this era Jews were released from the fear that had pervaded their lives under Stalin's terror (Zaslavsky and Brym 1983, 37). Khrushchev himself is not remembered with fondness, but many informants discuss the years of his regime with affection and pride of their accomplishment—in completing the task of rebuilding their country, in the Soviet Union's scientific advances, and in a general improvement in the standard of living, particularly exemplified by the exuberance of moving from a communal apartment to a newly constructed cooperative.[24] They were happy to have a renewed opportunity to participate fully in Soviet life.

The Sixties, the Seventies, and the Emigration Movement

To a great extent, Khrushchev's policies of normalization continued during the Kosygin-Brezhnev years. Zaslavsky and Brym (1983, 106) call this period "the great stabilisation of all spheres of social life." Two notable exceptions to this state of affairs, however, changed the conditions for Soviet Jews: a break in diplomatic relations with Israel after June 1967, and emigration, first in small numbers and then in the thousands, of Jews from the USSR.

In 1967, when Israel emerged victorious after the Six-Day War, the government of the Soviet Union recalled its ambassador from Tel Aviv. Just prior to the war's outbreak and during the hostilities, Soviet media played up the fact that the armies of the Arab countries far outnumbered those of Israel and stressed the imminence of an Arab victory. Israel was depicted as an imperialist aggressor, and Zionism was equated with the policies of the Third Reich.

Maxim, then a Moscow University student, recalls his reaction to Israel's victory:

I went to the synagogue—the first time was in 1967 when I was a student. There was a big demonstration there. How did I find out? I don't really know—we all just knew. One friend told another. We knew it would be interesting to see old friends, meet new ones, and girls too! But seriously, we were so proud of Israel, that this country was fighting so hard—and winning! We set fire, I remember, to Arab newspapers. We were so carried away and so proud. The police did nothing then. But later some people set fire to *Pravda* and *Izvestiia,* and that was broken up quickly—that's very dangerous.

Jewish children, however, often did not realize how the Soviet state's anti-Zionist stance that they learned in school and their own Jewish identities conflicted, as Yakov recalls:

In 1967 I was around ten, eleven. Already then I was a good student and a good member of the Young Pioneer Corps. During the Six-Day War I came home from school . . . saying things about the Israeli aggressors doing terrible things to our Arab brethren. Then my father decided to do something about my [Jewish] education.

Whereas in the 1920s Lenin appointed Jews to sensitive state positions because he trusted them not to become counter-revolutionaries, from 1967 onward Jews were reminded of their connection to the capitalist-aggressor state, Israel, and increasingly felt themselves suspected of potential or actual treason. A former television news producer discusses the tension he lived with at work:

Everyone in the Soviet Union lives in fear, and everyone has one strike against them. But I have two strikes against me. I have to be extra-careful because I am a Jew. Every day I am afraid to make a mistake. I have to make sure no one thinks I am a Zionist. I have to show Israel [at my job as a TV producer] in the worst possible light.

In the 1970s, especially after the 1973 Arab-Israeli War, the thin line dividing the "good" Soviet citizens of Jewish nationality from "bad" Zionists had all but disappeared. Children internalized the equations that Jewish = Zionist, Zionist = bad, so that therefore Jewish = bad. Jewish parents recall how their children dreaded the day they were to bring their birth certificates to school and how they invented illnesses to avoid "everyone finding out that I am a Jew."

Some children cried and screamed to their parents that there had been a mistake, that they *were* Russians. One little girl, Svetlana, went so far as to become "blood-sisters" with a Russian friend, and then demanded that her parents change her birth certificate because she now had "Russian blood."

Along with a barrage of anti-Zionism in the press, in television reports, and at workplace meetings, came more drastic measures, both by Soviet Jews and by the Soviet government. With the 1967 Israeli victory, more and more Russian Jews began applying for emigration visas to join family members in Israel.[25] At the same time, Soviet Jews, whether they were preparing to emigrate or not, found their own and their children's life-chances increasingly curtailed. Professional advancement and university seats became difficult, if not impossible, to attain.[26] Concern that Jews might be Israeli spies or agents of Zionism, coupled with the threat of brain-drain emigration, provided officials with the rationale for imposing a quota system on Jewish university enrollment and excluding Jews from top managerial posts. Boris's interpretation of the situation, like that of many other immigrants, is somewhat different:

> As you know, I am sure, during the time of the Revolution, many of the most talented, professional Russians left their country. There was a large shortage of people in the professions. You know too that many Jewish people were active in the Revolution; they saw this as the opportunity for their own freedom—to come out of their little villages and join the wide world. As soon as they could, Jews came to the universities, to large cities and immediately filled the gap left by the Russian nobility. I think it is something hereditary; Jews are always like this, always go into the professions—scientists, doctors, lawyers. That was good, when the new Soviet Union had no Russians to put into jobs, then it was fine that Jews held them. Jews were in the government, the army, high echelons, the foreign service—they were everywhere. I would say 90 percent of high positions were filled by Jews.[27] So what happened? The Jews taught the *goyim* [gentiles], and the *goyim* decided they wanted all these positions back.

Jews reacted to these conditions—of feeling unwanted, of knowing that they would never go any higher than they were, and, even worse, of fearing that their children might not even attain the same professional status that they themselves had—by leaving in increased numbers.[28] Early in the emigration movement, Jews, primarily from regions where traditional Judaism lasted longer than in the Soviet heartland (the newly acquired Baltic republics, Moldavia, the West Ukraine, and the Republic of Georgia), responded to Zionist sentiments and the belief that life would be better and more fulfilling for them in a Jewish state.[29] As the movement gained momentum, more and more cosmopolitan professionals left as well. By the mid-1970s, options for resettlement outside of Israel had opened, and emigrants frequently decided on the United States and other points west as their destination (Gitelman 1982, 4), although many immigrants emphasized to me that getting out of the USSR was the most important thing—where they were going was a secondary concern.

A number of surveys have been conducted to delineate the major reasons for this emigration. Noteworthy is the survey taken by Zaslavsky and Brym among Soviet refugees in Rome awaiting clearance for the United States. This survey of 155 people, conducted at the peak of emigration (1978–79), indicated that the most widespread reason for leaving the USSR was to enjoy political/cultural freedom (39%). Least often cited was the motive of family reunification. Five to six years later, the Federation of Jewish Philanthropies of New York's survey of 233 Soviet immigrants revealed a somewhat different picture. Respondents cited ethnic discrimination (including the vague, all-encompassing term, anti-Semitism, 21%; fears for children's future, 14%; barriers to one's own future, 4%; and the wish to pursue a religious lifestyle, 4%) most frequently as their chief motive for leaving (43%). Economic reasons were least often mentioned (3%). (See table 3.)

My long-term contacts and extended conversations with immigrants reveal that all these reasons are interconnected, and depending on the day or the mood, one or the other will be mentioned as most compelling. In many cases, would-be emigrants experienced a general dissatisfaction with the regime, thought about leaving for a long time, and then a specific event pushed them to action, as in Pavel's case:

> What really did it for me, to want to leave, was the problem with my doctoral dissertation. I do not know the way it is with American universities, but in the Soviet Union, first you must find a sponsor. The

TABLE 3
Reasons for Leaving the USSR (Percentages of Total)

Reasons	Rome Survey	New York Survey
Political/Cultural Freedom	39	26
Economic, Material	25	3
Ethnic Discrimination	22	43
Family Reunification	14	21

Sources: Zaslavsky and Brym, *Soviet-Jewish Emigration and Soviet Nationality Policy* (1983), 49–51; and Federation of Jewish Philanthropies of New York, *Jewish Identification and Affiliation among Soviet Jewish Immigrants in New York* (1985), 26.

sponsor reads your prospectus for the dissertation and then either approves or disapproves it. Before you can form a committee you must have one major professor who will sponsor you. To put it in short, I was blackballed; no one would be my sponsor. This is because I have a Jewish name, because I am a Jew. When you write the dissertation it is supposed to be anonymous, but everyone knows who wrote what anyway. It took me a long time, but I finally found a professor. When it got to the committee, I was blackballed again. I knew that this fight would take years, and that it would probably amount to nothing more than frustration and aggravation. So I applied for an exit visa and sold my dissertation to a graduate student in Georgia.

The decision to emigrate was not easy to make; some informants confided that they really had not wanted to leave in the first place but eventually gave in to pressure from family members. Alex, from Odessa:

I want you to know, I didn't very much want to come to America. No, I didn't want to come at all. It's a funny story—my father wanted to come very badly. He hated and still hates that system—which he knows much better than I, having lived through World War II and having had his parents die—he wanted to leave very, very badly. I didn't; I was happy over there. I worked very hard to make for myself the kind of life I wanted. I was working as a supervisor of a group of economists . . . and, like a freelancer, I wrote stories and articles as a journalist. I had achieved some success. . . . I was pretty well set up.

Sofia, Vladimir's wife:

> I had to push my husband, he didn't want to come. He didn't know English, and he had always worked in the humanities, teaching history and geography. He said, "What will I do there?" He was afraid to start over.

A small number of people in the entertainment field speak longingly about the fulfilling careers they had as cultural figures in the Soviet Union. They left because they felt they had no other choice. Grigory:

> I became an "enemy of the people" (*vrag naroda*). I was blacklisted. My cousin with the same last name as mine left a year and a half before I did. When he left, suddenly my songs were no longer played on the radio; no one asked me to write anything or perform anywhere. This was very dangerous because unemployment is a crime in the Soviet Union. I knew someone else in this position, and they found him a job as a doorman. I knew that this was my future. I ceased to exist as a composer and musician because I had become an enemy of the people.

Anna, a thirty-eight-year-old singer:

> In 1975, and I was so surprised, all of a sudden I could find no work. I found out I was blacklisted and heard from my friends that the official word was that I was in Israel—I hadn't even applied! I guess that's the time they wanted to get all influential Jews out from Russia. . . . There were many people on that list—good people—so there I was, all of a sudden, with no work. I went to many places—Gorky, Tashkent— looking, and I had been living in Moscow. Finally we emigrated in 1979, me, my husband, my son, and my mother.

There were, in addition, those who emigrated with no specific reason; they were not actively anti-regime, nor had they experienced discrimination. Captivated with the idea of America, they were certain that the United States would provide them with everything they ever wanted. Bella, a group worker at a neighborhood Russian project, explains:

> You wouldn't believe how many people in Russia think of the U.S. as a fairy tale—that a fairy prince or princess will sweep them away to instant riches, instant success and complete happiness!

Nona gives her opinion:

> You know, sweetheart, many women came to this country for this rea-
> son: they thought their chances of finding a man here would be better. In
> Russia, men aren't even men, they've been broken by the system, and
> because of the war there are just less men than women. And from our
> knowledge of America—which is laughable—we thought that Ameri-
> can men would be better. Believe me, many women came here looking
> for husbands.

Over and over immigrants expressed the conviction that if the
Soviet government granted the right of free emigration to all its citizens, "half the country would leave." They point out that being Jewish gave them additional problems, but that Soviet life is difficult for
everyone.

Speaking not only for herself but also on behalf of many Jewish
professionals, Lera, who has been in America since 1983, summarizes
why so many have left the Soviet Union:

> It is important to understand that we did not come to America just to
> live—we were already living in Russia—but to live better. Sure we
> knew that an entirely new life awaited us, but to a person, everyone of
> us just knew that it had to be better. Materially, yes, that had some-
> thing to do with it, but I mean in all senses of the word—to breathe
> freely, not to have to make all sorts of deals on the black market, not to
> be afraid that one day. . . . And mainly for the future of our children,
> that they would have a choice about their lives. I can tell you honestly
> that I am not 100 percent sure that I want to put myself through
> everything it would take to reestablish myself in my profession. But I
> do know that I have that choice.

Irina expresses a more cynical view of the emigration:

> Don't kid yourself, Franushka. I don't think many left for the reasons
> you are stating [anti-Semitism, fear for children's future]. Maybe this is
> part of it, but a very small part. . . . A lot of people left because Jews,
> well, like many people, each one of them has his own *gesheft* [business,
> petty crime], you know what that means. This one has this job on the
> side, that one has that job, and many left to avoid the possibility that
> one day the KGB would find all these little "jobs" they have. And
> take, if you please, Natalya, why do you think she left? Her mother is

always telling me how she was surrounded by a circle of intelligentsia. You know why she left? Because it was fashionable—everyone who was anyone who was Jewish was leaving, and no one wanted to be the fool who stayed behind. . . . Just don't kid yourself about why people came to this country; you are giving them too much credit.

Many former Soviet citizens, like Maxim, believe that the Soviet Union holds no future for its Jews. What then is the fate for those who remain? Irina continues:

Most Russian Jews are very much assimilated, even to the point that they've lost their [Jewish] last names and look like Russians. Now let's take my family as an example: My grandmother and grandfather, that is, my mother's parents, came from Poland, Polish Jews. They had three children. Let's look at the children of these children. My uncle had two children, a girl and a boy, and each one of them married a Russian. My cousin,[30] my mother's sister's daughter, with whom I was very close all my life, married a Jew. And then there is Raisa's daughter, you know her—that's me!—and she is married to that whatever-he-is over there. So here you have an example of what I mean—of four grandchildren, only one has a completely Jewish family. I say in another three generations there won't be a specifically Jewish national group left in the Soviet Union.

The history of Soviet Jews has come, or so it seems, full circle, back to the two poles of assimilation and national identification. Perhaps it goes back further still, to the time when the Russian Empire housed no Jews, for achievement of both these ideals logically results in a Russia without Jews. Assimilation now means intermarriage and conferral of the non-Jewish spouse's nationality onto the children, and national identification has become tantamount to emigration. Ironically, retention of overlapping Russian and Jewish identities, the middle course between these two poles, becomes possible only for those who immigrate to Israel and America.[31] As they retain these identities in new sociopolitical contexts, they reshape them as well.

3.

COMMUNITY AS SOCIAL RELATIONS

Soviet Jews arrived in America believing that Americans, in large part, would be like themselves. Many, it seems, anticipated an English-speaking Russia that conformed to their imaginative ideals. Having learned to "read between the lines" of the Soviet press, these former citizens of the USSR logically assumed that the USA would be a veritable wonderland. It hardly occurred to them that the basic, seemingly "natural" ways of expressing oneself in this country would be different from those they used in the Soviet Union. They therefore expected Americans to have similar concerns and interests, to express friendship, anger, and indifference in ways identical to their own, and to hold the same basic truths and values. Certainly the newcomers knew that Americans speak English, that they live in greater material comfort than Soviet citizens, and that they have ready access to goods and information of all kinds. Learning another language and adjusting to material abundance, however, were not viewed as problems; after all, the former was expected and the latter, experienced in Vienna and Rome en route to America, was welcome.[1]

What they did not anticipate was to be regarded as and to feel like aliens, strangers in a country that they looked upon as their new home. They did not expect to find ways of social interaction and assumptions about daily life that directly challenge their own. In sociological terms, they did not expect their knowledge, the epistemological bases of their existence—how they see the world, their views of society and friendship, their ways of presenting self in public—to be inadequate or inappropriate in America. To paraphrase Berger and Luckmann (1967, 45), they expected their knowledge of everyday life to work in the American context, for their "relevance structures" to intersect with those of Americans. After all, they reasoned, educated urbanites from one great, modern world power moving to the greatest city in the other should have little problem fitting in.

Soviet Jewish immigrants ultimately found America to be quite different from the world they knew and the one they expected as they confronted "another society having a greatly different history . . . [and] an alternative symbolic universe with an 'official' tradition whose taken-for-granted objectivity is equal to one's own" (Berger and Luckmann 1967, 107–109). Their social responses to this confrontation play a critical role in the development of their sense of community.

BOUNDARIES: DEFINING THE "WE"

An exploration into the development of group identity among recent Soviet immigrants must consider the dynamic between their primary identity, Jewish, and their growing recognition that they, in the American context, are Russian as well. The uncoupling of their merged identity (Soviet-Russian-Jew, under the rubric of Jew) accompanies their encounters with American lifeways as the values, language, modes of interaction, and social meanings they internalized in the Soviet-Russian context become conscious. These once taken-for-granted approaches to life's problems, unremarkable in their original setting, take on new meanings in an unfamiliar environment. Russian language and Soviet concepts of ethnicity, for example, can become powerful symbolic materials for creating bonds among many disparate individuals, overriding differences that would have precluded a sense of solidarity in the USSR. Amorphous stirrings of (immigrant) group identity thus begun are confirmed and become solidified through social contacts. The social and symbolic boundaries that develop in the process delineate Soviet immigrants from Americans in general, American Jews, and other immigrant and minority groups in particular.

As described in chapter 2, to a great extent Soviet citizens of Jewish nationality are indistinguishable from their Russian neighbors.

Not only have they abandoned traditional garb, they have also given up Yiddish for Russian and become integral parts of Soviet urban life.[2] Owing to intermarriage, physical differences have lessened,[3] and name changes, reflecting rejection of a parochial identity, have allowed many Soviet Jews to express their identification with what they see as "internationalism" instead. All this "drawing closer" notwithstanding, Jews in the USSR are officially bounded into a specific national group and, by this juridical designation, are demarcated from other peoples.

State-imposed Jewish identity is not the only means by which Soviet Jews maintain a sense of groupwide belongingness. Much like the Lumbee of North Carolina (Blu 1980, 140–143), Soviet Jews point to their origins—their Jewish "blood" and "genes"—and their progressiveness—contributions Jews have made to Russian-Soviet society and to the progress of the world in general—as they construct and pass on their Jewish identity. This identity does not rest on backward-looking nostalgia for a particularistic, religiously based culture, but rather derives from two forward-looking characteristics they often apply to themselves: intelligence and cosmopolitanism. Strong values for social and scientific awareness, adaptability, and progress, qualities of intelligentsia everywhere, underlie the specific identity of Soviet Jews. They bring this identity with them to America, and it plays a large role in shaping their responses to the people they meet in their new country.

On February 10, 1985, "Radio Horizons" ("*Gorizont*") aired an interview with an émigré psychiatrist.[4] The psychiatrist addressed the theme of Soviet immigrants' sense of cultural superiority and chided them for their oft-expressed belief that Americans are "stupid people." He advised them to quit mourning the loss of the Hermitage and go to the Metropolitan Museum of Art instead, and to learn English and American culture before drawing conclusions.

Those émigrés who discussed this broadcast with me laughed at themselves but, nonetheless, reiterated their belief in Americans' stupidity. Over and over, unsolicited in conversations as well as when the subject of informal interviews, Soviet immigrants stress that Americans are stupid, not because they are mentally deficient, but because they are overly kind and terribly naive.

One of the major reasons for this belief is that immigrants from the USSR are awed by what they understand the Soviet system to be—slogans and lies to its own people backed by the might of a fiercely strong army whose goal is to spread communism throughout the world. They are appalled that Americans know so little about the USSR and that the United States government ignores the Soviet threat by allocating what they consider to be "only" one-third of the national budget to defense. A woman in her early forties, when I met her for the first time, asked me, as do many immigrants when they are introduced to me as "an American who speaks Russian,"

> Why do Americans think that the Soviet Union is only Siberia—a land of snow and bears? Why don't they know and realize that the Soviet Union is a world power? It is because they think the Soviet Union is a barren wasteland that they do not and cannot see that it is a real enemy, a real power.

During the 1984 presidential campaign, with few exceptions, Soviet immigrants supported Ronald Reagan, claiming that America needs a strong leader, not a "kind uncle" to deal with the USSR. Americans who regard the Soviet Union lightly, or who think that the Soviets want the same peace and freedom as do Americans are "stupid."[5] Having experienced the Soviet system and determined to leave it, these people have become sophisticated, suspicious, and cynical. They view Americans as their direct opposites—parochial, content, and incredibly naive.

Americans may be good hearted, but they are superficially so, according to most émigrés. Pointing to the institutionalization of the American smile, Soviet immigrants speak of Americans' friendliness as void of conviction. Rather than viewing Americans who "smile all the time" as courteous and polite, émigrés consider them ridiculous. In their view, smiles ought to be reserved for people to whom one wishes to express genuine affection.[6]

Americans' smiles, initially read as invitations to friendship, are great disappointments to Soviet émigrés seeking Americans' empathy and companionship. A forty-year-old embittered art historian complained, "Americans smile and smile and with that they say they will help. But they never help, they only smile." Soviet immigrants speak of the American smile as friendliness without friendship, cynically described as smiling "not with their eyes, just with their teeth." These empty smiles are thought of as analogous to America's stance in international affairs, an empty gesture. It is naive and ignorant, they believe, to think that a smile or a declaration of peace can produce friendship or good will if there is nothing—neither genuine affection nor real military power—to back it up.

Immigrants' attitudes toward American culture are consistent with their political opinions and their attitudes toward sociability; they find Americans exceedingly parochial. Several Soviet immigrants have expressed surprise that so few Americans can speak or even understand Russian. They point out that Soviet schoolchildren learn French, German, English, or Spanish from early grades and that in major cities entire schools are conducted in these languages.[7] Believing that Russian is the "second world language" (second to English), they expected that more Americans would know it. Of course, since the vast majority of Soviet immigrants arrived in New York with no working knowledge of English, much of this comparison is simply a defensive reaction to their own feeling of inadequacy in a modern country where everyone—even the street-cleaners—speaks English.

More appalling to them than the lack of linguistic competence in Russian is Americans' ignorance of Russian (literary) culture. That most Americans have never heard of Mayakovsky and Akhmatova—to say nothing of Pushkin, Tolstoy, and Turgenev—attests to their insularity and ignorance. Immigrants boast that in the USSR they read Shakespeare, Dickens, Jack London, Ernest Hemingway, and John Steinbeck, albeit in translation. The fact that American students do not read similarly great Russian authors is further evidence of the immigrants' greater worldliness and cultural superiority, demarcating them from provincial, uneducated Americans.

Coupled with the label, "stupid," is a longing on the immigrants' part for the seemingly effortless, relaxed way in which Americans live. A middle-aged factory foreman expresses his amazement: "I don't understand it. People at work never seem angry or harassed. They do their jobs, but they talk to each other, listen to the radio, and they produce so much more than Soviet workers." American-English phrases such as "Take it easy" and "Relax, enjoy yourself" are frequently sprinkled into conversational Russian. With these words, often accompanied by a laugh, the immigrants tell themselves to adopt American ways, yet recognize that this easygoing, superficially stress-free manner is alien to them and difficult to master. It is therefore at least partially in reaction to their discomfort with the America they find so appealing, as well as in continuity with the particular personas they developed in the USSR, that Soviet Jewish immigrants stress their great intelligence and cosmopolitanism. Americans' parochialism can then account for the immigrants' inability to express themselves in English or to find American friends. In their designation of Americans as naive, provincial, and stupid, immigrants, who may find themselves to be just that in the American context, reconfirm their own high status, worldliness, and intellect.

In the Soviet Union, Jews pride themselves on being smarter and more cosmopolitan than Russians (see chapter 5). In America, they add that the experience they have gained from living in the Soviet Union is further proof of their sophistication.[8] While in the USSR the "nationalities" Russian and Jewish are mutually exclusive, and thus a dual identity of Russian-Jew is inconceivable, in America, as immigrants, they come to see themselves as such. Contrasted with everyone else around them, Soviet Jewish immigrants become conscious of something that was taken for granted in the USSR—they are imbued with and identify closely with Russian culture. Most emphatically reject the label "Russian" as their primary identity (see Simon and Simon 1982, 76; Federation of Jewish Philanthropies 1985, 20; Kosmin 1990, 30), but they frequently invoke Russian-ness to explain differences between themselves and their American neighbors:

- Americans ask if you want something to drink. Russians, when you come to their homes, give you a full meal.
- Americans shake hands and kiss the air. Russians hug and kiss, real big kisses.
- Americans ask, "How are you?" and before I even begin to tell them, they're walking away. Russians like to sit and talk. America is a country of action, not a country of talk.
- Americans say, "A man's house is his castle." Everyone has their own lives. Russians are much more open with each other in their apartment buildings; everyone knows what everyone else is doing—and that's how they think it should be.

Their "Russian" warmth, friendship, hospitality, love of poetry and conversation, which in the Soviet Union were never distinguishing characteristics, emerge in the United States in counterdistinction to

American ways of being. In their new country, then, immigrants from the USSR reaffirm their Jewish image of self as cosmopolitan intellectuals, and they add onto this self-description "Russian" qualities of sociability and generosity.

Soviet Jewish émigrés demarcate themselves from American Jews in much the same way they differentiate themselves from all Americans; only the contrasts they see with their fellow Jews are more disturbing to them. Soviet-born Jews decry the fact that their American counterparts are mainly Democrats and tend to be liberals. Boris voices a common explanation for this difference: "We learned from our experiences with so many Jewish Bolshevik leaders. We saw what kind of revolution they made. American Jews haven't learned what communism, socialism, liberalism really mean." While the prevailing sentiment is that Soviet-born Jews are wiser than the American-born, some immigrants express their political differences not in terms of superiority but as alienation. A middle-aged woman whom I met just once was eager to explain, "In the Soviet Union I knew for sure I was Jewish, but here I'm not so sure of this. American Jews voted for Mondale. We Russian Jews voted for Reagan."

This political alienation is part of a larger problem of unanticipated exclusion of Soviet Jews from American Jewish social circles. New immigrants had expected American Jews to treat them as family, with warmth and friendliness, and to respect their accomplishments. They wanted to be greeted as long-lost members of the group, to be treated as equals and resettled into the same kind of living conditions that their American counterparts enjoy. Immediate acceptance into the American Jewish mainstream was thwarted, however, by the language barrier, the pressing needs of finding inexpensive housing and employment for thousands of families, and the different views of Jewish identity held by each group (Markowitz 1988b).

American and Soviet Jews express their Jewish identities in different ways. While Soviet Jews see themselves as a "national group" sharing history, "blood," and intellect, in America, Jews are defined primarily as a religious group and secondarily as an ethnic entity. While certainly not all American Jews equate their Jewishness with Judaism, most of the people with whom Soviet immigrants have personal contact are part of the affiliated Jewish community and consider themselves believers in the Jewish religion. From the moment of their initial interviews with Jewish resettlement agencies, Soviet émigrés are told about and urged to participate in New York's Jewish life—to attend synagogues and to send their children to Jewish schools. Maxim puts it like this: "American Jews want us to be Jews their way—immediately, on the second day we are here. They can't understand that we are Jews our way."

More irksome than the matter of religion on the second day—to which many would have been receptive if discussion of religion had been accompanied by acceptance rather than sanctimony—was the impersonal processing immigrants feel they received from their Jewish social workers. Precisely because their immigration and resettlement were aided by fellow Jews and handled through the auspices of Jewish organizations, the newcomers expected a familial, caring welcome and recognition not only of their emigration ordeal but also of their educational and professional accomplishments. They expected housing in middle-class Jewish neighborhoods and jobs, or at least intensive English-language courses and appropriate retraining related to their professions. Instead, because the goal of NYANA (New York Association for New Americans, the initial resettlement agency for Soviet Jews coming directly to New York City) is to make new immigrants (economically) self-sufficient in the shortest time possible, the resettlement strategy in the 1970s and early 1980s was to guide immigrants into finding the jobs and housing that were immediately available.

The understanding behind NYANA's resettlement strategy is that with time and experience these "New Americans" will work their way up, both in the housing market and at the workplace. Newly arrived Soviet émigrés, however, do not share this understanding, because in the USSR one's first job and first apartment are often one's last. Moreover, many Soviet Jews feel that they had already proven themselves with years of university training and work experience. They were dismayed to find that "American Jews expected us to work in their factories for the same low wages as blacks. They saw us as another cheap labor supply like the Spanish."

American Jews—neighbors, employers, social workers—were confronted in turn with Jewish immigrants who behaved in ways that were quite alien to their own notions of how a Jew—especially a Jewish refugee—should act:

> I wanted to hire a bookkeeper. So FEGS [Federation Employment and Guidance Service] sends me a Russian. She looks at my office and tells

me it's too messy. She looks at my books and says my system isn't right. She's telling me how to run my business! When I told her goodbye, she was so surprised that she didn't have the job!

It makes me feel ashamed to hear everyone on the streets speaking Russian and only Russian all the time. They should be proud to speak English now that they are here in America. Especially the educated, they know how important it is to make a good impression and set an example.

Arrogant and hostile. They think everyone owes them something. And we all know this. Look at my synagogue . . . the rabbi, even he says it—the only time they come to the *shul* is when they need something, when we're giving away something for nothing. Otherwise, they want nothing to do with it. They're not real Jews. I don't care what anyone says.

Consequently, American Jews responded to the dissonance between their expectations and the reality they faced by developing an overall impression of Soviet Jewish immigrants as non-Jewish "Russians," arrogant, pushy know-it-alls. Prior to their arrival, American Jews had imagined Soviet refugees to be much like an idealized image of their own parents and grandparents, who without help from any organization, learned American ways and the English language and took whatever jobs they could find.[9] Secularized, Russian-speaking professionals with their own ideas of what they want from life in America simply do not fit their version of what a Jewish immigrant from Eastern Europe should be.

Soviet Jews react to this clash of expectations, in large part, by claiming superiority over American Jews. Feeling rejected, they deride American Jews as parochial and stupid for not knowing that Russian Jews of the 1970s and 1980s are professionals from large, modern cities, not *shtetl* dwellers. A former engineer, now working as a draftsman, explains:

How hurt and angry we felt that all these people were looking at us as uneducated peasants. We lived in the modern world there—why is it that Americans don't know this? This drives a wedge between us— them thinking they are better than we are. Why don't they know that we are just like they are—graduates of universities, professionals, and so on?

While many admire Orthodox Jews for the tenacity of their beliefs, Soviet Jews often look down upon them for living in the past, stating like Vladimir, "While American Jews held onto the religious part of being Jewish, they lost the national part." When pressed to define just what this "national part" is, again and again Soviet immigrants state, "It is our blood, our genes, our history, our intelligence, our professional accomplishments, our international character." This international character differentiates them from their parochial American counterparts, and, coupled with the immigrants' dashed expectations of a warm, familial welcome in addition to a language barrier and different historical experiences, has resulted in the erection of a social-symbolic boundary between the two Jewish groups.

The greatest distinction Soviet immigrants draw is one between themselves and other immigrant and minority groups. They point to the speed with which they learn English, find good jobs, open businesses, and revitalize entire neighborhoods as proof. Lera:

Tell me something—why is it that Puerto Ricans, who are American citizens, speak only Spanish? I've been here two years and I speak English better than Puerto Ricans who have been here seven, ten, or more years. Those Puerto Ricans are terrible people. They beat each other, kill, and destroy things—houses, cars. And they are considered Americans, and we are not!

Iskra:

Before we Russians came here to Brighton Beach it was becoming a terrible neighborhood—with blacks and Puerto Ricans. We cleaned up this neighborhood, opened stores, made this a nice place.

While they feel no communality with other immigrants, Soviet émigrés like and respect Koreans, in whose fruit and vegetable stores they shop. They have no negative comments about other Asians— Chinese, Japanese, Indians—either. Soviet immigrants' contacts with them are minimal, confined primarily to short business transactions. Competition in the workplace is minimal as well. They see only that

Asian-Americans are hard-working, that they keep to themselves, that they do not commit crimes, and that the products they sell are of good quality. And for this they deserve praise.

Soviet immigrants may express a sense of communality with other refugees from Communist countries, as Maxim explains:

> Here in Brighton Beach we are getting more and more Polish people. The irony of this situation does not escape me. There is a long hatred between the Polish people and the Jews, but in this case, the hatred of communism, and maybe the commonality of language, brings us together. There is no feeling whatsoever with Hispanics, and certainly none at all with blacks. We feel something for other people who are also refugees from such a system [communism]—Cubans who fled from Castro, even Vietnamese and Cambodians, but especially other East Europeans.

But even this sense of solidarity or just identification as political refugees is weak. When they say "we immigrants," Soviet émigrés mean specifically Jews from the USSR.

Soviet immigrants most sharply delineate themselves from American blacks, explaining, "We do not feel toward blacks [any sympathy] like American Jews do—I cannot tell you exactly why, only that it has something to do with our history." Soviet émigrés, often prefacing their remarks with, "I am not a racist," and pointing to statistics, frequently comment on blacks' laziness, anger, mean-spiritedness, drug addiction, and criminality. Lera offers her opinion:

> I understand that the history of blacks in this country has often been difficult, but now it's over twenty years that their situation has been improved, not only on paper but also in practice. I can't understand how many of them are *zly* [evil, mean, bad-tempered], that they don't want to work and have bad attitudes about everything.

Igor Reichlin (1983, 11–12) and a number of other émigrés explain this anti-black attitude as a result of Soviet propaganda. Since Soviet media portray American blacks as deprived of civil rights, uneducated, and primitive due to the inherent inequality and racism of capitalist systems, that is precisely how former Soviet citizens see blacks when they come to America. They are shocked to find blacks in the same classrooms as their children and at their places of work earning the same salaries as whites. They explain educated, professional blacks as exceptions to the rule (see Aksyonov 1989, 93–95).

Others dismiss the Soviet causation theory of their attitudes toward blacks and, like Regina, emphatically state, "We learned our prejudices here by seeing how they behave." They cite as examples of blacks' disgraceful behavior muggings and robberies, the number of blacks on welfare rolls, and blacks' destruction of once-nice neighborhoods.[10] No one can understand affirmative action policies; having endured a long history of persecution in Russia and discrimination in their own lifetimes, and having worked harder than everyone else to achieve, they feel that blacks should do the same. Immigrants view affirmative action as reverse discrimination, unfair to all Americans but most unfair to blacks, who now feel "they are owed something and that they don't have to work for anything." What they see as blacks' laziness, lack of achievement orientation, and self-pity they find contemptuous. Because these qualities are in sharp contrast to their own strong values for high achievement, intellectual prowess, and hard work, Soviet Jewish immigrants feel no sympathy for, and certainly no common bond of oppression or minority status with, American blacks.

To summarize, Jewish immigrants from the USSR use the same central characteristics—intelligence and cosmopolitanism—that they invoked to distinguish themselves from others in the Soviet Union to draw boundaries around themselves in America. While in the USSR there were few readily discernible characteristics by which they were identified as different from the majority, in America language (or accent) is a sure sign of their non-majority status. Knowing that they are immigrants, rejecting and feeling rejected by other groups, Soviet Jewish émigrés have forged a sense of their own group identity. Whereas in the Soviet Union this identity arose in counterdistinction to a Russian one, in the United States Russian-ness becomes a key component of who they are and an added symbolic factor in creating a sense of community.

SOCIAL STATUS: HIERARCHIES OF HERE AND THERE

While Soviet Jewish immigrants will, in the main, agree that they are distinguishable as a group, they also claim many intragroup distinctions. It is these distinctions, unimportant to outsiders, that contribute to the body of knowledge that Soviet immigrants claim as their own. Immigrants assess each other's intelligence and cosmopolitanism by two major sets of criteria: geography and occupation. Place of residence and profession in America and in the USSR are considered in concert, but each status indicator is not necessarily given equal weight. The hierarchy is manipulable, and it rests with the individual to know the hierarchy, assess the situation, and present himself or herself in the most favorable light.

Crucial to feeling part of a community is to accept, understand, and use the status system other members employ to judge and classify each other. Because immigrants can play up or play down their past or their present, the status system provides an arena in which nostalgia for the "snows of yesteryear" is permissible and where adaptation to a new socioeconomic environment is encouraged as well.[11] This ongoing dialectic between notions of status derived from the Soviet experience and those learned in America demonstrates how "knowledge is a social product *and* knowledge is a factor in social change" (Berger and Luckmann 1967, 87).

The geographical status system of the USSR rests on a foundation of urban preference and Russocentrism. Urban preference is directly related to socioeconomic reality, since living conditions in the Soviet Union's largest cities are much better—in terms of housing, availability of consumer goods, and cultural amenities—than in towns and villages. It also derives from a strong value, in both Soviet ideology and Jewish culture, for progress and modernization.

Highest prestige thus accrues to Muscovites, followed closely by Leningraders; they are from the "centers" and are therefore considered most worldly and cultured. Muscovites and Leningraders vie with each other for the number one position. Those from Leningrad claim that their city is European and point to its Italian architecture, the Hermitage, and trading ties with the West dating back to Peter the Great. Muscovites declare that their city is *the* capital, home of the Bolshoi Ballet and the National Theater, sure signs of cultural supremacy (interestingly, never is the Kremlin invoked). The following is a conversation between Natalya, a Leningrader, and her cousin Mikhail from Moscow:

Muscovite: What are you crazy? It's Moscow! The National Theater is located in Moscow and that theater sets the [linguistic] standard for the entire nation.

Leningrader: Leningrad is a living museum, with unbelievable architecture, unparalleled except perhaps in Venice. The history of Russia, its art, architecture, and cultural richness are all in Leningrad.

M: Leningrad is just the provinces. You are slow-moving and slow-thinking, there—see how slowly she is speaking! Moscow is the heart of everything—the trendsetter!

L: The heart of everything? You don't have the theaters, the concert halls of Leningrad!

M: What are you talking about? We have the Bolshoi, and . . .

While Leningraders would willingly be placed together with Muscovites at the top of the geographic hierarchy, not all Muscovites and other Russians will accord to Leningrad equal top status.

Muscovites and Leningraders do agree on the status of people from Odessa. A common statement by immigrants discussing each other is that, "Ninety-nine [sometimes only ninety] percent of the people here from Russia are garbage, and the ones from Odessa are at the bottom of the pile!" Non-Odessans discuss Odessans' loudness, lack of manners, Ukrainian accent and poor grammar, bad taste, and extravagant manner of dress to make their point.[12] Maxim, from Moscow, recalls:

I was in Odessa once. It is a very strange place, very different from Moscow, so I found there very little in common. First, it is an old and dirty city—people still live there very poorly. I guess it is because people still live primarily in communal apartments—the absolute worst way to live, and there are still people living in basements. The apartments are very small, very cramped and terrible. The streets are filled with litter. And the most surprising thing to me was the way people shout across the street to one another, "Hey Fira! Come here!" No, in Moscow that is just not done; you just do not yell across the street.

Natalya, a former teacher whose contacts with Odessans began after having immigrated to New York, focuses her analysis on language, a telling status-marker:

In general, people from Odessa have a different accent. They speak so loudly, they don't even speak but shout. They have no grammar and mix up their cases. Maybe it's because it is a port on the Black Sea, and there are a lot of sailors, but it is the most horrible, ungrammatical way of speaking Russian I have ever heard.

People from Odessa acknowledge their status inferiority in the eyes of others by stating, for example, "No one, when they first meet me, thinks I am from Odessa because I don't have the accent," or, partially in jest, "That's right. I'm not a cultured intellectual—I'm a materialist from Odessa."

Most Odessans proudly describe the beauty of their city on the Black Sea, laud the cultural merits of its Baroque-style opera house, point to the major works of art produced in Odessa (by Pushkin and Tchaikovsky), and state that theirs is an international city, a former free port with its own stock exchange where Russian, not Ukrainian, is the everyday language. They talk longingly of the climate, the beach, and a relaxed way of life, which they consider superior to the iciness of Leningrad and Moscow. Vladimir explains:

> Odessa is a port; there are many sailors who come in and go out, and there is still a lot of initiative in the people of this city. Also, Odessa is a southern city, happy people there who love to talk. Maybe we talk too much and too loud, but we are a joyful people. . . . I think people are silent not because they are so smart, but because they have nothing to say!

Further down the status hierarchy are provincial outposts, such as Uzhgorod in the West Ukraine, and other small towns. Georgians, however, are assigned a special category of their own. Russian Jews often hold a positive impression of Georgians whom they consider to be proud, brave, freedom-loving, smart, hospitable, and tolerant, as well as good singers. Georgian Jews, although thought to be some-what clannish, are included in this description of Georgians, especially those from the capital, Tbilisi. Those from small towns are often regarded as "primitive." Georgian food is hailed as the very best, and many Russian Jewish homemakers pride themselves on their Georgian specialties. Soviet Jewish immigrants express great appreciation for Georgian music and toast-making.

Central Asians are at the very bottom of the list. A tiny minority of Soviet Jewish immigrants in America (most Central Asian and Georgian Jews who left the USSR resettled in Israel), they are known for clustering together, having low levels of secular education, and maintaining a religiously Jewish lifestyle. New York's Bukharans live in traditional Jewish neighborhoods, such as Borough Park, where they have established their own synagogue. They are mainly crafts-men, most of them shoemakers. Alex, a former Odessan who works in the American public sector, described the Central Asians to me and Maxim as we encountered several families at a Russian-speaking resort in upstate New York:

> They are called *chorniye* [blacks] by Ashkenazis [European Jews] be-cause they are dark and have black eyes. They were able to keep their customs longer than we in the West. And they are funny! Remember when we went on that tour of Washington, and just as we were walking out of the White House one turned to the other and asked, "*Gde my byl?*" [instead of *Gde my byli*, a grammatical error equivalent to ask-ing, in English, "Where was we?"]

Later, when we were alone, Maxim turned to me and stated,

> These two groups never meet and get together. They only look at each other and pretend that the other doesn't exist. Of course the Odessans think they are better than the Bukharans, who they consider to be more primitive and Eastern. You watch—not one conversation will take place between these two groups.[13]

Thus, the particular meaning system of Soviet geography, with its manifestation in Russian-language usage, plays an important role in determining one's place in the immigrants' status hierarchy. Moscow and Leningrad are the acknowledged centers, and their (former) resi-dents claim and are usually given top status. Former residents of Kiev, the Ukrainian capital, regarded as the most anti-Semitic place in the USSR, and Kharkov, the former capital of the Ukraine, are judged neither too positively nor too negatively; but they are univer-sally regarded as more provincial than people from the centers. Odessa, from which a large portion of New York's Soviet immigrant population comes, is mentioned frequently and negatively by former inhabitants of other Russian and Ukrainian cities, who believe Odes-sans to be materialistic, crass, and loud. Those from Central Asia and Georgian towns are at the bottom of the hierarchy because they are "primitive Easterners," having little knowledge of the "modern (Rus-sian) world."

Professions are assessed in much the same way, according to the intelligence and worldliness of their holders. Their ranking is not dependent on income. During the early 1980s in the USSR, a highly skilled metal worker earned 400 rubles a month, while an editor/translator made only 120, but the latter profession holds greater prestige. Professional, white-collar "scientific" work, for which an institute or university diploma is required, is distinguished from "black" work, manual labor, for the highest grades of which only as much as a *tekhnikum* (technical school, like a community college or vocational high school) certificate is requisite. Commercial positions and the service trades are sometimes ranked above and sometimes below workers. The uncertain position they occupy is due to the belief that although these jobs do not literally get hands dirty, their holders are often unsavory because they are more likely than not to be involved in shady (black market) deals: "A shop clerk is a big shot in Russia. She controls the goods. You want something, give her a little extra, and she'll put it away for you. You don't have something extra, too bad." This tradition of speculation (dealing *na levo,* on the left), whether it involves trading theater tickets for strawberries, penicillin for shoes, or cosmetics for meat, brings together people from all walks of life, professionals, service personnel, and workers. Resentments build, but they are dissipated, as the need for forming connections to gain access to goods and services takes precedence over class differences.

Wage differences aside, intelligentsia in Russia are provided for in many ways and receive reinforcement for the creative work they do. They are given almost free access to vacation spas and meeting places—including low-cost, good-quality restaurants—for after-work activities and, most important, greater access to severely limited information and cultural pursuits than all other Soviet citizens. Several immigrants pride themselves on having read stories by John Cheever, seen *E. T.,* and attended concerts of Western (rock and jazz) musical groups while still in the Soviet Union. Their riches, they insist, "were not in material things, but in spiritual things—like art, literature, music, discussions." Their high esteem for intellectual pursuits over materialistic ones was confirmed time and again by others like themselves in their friendship circles.[14]

Three distinguishable layers constitute the hierarchy: the intelligentsia (professions in the arts, sciences, teaching, engineering, and law), workers, and the commercial/service trades (which include shop clerks, hairdressers, truck drivers, restaurant personnel, mechanics, and some managers). The further one is from getting one's hands dirty, either literally, by farming or factory work, or figuratively, by dealing with money, the higher the status one holds.

Profession can counteract geography, but stereotypes insist that jobs and place of residence are interrelated. Thus, as Nona explains, white-collar professionals come from Moscow and Leningrad, and people involved in commerce come from Odessa:

> The cream of the Odessa crop, they are different from the usual Odessans, but there is still something about them. Like there is a difference between people from New York and people from Texas. People there, in Odessa are different; they have a commercial orientation.

Soviet Jewish immigrants are united by an understanding of ideal status in the Russocentric, progress-oriented world from which they come. They are part of a Russian-made hierarchy and use it to assess themselves and others in terms of geography and occupation. Whether or not they accept the place given to them by others, they do agree that at the top of the hierarchy, as it exists, is the Moscow intellectual, and at the bottom is the Central Asian craftsman, rivalled only by the Odessan *spekulant* (speculator, blackmarketeer).

In America, a parallel geographically based hierarchy develops. Since immigrants from Moscow and Leningrad have settled in large numbers in the Forest Hills, and Rego Park sections of Queens, while Odessans have tended to prefer Brighton Beach and Bensonhurst in Brooklyn, the former neighborhoods hold higher status than the latter, and Queens is generally regarded as more prestigious than Brooklyn. While no neighborhood is homogeneous in terms of its immigrant population, this status differentiation is recognized by all. Leningraders, Muscovites, Kievans, and Kharkovites in Brighton Beach speak defensively about why they live there. Oleg:

> Queens, no. I know that's where the intelligentsia lives, but I don't want to live there. All my life I dreamed of the ocean. Although I have no real friends here, no one really is my type, I like living here.

Natalya:

> I went to a party in Queens, and we are all arranging for rides home. Someone asks me where I live, and I say, "Brighton Beach." "In Brighton Beach? A woman from Leningrad, as intelligent as you are, in Brighton Beach?" a woman asks me. Then we took her home to her high-rent Forest Hills apartment building—and it's right across from a cemetery! And I told her that I prefer my Brighton Beach and the ocean to her cemetery.

Soviet Jewish immigrants have also made homes in suburban Westchester and Rockland counties, in New Jersey suburbs, on Long Island, on Staten Island, and in Manhattan—sometimes in luxury apartment buildings—as well as in Brooklyn and Queens. The top of the geographic hierarchy, listed above, conforms exactly to Americans' ideal. The middle rungs of the hierarchy depend on how "immigrant" the neighborhood is. While they proclaim their cultural superiority over Americans, Soviet émigrés also know that clustering in immigrant "ghettos" marks them as parochial and provincial. Thus, Rego Park and Forest Hills derive their status not only from the preponderance of Muscovites and Leningraders but also from the fact that there are fewer Russian-speakers in those neighborhoods than in some areas of Flatbush and in Bensonhurst and Brighton Beach. At the very bottom of the hierarchy are predominantly black neighborhoods, such as Coney Island, Far Rockaway, the Lefrak City development in Corona, Queens, and Crown Heights and Williamsburg, where Hasidim, American blacks, Hispanics, and Haitians live side by side.

The professional hierarchy in this country, however, differs from the Soviet one, for most immigrants claim that in America there is only one indicator of status, prestige, and success: money. While in the Soviet Union money was rendered unimportant because of commodity shortages and a prevalent fear of displaying too much wealth, in America money *can* buy everything and should be used to this end. Maxim, a formerly "poor in things, rich in spirit" Muscovite, defends his quest for a solid income:

> In America, to survive, money is a necessity. In the Soviet Union, no one had much money, so we talked and discussed, and with these talks

and discussions we could show our individuality and make links with the outside world. In America, there are many, many links with the outside world, all available to everyone, even in one's home—in front of the TV or by telephone. And all you need for this is enough money.

Some immigrants work hard to reestablish themselves in the professions they had in the USSR, striving to replicate their Russian-grown status on American soil. But sometimes musicians become salesmen, writers turn taxi-drivers, and promising physics students go into computer programming to earn "enough money." Victor, who has worked rather than attend college since his arrival in America five years ago, comments:

> Money is getting more important than profession among many people in the Russian community. I know a man, an engineer, he was making four hundred dollars a week after taxes. He was working in his profession. Then he decided to get rid of this profession and go into business, where he now makes about two to three thousand a week.

Because money, in the eyes of Soviet immigrants, replaces education and intellect as the key measure of social status in America, some willingly forfeit their place in the Soviet hierarchy for an equivalent or higher one in what they perceive to be the American system. Those who, as a result of emigration, unwillingly lose their positions in the Soviet status system, in theory at least, can recoup their losses through the buying power of their American wages.

Edgar Goldstein (1979, 260), whose research among Soviet émigrés was conducted during initial phases of resettlement, pointed out that coping with the American socioeconomic system is difficult for "those whose profession, education and position in the hierarchy of society became a large part of their identity." Starting over, and at the bottom, threatens the very crux of their self-esteem. Goldstein predicted two opposing reactions of Soviet émigrés to life in this new system: self-realization, with resulting integration in society and reconciliation of the identity conflict; and blaming the conflict on American society, accompanied by resulting self-hate and compulsive clinging to past experiences while creating new idealizations of them (1979, 262).

Turning now to the situation five to six years after Goldstein's article, it appears that most Soviet immigrants have arrived at some resolution of this work-related identity conflict. The Federation of Jewish Philanthropies of New York (1985, 18) reports that the vast majority of émigrés are satisfied with their jobs. Two-thirds of the immigrants surveyed like their jobs a lot. An additional 30 percent are moderately satisfied with their work. Only 4 percent have expressed outright dissatisfaction. Some have successfully transferred their occupational skills and status to America; others have not, but it may be that the buying power of their salaries and the pleasures they derive from non-work-related pursuits contribute to their feelings of satisfaction (see Rogg 1971, 477–481, for similar findings among Cuban refugees). Several immigrants offer explanations for their identity-conflict resolution:

> There are many of us like this—driving a cab gives a good salary, and the musical instrument becomes a good hobby.

> *There,* in Moscow. *Was* a lawyer, *was.* At first it was hard for me to say this. Language was difficult for me—all my life I worked with language to express myself. All of a sudden I am no longer an intellectual but someone who can hardly make a grammatical sentence. It took time, but I've started working now at the police department—translation, and like a case aide. I enjoy it a lot.

> I was a construction engineer in Moscow. I came here absolutely without language—not a word of English. We're here now two and a half years, and now that language has started to come, I decided that I don't want to go back to my old profession. In Moscow I gave massages as a hobby, and [when we came] I found a job as a masseuse in a very good health club, and I like it very much.

While Soviet Jewish immigrants' status hierarchy is manipulable, allowing individuals to reconstruct themselves in America by selecting from among several reference points in their presentations of self, once most immigrants have been in the United States for over five years there is an increasing reluctance to confer high status on the basis of the past alone. Working is the norm, and many immigrants work at jobs they once considered to be beneath their educational and professional dignity. With time they have come to accept themselves in these positions and have, to a great extent, resolved the conflict between being an intellectual and working for money at a job that does not necessarily utilize their mental skills or advanced education.

The past can be invoked to bolster the present. The immigrants' social status system is based on reference points in two worlds, although it is increasingly grounded in the social reality of America. Intelligence and cosmopolitanism, as evidenced by Russian-language usage, place of origin, and professional training, remain very important. But those who sit at home, refused to work at jobs "below" them, blaming America for their loss of status, who exaggerate their past accomplishments and deride fellow immigrants as nothing but *spekulanti i meshchane* (speculators and materialists) find themselves increasingly isolated and falling to the bottom of the hierarchy. Consistent with their strong value for progress, it is more acceptable in immigrants' eyes to reject the past by learning English and starting anew among Americans than to completely reject the present. As Oleg puts it, "After all, any intelligent person knows that we are in America now. We can remain Russian intelligentsia if we wish, but we are also part of America."

Most Soviet immigrants take a middle course and learn to divorce their basic identity as intelligentsia from work roles that may be incompatible with this identity. The status hierarchy they have constructed allows émigrés to use backward-looking status indicators to complete this role disjunction and mitigate the psychological effects of perceived downward mobility. As a system of social meanings, the hierarchy therefore reflects a synthesis of prior knowledge with American social reality.

FRIENDSHIP NETWORKS

Friendships differ from virtually all other relationships because, although they begin and end on a completely voluntary basis, what binds them is the sentiment and trust that are most often associated with family and kinship. Friendships are formed and guided by the intangible understandings of what such relationships ought to be, which then generate expectations on both friends' parts to behave in ways, and be the recipients of behaviors, that contribute to a feeling of well-being. Who makes friends with whom is crucial for assessing where the boundary lies in demarcating Soviet Jewish émigrés from others and how rigid, or flexible, this boundary may be.

In order for one person to be a friend to another, both must agree on the actions—symbolic and material—that constitute the friendship relationship. Not surprisingly, immigrants' friends are mainly immigrants. Of the 233 individuals surveyed by the Federation of Jewish Philanthropies of New York (1985, 33), 79 percent report that their three closest friends are fellow immigrants. Only 3 percent claim no immigrants in their friendship networks (see also Gitelman 1984, 96).

Data derived from fieldwork confirm these findings. Construction of friendship networks for twenty-three people (thirteen married and ten single) reveals that the vast majority (89 percent) of their close friends are immigrants as well.[15] Consistent with the Federation's findings, American friends of these twenty-three immigrants are, with one exception, all Jews. Feelings of commonality, reflected and expressed through the formation of close social relationships, are shown first and foremost toward fellow immigrants and then, at a very distant second, toward American Jews.

Friendship networks were further analyzed to determine how geography—immigrants' present neighborhoods in New York and their cities of origin—influences their friendship choices. Interestingly, most immigrants' friends are not their neighbors (62 percent). Odessans are somewhat more likely to live near their friends (52 percent of the sample) than immigrants from other cities (29 percent of the Muscovites, 39 percent of the Leningraders, and 22 percent of those from Kiev/Kharkov). Looking next at place of origin, friendships are almost evenly distributed between people from one's native city and people from other places in the USSR (48 percent and 52 percent, respectively). Muscovites and Leningraders are more likely to select friends from their own cities (60 percent and 57 percent) than Odessans and Kievans/Kharkovites (37 percent and 33 percent), who often find friends from cities other than their own. In general, geography has limited value for predicting immigrants' friendship choices.

Do immigrants seek out and develop relationships with people they knew in the USSR? Some are not only reluctant to look up old friends but consciously avoid them because, as a former schoolteacher from Kishinev, now a caseworker in Brooklyn, explains:

We are afraid of something—jealousy. Let me give you an example: Let's say I am in this country a few years. I work hard, I save money. Then someone I know comes over, and he wants right away to open a business and says to me, "You have money. Give me money so I can get started." But you have your own kids, things you want to buy, and you don't want to give the money. Then there's an argument and you're no longer friends. It's better not to even get involved.

The other side of this coin is that when newcomers arrive, either relocating from another place in the USA or direct from the USSR, they may remain scared and lonely, finding old friends neither helpful nor supportive. Contacts with old friends often result in disappointment and sadness rather than in the companionship and guidance that were hoped for and expected. Boris, who arrived in late 1983, three years after the peak of migration, recalls:

When my wife and I first arrived here, it was very hard for us, especially for her, to leave everything behind and start all over with no friends. I went out on Brighton and I got a lot of phone numbers, and I called many old friends.[16] . . . This fellow who I knew, when I first came, he sees me and shouts, "Borya! You're here! It's so great to see you!" and that's it. Did he even invite us to his home for dinner? Did he ask if he could help me get a job or even give me some advice on how to start looking? No. Nothing—just, "Borya! Hi old buddy! Good to see you!" And that's all. This happened again and again.

Others explain that their old friends simply did not emigrate, or if they did, they live in Israel, California, Chicago, or Canada. Still others talk of drifting apart, finding new interests and different careers, with the consequence that the concerns shared in the Soviet Union are no longer important or relevant: "We just went our separate ways."

While almost two-thirds of émigrés' friendships are formed after people have left the USSR, some immigrants remain close with old friends. Muscovites are more likely than others to maintain old relationships (52 percent of the sample); a woman of twenty-seven who attended college and law school in America remains in close contact with her childhood friends from Moscow. These friends, who emigrated at about the same time she did, also completed their higher education in America and work in the professions; they have all "gone the same way." Another example illustrates a happy reunion between friends who had not seen each other in ten years. Boris continues:

> One day Slavik, just out of nowhere, called. He was speaking to some-one who knows the both of us who said we had arrived, and he took my phone number, called, and in the next few minutes was here to see me. Of all the many old friends from Russia, he was the one—the only one—who helped at all. I am not just talking about lending money and giving advice about life in America, I mean moral support, friendship—who invited me and my family to be with him and his family, as friends, real friends. He is it, the only one.

Immigrants' friendships then are not greatly determined either by geography or by the availability of friends from one's past. The majority of friendships are formed after emigration, with people from different places.

Immigrants tell of finding friends from three different sources:

(1) Those with whom they shared first experiences in the West. Although a very small percentage of this sample formed intimate friendships during their immediate post-migration period, many speak of *priateli* (the intermediate friendship category) made then. Boris and Lera provide one example of a close relationship: They arrived in Vienna from Odessa at the same time as another couple with a young daughter arrived from Moscow. After ten days there, the families travelled together to Rome, where they spent two months awaiting their American entry visas. The families found lodgings in different parts of Rome and visited with each other intermittently during their stay. Once in New York they settled several miles apart from each other in Brooklyn, but since they took the same English classes at NYANA, they shared the trials and tribulations of developing English skills, successes and failures in their job searches, and they consulted with each other when making major purchases. Two and a half years later, in 1986, they remain close friends; they visit in person on the average of once a week and frequently speak to each other by telephone.[17]

(2) Friends of friends (17 percent of the sample). When immigrants hold big parties of any kind, to celebrate birthdays, anniversaries, housewarmings, they invite all their friends and family. While sitting together at the table, enjoying food and drink, lively conversa-

tions develop among the guests. At the end of the evening, telephone numbers are often exchanged, and friendships begin. Irina recalls how she and her husband met a couple from Moscow with whom they now enjoy a close friendship:

> No, we haven't known them a long time, just a few months ago. . . .
> We were spending an evening at Tanya's, my husband's old friend, and they were there, too. We started to talk and immediately we knew that they are our kind of people. We saw them a few times after that, and then our friendship just grew. We're planning to go to Europe together.

(3) Those with common interests, expressed by participation in group activities (19 percent of the sample). Men may meet each other by playing volleyball, soccer, or basketball. Friendships begin during the summer on the beach, and by taking part in social, political, cultural, group travel, or other leisure-time pursuits. Irina describes the beginning of another friendship:

> We took a bus tour to Florida, and they were sitting near us. So we started to talk and found that we have a lot in common. It was a week-long trip, and we got to know each other, and when we came back to New York we stayed friends.

In all cases, development of friendships from initial encounters, including meeting up with old friends, springs from a somewhat intuitive feeling that "they're our kind of people." Two chance encounters developed into friendships as a result of this feeling, the first between two women in their thirties—a dentist from Leningrad and a technical-school graduate from Odessa—and the other between two men—a Leningrad engineer and a former Muscovite theater administrator:

> It's a funny story. She was shopping for a gift in this boutique I work in. One of the other girls was waiting on her, and I heard her talk, and I noticed that she had an accent. I was thinking, could she be Russian? There are very few Russians in this area. I started to talk to her and she to me—about the clothes—and then, I think I just came out and asked where she was from, and we exchanged phone numbers. I just had this feeling—and, well, you know how close we are—and our children.

> How did I meet him? It's hard to believe—on a bus. Yes, on a bus. Behind me I heard good, well-constructed Russian. I hadn't heard that

in a long time—where I live are a lot of workers and craftsmen—and here was someone speaking beautiful Russian. I turned around and started to talk to him.

More important than any one factor in the development of friendships is the combination of factors that leads people to think that they have something in common.[18] Feelings of commonality derive both from shared aspects of their former lives in the USSR and from their current ways of life in America.

Teenagers and children frequently include fellow immigrants in their close circles of friends as well. The Federation of Jewish Philanthropies' study (1985, 33) shows that although immigrants' children are more likely to have American friends than their parents, for the majority (60 percent), friendship networks are composed mainly of other immigrant children. Only 3 percent of the sample reported that none of their children's friends is from the Soviet Union. A fifteen-year-old high school student in Brooklyn explains, "It just happened. In my school the Chinese hang out with the Chinese, the Italians with the Italians, the Russians with the Russians. I don't mind at all. They're all nice kids, and we help each other a lot." An eleven-year-old, who was born immediately after her parents emigrated, emphasizes her feelings of ease and warmth when with immigrant friends:

> I never even set foot in Russia, but I feel myself most like the Russian people.[19] I don't know how to explain it to you, but they are so warm, so nice. Like with Svetlana and her parents—we just met them a few months ago, but now it seems like we've known each other all our lives. You know they will help you. Whenever we get together, it's so warm, all of us get along so well. And these other friends of ours, and their parents, also Russians, it's the same with them—always warm and friendly.

In Brighton Beach and Sheepshead Bay, and along Ocean Parkway, groups of Russian-speaking teenagers congregate to socialize. Some immigrant teens, however, avoid Russian hangouts because they reject the values and tastes of these groups. These teenagers identify more closely with their American-born classmates. Mark, the sixteen-year-old son of Irina and Oleg, explains:

> I just don't have much in common with them. First of all, because of dressing. I know that sounds funny, doesn't it? You would think it

doesn't make any difference what people wear, but it does. I don't like
the way they dress at all—the styles and all. Too showy. . . . To say
hello, yeah, but that's all. I just seem to have more in common with
American kids. Like music. . . . My idea of a good time isn't walking
on the boardwalk and eating sunflower seeds.

Soviet Jewish immigrants in New York have a huge field of potential friends from whom to choose. Friends, however, are not selected
at random, nor are they chosen solely on the basis of convenience.
The émigrés make judgments about the characters of the people they
meet and determine whether or not they have much in common. A
feeling of commonality derives from the perception that the potential
friend and oneself share a common orientation toward life—that both
occupied similar positions in the Soviet social system and have
adapted in like fashion to New York, or in the instances in which
friendships are made with Americans, that the latter understand and
appreciate the immigrant as a full person. Common interests and
common orientations are therefore most important in the development and maintenance of friendships, overriding such factors as territorial propinquity, city of origin, and even having been friends in the
USSR. When one friend changes course and thereby alters or elimi-
nates these commonalities, friendships are undermined. Irina comments on her and Oleg's friendship with another couple, Misha and
Ella:

We were very close, but then Misha just didn't have time anymore to
do anything. His English isn't so good so he couldn't transfer his job.
So he drives in a limo service. All he ever thinks about anymore is
driving, working to make money, more and more money. His orientation has changed, and we don't see them much anymore.

Friends satisfy each other's needs for acceptance and belonging.
They offer understanding and support, and through their interactions
friends create a feeling of mutual well-being for each other. By sharing joy and sorrow, as well as providing assistance in coping with the
mundane problems of daily life, friends validate each other, telling
each other that their lives are meaningful and worthwhile.

To best offer support, two people must share knowledge; each
one must know what is meaningful to the other. Therefore, it comes

as no surprise to find that friends are very much alike in a wide variety of ways (Jacobson 1973, 80–88; Jackson 1977, 59–61), and Soviet immigrants are no exception to this rule. They select as friends people who share a vision of self, and mutually confirm these selves through their interactions. Immigrants' selves are grounded in two worlds, and friends must appreciate and empathize with this dichotomy. Immigrants' friends are expected to understand who they were and what was accomplished in their old lives and that, in spite of having left the USSR, these old lives were not without merit. Immigrants want their friends to accept them in their new lives as well, to agree on the importance of work in the American context, and on how free time and money are to be spent. It is through interactions with people who share basic values, agree on priorities, live in similar socioeconomic circumstances, have a common history and sense of a common destiny, that the émigrés are able to integrate their identities. As intragroup friendship networks intersect and overlap, friends, and friends of friends, come to form a community of social interaction.

SECONDARY RELATIONSHIPS

Friendships, intense and intimate relationships, are like the bright colors that emerge in a child's scratch drawing; they must be carved out and developed. The black overlay is equivalent to a social field, the dozens of secondary relationships in which one takes part everyday. The roles played in these interactions—purchaser, neighbor, consumer, information-seeker and information-giver, and more—all contribute to one's self-image and to how one is viewed by others. The social field, in an impersonal way, helps shape the individual as it structures relationships with other people and a variety of institutions.

While friendships help integrate the self, secondary relationships force individuals to dissect themselves into parts. Some social theorists suggest that the variety of roles urbanites play may lead to a sense of disconnectedness and anomie (Wirth 1938; Durkheim 1951, 256–258, 323, 353, 368–369) and narcissistic self-indulgence (Simmel 1950b, 422–424). This role-playing, however, can also be viewed in a positive light, as it allows individuals to experiment with and express at different times diverse aspects of the self. How people navigate their social fields and how these fields constrain and structure people's navigation therefore contribute as much to the creation of community as does participation as a "full person" in primary relationships.

Like the second-generation Italian-American "urban villagers" Herbert Gans (1962) describes, Soviet Jewish immigrants in New York rarely complain of anonymity.[20] While the roles they play in the American workplace and those they play at home may differ, many immigrants view the dichotomy as complementary, not disorienting. In fact, the superficiality of American work relationships is welcomed by some as a respite from the intense social interactions of which they were part at their places of work in the Soviet Union. In a heated discussion about Americans' superficial sociability, a female engineer offered her views:

> And rightly so that Americans say, "Hi, how are you?" "Fine." and that's it. I remember at work in Moscow the entire morning was taken up with answers to "How are you?"—this one's husband drinks too much, that one's daughter got a 2 [failing grade] in mathematics, this one has stomach problems—no wonder work doesn't get done there. I prefer the American system—work at work.

These work relationships contrast with the relationships most have at home. While neighborhood in New York exerts little influence in the selection of immigrants' friends, it is a factor in defining the wider field of casual interactions. Especially for those who live in neighborhoods with high immigrant density (e.g., Brighton Beach and Sheepshead Bay, Bensonhurst and Flatbush, Forest Hills, parts of Rego Park and Astoria in Queens, several blocks of upper Manhattan's Washington Heights, and a small area in the North Bronx), home environment promotes continuation of Russian-style patterns of interaction. Although the roles of neighbor and shopper in the Soviet Union are not intimate, they are based on and aimed at increasing personal knowledge of one another as greetings are exchanged and business transacted.

The role of a neighbor is to know one's neighbors, to keep track of the comings and goings in the apartment building and in the neighborhood in general. Immigrants state that their reason for establishing personal ties with their neighbors is based on the Russian value of sociability, but this is not the full story, for knowing one's neighbors serves the individual well. Knowledge of neighbors' lifestyles and traffic patterns allows for better management of the immediate environment, thereby decreasing feelings of strangeness and lessening the possibilities of danger (Merry 1981).

Émigrés tell with disgust of a not-too-distant past when they, and most Soviet citizens, lived in communal apartments, sharing toilets, bathing facilities, and kitchens with their neighbors.[21] Even today, when apartment dwellers share only an entrance corridor, a courtyard, and a laundry room, neighbors in the USSR know each other very well. Most people keep kitchen windows open, so that "everyone knows what everyone else is having for dinner, who is having a family argument, and so on." Neighbors in the Soviet Union are intimately acquainted with each other and feel that this knowledge is their right and duty; after all, they are all living together in one home.[22]

In New York, Soviet immigrants remain overtly interested in the affairs of their neighbors. When moving vans park in front of apartment buildings in Brighton Beach, current residents inspect their contents and question their new neighbors. A fur-clad grandmother and her roly-poly grandson greeted me as I began to move into my apartment: "So many books! So many books you have! But where is your furniture? Is that all you have?" Neighbors also ask newcomers what kind of jobs they have, their salaries, how old they are, how many children they have (and if none, why not), and their nationality.[23] These questions are by no means regarded as prying into the private lives of others but rather as basic facts one should know about the people with whom one lives. Those who fail to find out about others in their building are viewed as socially incompetent, and if they are liked, neighbors will share information with them. A woman of my age living in my building wanted to gossip about another woman in the building and was shocked that I did not know who she was talking about:

How could you not know her? She's American, has a little boy around nine, and a German shepherd. A terrible mother—she goes out with all kinds of Puerto Ricans. I see them coming and going. And I've seen her coming home by car service very late at night. Are you sure you don't know her?

Neighbors use their knowledge of each other not only as a cognitive tool by which their immediate environments become more manageable but also as a way to gain access to services. Knowing one's neighbor provides informal channels to goods and services that might not be easily obtainable through formal routes. Maxim reminisces about relationships among neighbors in his former state apartment house:

> Let's say, for example, that I have a job as a bookkeeper, and I drive a car and wear stylish clothes. Of course my neighbors know that on one hundred rubles a month I cannot afford all this. So maybe they call the police, or maybe they come to me to get the same things as I have.

In America, neighbors, especially those over age fifty-five, congregate in folding chairs in front of their buildings and consult with each other about family matters, illnesses, current events, the best places to make purchases, and social welfare benefits (Supplemental Security Income, or SSI; Medicare; Section 8 housing assistance). They often ask younger neighbors to explain issues and to translate for them: "*Devochka* [Girlie]! I got this in the mail today. Is it important? What does it say? Do I have to do anything? Can I throw it away?" Younger tenants, too, sit in front of their buildings, often exchanging babysitting services and informally taking turns supervising their children, who play outside in nice weather.

Neighborliness among Soviet immigrants does not boil down to cursory greetings and sporadic exchange of specific services. The role of neighbor is to know thy neighbor; in the process of protecting oneself, one should look out for the welfare of others as well. Through neighbors' gathering and sharing of information about each other, they create a secure environment for each resident. When neighbors move away, those who remain suffer a loss. It decreases one's knowledge of the building and therefore lessens the amount of security one feels. Neighborly relationships are based not only on a personal relationship between two or more people but also represent an investment in bettering living conditions.

The same is true of business transactions between immigrants. In Brighton Beach, approximately one-third of the stores are owned by Soviet émigrés.[24] Of the remainder, many employ Russian-speaking salespeople and display Russian signs in their windows to attract immigrant shoppers.

In the Soviet Union, as described by immigrants, there are two kinds of business transactions: (1) completely impersonal ones that involve waiting, usually for a long time, in a line to pay for a product, then taking one's ticket to the product line to wait there for the purchase; and (2) those carried out through personal ties, either at the store, where special customers (friends, or those willing to "give something extra") can avoid lines by dealing directly with a sales clerk, or at one's home, where sales personnel, factory workers, and others will sell merchandise directly to friends. Everyone in the Soviet Union has "connections," for without them one could never obtain the goods that seem to be everywhere but in the stores.

In Brighton Beach, too, customers establish "connections" with sales help (or shopkeepers) in their favorite stores. While these connections do not always result in lower prices, they create an atmosphere of friendliness that encourages shoppers to return. Even those who may not have personal relationships with shop personnel often prefer to do business in immigrants' stores. Language is only one reason for this preference; shopping behavior is another. Soviet immigrants often enjoy haggling or getting a good bargain, even intellectuals from Moscow like Maxim: "Good, I'm glad we came in here first to try on the jacket and find out the price. The tag says $89.95. I'll come back later and get it for eighty dollars." In an English As a Second Language class, Soviet immigrants all bargained with the "sales clerk" as they role-played at making purchases. In fact, students called out from the audience to each other with advice as to how much the "merchandise" was really worth and expressed dismay when a Haitian student "bought" a sweater for the first quoted price.[25]

In addition to deriving pleasure from the feeling that one's patronage matters to store owners and from bargaining to get the best possible deal, immigrants like to shop at Russian stores because there they give and receive information. Outside the "International" (M & I International Foods), the largest Russian grocery-delicatessen-bakery in Brighton Beach, people always congregate. In small stores, too, gossip, along with goods and money, is exchanged:

—Will there be anything else for you today?

—No, but did you know that on my street there was a robbery today? One of the ladies—she was sitting right there in front of the building, a hunchbacked lady, you know her?—when they came in. She even saw them, but she didn't know they were coming to steal from her.

Within immigrant settings, then, so-called secondary relationships are at least minimally personalistic, for they are not merely quick, ritualized exchanges. Neighbors are expected to and do know each other, and store owners and their patrons establish ongoing relationships. It is not without irony that many immigrants remark about the village-like quality of their neighborhoods. A former Leningrader in his fifties comments:

> So we made our village, our colony here in Brighton Beach. Everyone here knows everyone—maybe not personally, but we know at least a friend or a relative of everyone else. Yes, it is funny that we all came from big cities and that we made for ourselves a village!

Émigrés who live outside the immigrant neighborhoods, even those who look with scorn at the "ghetto in Brighton Beach," have some ties to the enclave. Most Soviet immigrants have a friend or a relative living there, and virtually everyone goes to Brighton at some time for business or pleasure. A translator, living in Jackson Heights, Queens, remarks, "I never come to Brighton Beach. I can't stand it. Well, I do come once a month to shop—you can't get everything anywhere else, although there is a Russian store in my neighborhood." And a law student at New York University explains, "No, I rarely come to Brighton Beach. We live in Manhattan in the East Village, and my parents live in Queens. It's my uncle's birthday, that's why we're here. We always come to a Russian restaurant for family occasions."

Thus, virtually all Soviet immigrants have secondary relationships with other immigrants, either frequent or occasional, depending on where they live and where they work.[26] Those who live in immigrant neighborhoods have social fields more limited to fellow émigrés than those who live outside the enclaves. In either case, Soviet émigrés not only develop most of their friendships within the immigrant group but conduct casual interactions on an intragroup basis as well.

With few exceptions, Soviet immigrants also patronize American businesses and exchange brief greetings with American neighbors. Lera, a former Odessan living in Brighton Beach, likes to shop in Manhattan and at Queens neighborhood stores:

> It makes me feel like a person, a real person, to go into an American store where I hear, "Hello, can I help you?" and "Have a nice day," when I leave. I know that sounds funny, but to me it is nice. I am not a "Russian," not an immigrant, just a person like everyone else. It makes me feel like I belong here in America, not just in our Brighton.

Some will seek out American institutions, especially for banking and credit, specifically for this impersonal, efficient treatment and to ensure that their business matters remain private. These transitory transactions do not result in a feeling of disconnectedness but quite the opposite: They help Soviet immigrants—who have little if any possibility of returning to the land of their birth—in developing a sense of belonging to the wider new society of which they are part (see Hannerz 1986).

Through casual relationships, both with immigrants who share understandings of what it means to be a neighbor and business-owner or customer and with Americans who view neighborliness and sales transactions in a less personal way, immigrants confirm and reshape their social knowledge. By the simple fact that most interactions—on both a primary and secondary level—occur within the immigrant group, Soviet émigrés constitute a community of social relations. These social relations rest on a foundation of shared knowledge and understandings of what one should value and how one ought to behave.

4.

THE MORAL COMMUNITY

The question of society's moral base, that is, its values and common beliefs, has received considerable attention since the latter part of the nineteenth century as social analysts delineated differences between small-scale rural communities and complex, large-scale urban areas. Seminal theorists (e.g., Toennies 1957) suggested that community (*Gemeinschaft*), a group of people who intimately know and interact with each other; share interests, beliefs, and values; practice identical modes of livelihood; and are united by common territory, persists only in rural villages. In cities, rationally based society (*Gesellschaft*) replaces personalistic community; contract supersedes compact, law replaces tradition, and similarity of beliefs and occupations gives way to competition and diversity. Customs of small-scale societies, which unify the practical consciousness of their members (Giddens 1984, 4), or how they implicitly know how to "go on" in daily life, no longer implicitly guide behavior in societies of large scale but have been replaced by a rationally based codex of law, or by the constraints of technologically imposed space (de Certeau 1984, 40).

The works of Durkheim (1951, 1964), Toennies (1957), Maine (1906), Simmel (1950b), and Weber (1958) have inspired several generations of investigation into the sad condition of modern urbanites. Expanding on the themes of normlessness and anomie (in Durkheim's words) and alienation (in Marx's), those social analysts who declare "community lost" (Wellman 1979, 1204–1205) attribute the loneliness and insecurity of modern human beings to a lack of moral certitude deriving from an impersonal social world. In their "quest for community" (Nisbet 1969), it is claimed that urbanites become susceptible to totalitarian ideologies (see Langer 1951, 292; Marcuse 1966, xxvii–xxviii, 93) and over-conformity (Dewey 1930, 85–86; Riesman 1950) as they search for acceptance and belonging. Berger, Berger, and Kellner (1974) apply the image of a "homeless mind" to the uprooted urban-dweller who thinks and reflects but has no social grounding in which to share or verify these thoughts and feelings. Durkheim's once optimistic prediction that a highly differentiated large collectivity of people would develop a uniform morality based on mutual interdependence has not, according to the "community lost" view (and indeed, Durkheim himself), come to pass. Instead, the "freedom" that city life brings with its break from tradition is regarded as a prison that produces bewildered, lost souls (see Dewey 1930, 52) held together in a somewhat orderly fashion only by means of contracts and laws. Thus, "community lost" adherents conclude that no firm system of values and beliefs unifies modern-day city-dwellers.

Others, proponents of what Wellman (1979, 1205–1208) calls the "community saved" and "community liberated" viewpoints, dispute the contention that urbanites live in social and moral chaos. Although they agree that the city is not one big, unified community—or *Gemeinschaft* writ large—they propose that each city is composed of communities. These communities may be, but are not necessarily, neighborhoods (geographically bounded places where people reside); they are collectivities of people who share a sense of belongingness. This feeling of communality derives from agreement in values, attitudes, and what Redfield (1973, 80) calls social "oughts," played out in the structuring of everyday life and through personal relationships. It is precisely this moral base upon which urban communities rest: "At present, perhaps the most tenacious pull of the community concept is its moral implications. To share interests and live together requires agreement on rules, concern for others, and a commitment to the group" (Scherer 1972, 5). Or, in Koenig's (1968, 96) more concise terms, "a community can develop satisfactorily only when there are common values which determine its life."

Simply stated, social analysts who have located community within the urban sprawl point to shared value orientations that give meaning to social interactions and daily routines. This moral base, more than geographic proximity, economic interdependence, or any of a number of other factors, is the key to community formation and maintenance. While the majority of urbanites' interactions are indeed fleeting, impersonal, and rationally based, and while no one mega-morality unites all residents of a city, within each urban center communities of value orientations do persist.

Understanding the central concepts that subtly inform and are consciously called upon to provide the rationale for everyday life—what they are, how they are interpreted by immigrants, and why they continue to have salience outside the Soviet Union—provides insight into the directions that self- and culture change take among the Soviet émigrés. As they point to their principles of friendship, their ideas about "the collective" and about culturedness and intellectualism in challenging what they consider to be inappropriate behavior by fellow immigrants as well as Americans, and justify changes they see in themselves, Soviet Jewish émigrés unite themselves into a moral community that differs not only from other communities in New York, but also from those in the USSR of which they were once part.

FRIENDSHIP AND HOSPITALITY

Pessimistic accounts of the modern human condition that point to urbanites' loneliness, rootlessness, and alienation fail to consider friendship as an escape from this prison of anonymity and insecurity (Jacobson 1973 and Fischer 1982 present major challenges to the pessimistic stance). Former Soviet citizens, however, have never overlooked the importance of friendship and state that they value it above everything else. Time and again when I asked, "What is the meaning of friendship (*Shto takoe druzhba*)?" immigrants answered with something like, "Now you are asking the right question. This is it, this is the right question to ask. Friendship means, well, friendship is being a friend. This is most important to us, more than anything else in the world."

Friendship is almost never discussed in and of itself; it is always linked to the notion of escape, escape from a sociopolitical system that, like Western urbanism, may breed insecurity and estrangement. The contents of these systems, however, greatly differ. In American cities people are free to believe or not believe in creeds from agnosticism to Zoroastrianism, to select from a wide range of competing brands of products and services, and to entertain themselves in any of a broad variety of ways. No one "truth" is absolute or certain, and no one mode of behavior is dictated; the burden is placed upon the individual to make these often difficult choices. The Soviet state, at least prior to the Gorbachev regime, was an all-embracing "total system" present in every facet of each citizen's life.[1] This state, which called itself "the people of the USSR," owned and operated all industries, services, commodities, media, and art. It provided each citizen with housing, employment, health care, food, and entertainment. The government and party leadership of the USSR claimed that their country, by providing to its people everything they need, had eliminated alienation of people from one another and laid the groundwork for a utopian society. These beliefs were proclaimed in every city on huge red banners, engraved on the facades of factories and office buildings, and broadcast in newspapers, on radio and television, and in literature and art.

A problem, however, existed in the vast difference between Soviet rhetoric and the reality of everyday life. Immigrants speak passionately about the disconnection between government slogans and commodity and information shortages and its consequent psychological effect—an overall feeling of estrangement. Lera, who spent several years deciding whether or not to emigrate, looks back in disgust:

> There are so many unpleasantries [*nepriatnosti*], things to put up with all the time that remind you that you are not really a human being. All the time you are told that you live in the greatest country in the world, that we are a modern power. And then there are things like toilet paper. . . . Menstruation? You don't want to know about that. That's even worse than toilet paper. Every so often, after standing in very long lines, you might be able to find sanitary cotton. Otherwise, you just stay at home. And if you must go out, and there is nothing available, which is most of the time, use old towels and rags, and wrap them around like a diaper, and pray that nothing happens. Can you imagine how this feels? Even if nothing is visible, you feel yourself to be filthy dirty, an old hag from an ancient village—this, in the most forward-looking country in the world!

Sofia, Vladimir's wife, reflects with sadness:

The tragedy of everyday life in the Soviet Union is—what comes out from their mouths and goes on in their heads are two very different things—you always have to be careful to guard your real thoughts. What a terrible country!

While American urbanites and Soviet city-dwellers may share a feeling of disconnectedness vis-à-vis society, this feeling stems from different causes and contexts. Westerners may be overwhelmed by choice, but Soviets confront a Truth that contradicts the reality of their existence. Life in both these atmospheres of perplexity can lead to high rates of suicide (Durkheim 1951), narcissistic over-indulgence (Simmel 1950b), and mental illness (Srole and Fischer 1978). Other urban theorists have pointed out that insecurity and the range of choice available in cities lead people to create rewarding social ties through participation in voluntary groups (Wirth 1938), friendships (Fischer 1982), and helping networks (Stack 1974), which mitigate the dissonance. To counter the problem of feeling "not really human" in the Soviet Union, immigrants most often speak of two solutions, vodka and friendship, which not infrequently accompany one another.

Excessive drinking and alcoholism have been cited as the USSR's biggest social problem. During Andropov's, and in 1986–87 under Gorbachev's, regime, the state instituted crackdowns against alcoholism by ordering stores to deplete their stock of vodka and to cut back on the hours during which alcohol could be purchased. Immigrants laugh at the inefficiency of these measures, saying that workers would sooner slip away from their jobs before the shops close than find themselves without vodka. Should all else fail, they added, Russians would simply distill their own *spirt* (wood alcohol) or drink perfume.[2]

Soviet Jews often speak of the Russians as a nation of drunkards, but the Jews also imbibe. Their drinking behavior tends, however, to be more moderate than that of their non-Jewish neighbors, and alcoholism is rarely a great problem among them.[3] At a small gathering of immigrants to honor the fifth anniversary of Vladimir Vysotsky's death, the host, a personal friend of the iconoclastic songwriter and actor, answered the question of why he drank as follows: "Why did he drink? Better to ask, how could he have not? Listen, I once heard an anecdote about three surgeons. They were standing over a very ill patient, preparing to perform an operation with no good instruments and no anesthesia. As they were getting ready to begin the operation, they each poured themselves a full glass of vodka. 'How can you drink all that before performing such a delicate operation?' they were asked. 'How can we not?' they responded." Drinking is seen as a way to escape, albeit temporarily, the economic constraints and primitive living conditions that exist in a world that says such problems do not exist.

Friendships in the Soviet Union are viewed in much the same way as alcohol, as "total systems" of temporary freedom that form in direct opposition to the "total system" of the Soviet state. These relationships provide individuals with everything the state apparatus lacks or constrains: emotional support, material support, and, perhaps most important, the opportunity to display one's true personality. In public life, the collective is emphasized as all-important, and personality as such is repressed. Conversely, in the context of friendship, the individual is paramount, as Maxim explains:

> First I should say that friendship there was all-encompassing, both because you wanted it to be and second, because there was no other way for it to be. With your friends was the only time you could be absolutely yourself. Because they are your friends you trust them, and because you trust them, they are your friends. Friends help friends find something to eat—tell where you can get something—black market, so to speak. Friends help you find things to wear, places to spend the summer. These are just the practical things of everyday life—which are necessary to everyone and theoretically available to everyone but are not, except through connections. So friends provide this. Then there is the moral part, the emotional part. Friends are the people who you can share political jokes with—and that is the primary way of expressing yourself, especially in our circles—against the repressive system. But you have to know exactly who your friends are, otherwise you run the risk of getting arrested. . . . Friends then served many functions: They helped you provide physically for yourself and gave emotional and moral support. With your friends you can be you. It's the only time that your real personality—what makes you an individual—can be expressed. At all other times, you try to hide this.

Friendships in the USSR are intense, for they are the only areas in which people can be whole selves, individuals with particular joys, needs, and grievances. Their existence makes possible the daily routine of their public life, not only because these friendships help solve economic problems but, perhaps more important, because they enable people to express their inner thoughts and emotions. Within the context of a friendship, people are able to discard their public, emotionless "Soviet face" and give vent to their personal ideas and feelings.

Vladimir Shlapentokh (1989) demonstrates that public life and private life in the USSR are two sides of the same coin, each side working with the other to perpetuate the Soviet system as a whole. It might be helpful, therefore, to view Soviet friendships as states of communitas, or "anti-structure," opposed to yet deriving from the carefully constructed public behavior of structured life. In the state of communitas, interpersonal relations are based on spontaneity and emotion, as the total person, not one or another social role, interacts with others. This temporary suspension of the rules of public conduct allows individuals to disregard social responsibility and accountability to the dominant ideology and can prove to be dangerous. Communitas is a secret, often sacred, time out of time that encourages people to relate to each other without inhibition, with their feelings, not their rational minds (Turner 1969; also Myerhoff 1975).

Friendships, therefore, develop from a base of two opposing emotions, risk and trust. Within the context of a friendship, Soviet citizens who would otherwise not do so, called attention to the contradictions between rhetoric and reality in their everyday lives. Although everyone was well aware of these contradictions, great care had to be taken in expressing and resolving them because dealing on the black market (economic crimes against the state) and political jokes (slander against the motherland) were illegal and could have resulted in lengthy jail terms or labor camp sentences. People had to be certain of their friends, for within the state of communitas, where spontaneity and garrulousness replace the carefully chosen words of structured interactions, a mistake could have been costly indeed.

The risks one takes when developing friendships are eased by establishing trust. Trust is attained by friends baring their souls to each other, telling each other their history, their fears, their desires. That friends share completely is both expected and practiced; they share information, connections to material goods, whatever resources they have at their disposal. Most important of all is to share the essence of one's self, that which is hidden in all other interactions. Anything short of full disclosure makes the friendship suspect. Lera, commenting on the illegal activities of one of her old friends, concludes:

Either share it wholly, or don't say anything at all. And then be ready to accept the consequences of this openness for the relationship on both sides. . . . Each person has something in his character that is his own. You can either accept it or not—that is your choice. This friend of mine never tried to hide who she was—she told me everything, that is because we are friends. If it had been any other way, I never would have been friends with her.

With the test of time, as mutual trust is built and friendships intensify, risks diminish. Trust is the moral base on which friendships rest, both underlying and demonstrated by all the services one renders for friends. Galina, an architect in her early fifties, contrasts friendship in the USSR with daily life in the USA:

Friendship is something that is dearly guarded and very, very special because friendship means trust—trust to be yourself, to unburden your problems. In Odessa, I had my very close friend Zhanna, and whenever something went wrong, there I went to Zhanna. And she to me. There were no agencies, support groups, helping organizations— everything that was part of the government was suspect—only in the intimacy of a close friendship could you actually express who you are.

Friendships are cherished because they are a release from the structure of Soviet life, enabling people to free themselves, at least momentarily, from over-conformity and the denial of their problems. These friendships are so intense and multiplex, fraught with emotion, that any threat to their continuity is avoided at all costs.[4] To ensure the maintenance of friendship, to continue the excitement and satisfaction of "being oneself," friends try to anticipate and fulfill each other's every need. Friends give whatever they have to give, and in giving, as Nona sees it, they receive as well:

You asked, "What is a friend [*drug*]?" A friend, a real friend, is someone with whom you think as one. That means you don't have to explain yourself because your friend understands. That means you share interests and insights. And most important, to be a friend means you always think of giving, never of taking—how you can give more to this person—what can you do for him, not what he can do for you. That, to me, is the definition of a real friend.

Most immigrants speak of having had a circle of friends (*krug druzei*) in Russia, not discrete dyadic relationships. This circle is formed over the years from schoolmates, fellow university students, and colleagues in one's profession. Friends share friends as they share everything else, and with time, their circle becomes increasingly tightknit. The web of trust expands to about ten or fifteen people, providing a real cushion against the structure of the Soviet state. First Natalya, then Maxim, explains:

> We are always together—not just for parties, but to gather together, to meet, to discuss the news of the day, to be with each other, to share information. We had a very specific social life in Russia, centered on always being together. We would be with each other like a family, all the time together, as company for each other.

> Time after time there was the same circle of friends. Very rarely there were a few changes, additions, subtractions. Most people have the same friends for throughout their lives, from school, university, work. And not different little circles like we have here [in America], but one big one where your friends are also friends of each other. Number of friends is small, relations are intimate, and no matter what, they are always there.

Soviet citizens thus built their own small collectives in opposition to the huge collectivity that was the Soviet state. They forged social groups that came together spontaneously on a regular and frequent basis, and in which each member is a total person. This totality of total selves becomes so intimate and close that it even develops its own special language and modes of interaction that shut outsiders out. Commenting on a Moscow friendship circle retained over nine years of immigration, Yakov notes:

> Although they have this cosmopolitan outlook, they are a very closed group. I remember the first time I met them, I was very uncomfortable. . . . First of all, they were all talking so much and so loud that I could hardly hear myself, and not one of them. It seemed like their lines were already so well known to each other that there was no reason for any one person to pause to listen to the others. Finally someone noticed that I was there and not participating, and they turned to me and asked why I was so quiet.

Some informants note that these groups are "incestuous," meaning that many men and women within the group have been in sexual relationships with one another over the years.

Friends share food and drink along with everything else. Friendship circles gathered in someone's apartment, where they clustered around the kitchen table almost every evening. These meetings were not prearranged; friends just appeared, as first Victor and then Marina reminisce:

> There, every night, we would get together with friends, without fail. We would just know this. We would drink, but not so much, eat terrible *kolbasa* [sausage] and bread, and talk for the whole of the night. This was natural; no one called first. We just showed up and socialized together.

> It was a crazy kind of life over there, but I have many Russian qualities that I am proud of. The best of these qualities is, first of all, hospitality. The door is always open, and the table is always full. Whatever I have is yours, and you are welcome to it.

Friendship, then, is demonstrated by providing and consuming food for the body as well as the soul. Eating is requisite whether one is hungry or not, for to refuse offered food is to spurn friendship: "To come to my home and not eat—that is unheard of!" To feed is to love, and to eat shows acceptance and appreciation of the love offered. The magnitude of this love is demonstrated by the amount of food both served and consumed.

In America the tradition of feeding guests assumes new proportions, as good quality food is always available. Hosts feel obliged to show their friendship by offering an abundant variety of dishes. This newfound ability to prepare a groaning table filled with delicacies, however, has its consequences, as Victor points out:

> They are more conscious of their apartments here—they want to make sure that everything is in place and that they can put a lot of good food on the table before you come over. There, no one had anything, and the only thing that was available was terrible salami, so no one was ashamed or embarrassed—because we were all at the same terrible level. Here, no. There is the possibility to make a good table, to have

nice things in your home, so you want to be prepared when guests come.

"Dropping by" is being replaced by what the émigrés call the American way of socializing—telephoning prior to a visit. The spontaneous character of friendship in the USSR, seen by former Soviet citizens as linked to the material conditions of life there, is inhibited in America because it now becomes possible to plan an abundance of delicious foods to serve to one's friends. In the Soviet Union, full hospitality was constrained by lack of foodstuffs; in America, the only constraint is time. Immigrants find that in order to express their high value for hospitality, they must sacrifice, to some extent, their "open-door" policy. On a return visit to New York in 1986 I phoned Vladimir and Sofia, who had eagerly been reminding me to "keep in touch" and come to see them whenever I got to New York. Sofia's immediate reaction to my call was, "Of course we would love to see you, but now it's five o'clock and you want to come at nine. That's not much time. . . . Not prepare? Of course I must prepare. Come, it won't be much, but come."

Another effect of time constraints, coupled with increased possibilities to display wealth and generosity through hospitality, is the growing importance of special celebrations such as birthday and anniversary parties in the expression of friendship. Immigrants often choose to celebrate in Russian restaurants, where they treat their guests to a night of drinking, eating, music, dancing, and high-spirited company in lush surroundings. Some, not content with the already elaborate *prix fixe* offerings, order extra food items and provide entertainment in addition to the restaurant's floor show to make their party more lavish and memorable than all others.

Guests reciprocate their host's hospitality by paying their respects in a number of ways. First, friends must attend the parties to which they are invited. Failure to attend, no matter what the excuse, may be cause for family feuds or friendship dissolutions. Then guests demonstrate their affection and appreciation for their host through enthusiastic participation in dining, toasting, drinking, and dancing. Further, they come dressed in their finest, highest-fashion clothing and jewels because, as Nona explained when I invited her to my birthday party, "People judge each other by their friends, so I will look extra-special for you. I won't let you down." Third, guests present the celebrant with a gift, usually cash and a greeting card inside an envelope. Immigrants know implicitly how much to give to each person; gifts of fifty dollars per couple are the norm.[5] Anything less than fifteen or twenty dollars a person is grounds for offense, while gifts in excess of thirty dollars a person are expressions of special closeness.

The idea that more is better characterizes immigrants' views of hospitality and friendship. Marina offers an explanation:

> Some of these things you may think are funny—too much jewelry, too showy clothes, too much makeup. . . . Look, you have one ring on your hand. I have two. But what's the matter with you? You have five fingers! Why only one ring? . . . These are the traditions of the Russian *kuptsy* [merchants] on the one hand, and Russian *boyars* [noble families] on the other—more is better. And this carries over into entertainment. Big tables covered with so much food that you can't eat everything. Even if you don't have a lot of money, you must have a lavish table for your guests. . . . The point is to see [not only how much you can give but also] how many friends you have. The more friends, the better. During the time of feudalism the lords on their namedays sat and each one of their subjects would come and present him with a gift and congratulate him on this day. The more people who come, the more loved and the more important and powerful a person you are. This is where this tradition comes from.

Conspicuous display and consumption during festive events are major vehicles by which this value is played out. And in America where "more" is more possible than in the USSR, this value flourishes.

Immigrants are aware of many other changes that have affected the nature of their friendships since resettling in America. A common observation is that friends simply do not get together as frequently as they did in Russia; daily meetings have been replaced by telephone calls, and in-person socializing is often arranged several days or even weeks in advance. Many people cite distance, coupled with the longer length of the American workday and how tired they feel in the evenings, to explain the lessening of face-to-face contact among friends. Natalya explains her position:

> You remember the other night we had a little party? That is how it was almost every night, five or six in a week, in Russia. Distance didn't matter; one, two, or even five rubles for a taxi wasn't so much. What

was important was to see friends, to be together. You know, no one had anything there, no money, nothing, just each other. Now here, no I wouldn't say these friendships fall apart, they are just different. First of all, my very good friends, a lot of them live in Queens. Also, I work very, very hard, and when I get home, I'm so tired. It's very different.

Boris elaborates:

Another thing you should understand is the reasons why friendships in the Soviet Union and in the United States are different. This has to do with the work situation. In the Soviet Union, coming to work late is not only not so terrible, it is *normal*. And staying home absent from work is also expected. So if friends come over and stay until two or three in the morning, no one cares, because this is done by everyone. . . . What I am trying to tell you is that when circumstances change, people do too. Some people though cannot get used to these changes. They do not understand that people have to get up in the morning and go to work, and they become insulted when you refuse to party all night long.

These changes in the amount of time and energy spent at work as well as getting to and from work are part of a larger complex of structural changes that confront Soviet immigrants. They bring about a major transformation in their social lives, which, in sociological terms, means that their friendships in America become more diffuse and single-stranded. In the USSR, where helping agencies are either not to be trusted or simply nonexistent and no credit unions or banking institutions exist to give financial assistance, friends are the sole providers of these forms of help. Thus, one of the most important factors accounting for changes in friendships is the fact that in America, money, as opposed to personal connections, can buy whatever goods, information, and entertainment one desires.

Money, as Georg Simmel (1978), not to mention Karl Marx in *Capital* (see especially McLellan 1977, 436–445), notes, creates a situation of rational consumption and privatization as it mediates connections between people. Money separates producers from sellers and sellers from consumers, establishing a stronger relationship between persons and things than among people. In the Soviet Union, personal ties remain the route to goods because often there is nothing in the stores to buy. In America, things are available to anyone, as long as one possesses the money or credit line with which to make purchases. Personal connections recede in importance, while money becomes the major object of attainment, as it in and of itself is the path to all commodities. As a consequence, Soviet immigrants' friendships become disembedded from the economy, and their totality weakens. To obtain the goods that America makes so available, one must have money; to gain money, one must work, and by working more, one spends less time with friends. This phenomenon is noticed and commented upon by the immigrants themselves. Marina observes, "Now I am afraid that money is replacing friendship. Friends come second, money comes first. It was as though there friends could get you everything that you needed, and money there came second."

Not only does the American money-based economic system undermine the totality of Soviet-grown friendships, but the ability to express oneself freely in public contributes to its dilution as well. This newfound potentiality to express individuality—through words (e.g., letters to the editor, letters to Congressional representatives, conversations with co-workers and neighbors), dress, and behavior—in public weakens the compelling ties of friendship that had developed in opposition to the Soviet state. The friendship circle, once the sole arena for individualism, loses its grip when transferred to a society that emphasizes the individual and tells its members to "be yourself." Émigrés, like Maxim and Galina the architect, are quick to remark on the impact of American freedom on their friendships:

Here you can be yourself at any moment. You can walk down the street with green hair if you like, and no one cares. In Moscow, when I was eighteen, I grew a beard, and people, especially the old ladies, came up to me and said, "Young man, you have no right at your age to have a beard—shave it off!" When women started wearing pants, this was scandalous! They were viewed as prostitutes, and social pressure forced them back into skirts. Here you don't *need* this small, tight, close circle of friends to be yourself. You don't *need* friends here. They are a luxury. There, you needed them to survive—not only to allow you to express your personality, but also in terms of real, honest goods.

Now, here in New York, if you want to go outside with green hair or a purple face, please, go ahead. No one cares, no one will hardly notice. You can be who you want at any moment. There is a great deal of emphasis on individualism; that for here is normal and natural. Here you demonstrate your individualism; there you have no channel for its demonstration, except in small, intimate friendship groups, with people you trust. These friends become the only vehicle for self-expression. In America, friendships are more casual; you don't need friends to be yourself, and you don't need friends for all kinds of help—finding food, something nice to wear, and so much more. The relationship is now more diluted.

Claude Fischer (1982) has demonstrated that, social psychological theories of urbanism notwithstanding, the extrication of friendship from embeddedness in a total system can be very satisfying. When friends who share interests and similar ideas of having a good time, get together on weekends, they free themselves from the daily routine of workaday life. Relationships at a moderately intimate level, rather than as an all-embracing system, allow for greater choice. Friendships with a variety of people, Fischer argues, permit each individual to express and share different aspects of the self.

Soviet immigrants often recognize the advantages of having separate friendships rather than one circle but are ambivalent about the changes that have occurred in the content of these friendships. Some, especially those who, like Maxim, have some American friends in addition to immigrant friends and work at demanding jobs, view their variety of discrete friendships as liberating:

> I told you about the good and bad sides of friendship according to Russian ways. This is one of the bad sides—very demanding obligations, expectations. This I do not like at all. The kind of [American] friendship, without obligations, where we see each other without being pressed into it, this to me is real friendship, different from that in Russia where there was no other way or no other choice. . . . I am beginning to understand the American version of friendship—a tie, a feeling of warmth, without expectations and obligations, a sharing of spirit. I told you sometimes I miss the old way of absolute friendship, living not really for yourself but for your friends as well. Other times, and now more than not, I thank God that those days are over and that friendship has reached a new level.

More often than not, even as they reflect on the changes that their friendships have undergone, émigré friends in America continue to rely on each other for more than a "sharing of spirit." They lend money to each other to facilitate the opening of businesses; they exchange babysitting services; they share information (e.g., about the availability of scholarships, interest-free or low-interest loans, government benefits, as well as news from the USSR); and they accompany each other to lend physical and moral support in making purchases, doing home repairs, and preparing food:

> Allochka, my sunshine. This is Valya. Fine, fine. Listen my dear, I am still in Manhattan, and I have a big favor to ask of you. When you go for Misha after school, will you please take my Tanya home with you too? You will! Thank you, my sunshine. I'll see you later this afternoon. A big, big thank you!

> Of course I will feed your cat for you. You know that I love animals. Only one thing—I cannot take money from you. This is friendship, and I will do it for you as a friend. Forget about the idea of money, and if you even try, I will be very insulted.

> We helped them buy all the things they need to fix up their apartment—paint, varnish, things like that. They know all about this, but they asked us to help. No, I'm not so wonderful. If someone needs help, give it, and then it will come back to you, too. It's no big deal.

Service-provision among friends, however, differs from the Soviet to the American context because in America people feel that they are freely giving of themselves. Knowing that their friends could find other routes to these services, they provide them to demonstrate affection. In the Soviet Union, there is no choice; friends are forced by material constraints to rely solely upon each other. In America, the value of giving, now divorced from a context in which giving is necessary, has not faded; indeed, with voluntarism and alternate paths to the same services, it has become an even greater expression of friendship than it was prior to migration: "Why didn't you ask me [to do it]? You should be ashamed of yourself to think it would inconvenience me. What are friends for if not to help each other?"

Another difference between exchange of services among friends in America and in the Soviet Union is that in America one dense network is no longer relied upon to fulfill every need. Certain friends are asked for one kind of favor, others for different ones. Since the risks of friendship are no longer great and trust is more easily established between people who share only some interests and experiences, Soviet immigrants, like their American counterparts, have been developing a number of not necessarily overlapping friendships (see pp. 76–79). Several immigrants report that they no longer have a "circle," because their different kinds of friends simply do not mix well, and that they do certain things with some friends and other things with others. While some are very happy about this division, others, like Nona and Regina, mourn the loss of their circle and the intimacy of a closeknit small group:

> Here we lost our circle; there are no places for people here. Nothing is centered . . . the circle isn't centered, and people aren't so close.

> Here I have good acquaintances [*znakomiye i priateli*) but nothing like it was there. Like, on my birthday. There, every year without me saying a word, there was a celebration for my birthday. I never had to call anyone; they automatically came over. Here, if I want a party, I call and invite people over, but it's not the same feeling of closeness.

Russkaia druzhba (Russian friendship) has become a code word or symbol in immigrant life. It describes a feeling of such closeness that boundaries between individuals are blurred, where people live only to give of themselves to those they love. Immigrants frequently invoke this term as a self-ascribed feature of "we Russian Jews" and as a characteristic that delineates them from their American neighbors. Although most émigrés have not recreated "real Russian friendship circles" here in America, the central traits of openness and generosity, intimacy and trust remain strong moral imperatives and the yardstick by which relationships are measured.

Sharing, empathy, and mutual assistance remain the underpinnings of Soviet immigrants' friendships in America, although the freer nature of American society has contributed to dilute the all-embracing character of *russkaia druzhba*. These friendships are no longer total systems that exist in opposition to the state, and friends no longer completely depend on each other for fulfillment of every survival need. Precisely because food, clothing, and some avenues of self-expression are obtainable outside the intimate circle of friends, friendships increasingly focus on the emotional and sociable sides of human life. Because they are now seen as "luxuries," friendships among Soviet immigrants may be cherished all the more. And although impersonal money now buys the goods that friends once provided, the value for intimacy, trust, warmth, and giving, united under the rubric *druzhba,* has not diminished and remains a strong moral force and knowledge base linking Soviet immigrants.

THE COLLECTIVE, PRIVACY, AND GOSSIP

The notion of the collective, the structure in opposition to which Soviet friendships emerge, forms the moral base of the Soviet state. Collectivist morality proclaims that the optimal social good is an egalitarian, sharing society. Such a society is dependent upon individuals' conscious and constant efforts to contribute their talents and regulate their behavior in accordance with the needs—economic as well as social—of the Socialist system. The cardinal principle of collectivism is that because each person is a social being, by making positive contributions to society, everyone will reap individual satisfaction. Collectivism therefore attempts not to downplay individual talents but rather to channel them into socially useful directions. To rid Soviet society of lingering remnants of bourgeois morality—which, according to the *Slovar' po Etike* (*Dictionary of Ethics,* Kon, 1983, 33–35), emphasizes an egotistic individualism derived from the negative emotions of greed, selfishness, and envy—the collectivist spirit must inform every facet of each person's daily life.

This conception of the collective is not alien to traditional Russian culture. Teodor Shanin (1972, 40–41, 140) notes that the Russian peasantry placed its highest value on self-imposed conformity, egalitarianism, and justice defined in terms of the communal will. Socialist Russia therefore did not require its population to undergo a radical moral transformation in emphasizing the importance of collectivism for the new state. What was needed was a method by which collectivist *Gemeinschaft* could extend from intimate village settings over a vast territorial expanse to include millions of ethnically diverse peoples.

While adults in the USSR were showered with slogans and incentives, attended work committee meetings, and were subject to their neighbors' scrutiny, which, all combined, induced them to be good collectivists, children learned by doing that their interests and those of the collective were one and the same. Parents were urged to follow Makarenko's popular child-rearing manual by identifying and satisfying their children's true (socially constructive) needs, discouraging egotistical, anti-social demands: "A morally justified need is, in fact, the need of a collectivist, that is, a person linked with his collective by a common aim, of the common struggle, by the living and certain awareness of his duty toward society" ([1937] 1967, 32). Children experienced affection and care in the family while they were taught to contribute to the demands of housekeeping, be cheerful and polite, play with other children, and perform well in school. Jewish parents often stressed these Socialist-international values to shield their children from their "different" identity as long as they could.

Urie Bronfenbrenner (1972) describes how the Soviet educational system, by using these same techniques of love and security provision, instilled and confirmed in children a strong desire to be accepted by the collective. Teachers encouraged children to work together to achieve, to take responsibility not only for their own actions but also for those of their classmates. No one was allowed to fail, and no one was allowed to show off; the accomplishments of one were considered the accomplishments of the group. Poor students were helped by brighter ones; children who tended to be late or slovenly were assigned prompt and neat buddies; sociable children were paired with loners to bring them out; and egotistical showoffs were softly chided by the group in class. Children who did not conform to the will of the group faced criticism and were temporarily denied love, affection, and security.

This collective education/upbringing, Bronfenbrenner shows, provided "strong sources of security, support and satisfaction" (1972, 69), and led not only to the child's internalization of society's values but also to "personal initiative and responsibility in developing and maintaining such behavior in others" (1972, 80). The values learned in childhood were reiterated to apply to each stage of the life cycle as the actual collective of which one was part—the school classroom and Socialist youth groups, one's university, one's profession, and the Communist party—grew in scope. Since security in the collective at any level depended on others' contributions as well as one's own, and since the behavior of one exerted a direct impact on the well-being of all, Soviet citizens learned to meddle in their neighbors' activities. Collectivist upbringing fostered a spirit of communal responsibility and created a feeling in each person that the interests of the collective were one's own.

By employing the techniques of collectivist socialization through-out the nation, the value of conformity to village norms was extended from small-scale closed groups to cover the expanse of the USSR. The same methods of enforcement used in the village—gossip, social pressure, and the threat of expulsion—were used by Soviet citizens to exact conformity to the interests of the collective. It was not only the right but also the duty of good citizens to look after and safeguard the values of socialism; that is, complete strangers should take an interest in and "correct" the behaviors of each other. Observers of Soviet life (e.g., Smith 1976; Shipler 1984) as well as Soviet immigrants report that good citizens told others to pick up the papers they carelessly dropped on the street, to give their bus seats to the elderly, and not to shove while standing in line. They also told women not to wear pants, to wipe off their makeup, and not to smoke on the streets. Young men were chastised for growing beards and wearing their hair long. It was correct, in fact laudable, for strangers to tell parents that their chil-dren were not warmly enough dressed and could catch cold. Fear of such censure by well-meaning strangers made instances of public non-conformity rare.

The comfort and security of the collective were reinforced by the state's interest in each citizen. Graduates of Soviet schools, institutes, and universities were referred to jobs that suited their qualifications, and unemployment did not exist in the Soviet Union. State-provided health care, living quarters, pensions for the elderly and disabled all ensured that each person would be provided for within the frame-work of the collective. Opposition to the social good was therefore foolhardy as well as wrong; individuals who contributed to the collec-tive were taken care of by it.

Order, predictability, and security characterized collectivist life in Socialist Russia.[6] For Jews, however, who were defined as noncon-formists simply because they were Jews, such security was often offset by reminders that they did not belong. Many émigrés left the Soviet Union precisely to escape the repressiveness of such an all-embracing system; they were told to follow all the rules and conform, but try as they might, they were never quite accepted and constantly were told so. A young woman, originally from Moscow, told me at our only meeting about this feeling of alienation from a collective to which she had no choice but to belong:

I'll give you an example, hundreds of these you can find. One day I was on the bus with a friend of mine, also Jewish, but she looks very Jewish . . . and this Russian woman, an older woman who I never saw before in my life, was sitting on the bus and asks me, "What are you, a nice Russian girl, doing with a Jew like her?" You see, this is her business. It's everyone's business. No one even thinks that this might not be the right thing to say, to ask, it just is. Of course I answered her, "I am Jewish too," and that put an end to the discussion. But the point is not what I said, what I answered. The point is what she said, what all Russian people feel they have a right to say.

Uncomfortable with constant public scrutiny, with the necessity of "putting on a public face," and with being defined as different (Jewish) in a society that cherishes sameness, many Soviet Jews came to America for "freedom." In some cases, rather than the relief they expected this freedom to bring, former Soviet citizens find chaos and disorder. This is especially true for some dissident writers who, because they had been hounded by the KGB, knew that they had something interesting and compelling to say. In America, these messages lose much of their appeal; American audiences are often uninterested in them, and immigrants usually turn to American media for news, information, and entertainment. More disappointing still was the discovery that no one in America really cares about immigrants from the Soviet Union; no government or community representatives come to welcome them as new citizens or new neighbors, to find out about their experiences or to give help and advice about life in America. A former journalist from Moscow, a woman in her forties, reflects:

> I came for freedom, and I understand now that this freedom is something I never thought it would be—the freedom to sit day after day in my apartment alone, absolutely alone. If I knew what I know now, I am not so sure what I would have done.

Without the collective to oppose, freedom is rendered meaningless. The overwhelming majority, who do not in the least regret their decision to emigrate, remain uncomfortable nonetheless with the permissiveness and laissez-faire attitude of American society. Even those who "thank God for America and the word privacy" point to the tragedy of the homeless, the scourge of subway crime, the litter and filth that mar New York's streets and wish that at least some part of the USSR's collectivist spirit would extend to America, as two middle-aged men comment:

> I love America and everything it stands for. What I don't like is dirt and disrespect—especially disrespect of the young for the middle-aged and elderly, and disrespect for the American system and patriotism. Crime—it's unpredictable, you never know if it will be you. And the homeless—I see them everyday on my way to work. It is scary and horrifying that such people exist, especially in a country as great as the U.S. They are a sign of the problems with this society—that people aren't responsible for each other or themselves.

> America is a great country, but it lacks humanity. People here don't want to give to anyone else. Here doctors are afraid to give first-aid because they think the person they help might sue them. This is the shame of this country.[7]

Lack of an ever-vigilant collective, although liberating, is also demoralizing because this license is interpreted by former Soviet citizens as lack of concern. The Soviet collective may be repressive, stifling individuality and making Jews feel bad about who they are, but it also provides security; it lets people know that they are not alone, that they will not end up homeless on the street or accosted in the subway.

While on the one hand, Soviet immigrants cry out for stricter laws to provide protection for the American citizenry of which they are now part, on the other hand, they often relish the opportunity to relax their public behavior. It is not uncommon to see émigrés of all ages smoking in movie theaters where smoking is not permitted and dropping candy wrappers on the streets. Their rationale: "If everyone does it, why can't I? This is a free country." Soviet immigrants thus come to interpret the moral rectitude of individuals' rights as justification for inconsiderate social behavior. It is no wonder that people who repressed their own wishes in favor of the "collective good" in the USSR would act out their individual desires in America. However, it is often the case that the same people who throw candy wrappers on the street mourn the loss of "shining, clean Leningrad."

Some people, especially those over age fifty, never abandon their task of supporting the collective and continue to fulfill their social obligations in America. They sit in front of their apartment buildings and watch, and comment on, all who pass by. Lara, twenty years old, describes her daily meetings with the guardians of her neighborhood:

> You know, everything here [in Brighton] is everyone's business. You know the ladies who sit in front of the building on the street? If you want information, go to them. They know everyone and have a bad word to say about everybody. When I come home from shopping, they call me over, "*Devushka!* What do you have in your shopping bag? Tell me, who is that man your mother is seeing?" They intrude in your life like you wouldn't believe. You don't know the half of it! They make everything their business.

These monitors of the social good, also referred to by the younger generation as "grandmothers with x-ray eyes," create a new collective in their neighborhoods. By making everyone's business their business, they establish predictability and order in at least their immediate environments. But gossip travels far beyond one's street, to friends and acquaintances one meets when shopping or strolling, and through telephone conversations; and it certainly is not confined to the over-fifty set. In this way, the collective, or community, extends to immigrants outside the enclaves as well.

Informal word-of-mouth communication is not the only form of "gossip" that serves to unite Soviet immigrants into a moral community. Two formal channels are also used to spread information and cement community opinion: printed media and the radio. Established at the turn of the century, *Novoye Russkoye Slovo,* New York's Russian-language daily newspaper, is a widely read source of international, national, and local news (read by 82 percent of the immigrants surveyed by Federation of Jewish Philanthropies 1985, 15). In addition to its news articles, often translated from the *New York Times* or UPI, the newspaper publishes letters to the editor, guest articles and commentaries about émigré life, a wide variety of advertisements, and death announcements from its readers. The death notices are important to immigrants because they allow family members to share their grief. Public receptivity to their loss tells survivors that they and their departed are not alone, that they matter to the community. The strong desire to count as a social being, instilled in the Soviet Union at an early age, emerges particularly at death, when survivors wish to remind

themselves that their deceased relative, and by extension they themselves, has not lived in vain. Maxim comments on his ambivalence:

> Like a zebra has a black stripe and then a white one, that is how I feel
> about this word, *privacy*. In Moscow, I had a false sense of how great
> and important I was; then, in America, I got a false sense of how
> insignificant I was. The black stripe is that if I get sick in America I
> could die in my bed without anyone knowing or caring, and this is
> depressing and sad.

These death announcements are reminders to all that each person is
part of a social group and not insignificant. They are proof that others
know and care and that the individual is not alone.

Not only does the newspaper tangibly symbolize the existence of
a collective in which each immigrant matters, it also shapes and for-
malizes the opinions of the collective. Recognizing the strength of its
position, *Novoye Russkoye Slovo* encourages people who are subjects
of its articles or who take differing positions to clarify their stances in
the newspaper. Individuals are thereby provided with the opportunity
to defuse rumors and gossip and to respond to the collective's
charges, enabling them to enter into dialogue with and contribute to
public opinion. The following example is a case in point:

Immediately after the murder of a guest occurred at the home of
a very successful immigrant businesswoman, a close friend expressed
his grief not only for the victim but also for the hostess stating, "Ugly
rumors have already started." The day after the murder, the businesswoman published a death announcement in which she and her family
mourned the "tragic loss." She further explained herself by publishing two articles several days later describing in detail the events of the
murder, and her horror, grief, and shock in the murder's aftermath.
She stressed how she had cooperated fully with the police and the FBI
in their search for the murderers. Recognizing the strength of public
opinion, that vicious rumors were afloat about her character, she
appealed to the collective, through the newspaper, to win its support
and sympathy.

Announcements on "*Gorizont*" ("Radio Horizons") focus on
positive events in the lives of immigrants for which they want recognition. Individuals or families pay for a brief broadcast by which they
include themselves into the wider immigrant community, gaining its

approval, and sometimes its business. Personal accomplishments are publicized because some families consider their successes to be meaningful only if they are recognized and confirmed by society. Some announcements proclaim familial happiness:

> A very happy twenty-fifth anniversary to my loving parents, Aleksandr and Evgenia Karpman, from their loving son, Vadim.

Others publicize post-migration educational and professional success:

> Congratulations to our beautiful daughter, Dina Berkovitch, on her graduation from New York University, from her loving parents, aunts, uncles, and grandparents.

> Congratulations to our wonderful son, Roman Goldshteyn, on passing the New York State dental examination, from your loving mama, papa, and sister.

In the absence of an all-encompassing social structure that cares about every action of every citizen, Soviet immigrants have created their own. This collective, however, differs from that of the Soviet Union in two significant ways. First, of course, is the voluntary nature of this community. Rather than operating as an arm of the state, it has arisen in opposition to what the immigrants perceive as America's laxity. It fills the void of uncertainty by setting standards of behavior and providing security in this pluralistic, individualistic society. And if, using Maxim's metaphor, the "white stripe" of the zebra of privacy should outweigh the disadvantages of the black, individuals are free to divorce themselves completely from the immigrant collective. They can, and in fact some do, opt to live away from the ethnic enclaves, avoid the Russian press, and never tune their radios to "*Gorizont.*" Complete dissociation from other immigrants, however, is quite rare; the number of people in Brighton Beach who had originally been resettled in Cleveland, Milwaukee, Atlanta, Connecticut, and New Jersey, not to mention Far Rockaway, the Bronx, and Queens, speaks to the strong desire to belong. Inna and Felix, for example, left Milwaukee for Brighton Beach a year after arriving in America: "We missed hearing Russian, seeing familiar faces. We felt as if we were in Siberia, so we came here." Although this couple arrived in the United States with quite a good working knowledge of English, they missed the familiar, and they missed concern for and from others. They felt alienated without social referents, without a collective to provide order and security in daily life.

The other important way that this community differs from the Soviet collective is that it is composed almost exclusively of Jews. While in theory the Soviet collective equally values all peoples and national groups, in practice Jews are viewed by the Slavic majority as nonconformists and are therefore seen as threats to group unity. While Soviet Jews have, to a very large degree, internalized the same values of communality and egalitarianism as their Russian neighbors, because of their Jewish nationality, their loyalty to the Soviet system is suspect. They are reminded of their undesirability throughout their lives, and are thereby estranged from the collective to which they have no choice but to belong. In New York, it is Jews who forge the community; based on values learned in the Soviet Union, this collective now validates the "different" identity of being a Jew. Soviet Jewish émigrés have, in fact, created the collective they imagine could have been and should have been in the USSR, caring, concerned, all-encompassing—while also prying, jealous and judgmental—and one of which they are unquestionably both an active and a passive part.

ETIQUETTE, POLITESSE, AND BEING CULTURED

Soviet immigrants arrive in America with a well-defined sense of correct and proper public behavior. This behavioral code, the under-pinnings of "progressive and collectivist Soviet society," derives from the concept of *kulturnost,* roughly translated as "culturedness" or "refinement."

During the Revolution and in the early years of the new Socialist state, mass dislocations and urbanization brought Russian villagers and city-dwellers into close contact. The new leadership appealed to the citizenry to establish order, a new order based on the intrinsic worth of each person, without class differences and behaviors that offend basic human sensibilities (e.g., spitting in public, vulgar language, hierarchical forms of address). Campaigns were launched to spread to the masses "cultured behavior," which, despite the rhetoric against bourgeois morality, was rooted in the middle-class background of many of the Revolution's leaders. Peasant/Marxist values of egalitarianism and the will of the collective were incorporated into middle-class values of civility, respect, and decorum in developing the ethic of *kulturnost* for Russian Socialist society.

In addition to campaigns against unseemly behaviors that were attributed to class injustices (e.g., wife- and child-beating, public drunkenness, and poor hygiene), Soviet citizens were urged to express their newfound liberation and self-esteem through their work. Expanding on Marx's notion of *Homo faber,* the citizenry was told that now that it controlled the means of production, each person would reap personal and social benefits and satisfaction from participating in the workforce. In the 1930s, as the Soviet Union underwent intensive efforts to modernize and industrialize, the ideal Soviet citizen was portrayed in the persona of a "Stakhanovite shock-worker," a self-sacrificing member of the collective whose primary goal in life was to fulfill and over-fulfill the central plan. As the need for technicians and professionals grew, however, work and job titles became increasingly fetishized. The satisfaction of work for the social good remained important, but people also worked for upward mobility, recognition, and status. "Cultured" work became the goal of many.

Vera Dunham's (1976) remarkable analysis of Soviet mass literature reveals the increasing embourgeoisement of Soviet society after World War II. Having suffered during the war and exerted a tremendous effort to fight off the enemy and rebuild their country, Soviet citizens began to demand personal rewards for their work; sacrifice and privation were understandable in the early days of the revolution and during the German occupation, but during a period of peace and victory Soviet citizens anticipated an abatement of hardships. Work was still to provide intrinsic satisfaction, but people expected material goods, recognition, and status as well.

Even in the 1930s, as the New Soviet Man was being shaped into a "shock-worker," an undercurrent of self-gratification and indulgence was being interwoven into the guidelines for ideal Socialist behavior. An instructive story in Makarenko's child-rearing manual ([1937] 1967, 282–321) shows that citizens should not be deprived of pleasures: a hard-working librarian is rewarded not with a medal or a paragraph of praise in a local newspaper but with a dress made of cherry-red crepe de Chine, a luxury item. By the 1950s, this undercurrent was made explicit, and Soviet citizens came to believe that because of their sacrifices in building socialism, they were entitled to not only good (socially productive) but also happy (materially comfortable and personally contented) lives.

This tension between the collective good and personal gratification lies at the heart of Soviet etiquette and civility. According to the *Slovar' po Etike* (Kon, 1983, 150):

> In the broad understanding of cultured behavior,[8] all facets of external and internal human culture enter: etiquette, the rules of treating people and behavior in public places, the culture of daily life, including the character of personal needs and interests, interrelations between people at work, the organization of personal time, hygiene, esthetic tastes in the choice of articles of consumption (the skills of dressing, decorating one's living quarters); esthetic characteristics inherent in human gestures, facial expressions and body movement (grace). Of especial significance is the culture of speaking [verbal etiquette], grammatical skill and the ability to express one's thoughts clearly and beautifully, to avoid the use of vulgar expressions.

Thus, while Soviet citizens are urged to think of others and treat them with consideration and respect, in order to do so they must pay close attention to themselves, to dress nicely, look after their personal hygiene and appearance, and develop eloquence. According to Dunham (1976, 22–23), these admonitions to be "cultured" sanction aspirations to material goods and self-indulgence. Being cultured is not solely an internal attribute; it requires demonstration, and demonstration demands clothes, cosmetics, jewelry, home furnishings, education, and participation in cultural pursuits. While in one sense it focuses and thereby serves the interests of the collective by providing standards and order, post-war emphasis on *kulturnost* also created a rather egotistical kind of citizen, one who is dignified and well dressed, a seeker of status, respect, and things, which were now considered one's due.

How does the concept of *kulturnost* and its associated rules of behavior manifest itself in and inform the lives of Soviet immigrants on American soil? As both a personal quality and one that demands a social arena for its demonstration, recognition, and salience, *kulturnost* helps to explain the direction of culture change among the émigrés, and why they accept and reject what they do of American ways.

To be cultured is to know, through having internalized, the correct way to act in public, that is, easy manipulation of rules of etiquette. Verbal etiquette is a key component of cultured behavior.[9] In the Soviet Union, volumes are devoted to this theme, and child-rearing guides always include many pages on this subject. These books on etiquette stress that individuals demonstrate their internal beauty (character) through the way they express themselves in words. Clear, grammatical, and skillful use of the Russian language is considered a primary attribute of the cultured person.

This skill includes not only mastery of grammatical principles and a large vocabulary but also the correct and appropriate use of forms of address (see Formanovskaya 1982). After the 1917 Revolution, titles of respect accorded nobility, gentry, and burghers (*gospodin/gospozha*, equivalent to "milord/milady," or "monsieur/madame") were eliminated and replaced with one title of solidarity, *tovarishch*, "comrade."[10] In conversational Russian, however, addressing someone as Comrade plus last name is considered somewhat contrived and stilted. Use of this form indicates distance and cold formality, as Vladimir describes, "Yes, *Tovarishch* plus last name, you can use this; it's all right, it's correct. But to greet someone on the street just like this, no, not really. It's not appropriate." The preferred construction, the one that conveys deep respect yet establishes a personal connection between speakers, is the pre-revolutionary formal form of the first name plus patronymic (e.g., Petr Vasileivich—Peter, son of Basil; Margarita Aleksandrovna—Margaret, daughter of Alexander). This term of address imparts respect in two ways: first, by the use of the full formal form of the first name rather than one of many diminutives, and second, by linking the individual to a family (specifically the father), according to him or her legitimacy, history, and a sense of place. In America, use of the patronymic is usually abandoned. Vladimir continues, "Oh, many people come in here, especially new immigrants and the elderly asking me my name and patronymic. I tell them just my name and say that the other isn't necessary. It just isn't used here."

Why is it that the most refined and respectful term of address disappears in America, when other values and social traits noted by the immigrants as Russian stubbornly persist? Central to the notion of *kulturnost* are the themes of modernity and progressiveness and very strong esteem for urban, or high, culture. In America, Soviet

Jewish immigrants become aware, by comparison and opposition, of customs that differentiate them from Westerners. Those that confirm core values of cosmpolitanism and culturedness as well as sociability are defended and upheld; those that they recognize as tied to village life and provincialism are discarded. Vladimir concludes, "Look, use of the patronymic, it's a tradition of the village. No one uses it here. It's no longer appropriate."

This self-conscious shedding of the peasant image is bolstered by two other issues linked to the use of the patronymic. One stems from yet another desire to expurgate feelings of shame, as Maxim explains:

> I remember when my boss wanted to embarrass me or call negative attention to me, he would call me by my patronymic—Abramovich. Many of us, who have good international-Russian first names, still have Yiddish patronymics, and Russians often use them to call attention to us and shame us.

The other is also an emotional issue. The patronymic is a reminder of family and place, and most immigrants have left behind some relatives whom they will never see again. Its use evokes filial guilt, especially on the part of those whose parents, living or dead, remain in the Soviet Union. Thus, self-conscious appraisal of the appropriateness of this verbal form for modern, urban American society, coupled with its highly charged emotional overtones have led Russian immigrants to abandon its use.

First names, which have always been regarded as reflections of one's *kulturnost,* continue to assume great importance in America. Soviet Jews choose "international-Russian" names for their children, avoiding Yiddish names (e.g., Lazar, Berel, Feige, Malka) and traditionally Jewish ones (e.g., Abram, Solomon, Sara, Esfir), seeking "modern, pretty" Russian ones without religious overtones (Ivan and Nikolai are rarely chosen for Jewish men; Maria is often avoided for women).[11] They shun altogether names they associate with the peasantry. Sitting around the dinner table, Lera, Boris, their ten-year-old daughter, Svetlana, and I discussed my name:

> —Don't call yourself Franya. It's not really a good name for you. It's a Polish peasant name.
> —What about Faina?

—No! That's even worse. More provincial.

—And what about Frunya?

—No! Worse yet. Look, you are a cosmopolitan woman. You must have a cosmopolitan name. Just use Fran.

Diminutives of these sophisticated first names must be used with care because, while some communicate affection, others signal disrespect. In her book for parents, I. I. Rydanova (1982, 36) instructs, "Courtesy in the family is demonstrated by never calling anyone Tanka, Vovka, Ludka. Children are to address their parents as mama, mamochka, papa and papochka, and not mamka and papka." This-*ka* ending, permissible only with very small children and intimate family members or friends, proclaims disrespect when applied to an acquaintance, especially when referred to in the third person.[12] Irina became irate at Natalya for precisely this reason:

> I want nothing more to do with Natalya. Imagine, we were talking by telephone, and she was calling me *solnushko* ["sunshine," a term of endearment], Irichka, and her mother walks by and asks, "Who are you talking to?" "Mama, it's Irka," she said. Is that a way to refer to me? My name is Irina, Irichka to a friend, or just Ira. To say, "Mama, it's Irka," shows her real feelings about me, that she thinks I am below her, that she has no respect for me.

Soviet-born parents, noting the importance of appropriate and cultured names for their children's self-esteem, usually select popular English names for their American-born children. Michelle and Jessica are now in vogue for girls, and little boys are named Allen, Michael, and Robert. Among immigrants, and especially by their grandparents, these children are often referred to by a Russified diminutive, such as Michellushka and Allenchik, but parents and children alike are very happy with their English names. A mother of two girls, renamed Rachel and Julie after arriving in the United States, justifies her decision: "Why should they feel different or be made fun of because of their names? Why shouldn't they have pretty, modern American names like everyone else?" Some parents have officially changed their children's names after emigration; some children use two names, their Russian one at home and an English name at school.

The ethic of *kulturnost,* which urges refinement and appropriateness, guides the desire to conform to American norms.

Kulturnost also informs immigrants' concern for their appearance. What Americans might consider casualness in dress and grooming, immigrants often view as sloppiness and lack of good taste. Lera was shocked by the appearance of a journalist who came to interview her boss at his university office:

> The other day at work, a television journalist came to see my boss. You should have seen her—a journalist should look professional and well groomed, shouldn't she? This woman was simply dirty. She had on a dirty skirt that only a gypsy woman would wear, and the hair on her legs was this long, and thick—like the simplest peasant girl from the most backward village. This is, after all, America, and it is not appropriate for a woman to go about like that here.

Jeans may be worn, but only those with designer labels, preferably of European manufacture. Women seldom venture outdoors without coiffed hair and made-up faces, and they usually dress stylishly just to take their children for a walk or to shop for groceries. They show each other, as they show themselves, that they are on the cutting edge of fashion, not dowdy Russian peasants. The requirement of *kulturnost,* to develop and display skill in dressing, is demonstrated by Italian shoes and leather pants, styled hair, manicured nails, fur coats, and the latest styles from *Vogue* magazine or media stars.

The high fashion often reaches such extremes that immigrants' dress becomes a caricature of the Westerners they seek to emulate, so that they are immediately recognized as "Russians." Often immigrants' clothes convey excess rather than elegance, and this irony is sometimes noted by immigrants themselves. Two men, Pavel, a data analyst on Wall Street, and then Victor, who works in an immigrant-owned business, comment:

> The way people dress and walk around—I can't stand it. Why do our people have to be so loud and flashy? Everyone else wears tan and khaki, and olive and gray, you know, the Yuppie look. I like this very much, soft, understated, and our people wear bright yellow and red, and so much jewelry and faces plastered with makeup. It's so, so nouveau riche; it shows no class at all!

Take our Russian women; you see them in restaurants. They think they are dressing and acting like Americans, but you can spot them for Russians miles away! They may as well just wear the price tag and forget about the dress. They dress so shiny and flashy and don't look at all like American women—but they think they do!

But they are not dressing for Americans; they are dressing for each other. Their clothes and jewelry tell fellow immigrants that they have succeeded financially in America and that they have developed a flair for dressing as they had always longed to—and indeed felt they deserved to—in the USSR.

This theme of being entitled to something simply because others have it, as Dunham (1976) has pointed out, is interwoven into the material application of *kulturnost*. Even those without financial means feel that since everyone else is dressing nicely, they not only wish to but deserve to do the same. Nona, who receives SSI, complains:

I am so depressed, I cannot tell you. Eyeglass frames went up again. Over the Medicaid, I paid thirty-five dollars. Now I could have bought a pair of regular, cheap frames, but they are *drek* [Yiddish for "crap"], and they would fall apart in a year anyway. And besides, I see all these other women who have no good [clothes] sense wearing something else, something nice, so why should I be without?

This feeling of entitlement informs many aspects of public behavior and courtesy. Everyone wants to be respected, and each person feels that he or she has the right to be accorded status and dignity. This often translates into demanding to be served first at social service agencies and grocery stores, trampling over the rights of others to exercise one's own. Older people in particular feel that they have earned the right to immediate service, and they will often fight to get it. From my fieldnotes of March 14, 1985:

The doors [of a social service agency] finally opened at 10:20, about twenty minutes late, and the fifteen or so people who had been waiting on the street crowded into the small reception room corridor as the supervisor stepped behind the reception desk. Each person was yelling to have his or her application taken, and many were complaining that they had been waiting and that they are not young and that they are freezing from the cold. The supervisor asked that they go inside and sit, but all these people continued to stand in the corridor. I took out sheets of paper and numbered them and called for order, asking to see who had the earliest appointments. People, these were mainly women in their sixties, were pushing and shoving to get to me. A younger woman, in her thirties or forties, had been standing outside before I arrived, and she showed me her appointment slip with an early time. An old woman started screaming, "Young girl! What are you doing? You, a young girl, and look at us! We are old and sick. You should be ashamed of yourself! You rude girl—why do you say that you must go ahead? You are young and healthy; it won't kill you to wait!" The younger woman turned around and said she had been waiting since 9:40 and that she had to get home to her children. The older woman started pushing, shoving, and punching the younger one, screaming all the while.

Discussion of this incident with Lera, in her early thirties, elicited an accounting of a similar incident:

I'm just sorry for them that they learned all their lives that this is the only way to get along. See what living in the Soviet Union can do to people? They think that the more noise and the more fighting they do, the better they will be. This happened to me the other day: I was in a fruit and vegetable store, Korean, and I was standing in line to pay and stepped away for a moment to get something. When I came back to my place in line, "Madame" behind me pushed to take my place. The cashier there said, "No, she," meaning me, "was first." I am glad this Korean doesn't undersand Russian because the things this woman said to me I cannot even repeat. Every terrible word, and then some. Because I am young, and she is old.

Here are instances that seemingly fly in the face of the concept of *kulturnost*, undecorous behavior, shoving, shouting, and swearing. Built into the notion, however, is not only one's own compulsion to follow the rules, but also the expectation that others will behave properly and accord to oneself the respect and correct treatment that each person feels he or she deserves. Many elderly, and not so elderly, immigrants believe, precisely as Dunham (1976, 14) describes, that because of their exertions during the war,[13] their sufferings under socialism, and their present poor health, they have earned the right not to equal, but to extra-special treatment, the right to go first. Young people who do not understand this behavioral rule, who do not accord proper respect to their elders, are in fact the ones who are considered uncultured, and they must be instructed and shown that such inconsiderate behavior cannot and will not be tolerated.

The concept of *kulturnost,* once a guideline for gentry and enfranchised urbanites to behave with decorum in polite society, was developed under the Soviet regime into a standardized model for correct behavior in all social situations. Individuals have interpreted this concept to mean that they personally deserve respect and rewards; by following the rules of *kulturnost,* at home, at work, and in public places, they become entitled to dignity, happiness, and comfort in their society.

While some Soviet immigrants, especially the elderly and those whose social status has dropped with no chance of recovery, cling without modification to the Soviet notion and practices of *kulturnost,* many immigrants have begun to challenge the idea that there is but one cultured way to act and that good citizens have the duty to chastise those who fail to conform. As they interact with fellow immigrants and other Americans, they notice differences in appearance, hygienic practices, and rules of etiquette that run counter to Soviet norms. The central place that concern for being cultured and behaving correctly occupies in their self-image and public presentations leads some immigrants, especially those at university or in the workforce, to question the appropriateness for American life of the Soviet standards and behaviors they know. Lera most eloquently expresses this position:

> What I am beginning to understand is the spirit of America and the idea of freedom here. . . . It is a whole spiritual way of viewing the world and other people that we may never know ourselves that makes life seem so easy for Americans. For example, when an American buys something and when an immigrant buys something, they may both buy the same thing, but for an American, it is a matter of course, whereas for us, it is a triumph. We are, in a way, without culture. Yes, I really mean it—as cultured a people as Russians are, we don't have modern, urban culture. Seriously. Sometimes I call myself a hick because of my ignorance of normal practices for Americans, like going to the dentist once a year, or going to the gynecologist once a year. Without being sick? Unheard of! Seriously, this is not a part of our culture. Or physi-

cal exercise and diet—especially among women—no, never! Diet? What do we know? Only that if something tastes good—eat it! And eat as much as you like because that's what food is for. No, wearing layer upon layer of cosmetics, that isn't culture, although so many of our women do this. It's a typical Russian complex—inferiority/superiority. One feels worse, so he pretends he is better. They don't know how to act, so they copy something. But they do it without the spirit, so the same thing looks different. . . . We don't know, but we are afraid to show our ignorance by asking. It's crazy—but that's how it is, a typical Russian complex!

Being cultured means one knows the rules of behavior, and only a peasant does not know how to act in modern, urban society. Being a new immigrant, however, places the individual in situations where rules are unknown. To avoid appearing the rube, Soviet immigrants refer to their *kulturnost*. In some instances this reference works to their advantage; in others, it works against them.

The strong value for progressiveness and cosmopolitanism that is an integral part of the concept of *kulturnost* predisposes new immigrants from the Soviet Union to accept changes in their lives and abandon some Soviet-Russian ways, especially those that they perceive as peasant customs or old-fashioned. Further, the idea that culturedness demands demonstration—in clothing, furnishings, and professional accomplishments—impels many to develop English skills, find work, and advance socially and economically in America after a remarkably short period of time (see Simon and Simon 1982; Federation of Jewish Philanthropies 1985; Kosmin 1990). There are, however, those immigrants who, steadfast in their belief that they are cultured and refined, blame uncultured America for the uncertainty they feel in their new environment. They may refuse to let go of the "truth" that Soviet cultured behavior is the only correct way to act. Their fear of appearing as peasants, as unknowledgeable provincials, precludes their asking about, learning, and accepting social conventions in their new country.

Thus, the intense desire to display one's culturedness and urbanity exerts a direct impact on post-migration experiences and underlies the formation of the Soviet Jewish immigrant community. *Kulturnost,* in its various manifestations, is recognized implicitly, if not overtly, as a major symbol that unites Soviet immigrants and separates them from other Americans. Among the immigrants themselves, only true intellectuals disavowed the notion of *kulturnost* in the Soviet Union. In developing their unique talents and critical abilities, they rejected state-imposed conformity for higher values, and they attempt to maintain these values in their new country.

THE MEANING OF *INTELLIGENTSIIA*

Soviet immigrants very proudly declare that within their ranks are many members of the intelligentsia, and not infrequently they point to themselves as prime examples. They note their group's high level of education (about 60 percent of New York's émigrés hold a bachelor's degree equivalent or higher, according to the Federation of Jewish Philanthropies 1985, 11) and their jobs in white-collar, scientific, and artistic professions as proof. Yet some émigrés scoff at this statement; they believe that education and occupational level notwithstanding, true intellectuals in this wave of immigration are few and far between. In fact, they wonder if any *nastoyashchiye intelligentniye ludi* (real intellectuals) are left.

The theme of how to define and demarcate the true intelligentsia occupied many hours of discussion during my fieldwork, as informants invoked this label in application to themselves or in discussing differences among people within the Soviet Jewish immigrant population. These discussions invariably revolved around the opposition between the categories *meshchanstvo* (petty bourgeoisie) and *intelligentsiia* (intellectuals); it was difficult if not impossible for people to describe one without reference to the other.

The *meshchanin* and *intelligent* are both products of Russian urban society (Dunham 1976, 19), the first referring originally to an individual from the low ranks of the tsarist burgher estate, the second, a thoughtful, brooding, philosophically inclined artist or aristocrat. Literary portrayals of both types abound. Turgenev, Gogol, and Chekhov (among others) have painted marvelous portraits of the *meshchanin,* but the character who best embodies current use of the term is Molière's Tartuffe, a money-grabbing hypocrite hiding behind the veil of respectability and piety in anticipation of getting property, things, and status. Ivan Karamazov, Dostoevsky's creation, epitomizes the Russian *intelligent;* intensely concerned with spiritual matters and moral dilemmas, he challenges all the people, institutions, and values around him as he searches for Truth. In more concrete terms, *meshchane* are self-indulgent, seeking to elevate their social status through acquisition of things and *kulturnost* and doing so without discrimination, as blind consumers. Intellectuals, through introspection and social critique, rise above themselves as they devote their energies to creation—of art, literature, ideas, of culture.[14] They are the remaining few thinkers who have not been co-opted to conform by the lure of luxury items and promises of a bright, collectivist, Soviet future.

Occupation, because it indicates educational level and amount of analytical skill used on a frequent basis, is often pointed to as a key criterion of *intelligentnost*. In the USSR, all "scientific workers" or white-collar technicians and professionals are officially counted among the ranks of the intelligentsia. But since "in the Soviet world, *meshchanstvo* appears at every rung of the social scale" (Dunham 1976, 19), occupation alone does not a true intellectual make. Not all professionals necessarily embody the spirit, character, and moral sense of *intelligentnost*. Thus, poets, professors, linguists, and others who are self- and state-designated intelligentsia may be denied this status by others if they fail to display creativity, reflection, and ethical consciousness. Worst of all and most open to censure, as Nona's comments indicate, are shows of poor taste and ostentation, *meshchanstvo* in its crudest form:

> She is not an artist. She is one of those *meshchane* from Odessa. You should have seen her! We were at an evening gathering. A circle of intellectuals met one night to have a discussion, and there she was with her teenaged daughter who she had dressed as a ballerina—just awful. She was flitting around from one person to the next as if she was such an important person. Have you seen her work? Her work is not art, but nonsense. She's not an *artiste* but a *meshchanka*.

As clothing and demeanor are important indicators of the intellectual spirit, so too are one's home furnishings (wooden antiques, muted colors, and many shelves of books are preferred to chrome, mirrors, brocades, and velours), manner of speech (soft, expressive, reflective, as opposed to loud, bombastic, opinionated), and place of origin. Muscovites are most hesitant to accord membership in the intelligentsia to people from anywhere but the two capitals (Moscow and Leningrad), for they stress that open-mindedness and cosmopolitanism are essential qualities of the intellectual, and they strongly doubt that a provincial from, say Kiev, Kharkov, Odessa, not to mention Kishinev or Gomel, can qualify.[15] Dmitri, a friend of Yakov whom I met for the first time, was astonished that I was living in Brighton Beach and explained why:

> Yes, I am from Moscow. You know, there really is a difference. I wanted to ask you something—how can you stand to be in Brighton Beach? What I mean to say is—I know that there is no intelligentsia out there. All who live there are Ukrainians from Kiev, Odessa, and other small provincial towns. If you are from Moscow, well, then you have a much more cosmopolitan and international perspective. You are exposed to more—art, literature, poetry, music—that links you to the rest of the world of culture. Those people out in the provinces, they just haven't had that kind of experience. So it makes them a different kind of person, primarily concerned with material things, buying new things for themselves, for their apartments, and I have nothing in common with such people.

In these discussions of *intelligentsiia,* several immigrants note that throughout their lives in the Soviet Union they thought that Jews and intellectuals were one and the same. They speak of their families' emphasis on intellectual growth and point to constant reading, discussions of art, literature and philosophy, and social criticism that occurred in the privacy of their homes. Many recall that they never had enough money for anything nice, including good food, but that they and their parents were not resentful of those who had. Instead, since "we had nothing but our minds and our spirits, we discussed," and the value of these discussions more than compensated for the lack of material goods. This kind of family ethos based on deliberation of moral questions, love of the arts, and a continuing quest for education and knowledge they considered the "Jewish way." Immigrants stress that intellectual pursuits more than anything else separated them from their Russian and Ukrainian neighbors.

Upon emigration, in Vienna, Rome, and then in New York, many found that not all Jews, and certainly not all Soviet Jews, are intellectuals. They found *meshchanstvo* in varying degrees, sometimes at the extreme, as part of the character and lifestyle of fellow émigrés. Pavel recalls his shock:

> I left, and right away in Vienna something really strange happened. I saw for the first time in my life something I had never seen before—Jewish people of the lowest sort. . . . This was a big shock to me—seeing these crooks, Jewish prostitutes, drunkards, the sort of people I never ever saw in my life. Among Russians, sure, but never before among Jews. All the Jews I knew, all my friends, were very highly educated, quiet, cultured, intellectual people. Now here were Bukharans from the East who were living in another century. And what I knew of Odessa—I had been there three or four times—was the opera house, the state theater, the music and drama school, refined people. And here were the worst, lowest sorts I ever saw, who were only interested in eating more bologna and drinking vodka.

Nona contrasts Soviet Jewish émigrés with her Moscow social circle:

> The people I worked with [in the USSR] all—the best. Intellectuals, educated, high-class people. After these people, I look at the trash here on the streets and all I want to do is stay inside my own world that I have built. This is the world that I love—the world of books, of art, of literature, of knowledge, of wisdom. . . . These people—I don't know what they are, maybe cockroaches, for they are neither Russians nor Jews—they are something new and different from anything that I ever saw in all my life in Russia. Most of my friends in Moscow were Jewish, or half-Jewish, or married to someone Jewish—the brightest, the most intelligent people. And these?

On top of confronting non-intelligentsia Jews within their migration cohort, which shook the belief that "the Jewish mug is the intelligent face,"[16] with few exceptions, those who were considered and considered themselves true intellectuals in the USSR are not accorded such status by Americans. Many of these people, especially those with no competence in English, found themselves without a profession and deprived of the identity as thought-provoking, creative intellectuals that they had developed in their home country.

New immigrants react in a variety of ways to this unanticipated and shocking uncertainty about their intellectualism. At one extreme are the few who pine for the USSR from which they escaped to "be free." In America they find that the burning issues that had propelled their creativity and their longing for freedom in the USSR no longer seem to matter, attract no audience, and therefore no money, something without which it was possible to live in the Soviet Union but not in America. Anna discusses the fate of such people:

> I knew a man who, in the Soviet Union was a writer. He killed himself here. No, not suicide, but he just pined away and died. He was a famous dissident writer in Russia, so famous that the authorities would not allow him to publish his books, so they were all *samizdat* [underground press]. He thought he could come to America, publish right away and have a big following. . . . Within a few years, he got sick and died, of cancer, or a heart attack, I cannot remember which. This is only one of our tragedies, but there are many, many more. Such good, intelligent people, they just don't know what to do.

Another woman, a former journalist, bemoans her own fate:

> I am a journalist by profession, and in the Soviet Union, unlike most of the people you see here, I lived in Moscow. I was a journalist and a dissident there, and I left for freedom. I left because some of the things I said and the circles I was part of got me into trouble. But oh, what a price I paid for this freedom! In Moscow, I already had a cooperative apartment, my profession, my friends, my family, my place. Here I am alone—completely and absolutely. . . . You see, in the Soviet Union, the political system is all powerful. That is what denies us freedom. In America there is another king, and that king is money. Without money you cannot be free . . . to enjoy all the culture that this country has to offer. Without it, you are confined to your apartment, your neighborhood, your job.

This withdrawal, self-pity, and even death at an early age are in one sense logical outcomes of confrontation with post-migration reality. The danger and excitement of emigration are over, and the new immigrant's task is to start living an ordinary life. For some this proves difficult because in the USSR, challenging the regime through social criticism and dissidence, the marks of true intellectualism, provided them with the will for life. Prior to emigration, they viewed America as a haven, not of comfort and complacency, but a safe place where they could finally publish their thoughts and be heeded.[17] For some, the realization that their ideas are not as sharp or compelling in America leads them to doubt, like true intellectuals, the entire meaning of their existence. Some turn their doubts into anger at America; some turn them inward and die of melancholia. Others, who do little but concentrate on past glories and deprecate the *meshchane* around them, turn into inert Oblomovs.[18]

By far the majority, however, are those who find new routes through which to express and use their intellect. Many recent immigrants work at jobs below their former professions and educational qualifications. While they may experience initial difficulty adjusting to this drop in status (see chapter 3; Goldstein 1979, 261), with time they often find alternatives to their jobs for self-satisfaction. Some actively seek "intellectual company" with whom they discuss poetry, travels abroad, classical music, and moral questions. Although they may no longer hold jobs worthy of their intellect, they keep their intellectualism alive and meaningful through the creation of a social circle.

One such circle, an informal group affiliated with no larger organization or Jewish center, comes together about once a month. The family that hosts it most frequently lives in a transitional neighborhood (once all white and predominantly Jewish, now predominantly black with clusters of elderly American Jews and immigrants from the USSR) in Brooklyn. The modestly furnished living room is dominated by a large black and white portrait of Vladimir Vysotsky, the well-known dramatic actor at Moscow's Taganka Theater and iconoclastic singer-songwriter who died in 1980. Another wall is filled entirely with wooden bookshelves on which volumes and volumes of Russian books—prose and poetry of Russian and foreign (translated into Russian) authors, art books, atlases, history books, dictionaries—almost burst off the shelves. Ukrainian and Russian folk art, wooden dolls, bowls and plates painted in red and black floral patterns, decorate the topmost shelves. Furniture is sparse—a couch-daybed and a couple of worn armchairs—so that when guests come for an evening gathering, most sit on the floor.[19]

These evenings focus on a major topic or activity. On a few occasions, the hostess showed slides of European cities she had recently visited and presented a narrative about each one, the industries, cultural life, history, standard of living, and look of the people, as she showed the slides. Once an artist displayed and discussed his paintings and sculptures; once an Israeli poet, originally from Moscow, came and read her works. On the fifth anniversary of Vysotsky's death, the evening was devoted to remembering his songs and his life. Each one of these gatherings is characterized by intense, lively discussions that ultimately touch on broader questions pertaining to their immigration experiences ("How do we begin to feel ourselves necessary and useful here?"), differences between life in America and life in Russia, and ethical questions and moral dilemmas. They give voice to their introspection, their quest for knowledge, and their permanent lack of complacency while searching for life's ideal, without which, as Dunham (1976, 20–21; also Pipes 1961) points out, the intelligentsia would cease to exist.

These former professionals—actors, lawyers, administrators, teachers, musicians—whose intellect and talent are not fully used or appreciated in wider American society, have banded together to create a milieu in which their Russian intellectualism remains a vital and meaningful part of their characters. Their unbridled intellectual curiosity and creativity find expression in these exchanges of information, intense discussions, and debates. Through their gatherings, these middle-aged immigrants continue to be intelligentsia in the spiritual, moral, and social senses of the word, although an occupational base and recognition from wider society may now be lacking.

Younger immigrants, especially those who received higher education in America, have been able to apply their skills to well-paying professional jobs and worry that they are losing their intellectualism. As they interact with fellow Russian Jewish intelligentsia, they cannot help but notice, as Yasha's friend Dima points out:

> There is something about America that changes our people, for the worse, absolutely. I mean, in Moscow, when we would get together, a group of friends, we would discuss poetry, songs, you know, Vysotsky, Okudzhava, spiritual questions. Here, I hate to say it, the bulk of our conversation now concerns mortgages, car loans, and so on, not to mention income tax.

The irony for this young man and many like him is that where the Soviet government failed through its heavy-handed ideological campaign to co-opt the intelligentsia, to buy off its rebelliousness and disaffection with promises of comfort and status, America succeeded simply by providing whatever is desired, as long as one has the money (or credit) to spend. Theoretically, in America nice things can be had without compromising one's morality; however, as immigrant youth find out, they may have to relax their rigid standards of spirituality and intellectual pursuit to get the things that money can buy. Young people find themselves faced with the moral dilemma of choosing between humanistic or research-related careers that offer small salaries, and opening businesses, becoming involved in real estate investments, or pursuing careers in law or medicine that will bring them high incomes. Money does buy the ability to take advantage of New York's cultural offerings and to travel, but to get it one must earn it and pay attention to how it is spent. For people to whom discussion of money matters was once anathema, their present concern with income potential, investments, and tax loopholes is disconcerting.

Self-conscious émigré young adults, partially in response to their reluctant attention to money and their realization of how Americanized they have become, may, like Yakov, reactivate their attachment to Russian high culture and the beauty of their native language:

> Many, like myself, have gone back to reading Russian literary classics. Right now I can honestly say that my English is better than my Russian, yes, really, especially professionally. And lately, when I've looked at what I've written [in Russian] I haven't been happy. So I decided to go back and develop my language. . . . Now that I feel I might be losing some of the richness of this language, I have the urge to go back to it and capture it. And I am rereading old favorites. Many of the people I described for you [intellectual youth] are doing the same.

These same intellectuals, as they feel increasingly secure in their educational accomplishments and professional positions in America, begin to embrace some of the less lofty aspects of immigrant life as well. Seeing, perhaps, that going to dance clubs, enjoying fine food, and dressing nicely have not marred the legitimacy or reputation of American intelligentsia, immigrant youth who, up to a few years ago, never would have set foot in Russian restaurants, repositories of *meshchanstvo* with their over-laden tables, loud music, and flashily dressed clientele, "are beginning to go back to the Russian restaurants . . . not as normal ways to spend their free entertainment time, but rather, as events. They go to enjoy the food, to laugh, and really let out inhibitions, to have a good time."

Having attained American recognition of their status as intelligentsia, these young people, many of whom were blocked in these efforts in the USSR due to their Jewish "nationality," have fulfilled their parents' and their own ambitions that led them to emigrate. Guided by self-discipline and the criteria for being intellectuals, they had little difficulty in mastering English, excelling in their studies, and finding academic or professional work. Already shaped by a strong preference for cosmopolitanism and progress and having developed esthetic tastes that come with involvement in high culture, these Russian Jewish *wunderkinder* did in five to ten years what it took the turn-of-the-century wave of Russian Jews three generations to accomplish: they have become Yuppies, highly educated professionals and discriminating consumers of life's finer things, part of both the practical and the cultural sides of American life.

It is not difficult to draw an analogy between third- and fourth-generation Americans who seek a return to the ethnic fold and these immigrant intellectuals as they turn to the literary, philosophical, culinary, and leisure-time traditions of their native group. Comfortable with their ability to navigate in America and the achievements they have made, both seek out group-specific practices, people, and institutions in symbolic recognition and reaffirmation of their ethnic origins (see Gans 1979). The major difference, however, between these two sets of "weekend ethnics" is the notion of *intelligentsiia* that informs and pricks the conscience of Soviet émigrés' lifestyle. "Weekend ethnicity" and occasional forays into classic literature do not satisfy their urges to be part of an intelligentsia that they once knew. As they buy truffles at Balducci's, wear Ralph Lauren Polo shirts, and plan tax shelters, they wistfully remember impassioned discussions of Vysotsky's lyrics and switch on their state-of-the-art stereo systems to hear his gravelly voice.

Finally, there are those who, crammed bookshelves, recordings of dissident singers, and disdain for *meshchanstvo* notwithstanding, decide that they have "had enough of being Russian Jewish intelligentsia." They look at the free-enterprise system, the ability to start a business, and other routes for making a living and expressing oneself in America as new challenges to their intellect. In a rather typical

Marxist mode of thinking, some argue that Jews became intelligentsia in the Soviet Union because they had no other choice. Looking back now, they do not idealize intellectual discussions but rather view them as superstructural masking of a debilitating economic and ideological system. Developing only one's mind to make sense of or block out spiritual and material deprivation is, according to Maxim, no longer necessary and has outlived its usefulness in America:

> I am sick and tired of being an intellectual. Sure, there in the Soviet Union we turned our heads to spiritual pursuits and intellectual matters. We had no other choice. Here we *can* own things; we can pursue business opportunities. I'm ready for them. I've had enough of being a poor but smart intellectual.

These immigrants have little interest in continuing membership in the Russian intellectual circles that form in America. They tackle English and develop new skills to meet the challenge of what America has to offer; for them, the mastery of their new lives is the ultimate expression of their intellect. Pavel, who has established himself quite comfortably in computer programming, tells of his plans for the future:

> I am the kind of person who lives to achieve. If I reach a goal, then I cannot say that I get bored, but I can say that I am ready to move on. My plans are to speak English as well as Russian, and tomorrow I start my level 7 course at Columbia University. Then, the next year, I plan to go for my MBA—I am very interested in Yale. This is how I always was and always will be. That is why I came to America. This is the place for me, not over there where they've already taught generations to be followers.

This subgroup of émigré intelligentsia do not invoke their *intelligentnost* to distinguish themselves from others. They have privatized their intellectual pursuits and are content to read, watch thought-provoking films (Pavel, quoted above, ended our conversation to go home and watch Fassbinder's *Alexander Berlinerplatz* on public television), attend concerts, and travel without sharing their thoughts and experiences in intense discussions with a Russian-speaking circle of like-minded friends. These people point to their desire to expand their horizons and broaden their friendships to include Americans of various ethnic backgrounds, not only Jews but also Italians and

Asians, in differentiating themselves from fellow immigrants. Pavel continues:

> You see, when you come to a new country, you have the responsibility to change not only your apartment, but also your mentality. Unfortunately, Russia gave to its people a slave mentality, and this makes me sick and angry that here they are in America, and they have a chance to change their mentality, to travel, to open up new worlds, to taste the freedom they longed for in Russia. . . . It disgusts me that they sit and have their Russian newspapers, they walk ten minutes to their Russian businesses, and in the evening, they listen to their Russian radio. They didn't immigrate; they simply changed apartments from Odessa to Brooklyn!

This small group is taking its intellectual search to what it considers its logical extreme, ridding themselves of "Russian slave mentality," the clustering together and sharing of every experience by which Russian immigrants gain others' approval to verify the self. They have transcended the fear of many Soviet émigrés—that due to their non-native command of English they will not be taken seriously as intelligent people—and are seeking out a broad array of friends, acquaintances, and experiences.

Russian Jewish intellectualism is rooted in a specific context that developed over several centuries, first under tsarism, and then in the Soviet state. The true *intelligentny chelovek* is one who lives to think and create, who is never satisfied with the status quo, and yearns to right society's wrongs. This intellectual spirit guides many immigrants' encounters with America, although it may lead in several directions. At one extreme are those whose creativity or social critiques are so rooted in the Soviet context that they can find no voice in America, and they pine away in mourning for their old days of dissidence and true intellectualism. At the other extreme are those who willingly rid themselves of the trappings of being a Soviet Jewish intellectual and channel their energies in new, American directions. In between these extremes are immigrants who express their *intelligentnost* in a variety of social and symbolic forms, by regularly gathering in "intellectual circles," rereading Russian literary classics, listening to the recordings of the provocative bards, Okudzhava, Vysotsky, and Galich, and remembering the past. It is in the present, however, that the spirit of intellectualism must live on—in one's quest for knowledge for knowledge's sake, critical inquiries into current events and political happenings or artistic creativity—if one is to be counted among the ranks of Russian intelligentsia. This realization is shared by most and is precisely the point when they ask themselves if any of the real intelligentsia are left. Whether one counts oneself within their ranks or not, it is this craving for the true Russian Jewish intellectual spirit that serves as a moral unifier among many Soviet immigrants.

5.

COMMUNITY AS HISTORY AND DESTINY

People removed from their ancestral homelands recognize commonalities with others when they discover that they or their forebears lived in the same town or region of a country, spoke the same language, and adhered to the same faith. These discoveries provide interesting conversational moments and nothing more if the people involved have no concern with their past and see no implications of a shared history for their present or future. Soviet Jews, a heterogeneous group who came to America from a variety of backgrounds and places in the USSR, put great importance on their past and stress their history in discussions of their present. These immigrants feel bound to each other not only because they came from the same country and speak the same language but, more important, because they attach similar meanings to their common past experiences, which underlie their interpretations of events and their actions in the present. Perhaps most important of all is their belief that this history shapes their common destiny in America.

Jewish immigrants from the Soviet Union agree implicitly on one thing: that being Jews makes them in some way different from others. While most are secular Jews and consider themselves nonbelieving members of the Jewish nationality, their Jewish identity and the particular interpretation they give it remain unquestioned aspects of the self even several years after immigration. The meaning they attach to being Jewish and the group-specific ways in which they express this identity unite them as they distinguish themselves from American Jews. Yet it is within the American Jewish community that they believe their destiny lies. The ways they attempt to transform their Soviet-made Jewish identity into an American version forge an even greater sense of intragroup commonality as these rites of transition remind them of their common history and propel them toward the destiny they chose by coming to America.

Political attitudes and orientations are, with few but notable exceptions, remarkably similar among the immigrants. Unlike many of New York's Jews and most first-generation immigrants, new Americans from the USSR ally themselves with the Republican party (Noonan 1988). During the 1980s, they were particularly attracted to President Reagan and the alleged "get tough" stance of his administration, because they wished to see stopped any movements that may have eventuated in the spread of communism. Linked to this concern is their loud support for "law and order" and crime prevention. Having chosen the United States over the Soviet Union, these immigrants have tied their own future to the destiny of their new country. They passionately defend freedom and what they perceive as the American way, while they emphatically proclaim that a free America can persist only if the Soviet threat is curbed abroad and criminals here at home are apprehended and punished with dispatch and severity.

Soviet émigrés themselves are quite aware that their interpretation of what it means to be a Jew and their political orientations differentiate them from the Americans around them, specifically from American Jews. These topics are frequently mentioned and explained in the course of conversations among immigrants. Even more revealing perhaps is that when immigrants discover "an American who speaks Russian" in their midst, they immediately ask about and discuss elections, the Goetz affair,[1] Jewish identity, and the implications of these issues for their future in America. Like it or not, I was pulled into many conversations on these themes and quickly learned of a remarkable similarity among immigrants from different cities, professions, and generations, and of the great importance that these issues assume in their daily lives. How Soviet Jewish immigrants interpret ramifications of membership in their religion, ethnic group, and the American political arena is important to our understanding of what forges a sentiment of group belongingness and community among Soviet Jewish émigrés.

EVREISTVO: JEWISHNESS

The Russian word *evreistvo* translates into English in two ways: "Judaism," that is, the beliefs, rituals, and liturgy of the Jewish religion; and "Jewishness," a broader term that captures the racial-ethnic-national-spiritual character, which may or may not include religion per se, of a people who define themselves and are defined by others as Jews. Jewishness in the USSR is considered a national category, which, in the seventy-plus years since the November Revolution, has become increasingly devoid of religious content. Soviet Jews, therefore, delineate religious Jews as a small subgroup of the Jewish people.

Blood, Genes, and the Bread of Affliction

Soviet Jews regard their Jewishness as an intrinsic component of who they are. Jews are born Jews, and no one in the USSR challenges or questions their own or others' Jewishness. As immigrants explain it, being a Jew is an immutable biological and social fact, ascribed at birth like sex and eye color. Zhanna, a bookkeeper in her forties:

> In the Soviet Union, I tell you, I never for a moment questioned that I was Jewish. I was just this, and that's it. To me, it was me, and a part of me that I just naturally accepted.

Maxim:

> We are Jews by our blood, our genes, our historical experiences. While one can change religion, it is very difficult, if not impossible, to change genes and blood.

These symbols of blood and genes, mentioned time and again (see also Rothchild 1985, 34), capture the unalterability of Jewish identity.

"Jewish genes" make Jews different from other people. Very often Soviet Jews will refer to their "Jewish appearance" as an obvious manifestation of Jewish genes. It is taken for granted that everyone recognizes a Jewish face, and many have explained that in the Soviet Union, "By my face, that's how they knew I was Jewish." When pressed further to describe Jewish appearance, informants usually sigh in exasperation, start with, "You know," and give their explanations:

Short, red-haired, big-nosed, he was, you know, a typically Jewish-looking man.

A friend of mine, also Jewish, but she looks very Jewish. What do I mean by this? Dark very curly hair, short, dark olive complexion, big nose—typical Jewish features.

These Jewish faces stand out in a country of Slavs where conformity is highly valued. Jews' dark or red curly hair and shorter stature contrast with the Russian ideal of black or blond straight hair, blue eyes, ruddy complexion, and stocky build.[2]

Not all Jews, however, have "Jewish faces." While I am far from Nordic- or Slavic-looking, my Russian Jewish hosts would often challenge my Jewish identity: "No! I never would have taken you for Jewish. You look English, or North European. Your hair is too straight, and you're just too, too tall." But "Jewish face" or not, all Jews have Jewish genes and blood. This blood, which they received from their parents, is sometimes interpreted literally, especially by children who, like Svetlana, may become "blood siblings" with Russian friends in order to get the blood that qualifies them, as they understand it, to be Russian.

Blood, however, as David Schneider explains in his analysis of American kinship (1980, 24), means much more than the fluid that flows through one's veins. It symbolizes permanence; a blood relationship is one that "can never be severed, whatever its legal position. Legal rights may be lost, but the blood relationship cannot be lost." When Soviet Jews speak of their "Jewish blood," it signifies that nothing can eradicate their Jewish identity. Although one may disavow the Jewish religion and change one's name, as did Leon Trotsky and many self-proclaimed atheists among the immigrants, or even convert to Christianity like the family of Karl Marx when he was six years old, such ideological transformations do not alter the biogenetic composition of an individual. Being born of Jewish blood makes one forever a Jew.

This notion of the biological unalterability of Jewish identity is a relatively new concept among Jews and non-Jews alike. Until the latter part of the nineteenth century, Russian Jews viewed themselves not as a nation but as practitioners of Judaism (Dubnow 1918, 2:222–223). Religion, unlike race or nationality, is alterable. During the reign of the tsars, conversions to the Russian Orthodox church did remake Jews into Christian Russians, as conversion to Catholicism saved Jews from the fires of the Spanish Inquisition. Although Jews were forbidden commissions of rank in the tsar's army and positions in the state civil service, former Jews who became Christians were granted full citizenship and the rights attached to it.

Not only did the Russians recognize converted Jews' change of identity, but their Jewish communities and kin did likewise. Rabbis placed excommunication bans, or *herems,* upon those who abandoned the faith (see *Encyclopedia Judaica* 1971, 8:353–355). Parents of converts marked the death of their child as a Jew by tearing their garments and performing mourning rituals. Jews who embraced Russian Orthodoxy disappeared from the Jewish community and became, in fact, Russians.

Only in the latter part of the nineteenth century, as religion began to lose its tight grip to science among both Christians and Jews, and as Social Darwinism took root in some of Europe's intellectual circles, did the idea of "Jewish blood" start to supersede the view of Jews as practitioners of Judaism. After the death of Lenin, the Soviet regime institutionalized the idea of Jewish nationality and made it a fact that Jews, including those who had long ago abandoned their Judaism as well as persistent believers, are Jewish because of their "blood." During the Nazi occupation, this view became further entrenched, as even Lithuanians, Latvians, Russians, Byelorussians, and Ukrainians learned that by virtue of having one Jewish grandparent, birth of Russian Orthodox or Roman Catholic parents and their own baptismal certificates were rendered void. These Christians were labelled and treated as Jews, discovering that Jewish blood has such force that it cannot be assimilated into or subsumed by that of Slavs or even Germans.[3]

Even more recently, in Stalin's 1948–53 campaign against "rootless cosmopolitanism," Jews were shown that they can never escape their blood. Russians of Jewish descent who had changed their names and disavowed their religions were referred to, for example, as "Zhelensky, born Apfelbaum" as reminders of their Jewish status. By the 1960s, Soviet Jews had internalized a socially constituted biological fact: whether or not they practice Judaism, Jewish blood and genes will always make them and their offspring inescapably Jewish.

As symbols of common descent, genes and blood bind Jews together in a kinlike identity. Jewish genes not only manifest themselves in the "Jewish face" but also explain feelings of closeness with other Jews. Soviet Jews speak of feeling ashamed, depressed, and sad when seeing Jewish prostitutes—"They are like sisters to me. I wanted to go over to them and take them off the streets"—Jewish criminals and drunkards, or any Jew who is not of high calibre. After viewing a poor performance by Russian Jewish actors and singers, Maxim confided, "It made me very depressed because it is like [watching] my relatives. You always want the very best for your relatives, and you feel that their accomplishments are your accomplishments, their failures, your failures."

In retelling the story of a Jewish woman who is a professor of foreign languages in Moscow and married to a non-Jewish man, Lera pointed out that although many Soviet Jews have become part of the Russian intelligentsia by virtue of their education and profession, "they still know and remember and remind themselves that they are Jewish. It's second nature, and I cannot explain this." This "second nature," Lera said, was inherited by the children of her friend's mixed marriage:

> Both children are officially registered as Russian on their passports . . . but what happened? Both of them found Jews to marry. No one else would do. They said to their mother that there was just something that bound them to marry other Jews, a feeling of comfort, a special something in common. Jewish remains Jewish—that's all there is to it. It's a special something that we all share no matter how hard some may try to lose it.

"Jewish blood" thus stands for what Durkheim (1964) calls the "collective conscious" and Shils (1957) and Geertz (1963) label "primordial attachments." This feeling of sameness, ease, and comfort with fellow Jews cannot be explained; it is simply part of the belief that Jews are all related, through genes, blood, and spirit.

Deriving from this "special something" is recognition of a Jewish character that is linked to the blood relationship. Schneider (1980, 25) explains, "A blood relationship is a relationship of identity. . . . It is a belief in common biological constitution, and aspects like temperament . . . and habit are noted as signs of this shared biological make-up, this special identity of relatives with each other."

The "Jewish character" has been portrayed in non-Jewish literature throughout the centuries in the persona of a money-grubbing,
treacherous trader or lawyer who is sneaky and conniving, sharp of
mind, and weak in body. In Russia, the image of the "dirty Jew" still
holds strong sway today; Jews are just a little too smart for their own
good and are therefore suspect. Russians explain away those Jews
who do not fit this stereotype as exceptions to the rule. Informants
relate that after proving themselves physically or socially among non-
Jews they have been told, "You're really not like them at all. You're
one of us [*nash chelovek*]; you may be a Jew, but we accept you as
ours." Jews are different by virtue of their blood, and if their behavior
does not accord with the way "dirty Jews" are supposed to act, then
those Jews are different; the stereotype does not change.

Jews, too, believe that a common character unites them, and
they accept amended versions of the Russian stereotype. Soviet Jews
speak of their exceptional talents and superior intellect. This high
degree of intelligence is the foundation for the two major character
types Jews attribute to themselves: the "noble Jew" and the "crafty
Jew."

The "noble Jew" is an intellectual in the full sense of the word,
ethically pure, socially conscious, and motivated by the good of hu-
mankind. Émigrés point to Marx, Freud, and Einstein as the best
examples of this type, and to early Bolshevik leaders, and to writers,
doctors, scientists, and others they know who "help people" and
contribute to human progress. The "crafty Jew" is just as smart as the
intellectual, but rather than naively and altruistically dedicating himself to a lofty cause, he uses his intellect to "go around" (*obkhodit*)
the obstacles set in his path by the majority society. Jewish intellect in
this case is seen as an innate talent to find a way through or a solution
to any problem and underscores the attractiveness of such characters
as the Robin Hood–like Jewish thief Misha of Odessa (the prototype
for Isaak Babel's Benya Krik), several modern-day black marketeers,
and a host of professionals who have found places for themselves in
Soviet society. While some Soviet Jewish immigrants recognize both
"types" of Jews, others are certain that only one Jewish character,
either the intellectual "noble Jew" or the street-smart "crafty Jew"
typifies the Jewish group. The following conversation occurred between Galina, a middle-aged architect, and her artist husband in their
Brooklyn apartment:

Husband: It's unbelievable what we Jews have done with Israel, that it's been turned into a flourishing country. This you can see wherever you go. Then my friend told me about the Sinai. When it was in Israel's hands, it too became green and fertile. And as soon as Israel moved out, the Egyptians dismantled everything, and it has become a desert again. Yes, Jews are an uncommonly talented people.

Wife: Jews are not necessarily an especially talented people; they are especially pushy. Where others go in a straight line, the Jew can find another way around. For this they have a talent.

Husband: No, Jews are just that—talented. For example, while only 3 percent or less of the Soviet Union's population is Jewish, 30 percent of the Writer's Union is Jewish.

Wife: Fine, this is true, but I will not say it's a special creative talent. They know how to push, to find new paths, to get where they need to go.

These two character types emerge in jokes Jews tell about themselves. Sometimes the types are reconciled into one ambiguously "smart Jew":

Three men and a woman are abandoned in a desert. One of the men finds an orange and gives it to the woman. The other two men, both Russians, are trying to determine the first man's nationality: —He must be an Englishman because he is so polite to give the orange away. —No, he must be a Frenchman because he is so gallant. —No, he must be an Italian because Italians love women more than life itself. They thought for a few moments, and finally one says to the other, "No! I've got it! He must be a Jew. Who else would find an orange in the desert!"

Soviet Jews express a mixture of shame and pride in telling stories of the "crafty Jew." Intellect is something that is part of the Jewish character, intrinsic to the Jew like Jewish blood, and of this they are exceedingly proud. Craftiness, wiliness, and business acumen, often viewed by Soviet Jews as undesirable Jewish traits, are explained as reactions to being unwanted, despised strangers in European lands. That Soviet Jews have internalized the undesirability of Jews' proficiency as usurers and capitalists is not at all surprising, since Marx himself in his 1843 essay (1975) designated these characteristics as incompatible with a humane world. Soviet Jews argue that Jews' native intelligence allowed them to develop these survival skills, but craftiness as such, they believe, as Sonya, Natalya's friend from Leningrad, relates, is not innately part of the Jewish character:

> Listen carefully, you will find this interesting. Georgians, Armenians, they have their republics. Georgians are not so very smart, but hospitable, the most hospitable people you will ever meet. . . . Now Armenians are different—these two peoples are similar, both live in the Caucasus, but they are different. Armenians are smart, or rather, cunning, daring; they have very good business sense. Now, listen carefully—the difference between Armenians and Jews is that among Armenians, this street-smarts, their cunning, developed within the confines of their homeland, in their republic. It is a part of their character, their natural, internal character. Jews are in no such position [of having a republic]. Now they have Israel, a beleaguered country, always threatened by those terrorist Arabs sitting on her borders. And in the Soviet Union—no republic; we were dispersed everywhere throughout that country. And always unwelcome, always in danger of being chased out. So Jews developed their smartness in reaction to those circumstances. Do you understand this? Jews are an unhappy, unwanted people—to survive dispersed, they developed these skills. That is the difference.

To be a Jew is to suffer, for it means dwelling among strangers as a mistrusted, despised minority. To be a Soviet Jew is to live with the reality that oneself, one's family, and one's entire nationality (ethnic group) are considered different from and worse than all others, to know and be reminded every day that Jews are unwanted and hated simply because of their "Jewish blood." Along with the pride they feel in the belief that Jews are smarter than everyone else is an equally strong, if not stronger, feeling of shame, worthlessness, and self-hate attached to their Jewish identity. These negative feelings are internalized early on, as their Russian and Ukrainian schoolmates, colleagues, and neighbors, as well as the Soviet press, unrelentingly tell Jews that they are bad. Mark, Boris's brother-in-law, looks back:

> I have to tell you that all my life I was aware of being Jewish and of being ashamed of this. As children—all children want to be like other children, and when they find out that they are different, they hate this. And children learn from parents what is and is not different. I went to summer camp, and I had been circumcised, and each summer at camp I was the laughingstock. Oh, they had a lot of fun laughing at me. Why?

Because I was different from them, and they had already learned from their anti-Semite parents that being Jewish and being different are to be hated.

Maxim recalls:

As for me, ever since I can remember I knew that I was different from all others, that is, Russians, because I was Jewish. And how did I know this? Because the other boys who played in my courtyard called me "dirty Jew."

And two young women, one from a town in the Ukraine, the other from Moscow, express their childhood memories:

I was the only Jewish kid in the whole class, and, I told you this before, about my hair and other things. I made my mother do the weirdest things to me to make me look Christian. I felt, "Why do I have to be ashamed?" but I was. . . . In Russia, you had to hide this away—the confusion and insecurity of being a Jew.

Only that being Jewish makes you worse than everyone else. . . . This is what a Jewish identity means in the Soviet Union—feeling worse than those around you, and those around you having the right to tell you that you are worse.

Even those immigrants who downplay their confrontations with anti-Semitism in the Soviet Union reveal their pain. Many, like the next speaker, Alex, an economist from Odessa, and Lera, who follows, have said, "I personally did not suffer from anti-Semitism" yet speak of incidents and daily occurrences that remind them that being a Jew did have negative consequences:

I didn't think it [being Jewish] made me any better or any worse. Oh sure, sometimes I would hear "*zhid*" [kike], but for me personally, I cannot say that I encountered any direct anti-Semitism.

She was my best friend, and like most of my friends, she was Russian, not Jewish. At work I never had any problems either. The only problem I ever had was when I first looked for a job. . . . I called and set up an appointment with the director. With the director at the interview was a very unpleasant sort—obviously KGB. The director asked me a series of questions about my schooling and work plans, but the KGB-man asked questions about my family and about my allegiance to the Soviet Union and my opinions on Israel. It was the biggest shock of my life. A few days later I was called and told that "my kind" wasn't wanted at that place. It took me some time to realize what "my kind" meant. But this was the only unpleasantness that ever happened to me.

In a country where anti-Jewish sentiment is pervasive, Jews themselves came to accept the belief that they are worse than Russians. It was simply part of the reality of their situation, and as much as they may have been confused by or rebelled against this negative self-appraisal, it was not to be avoided. The ultimate effect of growing up in a country that distrusts Jews and constantly (through the media) attacks Zionism and Israel, is a gnawing feeling of self-consciousness and insecurity among Jews, "This is something that is with you your whole life—a terrible feeling always to hear bad things about who you are." To be a Jew then is not only to be hated and unwanted, but also to hate oneself and to suffer for it, because, try as one might, there is no escape from the stigma of this identity.

Nonetheless, Soviet Jews do try to escape these negative feelings, often by submerging themselves in their studies and their work. Professional accomplishments ease feelings of worthlessness, although Soviet Jewish immigrants, in reflecting, are conscious that anti-Semitism does not go away just because Jews have proven themselves occupationally meritorious. But back there, back then, many, like Maxim, relate that they made it their personal mission to prove themselves, and by extension all Jews, to be not only as good as Russians, but in fact, better:[4]

> These boys called me "dirty Jew" but instead of wanting to wash my hands to become a clean Jew, I then and there decided that this dirty Jew would work harder and become better than them all. All I know is that at a very young age I decided that to be Jewish means I must be better than everyone else. And that is what I did. I worked harder, studied harder, spoke and wrote Russian better. This is what I understood I had to do.

This compulsive dedication to excellence in school and work (Goldstein 1979, 260–261) masks the suffering but does not eliminate it. In the back of Jews' minds, and often pushed to the forefront, is the fear that one day their Jewishness will counteract and eliminate the individual professional achievements they have worked so hard to attain. A former Moscow television producer explains:

> It means that you are marked, set off as different, but not only as different but worse, as a potential traitor. What Jews know is that there is discrimination—in universities and regarding jobs. And they also know that because they are Jewish, if they should do something wrong, it will be doubly bad. First the crime, and then that they are Jewish—so it's like being tried twice.

After emigration, Soviet immigrants' social position as Jews changes dramatically. Among their first impressions of America is the startling realization that Jewish institutions are part of the public landscape and that Jews are treated with respect, as just another one of America's many ethnic groups. Zhenya, who originally resettled in the Midwest before coming to New York, was pleasantly shocked by a Jewish building:

> I remember one of my first impressions [of St. Louis] was when I saw this great, big hospital, a Jewish children's hospital right in the middle of the city. "Oh my God!" I thought, "What a country that allows you to publicize being Jewish!" And what a grand hospital it is.

Mark, Boris's brother-in-law, was happily surprised by the Jewish holiday greeting he received when on a job interview:

> Now I want to explain to you what personnel office means in the Soviet Union—it is filled with party cadre and KGB. The first thing you are asked for is your passport, upon which it is written, "Jew." So here I was, in Connecticut, in a personnel office, and I was in shock. A nice man came out and started to talk to me like I was a human being. He heard that I have an accent and saw that I was from the Soviet Union, so he thought I was Russian, like a defector. I began to explain that I wasn't Russian but Jewish and started to explain some of the reasons that I left the Soviet Union because of this. . . . When I was telling him I was Jewish, he put out his hand to shake mine because that day was some Jewish holiday, I think it was around the time of *Pesach* [Passover]. There we were in a personnel office, and the man I am talking

with shakes my hand to congratulate me on a Jewish holiday. I knew for
sure I was in a different country then!

In New York City the ethnically diverse nature of America's
population is acutely noticeable, as is the plethora of organizations
and institutions that demonstrate the acceptability of ethnic and religious pluralism. New York's Jewish life in particular is very rich, and
Jews—from Ed Koch, who was the mayor of the city from 1976 to
1990, to traditionally garbed Hasidim—are visible everywhere. Jewish schools, hospitals, and charitable institutions abound; Yiddish and
Hebrew newspapers, to say nothing of English-language Jewish periodicals, are sold at local newsstands, and kosher and kosher-style
butchers, bakeries, and restaurants are found throughout the city. A
multitude of synagogues, ranging from the cathedral-like Temple
Emanuel overlooking Central Park on Fifth Avenue, to little Hasidic
prayer houses in Brooklyn, make New York a city openly and proudly
characterized by a large and varied Jewish population. To be a Jew in
New York is to be like everyone else.

Soviet émigrés are quick to recognize that their status as Jews has
changed as a result of their migration, but, like Maxim, are usually
unable to specify how, except to underscore their new elation at
feeling "normal":

> I am not really sure I can tell you what it [Jewish identity] means for me
> here—except that I can find out more facts about Jewish people and
> history. Here it is just something, like everyone here has something.

Precisely because being Jewish is just like being anything else and
because the Jewish community offers an array of opportunities for
Jews to demonstrate and express their Jewish identity, in America the
burden is placed upon the individual to prove one's Jewishness. Jewish birth is necessary but not sufficient to be a "real Jew." In New
York, where anti-Semitism does not make people of Jewish descent
unalterably Jewish, where Jews have the possibility of changing their
names, noses, and lifestyles to pass unnoticed into the American
mainstream, they are told, "You can't be a Jew just out of a book or
just by buying bagels and lox."[5] To be a good Jew, one must do
specifically Jewish things.

Soviet Jewish immigrants, especially as they look around at fellow Jews in New York, acknowledge that they have lost much of their Jewish culture and religion as a result of having lived in the USSR. What they do not accept is that this lack of Jewish religious knowledge and faith makes them any less Jewish. Soviet Jewish immigrants are appalled when they find themselves in the ironic position of being labelled "Russian" by their American Jewish counterparts once they arrive in New York (Markowitz 1988b). Vladimir, for one, becomes quite emotional when discussing this subject:

> I completely reject the label, Russian. We are in American eyes Russian, but we are *not* Russian. All our lives it was underlined that we are Jews. Jewishness is more important in some circumstances than Judaism. To be a religious Jew is one category of being Jewish. We grew up in Russia not religious but as Jews. My self-consciousness [*soznaniye*] helps me feel close to any real Jewish person. I do not feel inferior that I am not religious. Some American Jews are religious, some are not. I've always been proud that I am a Jew. . . . The main misunderstanding is that religious Jews think in order for a man to be a Jew he must be religious. But any real Jew should respect my Jewishness.

While they may have abandoned many of the distinctive practices of Ashkenazic Jewish culture, especially as regards religion, Soviet Jews never did, of course, lose their Jewish genes and blood. By virtue of their biogenetic composition alone they claim full Jewish status. But, on top of that, Soviet Jews invoke their consciousness of Jewish identity and their feeling of a bond, which rests on shared suffering and survival, with all Jews throughout history as further evidence that they are complete Jews. The following conversation between Maxim and an acquaintance, Misha, illustrates these points:

> Misha: We Russian Jews are different from other Jews, not just from American Jews, because we see ourselves as Jews because of our ties to the history of the Jewish people. We see ourselves as the descendants of that group of people who came out of the Sinai thousands of years ago and all they've been through since. We are part of that history, of that tradition, but we don't believe in God. An Italian can be an Italian if he is Catholic, Protestant, or Communist. To me, it is the same with being Jewish: it is part of me, my history, and the history of my people.
> Maxim: No, that's not enough. I think being Jewish has much to do with anti-Semitism, and that maybe someone, like Karl Marx, who

doesn't want to be Jewish but still is, or, according to Hitler, where you have no choice in the matter. I think with anti-Semitism there is no choice, and it doesn't matter if you believe in God or not, as long as you have something that others see as Jewish—like a nose, or a name, or a manner—then you are Jewish.

Suffering, as Walter Zenner (1977) eloquently describes, is a central motif in Jewish culture, uniting all Jews, symbolically or actually, through a history of dispersal and persecution. American Jews, who are in the enviable position of having suffered hardly at all, remind themselves of the dire plight of fellow Jews through museum exhibits, scholarly research, their daily prayers, marches to free Soviet Jewry, donations of money to Israel, and Holocaust memorials. Soviet Jews, on the other hand, lived through discrimination and persecution, and in the case of those over forty-five, barely avoided annihilation. Every one of them had a family member perish at the front or as a result of the Nazis' "final solution" during World War II. In America, while they no longer suffer as Jews, their past suffering and that of their parents and grandparents remain a core part of their Jewish identity.

Reminders of their suffering do not diminish as time passes. In fact, as life in America becomes increasingly easy for Soviet immigrants, the pain of the past becomes all the more acute. During a bright spring day, walking through the Brooklyn Botanical Gardens, Boris's mother, Shura, a woman in her sixties, looked around and said:

> Oh, it's so beautiful here! But I just can't help myself. Whenever I see so many flowers, I am reminded of acacias. Do you know these flowers? They are white and sweet. I lived through three terrible famines, 1933, during the war, and then in 1947 when I was pregnant with Borya. Oh, that I lived through all that to come to this beautiful country, I am very thankful. During the famine of 1933, we were young girls then, my friends and I went into the forest every day and gathered acacias. This is how we survived, by eating acacias. That is all we had to eat. Now, although they are beautiful and smell so sweet, I cannot even look at these flowers.

Other happy moments evoke painful memories of the past as well. At the Bar Mitzvah service for Vladimir's and Sofia's son, while the boy chanted his *Haftarah* portion inside a synagogue, middle-aged female relatives began weeping and said to each other, "This is so beautiful. Oh, to see these children take part in Jewish life is so wonderful. They destroyed all that in the Soviet Union so that no children know any of the Jewish prayers and songs there. Had we stayed in the Soviet Union we never would have seen this day. So beautiful! So beautiful!"[6]

The solemn holiday of Yom Kippur, the Day of Atonement, provides a ritualistic moment for Soviet Jewish immigrants to mark for themselves and for American Jews the suffering that they and their relatives have endured. At around midday on Yom Kippur, a memorial service (*yizkor*) for the dead is held. In contrast to regular worship services, about an hour before its start, Russian-speakers fill the synagogues of Brighton Beach beyond capacity and ask each other, "When is *yizkor?* Has it begun?" Finally, as the cantor begins to intone the *kaddish* (prayer for the dead), a plaintive wail breaks out throughout the packed hall. Women sob and moan, pressing handkerchiefs to their eyes as they weep during the prayer. This ancient, mournful dirge evokes memories of dead loved ones, buried in the Soviet Union, never to be seen again, of World War II, the famines, the labor camps, and of course, all the pain that they themselves lived through as Russian Jews. As they cry for the people they have known, they mourn as well for the Jewish people as a nation, as an extension of themselves. This pain and sorrow is their link to Judaism, their proof of full Jewish status.

Ritualistic invocation of Jewish suffering also occurs at funeral services for Soviet immigrants. The most important last deed one can perform for loved ones is to bury them as Jews, to return them to their own people. In the Soviet Union, especially in Moscow, this often proves difficult since the Jewish cemeteries are overcrowded. Making other arrangements, such as having the corpse washed and dressed according to Jewish law, requires a great deal of commitment to one's Jewish heritage, since ritual specialists are hard to find in Soviet Russia. In America, however, Jewish funerals can be arranged by making a telephone call to any one of a number of Jewish funeral homes. In sharp contrast to the difficulties of being a Jew in the USSR are the ease and comfort with which one can live and die as a Jew in America. Immigrants remind themselves that life in America notwithstanding, suffering is part of who they are as Jews. Eulogies for the dead emphasize this theme:

> He lived a good Jewish life, surviving the harshness and terror of a Nazi concentration camp, where he lost his first family. After this terrible tragedy, he returned to his native city and . . . rebuilt his life. . . . Finally he came to America, where he was able to see his daughter marry and the birth of his grandson.

> She came to this country from Russia, leaving her friends and a way of life that she knew in order to remain with her children and grandchildren. She made this sacrifice for the sake of the future generations. She lived in Russia through such famines, and then the war. Yet despite all this, she raised a wonderful son and such grandchildren! Her last several days were especially difficult . . .

To have lived a Jewish life is to have suffered. Having suffered makes one a Jew. Although many of their Jewish traditions were undermined and their knowledge of Judaism weakened, having endured persecution and pain simply because of their "Jewish blood," Soviet immigrants know, and demonstrate to themselves and to their American counterparts who question their claims, that they are more than entitled to full status as Jews in life and in death.

Rites of Expurgation

Soviet Jews' blood, genes, and history of sorrow bind them to Jews throughout the world and provide them with legitimate claims to membership in the American Jewish community. However, they left the USSR precisely to rid themselves of the pain and insecurity attached to their Jewish identity, never believing that these negative feelings would remain and be important to them in America. Inspired by Israel's 1967 and 1973 military victories, which controverted the stereotype of the meek, weak Jew, and tales of Jewish prosperity in America, Soviet Jews fled their homeland to exchange their debilitating Jewish identity for a positive one. They came to New York, not to prolong their Jewish pain but to live as American Jews, to discard the past of self-consciousness and insecurity for the future of self-esteem and comfort.

However, instead of being welcomed by fellow Jews and automatically included in the American Jewish community upon arrival (Markowitz 1988b, 82), Soviet Jews often found their Jewishness called into question by rabbis, social workers, and neighbors, who demanded that the immigrants prove their Jewish descent and ethos. Rather than disappearing in America, the self-hatred and uncertainty attached to their Jewish identity thus remained. In the Soviet Union they were ashamed and suffered because they were Jewish; in America they were shamed and made to suffer because they were deemed not "Jewish enough" (Gitelman 1984, 97).

Soviet Jewish immigrants, through ritual processes, have been attempting to regain their lost knowledge of Judaism and Jewish culture and transform their membership from the historical Jewish community of sorrow and shame to a proud and noble Jewish community of destiny. These rites of expurgation, because they make explicit the break between the contradictory meanings of Jewish identity in the Soviet Union and the United States, are a symbolic bridge, which once crossed, facilitates immigrants' shifting of their Jewish identification from the Soviet context to the American and consequently results in the legitimation and confirmation of their claims to American Jewish status.

A visitor to Brighton Beach or any large gathering of Soviet Jewish immigrants would be struck by the number of people, old and young, male and female, wearing Jewish emblems as jewelry. They decorate themselves by displaying Stars of David, the Hebrew letters spelling the word *chai* (life), and facsimiles of the Ten Commandments worn on chains around their necks.

This public display of Jewish identity is an inversion of the way Jews treat their "nationality" in the Soviet Union. There it was "something to hide," and, although a Jew could never escape from his or her Jewishness, it was downplayed as much as possible. In America, Soviet Jews voluntarily don pendants made of precious metals, sometimes inlaid with gemstones, that proudly display their Jewishness. Not only does this jewelry tell American Jews that the immigrants are just as Jewish as they, but through the medium of gold and silver, former Soviet Jews tell themselves that their Jewish identity is precious and worthy of display.

For males, this form of expurgation is particularly striking, for their Jewish jewelry is worn also as a sign of machismo. Emulating

Italian male role models, they wear partially unbuttoned shirts that reveal thick gold chains and heavy pendants nestled against their hairy chests. By wearing Jewish stars in this way, they counteract old Russian and Ukrainian schoolmates' taunts that Jewish boys and men are weak, cowardly, and lack virility and show instead that Jews are as tough and masculine as anyone else.

Some Soviet Jewish immigrants, especially those in their late forties and fifties, seek work and residential situations where they can use Yiddish in everyday life. Many more, in describing their initial post-migration experiences, boast that their fluency in Yiddish enabled them to get around in Vienna and find apartments and first jobs in New York. Finding public voice in a language that was all but purged from the Soviet Union in 1948 counteracts negative feelings that arise from this suppression of a Jewish language:

> French—do you know what it means in Russian when someone asks, "Do you speak French?" That's our joke among Jewish people, a code for asking if you speak Yiddish. There are many such jokes in the Soviet Union. I do not have to tell you what the situation is like there for Jews.

Polina, a former Muscovite in her early fifties, works in Manhattan's garment district, where she communicates with her boss and fellow employees in Yiddish. She recalls that in the USSR she spoke Yiddish only at home with her parents and their friends—never in public places: "No, of course not! If I would speak Yiddish on the streets of Moscow, they would call me *zhid* and spit in my face."

In New York, this Jewish language becomes the *lingua franca* of many Soviet immigrants, allowing them to communicate in public arenas with Americans.[7] This dramatic transition in the status of Yiddish, from a secret Jewish code to a public language with its own press and radio stations, attests to and verifies the change that the immigrants' Jewish identity undergoes as a result of migration. Elevation of Yiddish to one of the several languages used in public by New York's varied ethnic and immigrant groups legitimizes its speakers as well.

Soviet Jewish émigrés perform Judaic rituals in confirmation of their Jewish identity and as ways to tell themselves that this identity, including its religious aspects, is noble and good. In fact, the American context is used to regain knowledge and practices lost or buried in the Soviet Union. Passover celebrations are a good illustration of this point, for they are held yearly in the large majority of the American homes of these former Soviet Jews (Federation of Jewish Philanthropies 1985, 28; Kosmin 1990, 47–49). Most immigrants, however, did not observe this holiday in the USSR, and among those who did mark the occasion of Passover, many, like Maxim, did so more as a political statement than as a religious observance:

> No, we didn't have a *seder* or a special meal, but we knew to eat this matzoh—which was very hard to get—instead of bread. Earlier I would get the matzoh from a friend, but in the last years there I would personally stand in line and wait. This was also a way I showed I was proud of being Jewish.

Several others, Marina and Nona, for example, have hazy childhood recollections of Passover at their grandparents' homes:

> I remember, maybe, when I was very little, going to my grandparents' for *Pesach,* but besides that—that's it.

> My father's mother was religious, and when she was alive we went to her for *Pesach*—gefilte fish and *khremsele* [traditional Passover foods]—and celebrated with her.

They use these memories of familial togetherness and special Jewish dishes served only at this time of the year to guide the celebrations they make in America.

Just as their memories rarely include chants and prayers of the Passover service, Soviet Jewish immigrants do not, as a rule, read from the *Hagaddah* (the religious text that structures and retells the story of Passover) during their observances. Some heads of family will discuss the significance of the Jews' exodus from Egypt, "like a history lesson," and explain how it relates to their own emigration from the Soviet Union. Occasionally children who learn portions of the Passover service in their Jewish schools will be asked to recite part of it, just as they might be called upon in other circumstances to sing a song or recite a poem.[8]

What is emphasized in Soviet émigrés' Passover celebrations is the food. Women recreate their mothers' and grandmothers' recipes and turn out gefilte fish from freshly killed carp, apple-stuffed goose or duck, *khremsele* (unleavened crepes or dumplings), and other holiday specialties. Much of the evening's conversation concerns their food, as the women explain how each of these items is as correctly prepared (i.e., according to Jewish dietary rules) and much more delicious than the "tasteless" ready-made kosher-for-Passover products used by Americans.

Immigrants self-consciously reflect on the disconnection between the wealth of Judaic knowledge they possess in the informal sphere and their lack thereof in the formal realm. Irina invited me to her family's Passover celebration, explaining, "You know we are not religious. There will be no prayers, no *seder* plate, but it is our Passover meal. And of course there will be matzoh, and gefilte fish—all the right foods." Raisa, Irina's mother, who had prepared the traditional meal, almost as we were seated proclaimed:

> We know what to do—and right. But in these religious matters, you understand, there are no Jewish schools in the Soviet Union, and it is hard for us to understand these prayers and their meanings. We learn from our parents. I learned from my mother how to prepare.

Jewish food traditions have persisted in the minds and kitchens of women long after closed synagogues and religious schools could no longer provide formal instruction in Judaism to men. The informal domain and the products of this knowledge, along with the sentiment attached to them, are often pointed to by Soviet Jewish immigrants as the manifestation and legitimization of their Jewish identity.

Not all immigrants, however, recognize such disconnections. A striking example occurred at a community *seder* held in an Orthodox synagogue in Brighton Beach for Passover 1984. An ersatz *seder* plate and a dish of matzoh were placed in the middle of a large table shared by several immigrants of all ages. Ordinarily a *seder* plate is made of porcelain and is decorated with gold-leaf and holds small portions of food items on designated spaces. The Hasidic Jew who placed a paper plate holding a boiled egg, cooked potato, lettuce leaf, horseradish, etc., on this *seder* table offered no explanation of what this "*seder* plate" meant. As soon as he walked away, the immigrants, unaware of the symbolic nature of these food items, started cutting up, handing out, and eating tiny pieces of the boiled egg, potato, etc., not knowing about, and therefore not waiting for, the blessings to be incanted.

Some émigré families are not content with only remnant knowledge of their Jewish heritage. Adults frequently confide that they themselves are "lost to Judaism" but wish to become integrated into the wider Jewish community through their children. During a discussion among a group of friends about their reasons for having emigrated and the meaning of the word "freedom," a cosmetologist from Moscow announced, "Freedom for me is giving my son a *bris* [circumcision]." Within weeks of arrival in New York, her then ten-year-old son was circumcised; three years later he became Bar Mitzvah in a local synagogue.

The Jewish circumcision ritual (*bris,* or *brit milah*) is traditionally performed on the eighth day after birth as a physical reminder of the covenant between God and the Jewish people. Males, although born of Jewish mothers, are not considered fully Jewish if they remain uncircumcised.[9] In the USSR, circumcision is viewed in official and "cultured" circles as a barbaric and savage practice performed by uncivilized peoples, and many Jewish parents, rather than marking their boys as different and adding to the indignity of their Jewish identity, simply do not have this rite performed (see Rozenblum 1982, 96–97). Once in America, however, Jewish parents may feel compelled to confer full Jewish status on their children and arrange for their young sons to be circumcised.

Both the Lubavitcher Hasidim and the Agudath Israel, two ultra-orthodox Jewish groups,[10] provide rabbis and *mohels* (ritual circumcisers) to perform circumcisions free of charge to new immigrants. Rabbis check the children's genealogies (*yikhes*) to make certain that their matrilines are completely Jewish. An Agudath Israel rabbi explained that a thorough check is necessary because "circumcision is often used as proof of being Jewish when people die and [their survivors] want a Jewish burial in a Jewish cemetery."[11] He added that it would be a terrible shame to give proof of Jewish group membership to someone who was not a Jew. He explained that his organization turned away several "Jewish" immigrant boys because a Russian maternal grandmother or great-grandmother was discovered when tracing descent.

The result of these *yikhes*-checks is that being a Jew is treated as a privileged status; no longer is it an unquestioned, undesirable identity that one has whether or not one wants it.[12] Undergoing circumcision, becoming a "full Jew," gives to the initiates the right to proclaim unquestioned belonging with a worthy people. Fear that they may not be "Jewish enough" in their uncircumcised state and the desire to resolve ambivalent feelings about their ethnic identity impels Soviet immigrants to (have their sons) undergo this operation.[13] Yakov, who immigrated to America at age seventeen, explains why he chose to be circumcised after arrival:

> I had a *bris*. I was eighteen. This was something I really wanted to do. I felt I wanted to belong. . . . When we first arrived, I fell in with the Hasidim, the Lubavitch. I thought it was great—here they were, real Jews, and I thought that I too wanted to be one of them. I listened to what they were saying about the "Jewish soul," and I spoke to my friends about their message. I had this *bris* and felt very good about myself. What do they say? You have to give up something to get something!

Many parents opt to enhance their children's knowledge and sense of Jewishness by providing them with religious education. Upon arrival in New York, the Board of Jewish Education offers immigrants tuition scholarships to enable their children to attend yeshiva or Jewish day school. Although few parents themselves had any Jewish education (Kosmin 1990, 39; Federation of Jewish Philanthropies 1985, 34; Simon and Simon 1982, 65–66), one-third or more of all Soviet immigrants surveyed at different times and different places, send their children to Jewish schools (Federation of Jewish Philanthropies 1985, 34; Gitelman 1984, 97; Simon and Brooks 1983, 62; Gilison 1979, 21). Those who do not, or who transferred their children from yeshiva to public schools, express fears that "immigrant yeshivas" do not provide ample English instruction or adequate education in mathematics, science, literature, and art, and that the instructors (rabbis and rabbinical students) are not sufficiently worldly to provide the skills that all American children require, including physical education.[14] Some parents mention, too, well-founded apprehensions that their children might come home from school, challenge their nonreligious lifestyle and create tension within the family. Lera, the mother of ten-year-old Svetlana, explains:

I would like her to know, I would like her to get an education about the Jewish people—culture, history, this is very interesting and important for her to know about. But not all the religion, not a half-day of religious studies every day. I do not want her coming home from school—and this happens in many families—telling me that what I have in my kitchen is wrong and that I do not do things right as a Jew. I don't want that to come between us. I want her to learn history and culture. This will make us a stronger family, but not to learn things that will push our family apart.[15]

Other parents, however, are not averse to changing aspects of their lifestyle. Anatoly, Vladimir's brother-in-law, explains:

I don't have pork in my house, and about 60–70 percent of everything we have in our kitchen is kosher. It's funny how this happened. When we first came, we bought everything, just for the sake of trying it, and we had pork and everything else you can imagine. Even now sometimes if a friend comes and brings some sausage, we will have it, but we just don't buy it ourselves to bring into the house. I was sending my son to Hebrew school, a religious one because I want him to learn the right way, and he would come home and say, "We shouldn't have pork in the house," and he refused to eat this. I started to think about this and said to myself, "You know, he is right." Here I was sending him to Hebrew school so he would learn, so I decided that we didn't need pork any more, and from that day forward we don't buy it.

Whether or not their children attend Jewish schools, many immigrant parents make Bar/Bat Mitzvah celebrations for them.[16] Some of these ceremonies are performed according to Jewish tradition in the synagogues on a Saturday morning and the child is called to the Torah and chants a portion of the *Haftarah* to make his or her debut as a Jewish adult.[17] The traditional Bar Mitzvah requires long preparation: several years of Hebrew language study, familiarity with Jewish prayers and practices, and intense training under a rabbi's supervision to learn the *Haftarah* portion. Those parents who deem it important that their children confirm their Jewish identity but reject traditional Judaism, opt for a modified version of this rite. Brighton Beach's Russian restaurants provide lists of liberal Reform rabbis who ignore the pork and seafood dishes served and perform Bar/Bat Mitzvah ceremonies in these restaurants. The rabbi meets with the child and parents once or twice before the ceremony to prepare them for the rite and drops off a cassette, which the child listens to and memorizes.

This form of Bar/Bat Mitzvah is a joyful celebration in which the rabbi lauds the child's beauty, talents, and intellect while confirming his or her membership in the Jewish people. English explications are accompanied by Hebrew prayers and chants and manipulation of religious symbols. This religious ceremony is followed by a birthday party in which candles on a big cake, often in the shape of the Ten Commandments or decorated with Jewish emblems, are ritualistically lit by friends and relatives of the Bar/Bat Mitzvah child. Symbolically blending and reconciling Jewish and American identities in the context of a Russian nightclub/restaurant demonstrate that the child, and by extension the family and all others present, are fully accepted as Jews in America, and also, that being Jewish is worthy and fun (see Markowitz 1986 and 1988a for in-depth descriptions and analyses of such Bar/Bat Mitzvah ceremonies).

The same clean-shaven, liberal rabbis perform Jewish weddings in Russian restaurants. In the Soviet Union, Jewish couples, along with everyone else, have a brief civil ceremony and register their marriages at the state Marriage Palaces. After this ceremony, they celebrate the wedding with a feast and dancing, usually in a restaurant. It is rare to have a rabbi marry a couple according to Jewish law, not only because of the dearth of rabbis in the USSR but also because such a ceremony, were it discovered, could have negative consequences for the couple at their workplaces or in their universities (Rozenblum 1982, 100). In America, however, Soviet Jews embrace the opportunity to marry under a *chuppah* (Jewish marriage canopy), as Irina explains:

All Russian immigrants are now giving their children Jewish weddings. In the Soviet Union this was very rare, but more and more Christian couples are marrying in churches there and almost all of them are having their children baptized. Here in America, we have a *chuppah,* a big celebration, and our party in a restaurant.

For Raya, the most visible grandmother in my apartment building:

This is the most important thing. Anything else doesn't matter so much. But Jews should marry Jews. And you and your husband? Married under a *chuppah,* outside, and by a rabbi? Beautiful! You will have a good life together!

Like the Bar/Bat Mitzvah, the wedding ceremony is not only a rite of passage but also a rite of explication. The rabbi explains each part of the ritual process, thereby including the bride, the groom, and all the guests in the Judaism from which they were estranged. Like the Bar/Bat Mitzvah, these Jewish weddings emphasize the new identity of former Soviet Jews in America. The rabbi calls attention to this by contrasting the Soviet and American contexts as part of his speech to the couple mentioning their "thankfulness to get married here in America, according to the laws and tradition of their Jewish people without fear of persecution."

Perhaps the most dramatic rite of expurgation occurs when Soviet Jewish immigrants encounter Hasidim in the streets of New York. Most immigrants express mixed feelings about these ultra-orthodox Jews. Vladimir:

> When I walk in the street and I see Hasidic children, it brings me joy. I ask them to forgive me—I respect them, but they are a primitive people. They could become part of the modern world, but they decide not to.

Zhanna:

> When I see Hasidic Jews, this gives me a strange feeling—like seeing something from the past that is like an anachronism. We Jews came to big cities, study in universities, and have good jobs. It is strange to see that in a country as modern and great as America they would still live this backward way. I can only say, "God bless America" that they can live like this.

Soviet Jews view Hasidim, in principle, as a living remnant of the now-defunct Eastern European Jewry that their parents, grandparents, or they themselves fled. The Hasid, then, embodies the restrictive, parochial, superstition-enshrouded past upon which cosmopolitan, educated Russian Jews look with fear and contempt.[18] On the other hand, however, Hasidim also represent the triumphant continuity of Judaism, showing Soviet immigrants that the Jewish people, in its fullest, most traditional sense, is still alive and flourishing. They take pride in the fact that old-fashioned Judaism thrives in the largest city in the most modern country in the world and that the *shtetl* is now a thing of the past.

One day, Boris, who had repeatedly said he "simply wasn't interested in religion" in the USSR, returned home from work in an exceptionally good mood. His eyes were twinkling and a broad smile crossed his face as he announced:

> Today I had a Bar Mitzvah! Right on Fifth Avenue. Seriously! Really! Right in the middle of Manhattan on its most famous street! A few Hasidim were standing in front of their van, and one asked me as I walked by, "Are you Jewish?" "Sure I'm Jewish," I answered him. "Do you want to do a *mitzvah* [one of the 613 deeds required of Jews; also now means 'good deed']?" he asked me. "Sure I do," I said to him. And he took out those little boxes with the straps [*tefillin,* phylacteries], and right there in the middle of Fifth Avenue, he put them on me, one on my arm, one on my head, and gave me a prayer to say. In the middle of Manhattan with these Hasidim, there I was having my Bar Mitzvah! If I had heard of such a thing in the Soviet Union, I never would have believed it!

Through this brief meeting, the worldly, de-Judaized Jew and his alter ego, the traditional, religious Hasid blended into one Jewish people. Each man's recognition that they share "blood" permitted them this spiritual merger through prayer. More compelling to the Russian Jew than the blood tie itself is the location at which this meeting took place—in the middle of Manhattan on its best-known thoroughfare. The Lubavitchers' "mitzvah mobiles" are treated as a normal part of the landscape on the Friday afternoons they occasionally park in Brighton Beach. Brighton Beach is a predominantly Jewish neighborhood, and there is nothing special about seeing Hasidim there. Hasidim working in the diamond business and among cameras and computers as well as "lighting the Jewish spark" among secularized Jews in the shadow of the Empire State Building and Rockefeller Center, however, show religiously estranged Soviet-born Jews that Judaism and the modern world are not incompatible. The irony of Jews openly performing religious rites in such a public, fast-paced milieu, attracted the assimilated, cosmopolitan Jew to reveal himself as Jewish as well. It was, in a sense, sweet revenge against the Soviet system, which always proclaimed religion and modernity to be at odds and as a result pushed Jewish life underground. By donning phylacteries for the first time and performing a religious act in the midst of the most contemporary city in the world, the former Soviet Jew, at least for the moment, shed his self-hate. Through this ancient ritual, conducted on a busy Fifth Avenue intersection in the company of Hasidim, he became good enough—as a Jew among non-Jews, and as a Soviet-born, de-Judaized Jew among American Jews.

POLITICS

Soviet Jews are politicized the moment they begin to think about the possibility of emigration, if not before. As a rule, from earliest childhood Soviet citizens internalize the belief that their country is the greatest, most progressive and egalitarian state of all, and that one day in the not-too-distant future, all peoples will join together to overthrow their conflict-ridden, oppressive governments and embrace communism (see Bronfenbrenner 1972). Just thinking about emigration, imagining an alternate system that could possibly be better than the best, challenges the cornerstone of the Soviet state's legitimacy.

Many Soviet immigrants speak of having believed in communism and of being loyal and patriotic to the motherland (*rodina*) in their earlier years. Some admit that when Jews first began to leave the USSR in the early 1970s, they looked upon these emigrants with contempt, considering them treacherous deserters. Maxim presents a typical picture of pre-migration political orientations among Jewish professionals:

> I don't think I was anti-regime at a young age. I was active in Pioneers, a group leader, and later in *Komsomol*. At my workplace I was president of the *Komsomol* club, very active in that organization. I was a straight-A student in all my politics classes, and I was always invited to come and give lectures to other students and youth groups.

That Soviet citizens took pride in their country's accomplishments and the egalitarian nature of their society is not surprising, given the paternalistic security the state provided. Their gratitude for the education, work, food, and shelter they received was reinforced with frequent television broadcasts that showed capitalist America's unemployed factory workers, pockets of rural poverty, urban decay, homelessness, and countless other calamities that daily seemed to befall the United States.

Some Soviet citizens, and certainly most who decided to emigrate, came to see a discrepancy between high-flown rhetoric and harsh reality in the USSR. Applying Marxist dialectics to their own lives, they began "to get annoyed by all the lies we live with everyday . . . for example, the idea of 'temporary difficulties' in the path of communism, first ten, then twenty, then fifty, and soon now seventy years after the Revolution." The disaffected and would-be emigrants then began to develop the notion that everything the Soviet regime says or shows is false. Carrying this inversion to its logical extreme, they concluded that America must indeed be the Golden Land; if the Soviet media portrayed it as a terrible place, it must in fact be great.

To build confidence enough to reject the security of a state that nurtures and provides for its citizens throughout their lifetimes and touts itself as the best country in the world, Soviet Jews constructed an idealized reality of the United States. When they finally did leave their homeland to make new lives, they expected the West to be as beautiful, friendly, prosperous, and worry-free as the images they momentarily viewed in Hollywood films and made permanent in their minds. Most arrived in New York excited and enthusiastic about being in the West and already as American patriots.

This American patriotism frequently persists despite the fact that Soviet immigrants quickly realize that silver-screen America is not the same as life in their urban neighborhoods of Brooklyn and Queens. There they encounter language difficulties, problems of occupational transfer, dirt on the streets, crime and danger; many of the images they saw on Soviet television turn out to be real. But their faith in America usually endures, especially for those who are able to make satisfying new lives for themselves.

New immigrants, no matter how content they are in their new country, are by no means blind patriots; they are quick to point out shortcomings of the American system. A forty-year-old art historian, for example, took the opportunity of an interview to list complaint after complaint about American schooling, health care, affirmative action policies, crime, the lack of police protection, and economic class inequalities. At the conclusion of her thirty-minute critique, I asked, near exasperation, "Well, then, which system do you prefer, the Soviet or the American?" She smiled, opened her eyes in wide amazement, and broke out into an ironic laugh, "How can you ask? The American, of course! Just the fact that we can stand here together, that I can tell you all my complaints, makes this country one hundred times better than the Soviet Union!"

Freedom, the ability to form one's own values and beliefs from a plethora of information, the ability to live according to these values and beliefs, and the opportunity to express and debate them in public, differentiates the United States from the USSR. Without labelling it ethnic pluralism, many Soviet Jewish immigrants speak fondly of seeing newscasters of varied racial backgrounds on national and local New York television broadcasts and remark with pleasure that the difference between Russian restaurants in America and those in the USSR is that in New York orchestras play an assortment of Russian, Jewish, Italian, American, Gypsy, and underground Odessa "thieves' " songs throughout the night rather than the Soviet state-selected repertoire. They cherish these expressions of freedom and exclaim "God bless America" for this alone.

The problems Soviet immigrants see with the United States derive, they believe, from Americans' lack of appreciation for their liberties. Rather than safeguarding democracy, Americans have come to take it for granted and, in the process, have turned the principles of freedom into a laissez-faire free-for-all. Soviet émigrés contrast Americans' ignorance of European geopolitics, and their complacency and blasé attitudes toward the Communist threat with the history and political-economy classes that were taught in Soviet schools, the ominous slogan *"Proletarii vsekh stran, soedinaites!"* (Proletarians of the world, unite!) on every issue of *Pravda,* and mammoth displays of weaponry in gala parades during Soviet festivities. Some further stress the pervasiveness of militarism by recounting how children learn to load rifles as part of the school curriculum and are rewarded for good grades by serving as armed honor guards at tombs of unknown soldiers on memorial days. A recent émigré remarked that she never sees men in military uniform around New York, whereas in the Soviet Union, where all men are required to serve a tour of duty in the armed forces, they are a sight everywhere. Americans' lack of vigilance in defending and protecting their freedom has resulted, they claim, in Cuba, and more recently Nicaragua, "becoming communist," and at home in graffiti and dirt everywhere, schoolchildren who learn neither mathematics nor respect, and crime as a normal occurrence.

Rather than berate the United States for its problems, Soviet immigrants frequently proclaim their love for their new country and propose remedies for its ills. Having abandoned the USSR, which they once believed to be the greatest country in the world, to cast their fate with America, it is very important to them that their faith in the United States not be misplaced.[19] At least partially in response to their fears that freedom-loving America, and thus they themselves, may be vulnerable to contervailing forces, émigrés suggest that the United States (1) increase its military strength to exceed that of the USSR,[20] and (2) arrest all lawbreakers and punish them with severity and dispatch.[21] These two themes pervade immigrants' political discussions.

Soviet Jewish immigrants during the 1980s were greatly attracted to the Republican party and especially to the persona of President Ronald Reagan. During the 1984 election season, Project ARI (Action for Russian Immigrants), housed in Brighton Beach's Shorefront YM-YWHA, conducted a registration drive aimed at involving new American citizens in the electoral process. Of the several hundred Soviet immigrants who registered to vote, perhaps 2–3 percent enrolled in the Democratic party. In fact, several Russian-speakers arrived at Project ARI inquiring, "Is this where I come to sign to vote for President Reagan?"

Ronald Reagan was immensely popular among Soviet émigrés because they admired his "get tough" stance and agreed with his designation of the USSR as an "evil empire," They supported his appeals for military buildups and his hard-line rhetoric against communism. They lauded his decision to invade Grenada and added that had President Kennedy invaded Cuba in 1960 the Western hemisphere would have been safe for democracy today. They pointed to Reagan's strong style of leadership as necessary for America's survival against its formidable and rapacious enemy, the USSR.[22] Below are several statements from immigrants that explicate these views. The first is from a middle-aged house painter, the second is from a former manager now retired, the third from a Project ARI group worker in her late forties, and the fourth from a single, male teacher in his early thirties:

> This country needs a strong, decisive leader who won't give in to the communists. You saw what happened under Carter—Afghanistan. They won't stop there. They wanted Grenada. Thank God for President Reagan! They want Grenada, and Nicaragua, and Salvador—but not with a strong man like Reagan for president they won't!

> The Soviets are liars. The system is run by lies. This Reagan, and he alone, understands. That's the reason why so many of us immigrants are 100 percent behind Reagan. . . . I agree [with you] that Reagan isn't for the ordinary person and that he has cut a lot from education, but the most important thing is not internal policies but relations with the whole world. Nuclear war—this no longer means armies, but the atomic bomb. One *k'nok* ['knock" or "bang," in Yiddish] and that's all it takes. For this reason, the Soviet Union must see the American president as a very strong man so they won't take advantage of the situation. This is how they see Reagan, and they wouldn't dare start with him because of this. A weak man as president is very dangerous— not only to this country, but to the entire world.

> I was an anti-Communist there, and I am still an anti-Communist here. America must talk in terms they understand, for surely they are determined to take over the world. Why do you think they went to Afghanistan? It's just one step. And Latin America? What is going on in Nicaragua and Salvador—they have a plan of attack. You don't believe this, but this is because you never lived there. You don't understand how their minds work, how their system works. Without the strength of President Reagan, this world is in big trouble. I have two sons, and that is why I am voting for President Reagan. I am voting for the man who is most likely to make this world safe. The way to ensure that the atomic bomb will not be dropped, the way to ensure that there is no war, is to show that we are strong—and stronger—than they are. Because if they should think for one minute that we are not as strong as they, then they would attack, and that would be the beginning of the end.

> I am not a political person—I wasn't very political in Russia, and I am not very political here either, so when people ask me who I am for, I

say I don't know. . . . In a year I will be a citizen, and now I don't even have the right to vote. What I do understand is this—on a national perspective, in my heart, I feel closer to the Democrats—their policy about helping all people, encouraging education, research, and lending a hand to those less fortunate, yes. But I have to agree with President Reagan on his foreign policy. I cannot describe the Soviet Union better than the two words, you know them, that he used, "evil empire." Yes, this is what the Soviet Union *is,* an evil empire. I tell you this because I lived there, and I know. There no one can think for himself, discuss anything worth discussing without being in fear. And this evil empire understands only one voice, the voice of strength. As many have said before, a *dobry dyadya* [kind uncle] is not what this country needs in its relations with the Soviet Union. It needs someone as strong and as tough as the bear. This is where I completely agree with Reagan.

When Russian Jews leave their natal country, they do not leave it behind. Their budding disillusionment with the Soviet system develops, in many cases, into full-scale fear and revulsion once in America. Yet this anti-Soviet stance is pervaded with great respect, even awe. They believe, and proclaim that they know, that the Soviet threat to the free world is real. This knowledge, gained as part of their socialization experiences, informs their views of the United States and the USSR as adversaries. Although they rejected Soviet citizenship for American, they often continue to identify with Soviet rhetoric. Old feelings of pride in post-revolutionary accomplishments, the unfailing destiny of communism to spread worldwide, and the belief that the USSR is the most powerful country in the world (see Menashe 1985; Howells and Galperin 1984) are reworked and expressed as fear of Soviet expansionism and a hawkish allegiance to America.

Immigrants from the USSR are therefore drawn to a president they believe can match or better the leadership style of the Kremlin. They are certain that with their votes for Reagan they improved and strengthened the United States. They supported Ronald Reagan because he symbolized for them a free and tough America, and because they believed that he could best intimidate Soviet leaders, hold them at bay, and avert a global catastrophe. Indeed, in the latter part of the 1980s, and as recently as August 1991, several émigrés were quick to credit the downfall of Soviet communism to Ronald Reagan's—and later George Bush's—political acumen.

While Soviet émigrés place greater emphasis on international politics than on specific domestic programs, no observer of Soviet immigrants can possibly overstate the extent to which these newcomers are appalled by crime in America. This horror does not stem directly from their relatively limited personal confrontations with criminals but rather from the prevalence of newspaper features, television programs, movies, novels, and nonfiction accounts that focus on this subject. Unceasing discourse about crime makes the threat of it very real in the minds of the immigrants, especially as it contrasts so sharply to Soviet society, where crime was a non-subject; until 1987 prostitution, drug addiction, extortion rings, etc., were not acknowledged to exist. Émigrés state that as Soviet citizens they felt safe to walk on the streets and ride the subways at all hours of the night. In contrast, New Yorkers are continually urged to take precautions against making themselves vulnerable to theft and attacks on their persons. "America is a wonderful country," they say. "Wonderful—except for crime."

By and large, former Soviet citizens blame what they see as the profusion of crime on America's laxity in safeguarding freedom for the good of the majority. They are amazed at the care that police officers must take in arresting criminal suspects and are positively horrified that perpetrators of crimes may walk away scotfree because of a legal technicality. Just as perplexing to them is the system of bail, the presumption of innocence, and the state's responsibility to prove the guilt of suspected offenders. During a session in an English As a Second Language class, students reacted in amazement as I explained that in America, unless an arrested party waives the right to do so, the first person he or she speaks with after arrest is a defense attorney, not the police. In the Soviet Union, students explained:

> First the criminal is arrested, and for three days sits in jail. He talks first and only with an investigator from the prosecutor's office. This investigator gathers the facts of the offense, and if there is a reason for a case, that is, if the investigator thinks the person is guilty, they go to court. The person who is under arrest sees his defense lawyer after these three days, right before the court appearance. If there is no case, the arrested person spends his three days in jail and is then released.

The major difference immigrants see between the two systems is not the moral question of whether to presume guilt or innocence, but the fact that the state takes an immediate and direct role in prosecuting offenders in the Soviet Union, so that Soviet citizens, unlike Americans, are protected against criminals. Émigrés justify unwarranted arrests and the days spent in jail by innocent people in the USSR as the price a few must pay for the well-being of the majority. In fact, when speaking of the criminal justice system in the USSR, Soviet immigrants usually gloss over the abuses that occur there in the administration of justice because, compared with the proliferation of crime they now face in America, apprehension of hooligans and criminals takes on greater importance than the unjustified arrest of a few.

During a conversation I had with Regina and Joseph about the problem of crime in America, Regina suggested that "the answer is for America to have a stronger codex of laws. And something like what we had in the Soviet Union. There they have a very good legal code, which is abused sometimes I will admit, but not often." Her husband, Joseph, reacted in astonishment, remembering very well an abuse that almost resulted in the death of Regina's own brother. "What are you saying?" he exclaimed, "The problem is that it is abused very often!" Regina, after recounting the story of her brother's arrest, remained adamant, explaining that this was a rare situation, one of the few isolated incidents when the Soviets arrested a Jew on trumped-up charges to remind others not to stray from the party line:

> This is an unusual matter. Your are already aware of anti-Semitism. Every now and again it gets very bad, and the Russian government chooses someone for an example. This time, it happened to be my brother. It was in 1968 or so. My brother . . . was pretty well set up, a respected member of the community. What happened is they accused him of murdering someone. Of course he didn't do it, but the police came to his home, read him the charges, and he disappeared—they brought him to jail.

Despite her brother's unjust arrest and eight months of imprisonment for a crime he did not commit, Regina continues to uphold the moral rectitude of the Soviet codex of law and its enforcement policy. In retrospect, the abuses pale in comparison to the lack of security New Yorkers feel, knowing that their streets are far from safe.

Regina is not alone. Many immigrants discuss how terrible the Soviet system is and then add, "That system is wrong in many ways, but not in how they punish people who commit bad crimes." In the same English As a Second Language class mentioned above, students were asked to suggest appropriate measures for people who commit crimes. The list was mainly proscriptive, characterized by denying criminals any kind of pleasure and free time. Rehabilitation of law-breakers is rarely suggested; émigrés strongly believe that criminals are to be punished for their acts against society:

1. No relations with the opposite sex. Many laughed and complained that American prisons grant criminals conjugal visits, calling them one more way America pays attention to the rights of the few—criminals—at the expense of the many. "This is what the state pays for! Criminals who sit in jail, play cards, play basketball, eat good meals, and have women!"
2. Hard labor, twelve hours a day, "such hard work that at the end of the day they have no strength for women, for recreation, for television, nothing—just sleep so they can get up and work another hard day."
3. No television, no recreation.
4. Bad food—"just bread and water, enough to keep them alive to work."
5. "The chair"—"Whoever murders someone should be murdered, too. Look at that madman [Charles Manson] in California who murdered so many people so brutally. Why is he still alive?"

It is the lack of such strong punitive measures, Soviet immigrants believe, that is responsible for the proliferation of crime: "Crime does pay in America. Someone commits a crime, if the police finds him and he gets caught, which is far from a hundred percent certain, then they put him in jail for two years, where he eats chicken!" They are, in the main, opposed to New York Governor Mario Cuomo, whose stance against capital punishment gives them yet another reason to support the Republican party.

Former Soviet citizens came to America "to be free," and they love the freedom they find here to consume, discuss, display their Jewishness, travel, and so on. They so deeply cherish these freedoms that they resent having them curtailed. In the United States, as they see it, it is not the state but the threat of crime that challenges their freedom. They become passionately angry when they explain that their freedom is limited because of the few delinquents who are allowed to run rampant and spoil the liberties and enjoyment of everyone else. They see no logical reason for being unable to take a midnight stroll and for the "four locks on my door. Here, it's like a fortress. In Russia, my door was always open." In their desire to take full advantage of America's freedom for ordinary citizens, they advocate placing limits on the rights of others (i.e., criminals, hooligans, and all those whose behavior is threatening to ordinary people, as well as those suspected of illegal acts). The good of all, they believe, should take precedence over guaranteeing the rights of a very few. It is not surprising then that many Soviet Jewish immigrants view Bernhard Goetz, the tabloid-dubbed "subway vigilante" as nothing short of a hero.[23]

Soviet immigrants lauded Goetz's actions—shooting the four black youths who menacingly clustered around him, asked him for the time and then for five dollars—as self-defense, pointing out that all of these teenagers have criminal records and carried sharpened screwdrivers in their jackets. Having shot them, they claim, Goetz gave a lesson to hooligans that they cannot get away with harassing ordinary citizens. This is a point that many immigrants, long-term acquaintances as well as people I was meeting for the first time, wish to express. At a funeral reception, a middle-aged man I had never seen before came up to me and declared:

> I want to talk to you about this incident on the subway with Bernhard Goetz. What do you think, was he right or wrong? Wrong—like all Americans of your generation—liberal and naive. Wrong you say? Well, I think it is wrong for young, healthy boys to be wandering about the subway demanding money from people. This would not be tolerated in the Soviet Union. Such hooligans would be treated appropriately, and if they had no jobs, work would be found for them. I think as long as people . . . give what they demand and only later call the police, this will only encourage hooligans and bandits to continue to do what they are doing. If I were Bernhard Goetz, I would have shot them, too.

Boris agreed with this man, adding:

> Sure I think Goetz was 100 percent right and even a hero to stand up to those hooligans. If I had a gun in my pocket, I would have shot them,

too. There is only one thing that these hooligans and bandits understood, and that is force, very strong force. They will try to get away with whatever they can—until they see that this behavior will not be tolerated.

Others, at other times, expressed similar opinions:

If I had been in Goetz's shoes, I would have done the same thing. The only way you teach criminals that they cannot get away with their criminal acts is to use force, to show that people will not submit to them.

What do you think of the Goetz case? I think—the problem with America is not freedom—but that here there is too much freedom. He was right to shoot those hooligans, those bandits. Did you ever sit in a subway car, and here comes a brigade of young black boys? God knows what they would have done to him—for what reason did they have screwdrivers in their pockets?—if he didn't shoot. They have to learn that they cannot just go around and take five dollars from others whenever they want.

And finally, Lera, a "liberal" voice:

Now, America is not perfect, and I have to say that I agree with the majority of Russian immigrants who wish that America would follow the example of the Soviet Union in regard to controlling crime and dealing with prisoners. Goetz, I think, was not legally right to have a gun and shoot those delinquents. But they are bandits, and they have already learned that they can get away with whatever they do because it's no big deal to go to jail—it's not such a terrible place to be. That's why if American prisons were made harsher—like Soviet labor camps— potential criminals would think a little more before they commit crimes. In all of this, I agree.

Soviet Jewish immigrants came to America to escape anti-Semitism and pursue freedom, to build a better future than their past. While they have, in general, found the peace in which to "breathe freely, to be myself," feelings of vulnerability check their sense of well-being. Their fear of a Communist threat, which they insist is real ("I lived there, I know"), and, more immediate and closer to home, the pervasiveness of crime, lead them to believe that America cannot remain a free haven if it persists in naiveté and "too much freedom."

To counter these fears, Soviet immigrants use the knowledge at their disposal to propose solutions to the problems they see with America. Because the problems they delineate reflect Soviet discomfort with ambiguity (see Bauer, Inkeles, and Kluckhohn 1960, especially 157–167, for similar findings for an earlier cohort of Soviet immigrants) and the remedies they suggest mirror Soviet strategies, it is tempting to attribute émigrés' political orientations to the lingering power of Soviet culture. But this explanation tells only part of the story. It must be kept in mind that these same individuals challenged their culture of origin first by envisioning an alternative way of life and then by acting on this vision and leaving.

America did not turn out to be the ideal that many former Soviet Jews conjured up in their home country. But it did turn out to be a place where they could be critical and could freely express their opinions. The two-party system and current debates between liberals and conservatives establish an arena in which immigrants can evaluate and give voice to their political views. Soviet émigrés find that although their politics may differentiate them from their Jewish neighbors in the liberal Democrat tradition, their assessment of America's state of affairs is very close to the dominant mood of their new country. The Republican party, in articulating concerns quite similar to their own, provides Soviet immigrants with a new but familiar idiom for reinterpreting their political beliefs. Having cast their fate with America after rejecting the Soviet Union, it is not surprising that they ally their political identification in the United States with those in power.

Soviet immigrants' politics, then, cannot simply be reduced to the orientations they developed in childhood. Certainly their desire for security, developed to a fine edge in the USSR, informs their view that the United States is weak militarily and too soft on criminals, but so, too, do Pentagon analyses, crime-bureau statistics, and daily reports in the media. Their history and destiny thus merge in their politics, "No, neither do we want the Soviet Union in America. We just want America to remain great and strong."

Soviet Jews' *evreistvo* (Jewishness), forged in a world without synagogues or Jewish communal organizations, and their political orientations and opinions, initially formed in a one-party state providing no official channels for challenge or dissent, developed anew in the United States. Remarkably, while Soviet Jewish immigrants represent a variety of geographical areas of origin and professions, their ideas and attitudes about Jewish identity and American politics have developed in quite a similar fashion. As they discuss the subjects of religion and politics with each other and with people outside of their immigrant cohort, internal agreement on these important subjects comes to outweigh intragroup differences. Lines between former Muscovite editors and Odessan factory managers fade as they converse about presidential elections, crime on the streets, giving their children a Bar or Bat Mitzvah, and their encounters with American Judaism. With these discussions, group consciousness and group cohesiveness grow, and the community takes on a character that previously did not exist.

6.

THE RHYTHM OF DAILY LIFE: COMMUNITY AS LIFE CYCLE

Anthropologists have long recognized that while families, age hierarchies, and sex role differentiation are cultural universals, the particular ways in which these forms are expressed differ cross-culturally.[1] They have remarked as well that different, geographically separated cultures with similar forms of social organization and levels of economic complexity are often characterized by family and gender structures that are also alike. Since Soviet émigrés come from large cities in an industrialized country, one might expect their notions of sex roles and family to be similar to those of urban Americans. And to a large degree this is the case. Yet as Ulf Hannerz points out for black American ghetto-dwellers, while they share some values about family and marriage with mainstream America, "there is something specific to the relationship between the sexes in this community" (1969, 71).

Soviet immigrants, on the one hand, notice many similarities between their conceptions of family life and gender distinctions and those of their host society. On the other hand, they differentiate themselves from "cold" Americans, who downplay the importance of the family unit, abandon their elderly parents, and ignore what the émigrés consider to be critical differences between the sexes. Thus, émigrés' views on such matters bind them into a community based not only on mutual understanding of what male/female and parent/child mean, but also on the ways by which they express these understandings in daily life.

FEMALE, MALE, AND MARRIAGE

Soviet immigrant women are far from the dowdy, mannishly garbed, asexual Western caricature of the Bolshevik female. In fact, these women take great care and pride in their personal appearance. In New York, émigré women regularly patronize hair stylists and skin salons, where they choose fashionable coiffures and have their fingernails manicured, legs waxed, and faces massaged; they apply bright cosmetics, wear a great deal of jewelry, and don stylish clothes for work or even for just strolling around the neighborhood. While much of this preoccupation with personal furnishings may be attributed to the Soviet notion of *kulturnost,* it is linked as well to Russian ideals of femininity and the ways of demonstrating them that have developed over the centuries (see Atkinson 1977; Hubbs 1988).

The position of women in Russia's Jewish enclaves differed somewhat from that of Christian Russia. Jewish women, like their Christian counterparts, were not considered full persons unless they married and became mothers: "To be a spinster is a dreadful fate which fortunately occurs far more in the anxious forebodings of girls and their parents than in fact. The *shtetl* does not provide a place for an 'alteh moyd' [old maid]" (Zborowski and Herzog 1952, 129). The major difference in the position of women in Christian and Jewish Russia was that the woman's role as helpmate was explicitly valued and rewarded by Jewish men. While Judaic ideology, like Christianity, is male-centered and views woman as potentially sinful because of her powerful sexual attractiveness, Jewish men and women in everyday life shared in household power and control of economic resources (Zborowski and Herzog 1952, 132). Furthermore, Jewish men rarely mistreated their wives, and when abuse occurred it was condemned by the community. Far more typical was the man who, recognizing that woman is a corporeal being deriving pleasure from pretty things, bestowed jewelry on his wife, which she proudly displayed each Sabbath and on festive occasions. Woman, as daughter, wife, and mother, was the ornament of the Jewish family (Zborowski and Herzog 1952, 138).

No matter how devoted and religious a person may be, Judaism recognizes that all men and women have a physical, sensual side, and early marriages were encouraged in the *shtetl.* Judaism has no monastic tradition, and sexual enjoyment for both partners—in its prescribed marital context—is considered healthy and good (Zborowski and Herzog 1952, 136).

In families of means, Jewish women controlled domestic and pecuniary affairs, while men devoted themselves to the sacred world of religious study and prayer. Very few men, however, could afford to devote themselves completely to study, and the majority considered it their primary obligation to provide for their families. Their wives usually participated in business with them, selling manufactured products to peasants, keeping records, or running the inn or store while their husbands were away on business trips. Jewish wives always controlled household expenses.

Unlike their Christian counterparts, Jewish girls received an education. Prior to 1870, because official ideology deemed women too ignorant to think, Russian Crown Schools educated boys only. Women in noble households were tutored by private governesses, but they were the exception. Jewish girls, however, often learned to read Yiddish and to understand the rudiments of Hebrew and were taught the basics of Jewish law with an emphasis on women's specific religious obligations. Moreover, because of their position in business, many Jewish women were fluent in the language of the land and well versed in arithmetic.

During the nineteenth century, Jewish girls in well-to-do families studied music, German, and French (Zborowski and Herzog 1952, 128), emulating the Russian gentry. The daughter of a Lithuanian rabbi, one of three Jewish girls allowed to attend the local Russian gymnasium (classical high school) just prior to the Revolution, became fluent in Russian and German. She managed her family's international travel and business affairs when she was still a teenager. She recalls her father's greatest compliment: "My father always told me that I was his smartest child and that it was a shame that I was a girl because I have a man's head and am more suited to be a rabbi than my brothers."

The ideal Jewish woman, however, was not necessarily a good economist, business manager, and polyglot. Although these traits were appreciated and valued, of much greater importance was the wife who kept her home in accordance with Jewish law, fulfilled her womanly obligations, was a good mother, and helped the men of the house fulfill their array of responsibilities to God. In the *shtetl*, women were viewed as necessary to men; without their assistance, men could not lead the religious life that was their right and duty.

By the end of the nineteenth century, several social movements spread from Western Europe to Russia, including feminism. Socialism and feminism appealed to a small number of educated elite women, Jews and Christians alike, and they took an active role in revolutionary activities. After the Revolution, these women continued in their struggle to revolutionize the thinking of the masses, turning Christian, Jewish, and Islamic notions of patriarchy on their heads. As part of the Marxist platform for the new Socialist state, full citizenship rights were granted to women—including the conferral of their own identity documents and passports, the right to maintain their own family names after marriage, the right to vote, the right to education, the right to work—and the abolition of church-officiated marriage ceremonies because of their anti-female bias.[2] Women, who in tsarist Russia were completely dependent on their fathers or husbands for shelter, food, and their very identity, were now, according to the new law of the land, liberated.

But were they? After the Revolution, Russian feminists, while of one mind in their desire to eliminate all institutions that perpetuate male/female inequality, had a difficult time agreeing on a lifestyle for the New Soviet Woman. Despite initial explorations into radical, egalitarian forms of relationships between the sexes, such as elimination of the traditional bourgeois (nuclear) family, "free love," and temporary unions based on mutual attraction, "By 1926 the party leadership had swung toward the more traditional position, because they disliked the instability produced by the new morality, because they had never accepted the liberal attitude toward sexuality of Engels, Bebel and Kollontai, and because they did not think they had the funds to support the offspring of unregulated sexuality" (Clements 1979, 235).

Woman-as-mother was never seriously challenged either. Farnsworth (1977, 161) notes that Bolshevik feminists, spanning the spectrum from right to left in socialism, "all believed in the maternal instinct." Rosenham's content analysis of children's books used in the early grades of the Soviet school system almost fifty years after the Revolution confirms the "cult of motherhood" hypothesis; she found that "the hierarchy of involvement as it emerges from these series is clear. Women are mothers first and 'something else' second" (1977, 301). Soviet leaders' rejection of radical alternatives to the traditional family while they urged woman to enter the workforce resulted in her remaining primarily mother and homekeeper *and* gaining additional roles and responsibilities in the public domain (Gray 1990).

Contemporary Soviet sociological inquiries into the "woman's question" reach the same conclusion as Western research: woman is first and foremost mother whether at home or at the workplace. Zoia A. Iankova (1978) rejects the biologically based premise that females are the weaker sex but accepts the notion that their anatomy makes their personality and social roles different from those of men: "Personality always includes a diversity of functions. This is all the greater for woman with her specific socio-biological role of mother" (p. 123). Five years later, E. I. Martynova says essentially the same thing: "Woman's fulfillment of family roles significantly enriches the contents of her inner world, adding to it a particular coloring and specificity" (1983, 82). To be a full person, to contribute to society and receive maximum personal gratification, woman must use all her natural endowments, those that she shares with man, *and* those that are specifically female. "The function of motherhood formed and forms in woman character traits like sensitivity, attentiveness, thoughtfulness, softness, emotion. . . . Most important, many traits of woman-mother manifest themselves in her professional and social-political activities—in the workplace, the social-political collective, in womanly advice, in the process of guiding the young, in cooperative forms of everyday life, etc." (Iankova 1978, 123).

Woman's "natural" role as solicitous, other-oriented caretaker, in spite of her juridical and economic equivalence with man under socialism, has not changed since medieval Russia entered Christendom. The official Soviet view of the "woman's question" is that it has been resolved in the USSR, where woman's equality with man is recognized and enforced through legislation. Equality, however, does not mean uniformity; woman is different from man, and the Soviet Union acknowledges and encourages the difference. Women have both the right to work and the moral duty to have children. While in theory women have the choice to forego their biological destiny, those who try to deny their femininity—their maternal instincts and the personality traits that derive from them—are viewed by men and women alike as asexual and unnatural.

A recent Soviet film, *Sluzhebny Roman* (*An Office Novel*), nicely illustrates this point. It focuses on a dowdy, unattractive, mannishly dressed, sexually repressed Bureau of Statistics director who is liked by none and feared by all. She is juxtaposed against all the other female employees, who are frequently shown combing their hair, applying makeup, trading blouses for sheer stockings in the ladies' bathroom, and looking at dress patterns in women's magazines.[3] An attractive, middle-aged man is the Bureau's assistant director and conspires with a scrawny male friend to have him court the director. They agree that with attention from a man she will "soften" and both their careers will improve. The director does indeed change with a man's attention, and a hilarious scene shows her, under the tutelage of her feminine secretary, learning how to dress, walk, and converse "like a woman." At the film's end, despite the tragic turn that the affair takes, her Bureau's productivity has increased, relationships among the co-workers have improved, and the director herself, now a feminine woman wearing stylish clothing and a contoured hairsyle, has friends and companions in the collective. The film's message: Women can work in any profession and hold positions of authority, but they must remember that they are first and foremost women. To forget their maternal instincts, to deny the soft, tender, solicitous side of their personality is unnatural and will result in social pathology (Atwood 1990).

Soviet women do not and will not forget this lesson and have internalized the hierarchy of roles that puts their wife-motherhood first. Even self-indulgence, the pleasure of wearing stylish clothes and cosmetics, is connected with an other-orientation, attracting and keeping a husband. In this respect, New Soviet Woman differs little from the Russian martyr/mother who derives personal gratification from making others happy. It is precisely this "need" to be self-sacrificing and solicitous while also carrying out tasks once relegated to men that differentiates Soviet Woman from Soviet Man (and from pre-Soviet Woman) and makes her believe that she is better and nobler than her male counterpart (Shlapentokh 1984, 180–186); Gray 1990).

In America, this image of superwoman-mother lingers. As in the Soviet Union, émigré women take as given the idea that they can receive all the higher education and enter any profession for which they have the talents and desire. Several women reported that they were shocked when their social workers at NYANA were reluctant to help them find jobs because their husbands had good professions. "At NYANA they said to me, 'Your husband has a good profession, and you have two children. Why do you need to work?' and they didn't want to help me at all." Others reported that social workers suggested retraining because their professions—engineering and other technical fields—were inappropriate for American women. But marriage, and marriage to a good man, takes at least as much effort as preparing for a prestige job. Mothers teach their daughters to look pretty and carry themselves in a feminine manner and encourage them to take an interest in fashion and develop a sense of style. Their female relatives further socialize girls into their future mother role by addressing them as *mamochka* or *mamaleh* (Russian and Yiddish for "little mother").

Soviet Jewish immigrants note that college-educated Americans often postpone marriage and family until their late twenties (and sometimes thirties) because they go away to college or rent their own apartments to establish independence. This trend stands in sharp contrast to the lifeways of Soviet Jewish students, who usually remain in their home cities and commute to a local university or institute. In a country riddled with housing shortages, it is the extraordinary single person who has an apartment apart from parents. Marriage is the way to establish oneself as an adult, and although many newlywed couples live with one set of parents, one spouse has an entirely new place to live, and both are accorded some privacy (e.g., a curtain to divide a room if not a room of their own) to mark their adult, married status. While they are aware of the American pattern of delayed marriage, immigrant women, in the main, still marry early and look for husbands with a sense of urgency. Nona, holding up a five-year-old photograph, comments on the upcoming marriage of her daughter's twenty-year-old friend:

> We've known her since we arrived, when she and my daughter were fifteen. Luba's mother had one thing on her mind for her daughter, marriage, and she has been preparing her for this all these years. Look at these pictures. See how seductively Luba is dressed, see her hairstyle and makeup. . . . Now she is getting married. At age twenty her mother tells her she can't wait too much longer or she will be an old maid.

Those who marry at an early age are not only women from blue-collar families, but include women from the educated elite (like the one described above) who pursue college education and plan professional careers. In the United States fears linger that stem from growing up female in Russia, where women outnumber men and where spinsterhood is stigmatized, and it is not uncommon for immigrant women to marry when they complete high school or during their college years. A fifteen-year-old girl explains:

> Believe it or not, a lot of my friends who are, let's say sixteen or seventeen, are planning to get married. Yes, really. They are either going steady or engaged. You see, Russian girls go out with boys much older than American girls go with. My friend who is seventeen just got married to a guy twenty-eight. That's eleven years older, right? It works out very well. He is able to support her. He already finished school, and in a lot of other situations they have also finished college. Then, after the girls finish high school, they go on to college while their husbands work. I don't think it's such a bad idea, only I'm not at all interested in that now![4]

Lara, who is twenty, complains that neighborhood women are constantly asking her if she is engaged and warning her that she is not getting any younger. When she insists that she wants to complete college before marrying, they look at her with amazement and ask, "What does one have to do with the other? You can't go to college and be married at the same time?"

At least as important as finding a husband, and perhaps even more so, is having a child, someone of one's own flesh and blood to love. While a man's love may be fickle, mother-child love is understood to be permanent. Most émigré women have had a baby within a year or two of their weddings, so that a woman of thirty usually has a child between six and ten years of age. It is rare indeed for a married woman over twenty-five to be childless. When such an anomaly occurs, as was the case with me, women of all ages, from schoolgirls to young matrons to elderly grandmothers, demand:

> When will you have a baby?

> I will talk to your husband about this—you must have a baby soon! You are young, but not so young!

> Why haven't you had a child yet? Is there something physically wrong with you?

Those women who do have physical problems that prevent them from becoming pregnant are greatly pitied. Nona discusses a friend's state of childlessness: "She has a big problem. She can't get pregnant. She had all kinds of tests, and she is perfectly normal. It's her husband. This is a terrible thing because she, like all women, wants more than anything to have a child." Their plight is disastrous because motherhood, and the array of emotions connected with it, is the crux of womanhood that absolutely differentiates women from men. To be denied this is to be something less than a full person.

Because only woman is able to conceive and bear children, the woman's body is thought to be fundamentally different from that of a man. On the one hand, women are believed to be the stronger sex, due to their greater capacity for endurance. Vladimir speaks ironically about Soviet society's recognition of this fact:

> Yes, there is equality in the Soviet Union between men and women—women do all the hardest work, and they have more jobs than men. On the *stroika* [construction site] they have the jobs that call for dragging and pulling, while the men sit in cranes and other machines. At work, they have the same jobs as men, but after work they have additional jobs—standing in line to buy groceries, preparing meals, taking care of the children and cleaning the apartment. What do men do? They are tired at the end of the working day, so they sit on the sofa and have a before-dinner drink.

Women themselves, like Lera, comment on their strength as they carry heavy shopping bags filled with purchases for their families: "I'm a strong Russian woman! I would feel naked walking on the street without dragging a shopping bag!"

But, perhaps because of the fact that the woman's body can bear children and tote heavy loads, it is susceptible to stress, especially what immigrants label "stress of the nervous system." Many women complain of severe headaches and early onset of menopause as their female-specific reactions to the strains of migration. Some seek a doctor's care and take *tabletki* (little pills) to ease their "nerves." Massage is also viewed as therapeutic; strong, trained hands know how to work out kinks, stresses, and irritation to one's biological system. Semyon Lasky advertises his "electrical hands when medicine brings no results" in a New York–based Russian-language women's magazine, *Tochka Zrenya* (*Point of View*):

> Treatment of woman's illnesses:
> inflamed extremities, fibromas, benign and malignant tumors, headaches, irritation in the function of the extremities, post-abortion complications, rejuvenation of the skin.[5]

A woman's physical and emotional well-being is dependent in large part on her sex life. A rosy, vibrant, happy woman is one who is sexually active. If a grown woman is skinny, scrawny, sallow-skinned, and dull-eyed with no spark to her personality, she may be labelled "under-fucked" (*nedoyobenaya*).[6] It is a woman's right to have a satisfying sex life. A man in his forties explains his friend's affair with a married woman as a service he is rendering to both the woman and her husband: "Her husband is impotent, and [my friend] goes to see her every morning after her husband leaves for work. He is doing them both a favor. A woman has a right to be satisfied, doesn't she?" Marina, who is in her late thirties, discusses her two boyfriends, one a "nice guy," the other someone to sleep with:

> He is a perfect gentleman, a very nice, kind, and generous person. But I don't think he's the man for me. He's older, and that's okay, but I just don't want to sleep with him. He has broad interests and tastes, which I like, and I like him a lot, but not in that way. And besides, I do have someone else, but I can't tell him that. This other one is good for sleeping with, but that's all!

Sexual desires are normal and natural, and women, to be physically healthy and emotionally content must partake of satisfying sex. Celibacy, for which there is no tradition in either Russian Orthodoxy or Judaism, is wrong because it endangers woman's well-being. And besides, it precludes motherhood, woman's most important role.[7]

Women know that they are different from men not only physically but in personality as well. As mentioned earlier, Soviet immigrant women are convinced that they are better than men because of these differences. Lera notes:

> Women are stronger and more cunning than men, and smarter than men. Men might talk louder and seem tougher, but it is really women

who are the backbone of their families. Men don't realize this because they don't want to.

Because women are smarter as well as softer and more caring than men, only women are able to, and therefore must, perform the triple role of wife-mother-worker, as demanding and demeaning as it might be. Lera continues:

> You have to understand something—men and women are different. It's natural. And in regard to the home and the family, men and women do different things. Everything concerning the house is woman's work—preparing the meals, washing dishes, doing laundry, taking care of children, and cleaning. . . . This is the way it has always been, and this is the way it will always be—house chores belong to the woman. If your husband helps you at all, you should be grateful.

The home remains the sanctum of femininity, "the romantic sentiment . . . that functions as an effective antidote to the unrelieved seriousness, the pressure of making one's way in a harsh difficult world" (Brownmiller 1984, 14–17). By creating this haven, women build a legitimate strand of resistance into official Soviet culture and find a reprieve from their burdens (Markowitz 1991b). But they do so at a high cost.

When women, as sometimes occurs after migration, are freed of their triple role, they may discover not that they feel liberated but that they are depressed. Having internalized the value for other-orientation and self-sacrifice, Soviet-born women can feel useless and unwanted when they find that they are not needed in one or more of their usual domains. With homemaking tasks much less time-consuming in America than in the USSR, unemployed women begin to feel extraneous. Yet, those who are eligible for state assistance or whose husbands earn more than adequate income have no externally imposed reason to work, and they often succumb to inertia. They need to be needed; having learned to look after others, many Soviet émigré women do not know how to be self-initiators. They find it difficult, if not impossible, to rouse themselves from depression, and require that someone else, a close friend or family member, take the responsibility for pushing them toward a job or training program. Recognizing that she cannot do it alone, Nona expresses her need for a push, a sign that someone else believes in her worth and will help her find a way to regain a place in society and her self-esteem:

> This is the first time in my life that I need help. I was always independent and people were always dependent on me, and now, after all this . . . for me to be dependent is almost more than I can take. For me to ask anybody for anything is like killing me. . . . My soul and my mind were keeping silent all these five years, and this was a very painful thing for me. . . . I am ready now to go out and do something, but I need help, a push, to get me moving. I cannot do this alone.

Part of woman's "natural role" of tending to the home and family involves planning the household budget, which is also a continuation of her role in East European Jewish *shtetl* life. Each woman must be fully apprised of her husband's financial affairs and know how much he earns and what his business is worth so that she can help with these endeavors and safeguard the family's economic well-being. Soviet Jewish immigrants objected to Geraldine Ferraro as a candidate for vice-president in 1984 not because she is a woman, but because she claimed no knowledge of her husband's business affairs. They deemed her incompetent in her wifely role and therefore reasoned that she could not possibly handle the complexity of high office.[8] Several women, like Regina, reacted thus: "Imagine, a woman who says she knows nothing about her husband's business affairs! If she doesn't even know what's going on in her own family, how can she be capable of running a whole country?"

In short, immigrants from the Soviet Union regard women and men both as human beings, each possessing equal capacities for higher education and the potential to work in any profession. Woman differs from man, however, because in addition to the need to work, which she shares with him, she is "naturally" in charge of the domestic domain. These "natural roles" create in her a set of personality characteristics—tenderness, solicitude, and self-sacrifice, coupled with deviousness, seductiveness, and hedonism—that are motivated by and feed into her deep need to care for others. To be a woman in every sense of the word means to recognize these differences and play them up to one's advantage. A woman who is unable or refuses to cultivate each aspect of her womanly character, attractive–solicitous–socially useful (wife-mother-worker), is viewed as unnatural and to be pitied.

And what of man? While women have two domains—the workplace and home—in which to make contributions and reap personal satisfaction, men are often peripheral, if not extraneous, to the inner workings of domestic life. Man's role as contributor via the public domain is magnified because in his household he is only a consumer. As Maxim puts it, "Men need to have their work be the most important thing and to have their work appreciated by their women. No, it's not the same. Man *needs* this, the woman does not." The man has no responsible adult role at home; his wife cooks, cleans, washes clothes, and makes a comfortable living environment for him and believes that it is her right and duty to perform all these household tasks. The husband is not expected to participate in domestic labor and occupies the same role as a child while at home. The difference between the husband and a child, however, is that the man works outside the home and brings to his family an income, status, and prestige. For this he deserves and demands appreciation.

Men and women alike point out that the Soviet system as it operated through to the 1980s had thwarted man's performance of his key role as provider. Besides the laws prohibiting "parasitism," life in the USSR is very difficult indeed for a one-worker family, so that women as a rule also work, whether or not they or their husbands prefer that they stay at home. Soviet men cannot be perfect men, since the system precludes them from fully supporting their families. An immigrant from the republic of Georgia expresses the dominant view of ideal man, noting that its practical application in Soviet Georgia differs greatly from that of the Slavic regions of the USSR:

> I am married. About six years ago I found my wife, and we have a five-year-old child. No, of course she doesn't work! She is at home with our child. Why should she work? In Georgia, no women work . . . only the poorest and lowest women work. It is a mark against a man if his wife is working. It shows that he is not a real man. You know about Georgian men; they are very proud and very strong and want their women to stay at home. And they work to make certain that their women stay at home. This is another way how Georgia is different from Russia. In Russia, without the two salaries, it is impossible to live.[9]

By denying them their "natural" right to support their families, the Soviet system has broken its men, according to former Soviet citizens. The powerlessness that men feel is often expressed in alcoholism and wife-beating, two ways by which men temporarily escape their emasculation and display their manly might. "Officially the husband has neither economic, cultural nor political advantages over the wife, but he does have the advantage of physical strength and uses it indiscriminately when drunk" (Kurganoff 1971, 118). Another way of undermining the ill effects of man's debilitation by the Soviet system, more widespread than excessive drinking and wife abuse among Jews and Georgians,[10] is to deal on the black market. Not only does underground speculation get back at the repressive system, it provides men with enough or more than enough money to support their families and gives them some degree of power over their lives.

In America, immigrant men can become ideal providers by earning enough money to give their families a comfortable lifestyle. Some, especially men with training in medicine, computer technology, and select engineering fields who work in their old professions, earn many times more money than they ever could have in the USSR. Others open businesses, drive limousines or taxis, or develop new skills to produce good incomes.

Men take great pride in their newfound ability to support their families in an opulent manner. Compensating for the long hours they often spend at work, they shower their families with possessions, a big apartment or house, stylish home furnishings, large television sets, clothes, jewelry, and toys. This means of expressing affection is usually but not always duly appreciated by wives and children, and lack of recognition for the sacrifices and contributions of the man of the house can lead to familial strife.

Another sore point deriving from the man's desire to fulfill his role as sole provider develops when men decide that their wives should leave their jobs to stay at home and tend solely to womanly pursuits. Reclaiming their position of family head through labor in the public domain, Soviet émigré men wish to relieve their wives' threefold burden. In America it may no longer be necessary that women work; because a man alone can make a decent living, the husband reasons that his wife should now stay at home and do what is "natural" for her—be female. Soviet man's ability to right the "unnatural" balance between the sexes is a great accomplishment for him and a source of pride. Women may willingly stay home to care for a baby, and couples who never would have dreamt of having more than one child in the Soviet Union may now have two or three. The decision to have a child ends the tension between spouses that develops when the woman wants to "do something" (work) and the man prefers that she stay at home. In cases that are not resolved by having a child, divorce may result. Marina is now separated from her husband:

> One thing he refused to understand is that I am not a baby without a profession. . . . I am a professional, and although I certainly know that I will never be a star, I do want my career, to find a small place for myself. And this he did not and could not understand, and every day I felt that I had to prove to him, and to myself, that he was wrong. And that was a great deal of pressure. He wants a Russian wife, to eat with, to drink with, and to sleep with, and that's it. And I cannot do this.

Other husbands, especially those who received higher education in America or who emigrated with wives who were well-established professionals in the USSR, are quite supportive of their spouses' careers and encourage them to make greater headway in their fields. Convinced that their wives will not feel like complete people otherwise, these husbands urge them to continue in their professions or to train for new ones. Both partners may downplay housekeeping duties by pointing to the fact that cooking, shopping, and cleaning are less time-consuming in America than they were in Russia so that a woman can easily continue to oversee her home while working. Rejecting the notion that performance of household chores makes a woman more feminine, younger, two-income, professional households ("Russian Yuppies") increasingly hire full-time housekeepers or part-time maids to clean, prepare meals, and look after children. Husbands in these families evince the same concern as husbands who want their wives to quit working; both wish to ease their wives' threefold burden. The difference is that some men favor divesting them of the traditional woman's role, emphasizing their wives' personhood, professionalism, and intellect over their place in the nursery and kitchen. (Supervision of the maid, and thus control over the domestic domain, remains squarely in the woman's hands.)

Among two-income families, which constitute the majority of Soviet émigré couples, the husband is usually the major provider

(Simon, Shelley, and Schneiderman 1986, 86–87), and he is quick to point out that his salary supports the family. The wife's job may be viewed along the lines of a hobby, something she does to keep busy, use her skills, and assert her personhood, but her job is not considered vital to the family's economic well-being, as Oleg proclaims:

> I make $12.50 an hour, and I have full medical benefits for the whole family, sick leave, and vacation. Yes, she speaks English better than I do, and she has an interesting job, but who do you think supports this family? There is no way we could live on her earnings; they are nothing! And who do you think pushes her in her work?

In America, Soviet man has an opportunity to reassert himself as household head through wages earned in the public domain, and very often he takes it. Soviet émigré men delight in having their wives well dressed and in stuffing their children's rooms with toys, computers, radios, and televisions, for besides feeling satisfied by making their families happy, they also receive prestige from the community for being good providers.

There are striking exceptions, however, to the rule that men be the major wage-earners. In some cases the wife explains her position as major breadwinner as temporary while her husband studies to establish himself in his profession. In other cases of successful and visible businesswomen, male and female immigrants alike explain, with a mixture of respect and awe coupled with disapproval, that these are women "with men's heads," for they have placed their jobs above their families.

Because some women may find themselves more successful than their husbands in reestablishing themselves professionally, not all men are able to attain head-of-household status for their work and income. In many cases those men feel emasculated and powerless to an even greater extent than in the USSR (see Steinfirst 1980, 7). Marriages in which the wife enjoys greater post-migration success than her husband may be unable to withstand the strain. At an evening gathering, Natalya points out someone and tells me about him:

> He's not too happy here. He was living in West Germany with his wife and two children. He is forty eight years old. . . . Well, his wife became a doctor there, and she began to lose interest in him. She was success-

ful, and then she began to look down on him. Not very nice, but it happens often.

In other cases, the woman simply perpetuates her triple burden, assumes much of the responsibility for her family and tries to downplay her husband's failure to attain the male ideal. Nona, after running into a haggard-looking acquaintance while we were on the bus, commented to me, "She's a very good woman, works hard. But her husband is not so good. I don't even know what he does. This is the case so many times with our immigration." In fact, it is part of the woman's role to bolster her husband's self-esteem and to hold the marriage together.

Men and women alike assume that men are inherently dissatisfied with monogamy, easily bored, and by nature promiscuous. Kurganoff (1971, 132) points out that in the Soviet Union, "Marriage fidelity is broken first and foremost by the husband. Research into divorces in the USSR shows that infidelity is not only widespread, but that nearly 20 percent of divorces involve a husband who had a second family on the side—another woman and other children." Because of her role as mother, the woman tends to be monogamous, and it is her responsibility to see to it that her husband remains faithful in their marriage. To ensure his fidelity, a wife must make herself attractive and attend to her husband's needs. Advice among girlfriends:

> Why don't you cut your hair and get a new hairstyle? You have to look more modern and pretty, and [your husband] will love you more.

> I am telling you this because I love you like my daughter. One month or two you can live apart, this is okay. But then you must go there and find whatever you can find, because there are many girls, and if you want to stay married you must look after your husband. A wife always goes to her husband and makes do with the situation.

As a result, women often blame themselves for their husbands' sexual wanderings, believing that had they been prettier, softer, more patient, accepting, and docile—in short, more "feminine"—their husbands would have remained faithful. When men express remorse for their misconduct, it is expected that their wives will welcome them back. Furthermore, friends and relatives wholeheartedly participate in attempts to reconcile a marriage. Lera provides an example:

Last night my husband came in very timidly and said, "I have something to discuss with you. I didn't want to mention this, but I feel that I
must. You know my new partner, Edik. He's been having troubles with
his wife. He had a lover, and his wife found out about this and said she
would divorce him. He told her that he cut all ties with this other
woman, said over and over again that he loves her, and promised that
everything would be fine between them." Understand that they have
two small children and that it would be a shame for a divorce to occur.
Only this Edik did not end the relationship, and his wife found out
again and told him that she will divorce him and never speak to him
again. Not one word has she said to him since. My husband and his
partner thought that if we invite them to our party tonight she will
change her mind and start speaking again. I will not sit in judgment of
them. All I can say is that I will always do whatever I can to help save a
marriage, especially when there are children involved, and I would
gladly do this for them.

Problems notwithstanding, it is considered better for men and
women to be married than to spend their lives alone. Although men
who cannot earn decent salaries and who have extramarital affairs are
viewed with opprobrium, the woman who rejects her husband because of his low income or marital infidelity is not looked upon with
kindness, either. Being single is unnatural and to be avoided at all
costs.

Being single is a difficult and socially awkward position for men
and women alike once they reach their mid-twenties. Although most
Soviet immigrants believe that it is easier for men to find dates and
potential spouses than women, single men do not necessarily agree.
Many argue that fear of crime in America makes the task of meeting
women more difficult that it had been in the USSR:[11]

There [in the USSR] people aren't so afraid. On the street if I saw
someone who looks nice, interesting, I could go over to her, say hello,
start a conversation, and invite her to coffee. Here, if you do that, she
might call the police, or not answer you, or think you are a pervert.

Even more disconcerting to single men is their feeling that Russian Jewish immigrant women are more interested in their income
than their character, more concerned about the money spent during

courtship than in enjoying each other's company. Three single men in their twenties and thirties offer their opinions:

> First, girls think they should marry either a doctor, lawyer, or a million-aire. I have enough money. . . . What a man does and how much money he has doesn't tell you everything about the man. There's more to it than that—his soul, his heart. I asked once, "What do you want, a man or a checkbook?" And then, they all expect to be taken out, not just for coffee or even dinner, but to a fancy restaurant and a show. If you don't do that they don't want anything to do with you.

> I can't date those girls from Odessa. They all expect me to drive up in a Cadillac, take them out for a night in a Russian restaurant, and give them presents. I can't afford it!

> Our Russian Jewish women are only interested in one thing—money. If you don't have enough money or don't buy expensive dinners or gifts, then they're not interested.

Maxim summarizes his disgust with émigré women's self-centeredness and lack of womanly concern for others by relating a personal incident. Not long ago he had a dinner date with a woman that ended abruptly because she preferred watching a television program to continuing conversation with him:

> I went out with a girl once, yes, Russian, on a Wednesday night. Shortly before nine o'clock she looked at her watch and announced that she had to go home now. I was very surprised and asked her why. "Because now it's time for *Dynasty,*" she told me.[12] Of course I never wanted to see her again because anyone who prefers a television program to me I have no interest in.

Although Soviet immigrant women are just as concerned as ever with finding men for themselves, émigré men note that these women have become more calculating and demanding in terms of what they want from a man in America. Now only certain men will do, those who make a good living, enjoy high social status, and are indulgent toward their girlfriends, giving care and concern as well as taking it.

Soviet émigré women have become more selective, owing to the influence of the media's portrayal of the ideal American husband and because immigrant men have become more demanding of themselves. These men are measuring their own status in terms of how well they can provide income and emotional strength to their families. Knowing that such men exist within the émigré community as well as outside of it, but knowing as well that not all émigré men meet these ideals, single women do their best to ensure that they avoid marrying a Soviet throwback. While they dress and make themselves up in the most alluring ways possible to attract men, they are looking for a certain kind of man. Therefore, they may rebuff men they deem inadequate providers of material and psychological support; a man who is too cheap to treat for a gala evening on the town or too self-centered to understand the importance of viewing *Dynasty* is not one they want for a husband in America.

In short, Soviet Jewish immigrants sharpen their perceptions and practice of ideal gender roles on American soil. Women remain first and foremost solicitous caretakers, intensely committed to the welfare of their children and husbands. Women's concern about their (potential) spouse's means of livelihood is not mere selfishness, it is part of the worry that their children from a previous marriage or as yet unborn, be provided for by their father. Émigré women have been relieved of much of the Soviet burden accorded to their threefold role of wife-mother-worker. With their husbands often earning more than ample salaries to support their families, Soviet Jewish immigrant women are no longer obligated to work full-time and are often encouraged to play out to its fullest their primary role of caretaker. Male/ female roles thus may change in response to the shift of duties within the family. As their physical burden lightens, Soviet immigrant women may find themselves increasingly economically dependent on their husbands and therefore less in control of their own fate. Marrying the right man is all the more important in such circumstances.

Men, conversely, who were denied the means by which to claim ideal male status in the Soviet Union, reclaim their role as provider in America. Men's earnings, in many cases, now allow them to support their families through their work, and they consequently feel more in control of their lives than they did in the Soviet Union.

In America, Woman the Mother and Man the Toiler have many avenues for expressing their primary roles and personalities as they create a social place for themselves, build financial stability, provide each other with emotional sustenance, and make a family. In the process, many couples, especially those in middle age, find that sex roles, particularly in the economic sphere, become sharper and more traditional. As a result, however, as man works longer and harder and woman's leisure time increases, major personality characteristics attached to these economic roles may reverse, with man becoming the self-sacrificing martyr/husband and woman reaping the benefits of his labor, for herself and her children.

PARENTS AND CHILDREN

Throughout the Soviet Union, people from every walk of life declare, "Our children are the future!" (Shipler 1984, 56; Smith 1976, 201). To government leaders and party ideologues, children represent the state's destiny and therefore have been raised to revere Lenin, become good collectivists, and oversee the evolution of world communism. When parents, however, speak of their children as the future, they see them not as anonymous building blocks in the structure of communism but rather as individual extensions of themselves, entitled to reap the benefits of post-war socialism. These views of the future, although different, are neither mutually exclusive nor separately attainable, causing the family and the state to join in implicit agreement to socialize and educate children toward both these ends.

The state's socialization task is to shape children into citizens who place the social good above egotistic desires. To this end, Soviet schools teach rules of etiquette, morality, and interpersonal relations in addition to academic subjects (see Bronfenbrenner 1972, 30–38, for a description of the specific character development tasks taught in each elementary grade). Parents are thus freed of these socialization duties, but teachers do hold them responsible for reinforcing the values and behaviors their children learn in school. The parents' duty is to encourage in their children "the development of a well-rounded personality characterized by 'love of work', 'discipline', and 'cultured behavior', and above all, [that] conforms to the ideological-political value system" (Liegle 1975, 24).

Soviet parents do support their children's internalization of state-provided "upbringing" (*vospitaniye*) for two major reasons:[13]

First, Soviet schools hold them directly responsible for their children's behavior and attitudes. Teachers are in frequent contact with pupils' parents and during public parent-teacher meetings shame those whose children are slipshod in their work, appearance, and attitudes (see Smith 1976, 196–199). To avoid their own embarrassment and censure, parents urge their children to obey the teacher and work hard at the tasks she assigns. Second, of equal if not greater importance, parents know from their own experience that conformity with regulations and obedience to authority are requisite for success in the Soviet system and thus instruct their children to follow the teacher's directions.

Parents' methods of reinforcing collectivist socialization differ from those used in state schools. At home, parents may spoil and pamper their children, dressing them better than they clothe themselves, feeding them the tastiest dinner morsels, and showering them with embraces, toys, cookies, and praise. Parents thus instill in their children a double standard of behavior which prepares them well for the split social world they will inhabit throughout their lives: at school and in all other public places, they are collectivists, while in the privacy of their own homes, they are indulged centers of attention (Pearson 1990, 41). Parents reward good school conduct by allowing their children to act in an opposite way at home.

As children grow older, parental anxiety intensifies, because children's school performance, at least in theory, determines their future. Parents, and this is particularly true of white-collar urbanites, do whatever they can to guide their children onto professional tracks; they oversee and assist with homework, present "gifts" to teachers and school administrators, shield children from their own doubts about or disappointments in the Soviet system, and spend their few extra rubles on private English classes, piano lessons, and specialized tutoring. Most important of all, early on parents begin cultivating a network of connections designed to assure their children places in university. Children come to understand that they are completely dependent on their parents, for the kind of lives they wish to have in the future, as well as the necessities of the present.

Jewish parents, like most other Soviet parents, readily accept this agreement with the state for their children's future. First, they have little choice in the matter. If they want their children to meet at least their own social status, they must play according to the rules. Second, it gives to the parents unquestioned authority and respect in their families. Children, no matter how spoiled, grow up knowing that their lives hinge on their parents' connections, and they treat them accordingly. Parents who may lack control over their own lives feel capable of guiding, directing, and guaranteeing those of their children. Third, on a historical note, Russian Jews have long been accustomed to compromising themselves (e.g., passing bribes under the table) to ensure their survival. Under the Soviet regime, more than ever before, they could see that the combination of their own hard work and obeisance to those in power pays off.

Fourth, and most significant, Eastern European Jewish culture predisposes parents to accept the Soviet deal for their children's futures because it views progeny not as independent, discrete human beings but as extensions of their parents. Charles Silberman (1985, 138) explains that in Ashkenazic tradition, "Children are the parents' *nachas*—a hard-to-translate term that means that children provide their parents with honor and fulfillment as well as joy. Specifically, the child's success and achievement becomes the parent's success and achievement—and the child's failure, the parent's failure." Having made compromises with the state themselves and seeing them, to a large extent, work out, parents encourage their children to do the same. Thus Jewish parents urge their sons and daughters to follow the proven path, for these children's lives are not only the outcome of their individual skills and talents but reflect those of their parents as well.

This very close identification between parent and child is influenced by demographic conditions as well as Russian and Jewish cultural factors. In the Soviet Union most urbanites, especially those in the Baltic republics, Jews, and the Slavic intelligentsia, limit their family size to one child, two at the most. Liegle (1975, 37) delineates three factors contributing to this low birthrate: general lack of living space, low standard of living, and full-time employment of women.

It is not only Western social scientists who view small Soviet families as the result of rational planning; parents themselves see it that way. Couples stop at one child because they want to give their children the best of everything and fear that, due to severe limitations on goods and resources, they would be unable to provide for two or more children. Lera explains, "There in Russia it was very hard to do the best for your child, not only because of money but also availability [of goods]. For that reason, I had only one, and many others also have just one child. With only one, maybe you can afford to do the best. With more, there's just not enough to go around."

Parents' close identification with their children derives in large part from their rational decision to have just one child. Parents have only one chance to raise a happy, healthy child, and this one baby becomes the focus of their love and hope. This point is brought home all the more when women undergo abortions to terminate untenable pregnancies.[14] Many women have had an abortion or two prior to the birth of their child, either because they conceived during courtship or because the married couple was not yet prepared to raise a child (e.g., still in university). It is not unusual for a Soviet woman to have several abortions after the child's birth (see Gray 1990, 20–21). These operations are performed to ensure the family's continuing ability to devote full attention, time, and resources to its only child.

Parents often consider a decision *not* to abort a pregnancy morally wrong if it would infringe upon the living child's opportunities to have "the best." Boris grumbles about his friend's pregnant wife: "It's not right. I don't know why she's so happy. They are just getting on their feet. Masha will be going to college next year and she needs everything they have. How can they afford a baby? It's not fair to deprive Masha."

With each aborted pregnancy, the bond between parents—particularly the mother—and child strengthen because they are reminded that they have chosen the one child they do have to keep, to cherish, and to love. It reinforces their pampering and protective identification with this only son or daughter.

The result of all these factors—Soviet upbringing, Russian Jewish culture, and post-war demographics—is that within the Soviet Jewish family, boundaries between parent and child often blur to the point that it becomes difficult to discern where one person starts and the other ends. This overdeveloped sense of intrafamilial identification contributes in large part to a family's decision to emigrate and the means parents use to inform, or not inform, their children of this action.

In the 1970s Soviet Jews saw their own or friends' children denied university admission despite their high grades and despite having played the game according to all the rules. Many parents, their own stable and prestigious positions notwithstanding, decided, without consulting with their children (see Markus 1979, 30–36), that, since the next generation of Jews had no future in their native land they had no choice but to emigrate.[15]

An unanticipated consequence of emigration is that once in America parents' absolute control over their children's lives crumbles. Parents find themselves in the difficult position of not really knowing how to "do the best" for their children. However, they are reluctant to cede authority or to give up their beliefs, inappropriate as they now may be, about correct behavior for their children. The situation is exacerbated by the fact that children, who in the Soviet Union were shielded from information by their all-knowing parents, discover that they may better understand American norms than their parents and therefore hold their own ideas about how to live their post-migration lives. Family dynamics frequently undergo alteration as a result of this new balance in knowledge and power.

Reactions to these changes span a wide range on both parents' and children's parts. Some parents recognize that they must expand their knowledge and immerse themselves in the task of understanding the complicated world of American schooling and professions. They work along with their children so that the entire family can adjust accordingly. Other parents simply will not or cannot change; in the most extreme cases parents abandon their child-rearing duties and reverse roles with their children. Certainly most families fall somewhere in between, with parents ceding some power and granting more independence to their sons and daughters while continuing to hold onto beliefs about children's behavior formed in the Soviet Union. These three broad types of relationships, all stemming from the tendency to view family members as interlocked with one another, are delineated below and illustrated with examples:[16]

(1) *Parents who continue to assume full responsibility for their children's character development yet modify the content of their child-rearing roles to correspond with the new environment.* These parents believe that the only way they can raise healthy, well-adjusted children is to provide them with a consistent role model in their own person.

Joseph and Regina arrived in New York with their six-year-old son Paul in early 1977. They avoided Brighton Beach because they did not want to live in a "Russian ghetto" and found their way to

Rego Park, Queens, where they were one of the first Russian Jewish immigrant families to settle. Believing strongly that "no one invited us here so we must make a way for ourselves," Joseph immediately sought work and soon found a job in his profession although he was barely able to communicate in English. As soon as they moved into their apartment, Regina and Joseph enrolled in English classes at the local Jewish center: "How could we not learn English? We have a son to raise! We have to help him with his homework, speak to his teachers, know what's going on in the world."

At the same time his parents were striving to master a new language and adjust to a very different work environment, Paul was struggling through school. "He went directly into the first grade with no preparation at all. Sure there were days when he would come home from school crying because he didn't understand a thing. We comforted him and told him this is painful now, but this is the best way," Regina explained. Just as she and Joseph readily threw themselves into the fray of making a living, understanding and adapting to the demands of the country they chose for their new home, so too was Paul expected to meet the challenge of his school. And he did, buoyed by the emotional support and affection of his parents, along with the examples that they were setting for him. This family tackled the task of resettlement together; knowing that their own and their youngster's self-esteem were intertwined in making the transition successfully, the parents set an example of hard work and perseverance, and their son followed.

Seven years later their familial relationship has not changed. On an early June day in 1984, Joseph and Regina were speaking rapid, colloquial English and discussing their plans for the summer. Paul, thirteen and the winner of the district championship in a citywide spelling bee and third prize in a competition for writing a poem about the Statue of Liberty, was to begin preparing for the college entrance exam (PSAT). Regina and Paul, joined by Joseph on weekends, were planning to spend the summer at a cottage "where we go every year." Along with enjoying fresh air and outdoor activities with other children, Paul was to spend about an hour each day going through the material in the test guidebooks with his mother. Regina and Joseph had already begun reading the guides and taking practice tests because they believe that if they are incapable of understanding the material and performing well on the exams they can be of no help to their son, and perhaps he too would be unable to pass.

This example of an enmeshed family demonstrates consistency between theory and practice of "doing the best" for one's child. Regina and Joseph strive to understand their new environment and every aspect of it that can contribute to their son's present and future happiness and success. The full burden of post-migration adjustment is not on the child; his parents provide a role model for him, achieving in their own right as they urge him to perform well in school, make friends, and take part in social activities. Thus far, at least, their efforts have paid off not only in each individual's social, linguistic, material, and academic/professional successes in their new country, but also in producing familial harmony, support, and love.

(2) *Parents who surrender their child-raising responsibilities and reverse roles with their children.* The debilitating process of role reversal, probably as difficult for the parent who abrogates responsibility as for the child who assumes it, occurs when parents, due to physical or emotional incapacities, are unable to give their families economic or emotional support. The child, often feeling responsible for the family's decision to emigrate in the first place, steps in and tries to fill the void.

Victor emigrated with his parents in 1980, when he was a first-year university student. He immediately abandoned his studies to take a job as a laborer: "My parents are old and sick, and my brother was in Israel. So I went to work. Not knowing any English, what could I do but heavy labor? I loaded boxes and crates." Now, four years later, Victor works in an immigrant-owned commercial enterprise earning a good salary. He is fairly content with his job, although his "heart is not in this work." Victor is interested in veterinary science and psychology, but he will not even think of quitting his job and returning to college: "First of all, my language is not good enough . . . and second, and most important, I am now able to support myself and my parents, but if I gave up my job, I would be unable to. And I can't do that."

Daughters more frequently than sons find themselves in role-reversal situations, particularly in cases in which the mothers are single parents.[17] Lara, for example, arrived in America at age fifteen with her mother Nona, a thirty-eight-year-old divorcée. In Moscow they had lived relatively privileged lives; the girl spent her time in school, and after school did her homework, took private English lessons, and ice skated. Nona worked among "artistic circles" and took night courses to earn a second university diploma. About two years prior to their emigration, Nona was hospitalized for "nervous problems," which she attributes to the stress of working at an organization newly filled with KGB agents and party *apparatchiks*.

Upon arrival in America, Lara, whose English lessons resulted in her ability to communicate rather well in that language, found a part-time, after-school job. Within a few months her mother also began working but in a position she considered well beneath her station. After nearly two years Nona became ill ("post-migration stress"), quit her job, and went on state assistance. While her mother rested at home and took English courses, Lara attended a nearby community college and worked for cash "off the books" in a local retail store.[18]

In September 1984, Lara transferred to a four-year college in Manhattan. In addition to her full course load, she continues working twenty hours a week and does most of the household chores. At the end of her school-work day, Lara is expected to chat with her mother to cheer her up from her solitude and boredom. The daughter increasingly turns down invitations to socialize with her friends because her mother throws tantrums, calling her a selfish egotist for going out and leaving her all alone. At the end of her first term in the four-year college, Lara was placed on academic probation. However, she categorically rejected a suggestion to attend an out-of-town state college where she would be able to concentrate on her studies. "How can I do that? Mom sacrificed so much for me in Russia. How can I abandon her? She even sewed up holes in her old pantyhose, doing without new ones, so I could have my English lessons. No, I couldn't do that. Everything will work out."

Another mother-daughter role reversal occurred in the aftermath of a very poorly planned migration. The mother's brother and his family had earlier emigrated to a midsized Texas city, and, despite his warnings that he could not support them, his sister and her daughter decided to join him. "When we arrived, my brother wanted nothing to do with us." Not knowing what else to do, they stayed in Texas and received public assistance:

My daughter was twelve and a half, maybe thirteen at that time. But because of everything I became sick, very sick, in depression. My daughter went to school, and after school she worked. It wasn't much, but she worked and earned some money. Everything there was opposite to how it should be—the daughter took care of the mother.

Eventually they left Texas and came to New York, "to be with more Russians." The daughter began high school, but after some time dropped out to work. Three months later they left for Israel, "thinking it would be better there." A year later they returned to New York and ended up in Brighton Beach seeking assistance from a social-working rabbi. Several weeks after their meeting with the rabbi, the daughter explained her family's current situation:

> Yes, we have an apartment now. Everything has worked out with that. But at Lincoln High School they will not give me all my credits. See I started tenth grade, and that April I left school to go to work. I worked three months and then we left for Israel, where I went to high school for a year. I know that I made a mistake, but all I knew then is that we needed the money, and I thought I would be all right. How was I to know? I was just a child. And my mother is an even bigger child in situations like that. Well, now I have to work very hard to make up all these credits, to take the Regents exams and prepare for college.

At the end of June 1985, the daughter received notification from New York University that she had been granted a full-tuition scholarship to begin in the fall. Mother and daughter stroll Brighton Beach Avenue arm in arm each warm summer night.

In the cases described above, the children express neither resentment nor contempt for having assumed roles that were once their parents'. They consider this burden of family support to be "natural" because they are young, healthy, and competent, while their parents are "old and sick." The fact that they have been raised in an enmeshed family situation propels and maintains this attitude, for they have come to believe that their individual desires and goals must include the good of the family unit. Since their parents are unable to fulfill their obligations, the children take the obligations upon themselves, almost as repayment in kind to parents who sacrificed throughout their lives in Russia on their behalf and then made the "supreme sacrifice" of emigration for their sake as well. Guilt and love interact to produce a need to look after the welfare of one's parents to the extent that one's own present and future happiness may be thwarted.[19]

(3) *Parents who believe that their children are reflections of themselves and that they are responsible for their children's development but cannot be complete role models.* They lack the knowledge and experience necessary to guide by example in America, and because of various factors—number of hours spent on the job, need for leisure time, or sheer inability—seek substitutes or intermediaries for, or sometimes even neglect, shaping their children into the kind of people they want them to be.

Soviet-born parents are frequently befuddled by the American system that tells them to "do your own thing" and that achievement is based solely on individual motivation. Parents want their children to achieve in school but fear that in so doing their children will lose "Russian culture" and become disrespectful of their parents' ways. They want their children to speak Russian but know that they must adopt English as their own to make it in America. Plagued themselves by ambivalence, many parents cannot help but send double messages to their children.

It is not uncommon to hear émigré parents complain bitterly about the American school system. Unlike Joseph and Regina, whose son was only six years old when they arrived in New York and had not yet attended school, many families, whose children had already attended Soviet schools, had become dependent on state-provided upbringing. (Soviet children are usually seven years old when they enter school.) They arrived in America used to reinforcing the "cultured behavior" and "collective spirit" their children learned at school. These parents quickly developed resentment at American public schools for giving their children "too much freedom" and viewed teachers who encouraged students to think out questions for themselves rather than giving them definitive answers as abrogating their responsibility to put children on the right track. Parents who must spend several hours a day at work and feel inadequate to the overwhelming task in America of developing their children's characters alone, express confusion and anger at public schools:

In my younger days in Russia, it was considered appropriate that both the family and the school develop the child. Children were different at that time—they were polite. Now schools consider that they only have to give knowledge, and that parents have to do the upbringing. Families cannot always give necessary upbringing because sometimes there is not enough time.

I am a mother who has two sons. I, like every mother, want to see my children strong, happy, and living in freedom, but they need time and attention. We don't have more time for them. Children come home early, and parents come home late. School is not responsible for them after three o'clock, and it's too bad that the school doesn't care about children after this time. We would be happy if we knew they are in a special group between three and six P.M., where they would do homework, play music, draw, participate in sports. Because there aren't such groups, I think that is why so many teenagers are criminals.

Some parents seek equivalents for the Soviet school system and enroll their children in private schools. The vast majority of immigrant children receiving private schooling attend Hebrew day schools, or yeshivas, where moral education is considered of equal importance to academic subjects. Discipline is quite strict and children are usually required to conform to a dress code, and yeshivas offer a longer schoolday than the public school, so that children and parents return home around the same time. In New York, about one-third of immigrant parents have or have had their children enrolled in a Hebrew day school (Federation of Jewish Philanthropies 1985, 34).[20]

Of greatest immediate and long-run concern to parents is their children's school performance, for they view education as the key to their children's future. Most parents, whether they opt for socialization help from yeshivas or not, arrive home from their full-time jobs fatigued. Many simply do not have the stamina or the ability to help with children's homework or even to listen attentively to their excited recountings, especially when they are delivered in rapid English. Even though some émigré parents often do sit with their youngsters and make certain that they are doing their assignments, sometimes checking their arithmetic and the neatness of their papers, they cannot always be sure that the assignments are correctly done. Nonetheless, parents expect their children to perform well in school. Indeed, they require it as vindication of all the hardships of migration. Parents readily show their children's notebooks, tests, and certificates of merit to "American friends who understand what these mean," enjoying as their own the accomplishments of their youngsters. Parents are usually grateful to their children for their success and reward them when they earn high marks on exams and bring home exemplary report cards. One girl received a gold necklace and fifty dollars for obtaining all A's on her last elementary school report card; another was presented with a portable television set for gaining admission to a special junior high school program.

Showing love, affection, and appreciation through gifts does not start and end with school performance. Some parents use elaborate presents to assuage their own feelings of guilt for having disrupted the formerly serene lives of their children and their inability to direct completely their new lives in America.[21] While usually convinced that children adapt easily and relatively effortlessly to immigration, some parents nonetheless feel the pain of their children's struggle to become "like all the other kids." Parents may then lavish their children with treats, toys, clothes, stereos, computers, to help them feel happy. A Queens mother of two girls:

> This is very important for her to have something new, to feel like everyone else, as it is for all children. But I think it is especially important for immigrant children, who feel strange to begin with.

Lera:

> All parents want the best, the very best, for their children, and they all try in the ways they know to give this to them. Maybe I spoil my daughter, but it's only because I want her to have all the things that make her happy. Why not? You're only a child once, and why shouldn't that be the most wonderful time in your life?

Parents receive pleasure when their children smile at the receipt of their gifts. It makes them happy, and vindicates them as well, to be in a position to give their children the things that, owing to insufficient money or simply a market "deficit," they were unable to give them in the Soviet Union. Moreover, they and their children are highly influenced by American consumerism and the "keeping up with the Joneses" mentality that commercials often utilize in selling their products.

Many of these same parents, however, decry their children's tendencies toward rampant materialism and cannot understand how initial appreciation for gifts turns into constant demands for more things. Lera complains:

> She is always saying, "Buy me this! Buy me that!" When I was little, I just don't remember at all asking my mother to buy things for me. It's constant, not just once in a while. Her whole perspective is this way. She wants—everything! A dog, a horse, these stickers, this kind of toy, that kind of toy, always—buy me! I must say, I'm getting afraid. . . . My daughter is a smart girl, and she reads, but I am getting afraid of this materialism.

Despite these fears, parents are reluctant to put an end to this bestowal of things, because their children have become accustomed to the practice, "need" new clothes and accoutrements to keep up with their friends, and would interpret its cessation as the withdrawal of love. (This interpretation is not at all surprising, since parents do use things as bribes, such as, "If you don't clean your room, you won't get. . . ." Thus, children come to believe that they have misbehaved or displeased their parents if they are not given something they expect.)

As illustrated above, parents who see their sons and daughters as extensions of themselves are usually unable to anticipate their children responding in ways that differ from their own responses to similar situations. This inability to see their children as individuals distinct from themselves can have serious consequences. A boy of fourteen was referred for psychological counseling after he was apprehended for stealing automobile parts. His counselor relates that the boy's mother was appalled by this behavior and was unable to understand how he could have done such a thing:

> She was in shock and disbelief and said to me, "All my life I taught my son that stealing from another person is wrong. I can't understand how he could do a thing like this." Meantime, she is working full-time here in Brighton for cash and also receiving food stamps, welfare, and Section 8 assistance. She didn't see at all that she was setting an example for her son by lying and stealing because she draws a distinction be-

tween stealing from individuals, which she sees as a crime, and stealing from the state, which is your due.

When parents discover that their children have misbehaved, they may project the problem elsewhere or react as though they themselves are the wounded parties of these actions. Soviet Jewish immigrant parents let their children know that their bad behavior insults and hurts them by asking, "Why do you make me blush from embarrassment all the time?" Parents try to modify their children's behavior by manipulating vulnerable emotions. Nona complained to me, in the presence of her nineteen-year-old daughter, about her poor performance in college:

> Her situation—as well as hurting her—is killing me. I can't take it! I can't stand by and see what she is doing. She is not very strong, and she must devote all her strength to her studies. When she doesn't do this— oh, my head! oh, my heart! But I must gather all my strength, all of it, to help her.

This kind of chastisement reinforces the lack of boundaries between parents and children in immigrant families. Children do not come to see their poor grades or antisocial acts as necessarily bad or wrong in an absolute moral sense but rather as problematic only if their parents find out about and are hurt by them.[22] In the USSR, where teachers and parents are in close contact, this socialization strategy may produce good students and well-behaved youngsters. In America, where the boundary between home and school is more entrenched, it can result in children feeling that as long as their parents do not find out what they are doing, anything goes.

In order to ease intergenerational communication and maintain their own sense of authority in the home, parents usually demand that Russian be the sole language of the house (Markus 1979, 58).[23] Within the family unit language often becomes a contested domain. Parents feel that conversing at home in English "is just not natural" because Russian is their and usually their children's native tongue. Parents complain about the rapid deterioration of their children's Russian vocabulary and their increasing inability to read and write in the Cyrillic alphabet, and they frequently make fun of their children's

Americanized accents and faulty grammar.[24] It is a rare parent, however, who tutors his or her child in Russian. As with many other practices of which they disapprove because they see them as contributing to the breakup of the intertwined family, parents simply mourn the passing of their language and shame their children for poor performance. Children, however, are not encouraged to laugh at their parents' accented English or insufficient command of this language and are expected to translate (especially television programs and movies) on command.

Characteristically, Soviet-born Jewish parents believe that families should spend their leisure time together and often include their children, small and grown alike, in their dinner parties, vacation trips (even during the school year), and cultural activities. Some immigrant parents will not send their children away to summer camp because they fear their own loneliness. Parents expect that their families will remain together throughout their lifetimes, and college-bound children, as a rule, seek admission to New York–area universities rather than leave their families to study away from home. Sometimes, however, immigrant teens and young adults come to accept the American expectation that they assert their independence by moving out. Vladimir's twenty-year-old daughter was about to graduate from New York University and had found a well-paying job to begin immediately after school ended. When she announced to her parents that she planned to find her own apartment once she began working, her father was indignant:

> Now my daughter says when she graduates from college she will move into her own apartment. Now, isn't that ridiculous? I can understand if someone goes to college away from home and lives in a dormitory, and I can understand young people leaving the provinces and coming to New York—of course they have to find their own apartments. But what does Julia need this for? She lives like a queen with us, and the apartment is her realm. She has everything she wants. If she will get married, of course she will go off with her husband. But until then, she should stay at home. When parents and children live in the same city they should live under one roof together.

Children in this kind of embedded family often tolerate their parents' demands, good-naturedly labelling them "old-fashioned."[25]

They listen, sometimes amused, to their parents' outmoded views and usually accede to their requests, reasoning that there is no purpose in arguing. The children know that they have the "American way" on their side and that they will eventually do what they want to do anyway. Just as parents in embedded families know how to manipulate their children to behave according to their will, so too have children learned how to placate and manipulate their parents.

Children in this sort of enmeshed family tend to look upon their parents with a mixture of pride in their accomplishments and pity for the fact that they are immigrants who are neither Americans nor Russians. They understand why their parents hold outdated attitudes and usually put up with them if they do not consider their parents' demands totally unreasonable. As an example, one weekday night the fifteen-year-old son of Oleg and Irina returned home at 10:05 P.M., five minutes past his ten o'clock curfew. As he stepped into the apartment, his father began to shame him in front of dinner guests, calling him to task for his tardiness. The boy mumbled, "Sorry" and went into his room and shut the door. A few months later, in a discussion with me about his friends and family, the boy summarized his feelings about his relationship with his mother and father: "My parents are all right. They watch too much TV and spoil my brother, and they're old-fashioned in some of their attitudes, but they're all right."

In America, the Soviet Jewish enmeshed family, depending on the form it takes, may be a warm and supportive environment for children's growth or it may thwart achievement of their personal development and autonomy. In all cases, the key parental responsibility and motivation is to "do the best" for one's children. Consequently, parents whose children do not live up to their expectations, who react against the rules of the house, school, or society usually deny or project elsewhere the problem of their son's or daughter's maladjustment (e.g., blame American schools for giving youngsters "too much freedom"). For if parents are unable to guide their children onto the right track, not only do their children have no future, but they themselves are without one as well, for they then have no one in whom to take pride, no justification for their emigration, and not a soul to look after them and give them comfort in old age.

OLD AGE AND DEATH

Soviet Jews usually leave their homeland in family units, bringing with them young children and aged parents. The elderly, as a rule, have little say in the decision-making process; they come to America simply to remain with their families. In many cases, older immigrants arrived in the United States as a result of Soviet migration policy. Emigration officials often refused to grant exit visas to productive, educated professionals whose old, sick, pensioner parents would remain behind. An émigré social worker explains, "They didn't want to leave Russia. They left only because of their children. You know, when you go for your exit visa, the police say you should take your old parents out, too. So they come, but they don't understand."

Cultural factors, too, exert a strong influence in impelling the migration of the Soviet Jewish elderly (after Petersen 1964, 280). Life in a tightknit, virtually boundary-less, three-generation family does not prepare people, especially those in old age, to live alone. Thus, leaving behind a familiar environment to stay with loved ones is a more attractive alternative to many than remaining in their native land without their children.

How do the elderly fare with uprooting and resettlement? As with younger émigrés, they experience a range of reactions and responses to their new lives in hitherto unknown environments. At one end of the spectrum are grandparents whose daily inclusion in family affairs, weekly attendance at senior centers, participation in neighborhood social life, and occasional travels abroad make their old age in America happier and more fulfilling than they imagine it ever could have been in the Soviet Union. On the other end are those aged immigrants who have been abandoned by family or have isolated themselves and live out their lives disoriented and unhappy. Older immigrants who cluster in émigré enclaves are more satisfied with their post-migration experiences than those who do not.

No matter where they reside, Soviet immigrants are forced to reevaluate their concept of old age once they arrive in America. Like Lera, they often note that Americans of their age appear to be younger, healthier, and more energetic than they:

> People in this country are a lot healthier and younger-looking than in Russia. Especially the middle-aged and elderly. My mother for exam-

ple, is fifty-five. By your standards, yes, she is still young, but she really is not. She has only one kidney, problems with her back, high blood pressure, diabetes, liver problems, not to mention her heart. People in Russia are much older than they are here.

Differing ideas about old age in the two countries are further underscored by legal definitional differences. In the Soviet Union, women receive retirement pensions at age fifty-five, men at sixty; Americans usually retire at age sixty-five. Thus, many old people from the Soviet Union arrive in the United States to discover that they are no longer "old" but middle-aged members of the labor force. Those who are neither old enough nor ill enough to qualify for SSI face an extremely difficult situation. Skilled workers have an easier time than most because their experience in the USSR is counted to their credit and language is not crucial to their job performance. Men in their late fifties and early sixties—one a furrier, one a house-painter, a third a mechanic—related with pride to me how they found their jobs in New York, that they belong to a union, that they never miss a day of work, and how much money they have already accumulated in their pension funds.[26] Most fifty-five to sixty-five year olds, however, have already psychologically "retired," and even if they wish to work, job prospects, especially for those without English-language competence, are poor indeed.

Many late-middle-aged immigrants, particularly those who survived World War II in camps or at the front, are disabled and eligible for SSI. Those sixty-five and over receive this state support automatically, because immigrants from the Soviet Union are granted refugee status by the United States government. This status, which places those fleeing (political) oppression in a much more privileged position than so-called economic immigrants, who are not immediately entitled to state support, gives to Soviet immigrants an array of social services, the ability to work, travel passports, and old-age benefits. Elderly Soviet immigrants regard these SSI monies as their retirement pensions. Most are grateful: "I receive SSI—$385.91 a month, and Section 8, and food stamps. God bless America! What a wonderful, beautiful country!" Yet they also consider these payments their due. They did, after all, relinquish their rights to pensions in the USSR when they emigrated and believe that after having worked their whole lives they are now entitled to the same (if not better) benefits in America.[27]

Acceptance of SSI and related benefits carries unanticipated consequences for Soviet Jewish immigrant families. First, the American social welfare system, unlike that of the Soviet Union, does not indiscriminately hand out total benefit packages to the elderly; only those "in need" are eligible for state awards. To get SSI, Section 8, and food stamps the old, the sick, and the disabled must demonstrate that they have no means of support—no job, no pension, and no family members to provide for them. Thus, a sixty-five-year-old woman who resides with employed children will not receive as much (if any) assistance as one who lives alone. Consequently, this welfare policy encourages the breakup of the traditional three-generation Russian family.

Elderly immigrants express happiness with the "American system" when, as is often the case, their children live nearby and frequently visit:

> My daughters and I live [in separate apartments] all on one street. We all live together on Brighton Third Street. My daughters work, and I come to their homes and prepare after-school meals for their children. So it all works out fine. I have my children and grandchildren. They help me and I help them.

> When we first came to America, we all lived in the Bronx. . . . Then, first my son found an apartment in Brooklyn, and he moved. Then he found an apartment for us close by, and we moved too. Of course we all stay together! That's the way they want it [son, daughter-in-law, and granddaughter], and that's the way we want it.

A son who lives in suburban Rockland County and visits his elderly mother in Brighton Beach almost every weekend explains why his mother and her cohort are quite happy in their new homes:

> Whatever they had in the Soviet Union, they have here ten times better. And they have all health costs covered . . . completely free! Our old people never had it so good. Brighton Beach is great—they have the stores, the boardwalk, and all other people who speak their language. Some children have forgotten their parents . . . but most of these old

people live near their children and have friends. You shouldn't believe when someone complains too much—they have this much, and maybe they want even more!

Family members who reside in geographical proximity often benefit from each other's presence. Working parents can rest assured that their children are being looked after by their grandparents. These grandparents, particularly grandmothers, retain their role as primary caretakers in their new country. This position of responsibility makes them feel needed in a context in which they might otherwise feel quite useless.[28] Some grandparents take English-language courses to communicate better with their grandchildren, enabling them to read them stories in English, help them with homework, and talk about television programs: "See how well I speak English! This is because of the grandchildren."

Some grandparents, however, are indeed too old, sick or worn out to care for children, especially active toddlers. Family friction may arise when children's requests for free babysitting services are not enthusiastically granted. Elderly parents find themselves in the awkward position of trying to assert their independence from their children, but they are usually unable to succeed. In their hearts, and from their experiences in the USSR, grandparents believe that it is their obligation to care for their grandchildren. They will often overtire themselves doing a job they really do not want to do and are physically unable to do because they are incapable of saying no within the family context. Furthermore, their worst fear is to cause ill will or hardship on their children. Lera explains the latest glitch in the relationship between her husband's sister and their mother:

Mila has created a very big problem in the family. She has decided to go back to work. This is fine and okay, but what she does is bring Robert to her mother's and leaves him there. Now, Shura is not a well woman. She was having problems before her husband's death, but now it's even worse. She is very tired, very upset, and the doctor says the best medicine for her is calm, quiet, walks in the fresh air, and pleasure. . . . Poor Shura was woken up by him this morning at six o'clock, and ever since she has gotten no rest. How to tell this to Mila? She has already tried, but Mila gets insulted. You see, she thinks it's her *right*— that a grandmother must look after her grandchild. . . . She has no idea of how tired and sick her mother is. And also, she looks around and sees grandmothers with grandchildren everywhere and feels that this is her right, too.

Some grandparents do indeed assert their independence and move away from their children. This is frequently the case when three-generation families find homes in the suburbs. Elderly immigrants complain that their children are at work, their grandchildren in school, that there is no street life and no one to talk to. Life far from the Russian crowd, in the privacy of one's own luxurious home, is boring. Some simply pack up and find their own apartments in immigrant neighborhoods. A woman in her late thirties, when showing her spacious house to her guests, pointed to "mama's room" and commented:

> She only stays here about four times a year. She told us that she felt lonely and isolated here because we work, and the kids are in school, and she had nothing to do. So she found herself an apartment in Brighton where she has friends, stores, and things to do.

Brighton Beach is a particularly hospitable environment for the immigrant elderly. Prior to the arrival of Soviet Jewish émigrés, Brighton Beach had already become a geriatric community, composed primarily of Jews. According to the 1980 United States Census, the median age of three of the neighborhood's census tracts is over sixty (64.4, 64.2, and 62.8). The remaining three ranged from 37.5 to 54.8. The Federation of Jewish Philanthropies of New York's (1984) *New York Jewish Population Study,* based on data collected in 1981, reveals that 63 percent of all people in Brighton Beach households are Jews; 41 percent of them are fifty-five or older.

The neighborhood's institutions, businesses, and services are all geared toward an aging clientele. Doctors, dentists, and pharmacies solicit Medicaid and Medicare patients; grocers take food stamps and provide delivery services, and savings banks make direct-deposit arrangements with customers who receive monthly Social Security or SSI checks. Until the latter half of the 1980s, landlords eagerly took Section 8 tenants and set their rental rates accordingly. Local synagogues direct their activities to the elderly, and the Shorefront YM-YWHA has a wide array of programs geared to the senior set. In nice weather, the standard practice in Brighton Beach is for older folks to set up beach chairs in front of their buildings and relax outside on the sidewalk. The neighborhood is regularly watched by police officers and a volunteer neighborhood patrol.

During the 1970s and 1980s, in response to the influx of immigrants to the area, émigré businessmen opened their own shops along Brighton Beach Avenue, and long-standing enterprises began hiring Russian-speaking sales clerks. In addition, Russian-speaking medical doctors, real estate and insurance brokers, travel agents, and lawyers opened offices in the neighborhood. At the YM-YWHA, Project ARI (Action for Russian Immigrants), with aid from JASA (Jewish Association for Services to the Aged), established a seniors' program, offering English-language courses and weekly entertainment-social gatherings. For elderly Soviet Jewish immigrants, Brighton Beach is institutionally complete (Breton 1964).

Long-term Brighton Beach residents initially greeted "the Russians" with enthusiasm and viewed them as potential saviors of their Jewish neighborhood. The two groups have much in common—age, Eastern European background, Jewish identity, and knowledge of Yiddish. With time, however, the "Americans" developed resentment against the newcomers, whom they came to feel were "taking over," replacing kosher establishments with non-kosher ones and substituting Russian for English and Yiddish. Old-time Brighton Beach residents were surprised by and not a little jealous of the almost overnight prosperity of the new immigrants. They grumbled among themselves that when their parents, if not they themselves, arrived in the United States, they were not given pensions and welfare benefits. This sentiment is piqued by the immigrants' forthright display of their wealth in home furnishings, clothing, and jewelry. Living modest lives themselves, Brighton Beach's "American" elderly attribute their immigrant neighbors' economic success to chicanery and fraud. A long-term businessman (who finally retired by selling out to immigrants in 1985) explains:

> Just look around you, and you'll know right away that this place is filled with liars and cheats. Go to any bank manager here and ask how they get the money to open all their stores. All around us there is counterfeiting, lying, cheating. Just like Gromyko—he can stand up and tell you something, calmly, placidly, and you believe every word he says and then, he turns around and does the opposite. Look at them, they have millions! Counterfeiting, opening stores left and right—where do

you think they get this money? There's a complete sense of lawlessness here. Look, their old people stand on line for free cheese. Then, within an hour they're on the streets trying to sell this same cheese. They have businesses, yet they pay with food stamps and live in Section 8 houses.

Irina's mother, Raisa, in her sixties, interprets the situation quite differently. She, like many other former Soviet Jews, invests her money in her comfort. She believes that home is the most important place for any person but especially for those who in old age spend so much of their time there. Thus, one's apartment should be filled with luxurious furniture and pleasing decorations. As she relates below, the difference between Russian Jews and "old Polish Jews" (Americans) is that the latter deprive themselves by sticking every penny in the bank rather than creating surroundings for themselves. It is this terrible lifestyle that is responsible for them ending up miserable and alone. It is no wonder, she believes, that the "Americans" are jealous of the new immigrants:

> You know, I hear people now in Brighton saying, "Oh, the Russians are coming. They're coming again." They say this with no kindness or happiness. You know who I mean—the old Polish Jews who as soon as they have one dollar, take it immediately and put it in the bank. They are so jealous of us because we know how to live. Sure, our people take a dollar and buy themselves something nice to wear or put it into their apartment. Let me explain this to you. An apartment is our home, and home is where you spend your time, the pleasant, enjoyable, relaxing parts of life. It gives me great pleasure to come to this apartment, to sit in my throne-like armchairs, to look at my shelves, to have nice things around me. This is my home, the most important place on earth. What good does a few cents do in a bank account if all you ever do is grumble and complain about the way you are living? Yesterday, I was waiting for the bus, and this little old lady asked me, "Do you speak Yiddish?" Of course I do. And she starts to complain to me about her son who never visits and her bare apartment and all these Russians who are here for three years and have big cars and wear lots of jewelry. Who is she to complain if she takes every penny and puts it in the bank? I am sick of them!

As this statement suggests, Brighton Beach's "American" elderly resent not only the immigrants' material wealth but also the fact that "Russian" families remain close-knit. Many of these "American" Jews see their children, who long ago fled the neighborhood for suburbia, a couple of times a year at the most. Their émigré neighbors, however, always seem to have a grandchild in tow and several visitors. This resentment is more basic than economic disparity; Americans, who first considered themselves in a privileged position vis-à-vis new immigrants, come to see that it is indeed the newcomers who are more prosperous, emotionally as well as materially. Thus, on warm summer nights, when all of Brighton's old people sit outside their buildings or on the boardwalk, two distinct social groups form. The "Americans" speak together in English and listen to baseball games or popular music on the radio. The immigrants cluster together, speaking in Russian and listening to the news of the day from "Radio *Gorizont.*" Although both circles could join into one by communicating in Yiddish, they choose not to, and "Americans" and "Russians" remain two distinct social and linguistic groups.

Jealousy is not confined to the boundary between elderly American and Soviet immigrant Jews. Some émigrés speak with disgust about their older neighbors' "typical Soviet behavior," their desires to know everything about everyone around them, and then to discuss people's good fortune with resentment. From time to time these discussions take the form of telephone calls to the police department or social welfare agencies; sometimes the elderly take the same actions in the United States as they would have taken in the USSR to report untoward behavior. When Shura's husband died, she received a death benefit from the Social Security Administration. Several months after the funeral she decided to use this money to travel to Western Europe. Lera, her daughter-in-law, instructed me:

> Don't tell anyone. We want everyone to think she went upstate to rest. You still don't understand? Some of our people think it's their business to call Social Security to say this woman doesn't need a pension because she used the money to go to Europe.

Within the immigrant enclave, the elderly continue to live in a manner similiar to the way they lived in Russia, remaining vigilant in enforcing the will of the "collective" by monitoring their neighbors and themselves throughout the course of daily life. With the exception of two major differences—easy access to material goods and an avid interest in television programs like *Dynasty*—older Soviet immigrants have not greatly altered their daily routines, their roles within the family, or their notions of responsibility to society. Boris's description of his parents' post-migration experience sums up the situation: "My parents? Sure they've adapted. But not to America. To our Russian colony in Brighton Beach!"

Not all elderly immigrants, however, find homes in Brighton Beach, Flatbush, or Forest Hills, and not all the aged Soviet Jews in these neighborhoods are integrated into family or community life. Social service workers tell of disoriented old people whose children have abandoned them, who are frightened and unable to take care of themselves. There are also those, albeit a small proportion, who isolate themselves, refusing to enjoy the last years of their lives as they grieve for their lost homeland. Their loneliness and privation are their penance for abandoning their native country, the graves of their parents, the ideals of their youth, and the only life they ever knew. Yakov describes his wife's grandmother's situation:

> She has an apartment up on West 105th Street in Manhattan. We suggested that she move to Brighton; there she would feel more comfortable on the streets going shopping since she doesn't know English. We also suggested that she move in with us . . . but she has refused. Although she is miserable, I think she likes this misery, this self-imposed isolation. And it is completely self-imposed. She won't listen to anyone, and I am afraid that she is not alone, that there are many other older Russian immigrants who are living in this exact way—like the fact that they left the Soviet Union makes it so that they should not lead happy lives.

When elderly Soviet immigrants die, their next of kin calls one of several Jewish funeral homes that advertise in the Russian press to arrange for burial services.[29] The ease with which Jewish funerals are arranged in America contrasts with the highly stressful search for ritual specialists and gravesites that occurs in the Soviet Union. At the funeral of a friend's father, a young woman turned to me and reminisced about her grandfather's death in the West Ukraine:

> My mother called and got my grandfather's body from the hospital. There you can't trust anyone to do anything right, and what they would do with a body if it was sent right from the hospital to be buried, you

can't even imagine this. . . . I remember how afraid my mother was that it would not be done right, and how she had to bring the body home and find the right person to wash, dress, and pray over the body. Here you can breathe easy because they take the body right from the hospital and do everything right.

In America, the frenetic activity that surrounds funeral arrangements in the Soviet Union disappears because the easily accessible Jewish funeral home performs all obligatory rites. Anxiety attached to giving a loved one a proper Jewish burial thus is dissipated, but without the intense activity that occupies next of kin in the Soviet Union, their grief, guilt, and doubts about their own behavior toward their parents may be heightened.

Death of an elderly immigrant is a moment of reckoning for the survivors. As they look back upon the life of the deceased, they examine their own lives as well. Funeral services encourage this self-reflection by reminding the participants that death is their ultimate fate, yet the content of the ritual assures them that death is not cause for despair. The rabbi's personal eulogy of the deceased complements the intonation of ancient Judaic chants, informing survivors that their parent, and by extension they themselves, count both as individual human beings and as members of a larger ethnoreligious unit, the Jewish people.

Rabbis interview the next of kin before presenting a funeral eulogy. Their speeches call attention to the specific circumstances of Soviet Jewish émigrés. They address the individual's long and difficult life as a Soviet Jew and the hardship of being uprooted in old age. (Specific eulogy texts are presented in chapter 5.) After lauding the deceased for his or her life of trials, the rabbi ends his speech on an optimistic note, announcing to all present that their friend or relative has now "come home" to rest in peace among his or her own people. This theme is accentuated by the Hebrew prayers and benedictions said over the body at graveside.

The rabbi's final comforting words are very important for the survivors, who were, in the main, responsible for having their parents undergo a major transition in old age. Children experience pangs of guilt at their parents' death, because they know that their parents came to America to witness opportunities for future generations, not to live out their own desires. No matter how bad it may have been, the life their parents left behind was the only life they had ever known. At death, next of kin recognize and laud the elderly for this sacrifice.

At the same time as they reflect upon their feelings of guilt and sorrow, survivors feel relieved and self-righteous to have been able to bury their loved ones in America. Here they are assured of a correct Jewish funeral, and they can oversee the maintenance and care of their departed one's grave. Having emigrated allows them to grant their parent's last wish—interment in a Jewish cemetery accompanied by Judaic funerary rites.

The funeral, in reminding survivors of the difficult position of Jews in the Soviet Union, serves to reinforce the correctness of the émigrés' decision to emigrate. For the elderly who left behind everything they had ever known, the funeral reminds them that their former way of life was a tragic one and not to be mourned. The eulogies tell middle-aged adults that despite their initial disorientation and loss of social status, their lives in America hold greater promise of comfort and happiness than those they would have had in the Soviet Union. In burying the dead, the future for the younger generation looks brighter still, for in the funeral ritual, Soviet immigrants depict the differences between the easy and prosperous life of a Jew in America, and the difficult lives their parents—many of whom barely escaped genocide—lived as Russian Jews.

In death the decision to emigrate is vindicated, and the Russian Jewish immigrant community finds expression. Not only do friends and relatives come together to pay their last respects, but immigrants' gravesites and gravemarkers perpetuate the community. Soviet immigrants bury their dead in plots adjacent to each other, not scattered throughout the cemetery. New York's Jewish cemeteries now have "Russian colonies" within them, whole sections where tombstones are engraved with Cyrillic lettering. When they "come home to rest," Soviet immigrants choose to do so beside fellow Jews who also lived in the USSR, spoke Russian, and shared in the experience of emigration. Even after death émigrés demonstrate their group identity, manifesting the symbolic boundary on the ground, in their sections of the graveyard.

7.

THE ELUSIVE SHAPES OF COMMUNITY

A community, at least in the everyday sense of the word, exists on the ground—as a neighborhood or formal institutions—as well as in the hearts and minds of the people who constitute it. Most Soviet émigrés, however, have no formal affiliations with any type of organization. With no religious institutions or social service networks to transplant from their home country, it is difficult at first glance to pinpoint any formal structure that might unite Soviet immigrants in mutual assistance or for group expression. The elusiveness of this community is precisely what journalists, communal service workers, social analysts, and the immigrants themselves cite when they wonder aloud if a Soviet Jewish émigré community exists at all.

COMMUNITY WITHOUT ORGANIZATIONS

One of the most perplexing social characteristics of New York's Soviet Jewish émigrés is their reluctance to join preexisting communal organizations, coupled with their steadfast refusal to form voluntary associations of their own. Their lack of formal channels for self-help and sociability stands in stark contrast to the intricate web of organizations founded and patronized by their forebears in an earlier wave of immigration (see, e.g., Howe 1976; Kliger 1985) and, more generally, immigrants throughout the world (Fallers 1967).

Certainly the conditions that faced the established Jewish community of New York and Eastern European Jewish immigrants in the early 1900s differed dramatically from those of the 1970s and 1980s, during which time Soviet Jewish newcomers arrived at Kennedy Airport from their transit point in Rome into a much more than passively hospitable environment. As contemporary political refugees, former Soviet citizens are placed in a privileged position vis-à-vis other (economic) immigrants (see Pedraza-Bailey 1985). Like the Hungarians who fled their country after the attempted 1956 revolution, the Cubans who poured into Florida during the 1960s after Castro's victory, and recent immigrants from Southeast Asia escaping Communist regimes, Soviet refugees are furnished with material assistance and support services by the United States government, to facilitate their resettlement (see Haines 1985: 4–12). This ideologically motivated aid had very real economic and psychological consequences for the newcomers and set the tone for their acculturation experiences.

From this brief overview, it is easy to conclude that Soviet émigrés do not participate in pre-existing self-help organizations or create their own simply because they have no need to. It seems quite logical that, supported economically by the U.S. government and Jewish communal organizations in their initial months of resettlement, granted medical insurance, food stamps, and housing stipends, Jews from the USSR would not establish replicas of the *landsmanschaft,* the typical turn-of-the-century Jewish mutual-aid society.

But this logic tells only part of the story, because despite the refugee resettlement assistance provided to them, Cambodians, Laotians, and Vietnamese are prolific in forming self-help societies (see Montero 1979; Indochinese Refugee Action Center 1981; Dunnigan 1982, 131; Dunnigan and Olney 1985, 122; Ebihara 1985, 141; Van Esterick 1985, 163–164), and Cuban-Americans not only participate in mutual-assistance organizations but have also formed strong political lobbies (Boswell and Curtis 1983, 169–173, 175–178; also Portes and Bach 1985, 304–305).

Other immigrant groups, such as the highly educated urban-to-urban migrants from India and Korea, have also created and actively participate in their own credit associations, social organizations, and political lobbies (see Fisher 1978, 1980; Kim 1981). To explain why Soviet immigrants have not done that which virtually all other immigrant groups have done,[1] it becomes necessary to explore the meanings Soviet émigrés attach to organizations and to describe their revulsion at bureaucracy. These meanings and their values taken in concert create a different kind of community—a community without organizations—than is usually formed by immigrant groups.[2]

It is important to reiterate, for a moment, that to be a person in the USSR was to make sense of and manage glaring contradictions. The sharp contrast between the icy, expressionless "Soviet face" of public life and the warm, effusive smiles among friends is, according to Soviet émigrés, a perfectly natural phenomenon "for there," where "bureaucratic encounters" (DiFrancisco and Gitelman 1984) are hostile and only close friends and family are safe. Many people in the USSR (everyone, as the immigrants tell it) devised ways to "get back at the system," and stealing from the state, that is, helping oneself to the products of the people's—logically one's own—factory, store, commercial enterprise, became a matter of course. Although defined as illegal in the codex of law and immoral in Marxist-Leninist ideology, such on-the-job pilfering was generally recognized by Soviet citizens as neither crime nor sin but as a rightfully deserved bonus in a system that promises much but delivers little.[3] In the post-war years, suspicion of the public sector grew, as Soviet citizens increasingly came to view bureaucracy, the collective, and the state as stumbling blocks rather than the means for fulfilling their needs and wishes, and people turned more and more to the private domain to satisfy their material and emotional needs (see chapter 4; Shlapentokh 1989).

The knowledge that the sociopolitical system in which one lives is a bundle of contradictions at best and a bald-faced lie at worst produces a certain kind of person. This person is not the New Socialist Man envisioned by the Soviet Union's founding fathers but more closely resembles a split personality enshrouded in duplicity. Suspicious of the state, of bureaucracy in all its forms, Soviet citizens assume an expressionless pose for the public. While some émigrés had taken active roles in *Komsomol* and then joined the Communist party, they did so primarily to advance their careers, not from a sense of political commitment. "Plain and simple," several émigrés told me, "that system produces liars and cheats. You have to feel sorry for them; they have no other choice."

Steadfast in this belief, Soviet-born Jews view social activists, especially those from within their own group, with a jaundiced eye.

Boris explains, "We learned from our experiences with so many Jew-ish Bolshevik leaders. We saw what kind of revolution they made." Immigrants are often happy to share their uncomplimentary opinions about prominent (former) refuseniks and "self-proclaimed leaders of Russian Jews." Some of the kinder commentators accuse these activ-ists of blind idealism doomed to end in failure. More often, however, remarks focus on activists' desires for attention, self-aggrandizement, and financial gain. From all this talk one message emerges: If people truly wish to help one another, they can—and should—do so quietly, personally, by giving of their hearts, souls, minds, and pocketbooks. Seeking publicity and forming organizations lead only to bureaucracy and hierarchy, which hurt, rather than help, the person in need.

It was precisely this type of assistance, associated with the pri-vate, personal domain, that Soviet Jewish émigrés expected from the American Jewish community when they arrived in New York. And, in the main, what they found instead was bureaucracy.

Soviet Jews, as political refugees, receive substantial material assistance from the U.S. government. The American state does not, however, dispense its benefits directly to them; it contracts instead on a matching-funds basis with Jewish social service agencies. In New York City, NYANA (New York Association for New Americans), a nonprofit organization funded by the national United Jewish Appeals campaign, directs and oversees the initial phases of Soviet refugee resettlement.

HIAS (Hebrew Immigrant Aid Society) and the Joint Distribu-tion Committee (which assist Soviet Jewish refugees in transit in Vi-enna and Rome), NYANA, and agencies funded by the Federation of Jewish Philanthropies of New York throughout New York City are the professionalized descendants of earlier Jewish self-help and welfare organizations. Following biblical injunctions to perform charitable deeds, these agencies have a mandate to provide material assistance and social services to immigrants and other Jews and non-Jews in need. But social workers and other staff who worked with recent Soviet arrivals in these settings were unprepared for Soviet Jews to be the type of "refugee" they are—secularized Russian-speakers in-tensely concerned with finding well-paying jobs in their professions, nice housing, and good schooling for their children (see Brodsky 1983; Dublin 1977; Hawks 1977; Rubin 1975). Moreover, they were surprised at what they perceived as the immigrants' demanding attitudes and developed negative impressions of them as self-seeking opportunists who wanted something for nothing.

Immigrants, in turn, were shocked at what they experienced as bureaucratic processing and grudging assistance from Jewish personnel:

> NYANA's biggest mistake is the way they give advice. They certainly did a lot for us, for our people. But the way they do this is completely without warmth, without caring, in a tone that we expect to hear from Soviet bureaucrats, but not from our Jews. This was a big disappointment. And they don't give us the kind of information we need. They all tell us that we must start from the bottom on account of language, and then they don't give us all the language we need. . . . It was a hard decision to leave, and then to be told that you are going to go backward instead of forward is even worse. It's this kind of manner and attitude on the part of NYANA that did a lot to embitter our immigrants. Show and provide training and instruction, and, most of all, warmth.

This antagonism between clients and providers also characterizes immigrants' experiences with the Jewish communal agencies in their neighborhoods. Wherever they settled, émigrés were urged, through the Russian-language press, flyers, and brochures, to make use of neighborhood organizations and the services they offer. Many synagogues and YM-YWHAs offered newcomers free membership for their first year in America. In areas that received a large influx of new immigrants, well-meaning residents initiated "Russian projects" to assist their new neighbors in the secondary phases of resettlement. However, along with such helpful services and social activities, Soviet Jewish immigrants are often given a distinct message that they are unworthy of such assistance.

On the one hand, then, the American Jewish community offers continuing resettlement services to Soviet émigrés, while, on the other, it expresses indignation that these immigrants make use of the proffered assistance. Agency administrators are perplexed by what they perceive as the immigrants' continuing dependence and wonder why they have not established self-help organizations of their own. Soviet émigrés respond to this double bind by referring to their prior knowledge of bureaucracy and may come to equate institutions of the "Jewish community" with the hostile maze of government offices in the

Soviet Union. Their experiences with unsympathetic staff reinforce the belief that all bureaucracies, including "our Jewish NYANA" and neighborhood centers, are either something to avoid or something from which to get as much as possible without owing anything in return. Thus, while they provided Soviet Jewish immigrants with support services, these Jewish welfare agencies may have thwarted the development of mutual-assistance societies among the newcomers and indirectly impeded affiliation with American Jewish institutions (see also Gold 1992, 227). Moreover, they reinforced and perhaps increased the immigrants' suspicions of formal institutions (see Gold 1987).

Several years after their initial experiences with the American Jewish communal network, Soviet immigrants, for the most part, continue to shun involvement with formal organizations.[4] Many refer to the so-called volunteer work they did in the Soviet Union—as students laboring summers on *kolkhozy* (collective farms) and as members of the workforce contributing their time for *subbotniki* (free-labor Saturdays) "whether we wanted to or not"—and near-mandatory participation in a multitude of citizens' committees as reasons for non-participation in American organizations. Most agree with Vladimir's assessment of the situation: "We don't want to spend our time in meetings anymore. We had it up to our necks over there. Now our time is our own." (See Gold 1985, 126, 153–156, 300, who finds the Soviet Jewish immigrants of San Francisco uninterested in forming or participating in formal organizations.)

Some immigrants, however, are unhappy with what they view as selfishness and lack of initiative on the part of their peers. They see a deficit of self-help organizations as indicative of a lack of communal spirit. Pavel, contrasting fellow Soviet émigrés with Korean immigrants, expresses a dim view of his group:

There is something about our people that makes them take the easy way out. . . . Russians are taught to be followers, not to initiate, not to innovate, but to follow, to be quiet and take the easiest way out. . . . No one really helps anyone else in this community except maybe family. There is no feeling of community; each person is running so fast to accumulate wealth for himself—to buy more jewelry and sausages—that no one else matters. I hate this so much I cannot even express this to you. I told you from my job that I have mostly American and Oriental friends. I love the Korean people—they are such hard workers and they know how to help each other. . . . As soon as Koreans come here to New York they go just exactly and immediately to their church . . . in these churches every member gives something like fifty or a hundred dollars, which goes into a general fund, and this fund is used by newcomers to open their own businesses . . . and then they put the money back and someone else uses these funds to open their shop. This is the way it should be—people helping each other like one community to get started.

What Pavel did not consider in his discussion, although he is well aware of it, is that as individual Soviet immigrants turn inward to their personal and family interests, they are forging friendship networks that, as in the USSR, are easily convertible into mutual-aid associations. To make down-payments on cars, houses, small businesses, to buy stereo equipment, television sets, or home furnishings, or to tide the family over in times of unemployment or failed business ventures, Soviet Jewish immigrants look to friends and kin for financial help. Trust, derived from sentiment and reciprocity, shared experiences and expectations, motivates and underwrites these loans. When requests are made, money is delivered in cash within days if not hours, and no promissory note is signed. Not only do immigrants share money, they also help old friends, and friends of friends, find jobs and places to live, accompany them to government offices, in short, assist them through the maze of acculturation. Denial of assistance is tantamount to rejection of friendship.

The very idea of formalizing these helping-friendship networks is anathema, for it undermines the egalitarian and trustworthy nature of social bonds that permit free giving and acceptance of assistance. Thus, when a credit union opened in 1984 under the name of an all-but-defunct immigrant organization, many émigrés grumbled among themselves that its founder was seeking self-aggrandizement and business opportunities rather than to provide a needed service for his community. Several people, nonetheless, investigated the possibility of procuring a loan. After obtaining information about the credit union's policies, procedures, and interest rates, Lera decided against this idea, explaining that its terms were not competitive with the commercial savings and loan institution in the neighborhood and also that "it's not a good idea to deal with Russians in these situations. In a day, all of Brighton will know our business." By the latter part of 1987, this credit union had closed.

While most immigrants do not participate at all in organizations, do not care to and evince no concern that they do not have a formal structure of mutual aid, a counter-tendency has emerged among a small number of émigrés who are attempting to play active roles in neighborhood and cultural affairs. The first concerted effort to this effect occurred at the height of immigration (1979–80), with the formation of JURI (Jewish Union of Russian Immigrants). A voluntary organization, it was developed by émigré staff with the encouragement of the American-born project director at a neighborhood Russian service center. Not long after JURI began to gain momentum, key members concluded that their organization and the funded Russian project duplicated each other's efforts and suggested that the two merge under the auspices of JURI. A power struggle developed between the two groups, and by 1984 nothing remained of JURI but a name and a letterhead. JURI is periodically revived by individual members; most recently its name was used to obtain funding from Federation of Jewish Philanthropies of New York for the federally sponsored credit union mentioned above.

In 1986 another effort at organizing Soviet émigrés to participate in community affairs showed signs of self-destruction before it even got off the ground. Responding to a call for "community leaders" by the same neighborhood Russian project, a number of successful émigré professionals and business people met and announced that they would be willing to donate money, if not time, to community service. Some of Brighton Beach's restaurateurs offered to host an organizational/fundraising dinner to attract more volunteers. Orthodox rabbis, social workers, and others involved in the Jewish Community Council, a co-sponsor of this nascent self-help group, rejected the offer because Russian restaurants do not subscribe to Jewish dietary laws. They suggested instead the shabby meeting rooms of the local YM-YWHA. The struggle went on for almost a year before the idea was abandoned.[5]

A somewhat different dynamic characterizes the formation of cultural organizations among Soviet émigrés. Initial resettlement services, vocational counseling, and English-language courses provided Soviet immigrants with the basic instrumental skills necessary for getting along in American society; with time, many found themselves materially well off but in something of a cultural void. Outside of their own books, video cassettes, and occasional concerts, some émigrés feel frustrated that they lack a forum for experiencing and expressing ties to the high culture they love. To remedy this state of affairs, every so often small groups of immigrants come together, and some even try to develop formal organizations, to enhance their connections to Russian literary and artistic traditions.

In late 1984, a new organization, the Cultural Center for Refugees from the Soviet Union, was created. Galina, an architect who emigrated in the mid-1970s and one of its founding members, explains why now, several years after the peak of immigration, she believes there is a strong need for such an organization:

> There are many people in this emigration who are dying for a place to express themselves, to express their Russian Jewish culture. . . . People came here, let's say five, seven years ago. When they first come, they are completely in love with America and everything American . . . but even those with American friends begin to feel that there is something missing. I would say after two, three years, people begin to feel that they would like to associate again with people in their native language with similar experiences. And then it is sometimes hard to find the same kind of people as oneself. . . . What I think is—it is important to have a good presentation to attract people, but what is more important is to have a place where people can meet and talk to each other.

Although immigrants frequently complain to each other about their lack of clubs, poetry circles, or artistic associations, many are skeptical if not downright cynical about the long-term possibility of the Cultural Center. Their negative reactions to the idea and predictions for this organization's failure are based on experience with past efforts at forming such clubs. Further, they emphasize as factors operating against the success of such a venture time constraints due to work and the variety and abundance of entertainment that America has to offer. Three people, Vladimir, Maxim, and a poet/translator express their negative opinions of the Cultural Center:

> Not enough people will be interested in this, especially in the center of Manhattan. No one has time for this anymore. People work all day. They are busy. They are tired. And here they have other forms of entertainment. Sure, in Russia they would talk and talk, but America is a country of action.

Participate? Absolutely not! This is, of course, just my personal opinion, but I don't think there will be enough people to make this continue. I think it's a little sick and ugly to try to continue what went on in the past. As for me, I have no time for this sort of thing at all. When I have the time I would rather spend it with close friends or with someone entirely new, Americans. I have no desire to sit around with them and drink wine. Maybe I would come if someone interesting is giving a presentation, but I am not interested in re-creating what was over there. I am too busy and I have a new life here.

This won't work anyway. Oh yes, it will get started and there will be a few nice events. But it won't last in the long run. I know this from experience with another club that was formed about five or so years ago when immigration was at its peak. It gave a few nice concerts, and then, that was it.

The Cultural Center staged four events in the first six months of 1985. The first two performances attracted large crowds, including two of the speakers quoted above. A film showing in May, however, drew only thirty people, all but a few of whom were over age fifty. The founders, undaunted, have incorporated as a nonprofit organization and applied for funding from local and state granting agencies. After a hiatus in offerings, the center staged a very successful performance in 1986 and cosponsored an exhibit of paintings and a poetry reading in 1987. They have also published some Russian-language books of émigré/dissident literature and are seeking to purchase a building for their permanent home.

Whether or not the Cultural Center can sustain itself remains to be seen. Its likelihood for success, however, seems more certain than an increase in Soviet émigrés' participation in Jewish communal organizations or the creation of formal mutual-aid societies. First, the Cultural Center is in no way connected with any other organization that can influence its policies or offerings. Second, and perhaps more important, is the strong value among many immigrants for continuing involvement with Russian culture. This, coupled with the minimal commitment of time and resources that going to a poetry reading or film screening a few times a year entails, ensures a small audience at the very least, for the center's offerings. The center's success is ultimately dependent on its founding members' continuing sense of mission to provide interesting offerings for themselves and fellow émigrés, as well as their own personal ties to others in the community. But it, too, will probably come to be seen—if it is not already—as just another choice in the range of entertainment pursuits, not as a vital rallying point or institution that will harness the energies of and make tangible the Russian Jewish immigrant community.

"Community," Robert Nisbet wrote in the 1969 preface to *Quest for Community*, "thrives on self-help . . . and everything that removes a group from the performance of or involvement in its own government can hardly help but weaken the sense of community. People do not come together in significant and lasting association merely to be together. They come together to do something that cannot easily be done in individual isolation."

As I have described it, the case of Soviet Jewish immigrants directly challenges Nisbet's statement. The community that they have constructed is by no means based on purposive action, institution building, or the consolidation of political power. Instead, it derives its value and strength from a personalistic orientation resting on shared knowledge, sentiments, and sociability. For Soviet Jewish émigrés, the community is the place—or arena of social relations—where individuals seek and receive verification of their personalities, preferences, and prejudices, and confirmation of the strategies they employ to create a new life in America. Past attempts to change the character of this community have ended in failure, and it remains likely that aggressive efforts by "self-appointed leaders" to aim the community toward institutionalized formal goals would either be ignored or fall apart after initial planning efforts.

Self-government, contrary to Nisbet's insistence, is not something that Soviet émigrés want. They are content to live as citizens, or citizens-to-be, in a country that sets limits for the public domain but does not control their personal lives. Within these perfectly acceptable boundaries, Soviet Jewish émigrés gather into a barely visible anarchistic community, one that is indeed directed at the simple goal of "coming together."[6] To this end, Soviet immigrants form a sociosymbolic community without organizations, created and maintained in defensive reaction to a new linguistic, social, and political environment and in response to their own strong value for informal, egalitarian relationships based on affect and trust. Its unofficial, anarchistic character and its lack of any strong institutions or formal organizations are crucial factors that make the community viable, although barely visible, for its members.

COMMUNITY AS SYMBOL, THE SYMBOLS OF COMMUNITY

Soviet Jewish émigrés constitute a community without organizations but within which they conduct mutual assistance and social activities on an informal basis according to individual needs or desires and groupwide understandings. The expressive side of their community follows the same pattern; Soviet immigrants participate in what they consider overtly "Russian" activities sporadically, in response to special occasions, personal longings, crises, and extraordinary events. The ways by which these individuals come together to articulate and reaffirm what it means to be "Russian" (Soviet-Russian-Jewish-immigrant) in New York make real the symbolic boundaries of this community and shape the contents of its meaning.

Two basic means of expression are available to Soviet immigrants for public display of their Russian-ness. One of these is the Russian nightclub-restaurant, where "Russian" food and vodka are liberally served and émigré orchestras play an assortment of "Russian," American, Italian, and Jewish music.[7] Reservations, instructions to waiters, and requests to the orchestra are all conducted in the Russian language, as are conversations around the long banquet tables. Although increasingly popular for the general public, these restaurants, twelve of which are clustered in the Brighton Beach area, are designed specifically for, and owned and operated by, "Russian" immigrants.

The other expressive form available to émigrés is the Russian cultural (literary, musical) event. Unlike the restaurants, some of which are open seven days a week, others of which serve the public on weekends only, concerts, poetry readings, and commemorative presentations occur intermittently, and each event is usually held just once. Participation in this arena of expressive ethnicity requires that one keep informed, through a network of friends, the Russian-language media, or both. It demonstrates a strong commitment to maintaining links with high Russian culture.

As is readily apparent, and not at all surprising, these two public means of expressing identification with the "Russian" community manifest a key tension, or what Kai Erikson (1976, 82) calls an "axis of variation" within émigré culture: the conflict between materialism, on the one hand, and dedication to the arts and sciences, on the other. It is this slide back and forth along the hedonistic-*meshchanstvo/* spiritualistic-*intelligentsiia* continuum that provides symbolic unity within the community and inspires the creation of satisfying expressive forums through which individuals can articulate their membership in this community.

Russian restaurants exemplify to an extreme the core value of hospitality, as they provide their patrons with comfort and sensual pleasures to excess. These restaurants are decorated with plush wallpaper, mirrors, flashing lights inlaid in the dance floor, long dining tables draped in linen and covered with china and flowers. Each of these tables is laden with a wide variety of colorful dishes of food in enormous portions, fruit baskets, and bottles of alcoholic and soft drinks. Food is consumed throughout the night, and vodka and brandy flow freely. The live music is loud and joyful, and couples crowd the dance floor to join in the merriment.

It is difficult to say what one notices first upon entering a Russian restaurant, the decor of the room or the dress of its clientele. Women arrive heavily made-up in shiny lipstick and thick, black mascara. Their hair is carefully coiffed, and they wear high-fashion evening dresses, often sequined or brightly colored. Plunging necklines, tight skirts, and high-heeled shoes are very much in evidence. Women are further decorated with sparkling earrings, necklaces, bracelets, and thick rings made of gold and gemstones. The men favor Italian suits, but some wear leather pants with open-collared European style shirts or fashionable knit pullover sweaters. They too wear jewelry—gold watches and neckchains and sometimes diamond rings. The air is redolent with a mixture of men's and women's perfumes blending with the scents of flowers and food. Lera describes her first visit to one of Brighton Beach's night spots: "Unbelievable! Waterfalls and waterfalls of diamonds! Where do they get such jewels? Waterfalls and waterfalls!"

People spend a long time at home preparing for a night in a Russian restaurant because, as another woman, six years in America, explains, immigrants go to Russian restaurants not only to enjoy the food and the music but to see and be seen: "If we were going to an American restaurant, we would be ready in no time. But we're going to a Russian restaurant—so we must get all dressed up."

The restaurants are institutionalized showplaces that bring Soviet émigrés together from all over. They attract their clientele, at least in part, because they provide arenas in which individuals can demonstrate success and measure themselves in terms of their fellow émigrés. In addition to the display of material success via personal adornment, the restaurant scene provides its clients with two other demonstrative avenues.

There is a semiotics of Russian restaurants, an understanding among immigrants of the meaning each establishment holds within the broader scheme. While the decor and the dinner courses all follow a similar pattern, some restaurants are more expensive and plush than others, some attract a more refined clientele, some serve higher-quality food. Everyone knows which restaurants charge eighteen dollars per person and which ones charge twenty-five, where the young, rich people go and where criminals congregate, so that the initial selection of a restaurant tells much about one's real or desired financial and social status. Restaurant owners also permit customers to order additional dishes to supplement the more than ample *prix fixe* meal; when a shellfish course appears, guests take note of this extra touch, and the added expense that their host has incurred increases his prestige.

The orchestra encourages yet another route for wealth display and generosity by accepting gratuities to play customers' requests. A young black female singer with a Russian band explains:

> I love it. I work here three days a week, and the money I make, well, it takes me through the whole week. They give me a salary, but that's not important. It's the tips. And sometimes—those tips! I've worked a lot of clubs before coming here, but this is the best. *Davai dengi* [give money]—I learned that!

Some orchestras "charge" more for English or Italian songs than for Russian ones and for playing the request immediately rather than at any time during the night. Victor elaborates:

> I will give you an example. You know, to buy a song usually costs maybe five or ten dollars normally. I went with some friends for a birthday . . . to [this restaurant], and my friends wanted to buy a

song—a popular Italian song. Since it was one of the most popular Italian songs, the band told them it would cost fifty dollars.

In dedicating a song to a friend or relative, the donor not only displays affection for the honoree but also demonstrates material success and generosity.

Evenings in Russian restaurants blend core values of generosity and hospitality with the belief that money is *the* measure of success in America, so that consumption and give-aways constitute much of the activity. It matters greatly to Soviet immigrants, who have lost their original sense of place and social status, that they have attained so much in such a short time. And they derive satisfaction from showing off and sharing these attainments with fellow émigrés for whom this material success has deep meaning. In these restaurants immigrants receive confirmation for the occupational choices they have made and for pursuing the idea that "more is better." The *meshchanin,* the nouveau riche materialist in everyone, can emerge openly, and whether or not one is privately disgusted or ashamed by such a quality, the restaurant scene gives it public approval and lets each individual know that he or she is not alone. Victor summarizes the powerful attraction these establishments hold for him:

Each time I go into a Russian store and have all those people pushing and acting impolitely, and each time I go to a Russian restaurant and see people drinking too much and acting like buffoons I say to myself, "This is the last time." And before I know it, I'm back. I don't really know why, except that I'm still a stranger here, and these Russian places make me feel part of something.

Just as Russian restaurants provide an opportunity to partake of the materialistic-hedonistic side of Russian culture, concerts, poetry readings, and lectures given by émigrés and occasionally Soviet performers enable people to express identification with the intelligentsia. In recent years (1984–86), some of these concerts have disappointed their audiences, leaving people with a greater feeling of cultural marginality than they had before the performance.[8] This, coupled with competition from an enormous range of leisure time activities offered in New York, not the least of which are one's own color television and VCR, explains why occasional concerts and literary evenings do not always draw large audiences. There are several exceptions to this rule: the Soviet poet Andrei Voznesensky drew an almost full house of predominantly young (under forty-five) people when he gave a recitation in 1985; a day of lectures and performances in memory of Solomon Mikhoels, the founder and main actor of the Moscow State Yiddish Theater, attracted over two hundred people; and Joseph Brodsky's 1986 poetry reading commanded an over-capacity crowd. Ordinarily, concerts and other cultural events at local Jewish centers attract about fifty to one hundred people, most of whom are middle-aged and older.

On February 11, 1985, a previously announced "literary evening sponsored by the journal *Mir*," at the Bensonhurst Jewish Community House drew an audience of well over two hundred people, over-flowing the auditorium. This was to be no ordinary poetry reading, however, for two days earlier, Alexander Alon, an émigré songwriter, had been killed in a freakish robbery at the quiet suburban home of an immigrant businesswoman where he was a guest. His murder served as an impetus for many to rethink who they are and how they might be united into a community.

On February 10, the lead story on "Radio Horizons" was a re-port of Alon's murder, and local New York television news broadcasts announced the crime as well. It was also reported on February 10 and 11 in New York's three daily newspapers and in *Novoye Russkoye Slovo*. At no time were public announcements made of a memorial service in Alon's honor; but on Sunday morning, February 11, tele-phone lines were busy throughout New York with émigrés telling each other, "It was decided that at three o'clock this afternoon in the Jewish center in Bensonhurst there will be a memorial service for Alon."

Alexander Alon's murder was not the first to occur among Soviet émigrés. In July 1984, a father of five got into a brawl with an off-duty police officer at his Queens housing project and was fatally shot. In October 1984, a thirty-seven-year-old émigré woman and her twelve-year-old son were found stabbed to death in their Brooklyn apart-ment. Newspaper accounts revealed that the man murdered in 1984 had sometimes abused his wife and was periodically unemployed, and conjectures about the mother-and-son murder linked this deed to the husband-father's involvement with "Russian mafia" loan sharks. While both of these murders received ample coverage in the Russian-language and mainstream press and were heatedly discussed among immigrants, no public commemorative services or demonstrations were held in these people's honor. In contrast, the literary figures who had long planned to read their works on February 11 quickly decided to open their program with a memorial service honoring Alon. Poet, soldier, loyal friend, and hard-working husband, his persona encapsulates how Soviet Jewish immigrants envision themselves.

After tearful greetings among friends, the program began with opening remarks from the editor of *Mir;* seated on stage with this man was an assemblage of poets, prose writers, and journalists, almost all of whom were dressed in dark grey or black:

> We have planned for some time to have this literary evening for the magazine *Mir,* to have an evening of poetry. But we will start today with a memorial service for Sasha Alon. It is very difficult for us today. Sasha was a genuine human being [*nastoyashchii chelovek*]. He led a beautiful life—a songwriter, a poet. . . . Let us now stand for a moment of silence for him.

As everyone stood, sobs and sniffles could be heard throughout the room. The editor resumed, "Yesterday the poet Boris Vetrov wrote a poem for him, which will now be read."

A diminutive blonde woman, a former actress in the USSR, a frequent performer at Russian émigré cultural events and a close friend of Alon, stood to recite the poem. Her husband accompanied her recitation by playing a Rachmaninoff piece on the piano.

> To Alexander Alon[9]
> I today
> again choked from pain
> I today—
> like a bitter, piercing
> moan.
> why, oh why
> did all of this happen to you:
> A poet.
> And a soldier,—
> Alexander Alon?

The Heaven of Yom Kippur
above you blazed
And the earth burned
But you were left to live,
And cursing
the bullet
which today
Here in New York
reached you.

And . . . a ragged string
Did not sing till the end,
You were killed at your take-off
Indeed, poets of the
Very first rank, always
Have such a fate
To live,
Like a grenade among a platoon.
There
Father will fall
And . . . will freeze to death in tears.

To never forget
Only perhaps through words
Can we communicate our pain,
Of the heart, this sorrow.
Forever,
Forever
You
Will remain with us
As a poet,
And a soldier,—
Alexander Alon!

The actress read in a quivering voice, choking back tears until her reading was almost complete. In the audience, several people, men and women, wept. One woman, sobbing, shook her head and declared, "He was so young, so talented, and we were just with him one week ago." When she completed her reading, the actress, wiping away tears, proclaimed, "He lived a wonderful life. He was surely a man of God. And as the Bible says, what God gives, God takes away. We will never have him again, but his songs, we will have always." She then swooned into her chair and dabbed her eyes with a handkerchief.

The next speaker, a journalist who had recently interviewed Alon for *Novoye Russkoye Slovo,* reminisced:

> He was in the tradition of Vysotsky . . . he wrote in that same style of the bards. I never thought that my article and my interview would be his last—such a horrible catastrophe! He least of all was preparing to die—to be a poet, and studying computer programming. He always lived with vigor. And as he lived, so he touched us.
>
> Each one of his songs was pure gold. Thirty-one years old, and one week ago he was my guest, and he sang for my guests. Listen to Sasha Alon as he played a few days ago.

Two of his songs were played, complicated texts set to simple melodies, one in honor of Jerusalem, the other dedicated to his wife. The women on stage wept as they listened to his voice, and others in the audience cried, too. One turned to another and commented, "He left the Soviet Union at age eighteen and lived twelve years in Israel. Listen—his Russian language is so beautiful, so good—unbelievable!"

At the songs' end, the editor of *Mir* admonished the audience, "We shall never forget this poet, Sasha Alon, who wrote such wonderful verse." He then called for a break, and the entire audience, all dressed simply in dark or neutral-colored clothes, moved into an adjoining room for coffee and cookies. They clustered in small groups and shared their shock and horror at Alon's murder.

The journal editor resumed the program by focusing his eulogy of Alon not on his poetry but on his military service during the Yom Kippur war in Israel:

> Everyone was in the synagogue when it started. No one was prepared for the horror of warfare on this day, and it was terrible. And Sasha Alon served in this war. . . . Sasha—was a wonderful person, a great person, and still, so young.

Then he changed the theme of his speech and talked about the literary journal *Mir.* About twenty minutes into his presentation, people around the room signalled to each other to leave, "Let's get out of here! Let's go! We are all going over to Nina's."

Moving the event from the public domain of the Jewish center to the private arena of Nina's apartment did not break the spirit of the evening. At its height, about sixty people, including the editor of *Mir* and the entire assemblage of performers, gathered in Nina's living room, where she had erected a shrine on a small round table. On this table she had placed a color photograph of Alon with guitar in hand, flanked by two white candles in silver candlesticks. In front of the photo Nina had set a jigger of vodka, and in front of that a small plate holding a crêpe folded into a triangle.[10] Meanwhile, vodka was being poured into small glasses for all present, and women were bringing food and plates out onto the dining table.

Nina, slumped in an armchair beside the small table, raised a brandy snifter, poured herself some Jack Daniels bourbon, called for attention, lit the two candles, and declared:

> He was our hero. This to me is evident. In general, life in migration is difficult for all of us. He made it better for us. I was always so afraid for him. Sometimes I would see him and just hug him and shake him and say, "Please Sasha, please." It was just too good to be true, and I was always so afraid, somehow, that we would lose him.

She compared Alon to the nineteenth-century Russian poets Lermontov and Pushkin, "who, unhappily for Russian literature, died too at early ages from unnatural causes," and in the same breath called Alon a "bard in the tradition of Vysotsky.[11] He was the spirit of our migration. He will always be in our hearts." She ended her speech by looking straight at her guests, raising her glass, and proclaiming, "We have lost you, Sasha. Now we are all we have left, and we must look to each other and draw closer to go on."

Sasha Alon arrived in the United States from Israel toward the latter part of 1983 and had just begun to gain recognition in émigré circles as a singer and poet. He had been publishing his verses in *Novoye Russkoye Slovo* and giving concerts at Jewish centers and friends' homes. In addition, he was learning computer programming in order to better support himself and his wife. Unlike the murder victims of 1984, Alon was an intellectual who had led an exemplary life. He was a soldier and a poet, a man of peace and song who did not shirk his duty to provide for and defend his family, his friends, and his people.

Sherry Ortner (1978, 3) notes that rituals "begin with some cultural problem (or several at once), stated or unstated, and then work various operations upon it, arriving at solutions—reorganizations and reinterpretations of the elements that produce a newly meaningful whole." Death is always a moment of crisis and reevaluation, but one person's death is usually not enough to pull a community together. Sasha Alon's murder struck deep in the hearts of Soviet émigrés because it unleashed problematic questions that are usually repressed but never stray too far from the surface.

The murder was a catalyst for immigrants to reexamine continuing insecurities about their lives in America. Alon did not die in a way all could envision and anticipate; he was not murdered after dark in a rough New York City neighborhood. He was, after all, a guest in a private home on Long Island. Soviet immigrants work long and hard to earn large sums of money with which to buy status, prestige, and security, and many aspire to own homes in suburbia. Now their reasons for amassing large sums of money were challenged by Alon's freakish murder. The murder confirmed what many knew but wished not to recognize—that nothing in (American) life, not even that which money can buy, is certain. In reminding themselves of this truth, they reminded themselves as well to temper their materialistic strivings and reassert their intellectual leanings.

The senseless irony of the death of a combat veteran in a peaceful home was rationalized by placing Alon alongside great Russian poets who also met untimely deaths. But this linking of Alexander Alon to the heights of Russian culture did more than rationalize his early demise. It joined Soviet immigrants to the cultural heritage from which they find themselves increasingly removed but with which they strongly identify. Alon, who, after leaving the USSR at the age of eighteen, continued to write lyrical poetry in the best of Russian traditions until his death at thirty-one, became a tangible symbol of the *intelligent* for all Soviet Jewish émigrés to emulate. If he was able to preserve his *intelligentnost,* his spirituality, his "beautiful Russian language" while serving as a soldier in Israel and becoming a computer programmer in New York, so, too, can they remain part of Russian intellectual life. Taking part in this memorial service for Sasha Alon allowed each person the opportunity to come together with fellow émigrés to mourn a collective loss and, in so doing, to express and solidify their membership in a community.

As territorial boundaries and social ties become attenuated in large urban centers, immigrants and ethnics increasingly find the strength of community in its "repositories of meaning" (Cohen 1985, 98) rather than as a social structure. These meanings—the themes, values, and goals that unify and lend coherence to geographically scattered individuals' lives—usually lie dormant or only latently inform everyday goings-on. They reach overt expression sporadically as what Herbert Gans (1979) calls "symbolic ethnicity" or, in a more diluted version of the same phenomenon, what Moshe Shokeid (1988, 99–103) labels "one-night-stand-ethnicity," through social displays, rituals, and performances in designated settings. How and where people express their ethnic identification and what particular traits are designated as deeply meaningful through such displays provide valuable insights into the nature of community among any group.

Soviet Jewish immigrants shape and articulate their collective identity through two overlapping constellations of expressive forms, Jewish rituals and "Russian" social dramas. As they play out their material success in the context of a Russian restaurant and exhibit their involvement with Russian high culture through attendance at a concert or "literary evening," Soviet émigrés make real and reaffirm groupwide values. In creating reasons and settings for coming together, individual émigrés give substance to an otherwise amorphous feeling of commonality. And in coming together to express these commonalities, Soviet Jewish immigrants are able to integrate the reality of their American lives with the values and self-image they have developed in a different context, giving shape and substance to their emerging community.

8.

A POSTMODERN COMMUNITY

TALK—CEMENT AND SUBSTANCE

Outside of occasional displays of Russian Jewish immigrant identity in the restaurants of Brighton Beach and at concerts and literary evenings, talk is what sparks, unites, and keeps alive the émigré community. Talk among friends, acquaintances, shop clerks, neighbors, and that which comes over radio waves and through the Russian-language press spreads through the boroughs, into the suburbs, and back again. This talk concerns current events, television programs and movies, workplace experiences, vacation travels, real estate, fashion, bringing up children, crime, cultural happenings, politics, health and medical care, plans for the future, and, of course, each other. Gossip, scandal, and what immigrants call "O.B.S. stories" (*odna baba skazala*, "one old woman said") have the power, as Max Gluckman (1963, 308) noted, to cement the group into a cultural unit: "Clearly they maintain the unity, morals and values of social groups. Beyond this, they enable these groups to control the competing cliques and aspiring individuals of which all groups are composed." Through talk people create and confirm their (social) reality, filter new ideas and experiences through it, and come to understand how they themselves fit into the world around them.

Certain events, like the 1985 murder of Alexander Alon, focus and intensify the talk that occurs among émigrés. In February 1987, talk about and among Soviet immigrants reached new proportions with the occurrence of an unexpected phenomenon. In the latter part of 1986 and the beginning of 1987, a few small groups of émigrés received permission from the Soviet government and returned to live in the USSR. About 150 people made the decision to re-emigrate. *Time* and *Newsweek* published articles about these "prodigal" or "disgruntled" émigrés (January 12, 1987), the *New York Times* and the *Washington Post* ran several stories documenting the returns, and ABC-TV devoted a *Nightline* program (December 29, 1986) and a portion of *World News Tonight* (February 23, 1987) to the issue of re-emigration. Why had 150 people captured such attention?

A well-publicized component of the United States's foreign policy toward the USSR has been the former's insistence on human rights, including the right of emigration, for Soviet citizens. Soviet Jewry in particular is often portrayed by the media as a captive people with no permissible outlets for ethnic or religious expression. Religiously committed Russian Jews, like the refusenik Iosif Begun, who were incarcerated for teaching Hebrew to small study groups, have become representative in the West of the plight of all Soviet Jews. These people who risked their livelihoods and their very lives in the struggle to emigrate demonstrated to the world that no Jew can be free in the USSR. Thus, the occurrence of even one (former) Soviet Jew wishing to return and then actually repatriating to a land from which thousands are striving to leave becomes an anomaly worthy of note and demanding explanation.

At the same time as the American press was reporting this return migration, the immigrants themselves were heatedly discussing it. In early January 1987, Lera telephoned me from Brighton Beach, "You must come back to us. Everyone is talking about the return of the immigrants, everyone." And what were they saying? "My husband's hairstylist said, 'These are not our people!' Others are talking about Gorbachev's new policy of *glasnost,* and some are talking about the possibility of going back—but just for a visit. Come and see."

In March 1987, I did return for a period of two weeks. Almost immediately after I arrived, Maxim told me his thoughts on the subject of re-emigration:

> Oh, the return of the immigrants. The big noise has died down, but it
> got a lot of emotions going, a lot of anger . . . because most of us, more

or less, are living not badly. And most immigrants are grateful to America for the chance we got. There were people who went to the airport to yell at the returnees.[1] There was a lot of bad feelings, no one could understand how this was possible. Many people have relatives, some close relatives, who have been refused, or who are waiting and waiting to get out. They know how hard it is for them and how much they are suffering. And to see these go back, they cannot understand.

While in fact the "big noise" had died down, people were still talking about this issue. Several times during my stay it was not I who initiated discussion about the subject; at a wedding one of the guests greeted me and asked, "Have you heard about this re-immigration?" and later, at another table, a group of young professionals were discussing the returnees' motives.

Many immigrants introduced their thoughts about re-emigration by declaring, "Point zero, zero, one percent, maybe even less [of the population]" or something similar, underscoring their belief that this return is insignificant and that the phenomenon has been overblown in the press and on the streets. Several people, and an article in *Novoye Russkoye Slovo* (March 8, 1987, p. 5), emphasized that return rates for Jews at the turn of the century and in the 1920s, when conditions were much more oppressive in Russia, were higher than this tiny ripple.[2] Further, many, like the hairstylist quoted above, stressed that "these are not our people" by pointing to important distinctions between the returnees and themselves: "Very few, almost none are Jewish, or if there are Jews, then they are of mixed families," or from the Caucasus or Central Asia.[3] Irina relates one story in circulation among the immigrants:

This story is one we call O.B.S., which means, one talks and tells another and another, until the final story, you don't know what to believe. This is about a family from Baku who owned taxi medallions [taxi ownership permits]. One story says worth 100,000 dollars, another 1,000,000, another 10,000,000—with each telling comes another zero. This family, the man, worked very hard for five, six years driving taxis, earning money, buying medallions. He has the money in a Swiss bank account, and in the Soviet Union will live from the interest. That's about four hundred dollars a month, which goes a long way there. Then, too, he was by training a shoemaker. And now, with the economic reforms, he wants to open his own shoe shop. So he came to

America to work and make money so he could go back to Baku with a lot of money and, so to speak, retire.

Another way Jews who return are portrayed is as deviants. Stories are told of alcoholics, drug addicts, "not normal" families:

> This family that went and then came back?[4] They are not a normal family. They emigrated many years ago. She, the mother, is the family matriarch. Her English is very good. . . . Her husband is almost completely without language. He worked here and there as a messenger or something like this. For them life was difficult, only on the one salary. But of course a person is dissatisfied if he does nothing! This country gives so many possibilities and opportunities; it is up to the person to do something. They have two children, sons, one nineteen in college. He is a very smart and talented boy. She [the mother] runs their lives. This boy is nineteen and has never been in New York City, just across the river. She is very protective of him. They left, oh, ten years ago. First to Israel, then to Switzerland, then to America, and never satisfied. Not normal people.

> Now let's take for example who it is who goes back. This woman, Katsap, who kissed the ground when she went back, she lived on my street. She is a drunk and a prostitute—that's what they say. She came with her mother, and her mother received a pension [SSI, Section 8 housing, food stamps]. They lived together in the apartment and rented one room to a man. She worked a little here, a little there, and on this and the pension, this unsatisfied woman travelled throughout Europe. . . . Now her mother died and she can't live the way she did, and she is alone, so she is going [back] to her daughter and granddaughter.

Those who have no personal acquaintance with any returnees simply look upon the lot of them with scorn and disdain:

> Slaves, lazy, old, lost a husband or a wife, lonely, alone. Less than point zero one percent. I am not angry with them. I hope they find the slavery they are looking for.

> Garbage—we have no need for them. These people are not necessary to anyone, not to America, not to Russia. They are people who go here and there and will never be satisfied.

Through their talk, "normal" hard-working people distance themselves from their former neighbors who did the unthinkable and returned to the USSR.

For some émigrés, mention of re-emigration does not necessarily elicit personal condemnations of the returnees but rather evokes bad memories of Soviet life. A woman in her sixties, in America almost ten years, recalls:

> People like this, I can't understand how they could forget everything. The famines, the waking up at five in the morning to stand in line for food products . . . and the terrible way of life. . . . Many people lived [materially] not badly there. But always in fear because of their deals, without which they could not have lived. But to go back—not to remember the lines, the famines, the pressures of the plan, the constant running to make a living, and the terrible fear, always with you—for me, that's impossible.

Another woman, who emigrated with her parents, husband, and school-aged children eight years ago, expresses her feelings:

> I can't understand it. I think it's terrible. I want to tell you what I think of. In Moscow I worked in a very large organization of architects, engineers, and so on. One old man who I worked with, an architect, got very little pay. And one time I was talking to him about this, and he told me his story: He was from a family of *boyars* [Russian aristocracy] and at the time of the Revolution they left Russia and lived in Yugoslavia. In Belgrade. There he studied, became an architect and married a girl from another one of these families. She was always sickly, and she told him that maybe if they went back to their home country she would feel better. In 1947 they went back. 1947—do you know what this means? The worst time, right after the war. A terrible time in Russia. They came to Moscow. They had nowhere to live. Some relative took them in but told them they could only have a place to sleep. They had to be out of the apartment from eight in the morning till ten at night— there was just no room. This man found work but for very low pay. . . . His wife was not educated and had no work. She went to sit in the park from morning till night. This was fine in the summer, but can you imagine in winter? She started to go a little cuckoo, mentally ill and physically ill. And no one would help them. Neighbors were unkind and said, "We have no use for you—you in our country's hard times left. You are—," they called them traitors. The man told them that he

had fought with the partisans in Yugoslavia, but they didn't care. How dare he have lived abroad during times when everyone in Russia suffered? And these were Russian people, not Jewish.

Natalya's reaction, despite her often professed love of Russian culture, focused on the alienation she had felt as a Jew in the USSR:

> And to return to an anti-Semitic country, where people in your building, on the street, in lines, on the bus, call you *zhid?* How can anyone return to that? No, I don't want to return, not even for a visit.

These memories are often supplemented by memories of an earlier period of liberalization, the Khrushchev years, which was then followed by a return to restrictions. Oleg, a non-Jewish émigré in a mixed marriage, who left behind his natal family, explains:

> Although my parents, brother, and good friends are in Russia, I have no thoughts whatsoever about returning. Memories are memories; now I have the ability to breathe freely, cross [national] boundaries. . . . Those who return will experience a new nostalgia, this time for America. No one asked me to come to America, I came here of my own free will, and I am staying here of my free will. I do trust that Gorbachev is sincere in making his reforms, but I don't and cannot trust that system. Who knows how long it will take before they arrest those people who went back and have them shot.

This sentiment is frequently echoed. Vladimir and then Maxim express their skepticism about Gorbachev's reforms:

> About this *glasnost* and Gorbachev. You see, this is like first with Khrushchev. First there was liberalization in the arts, in literature and rehabilitation of political prisoners. This now too will go on, for so long. And then—nothing. Take China as an example—liberalization for so long, and then, the end. You can't trust them, not Gorbachev, not the Soviet system.

> The way I see Gorbachev is like this—at first I was very suspicious and didn't know if these reforms were real, or only for the image abroad. Now I believe that he is for real, but I think it can end in only one of two ways. The first is that Gorbachev will work very hard to get his

measures across and slowly there will be reform. But of this I am not sure, because already, both abroad and at home, there are problems. . . . It can end in two ways—a new way of slow reform, or the old way of arrest and execution.

As if these speculations about the future of the Soviet system are not enough to eliminate any thoughts of returning to the USSR, rumors have already begun to circulate about the fate of those who did go back:

Dneprov, the composer, he had a heart attack at the border when he arrived and they [customs officials] confiscated his things. That mime [another returnee]—is now in a psychiatric hospital. That's what awaits them.

I have heard about some people. One, a couple with two boys, one seventeen, one fifteen, prepared to go back. They, when filling out their forms in Washington, were told to give a contribution to Chernobyl—no less than ten thousand dollars. This I heard they ask of everyone. Then, too, they paid in dollars for an apartment and a car. They bought lots of things to take with them. At the border, all this equipment was confiscated except one TV and one VCR. . . . Nothing good awaits them. They will not go back to their old apartments or their old lives. People will call them traitors, and they will not be happy.

And a snatch of conversation I overheard from a middle-aged man to an elderly woman on Brighton Beach Avenue:

Whores who went back! Nothing good happens for them. He wanted to go back to Tashkent. Well, what did he get? An apartment thirty kilometers from Tashkent in a little town. They get what they deserve!

Before 1987, when it was virtually impossible for former Soviet citizens to obtain tourist visas to the USSR, life in the United States, for better or for worse, was their unquestioned fate. Soviet immigrants exercised their right to freedom of speech and complained at length about the shortcomings of American society. They counterposed Americans' lack of warmth to caring friendship circles in Russia, fear of crime and subway filth in New York to the theaterlike metro of Moscow and Leningrad and the ability to take a stroll no matter what the time of day or night in any Russian city; they compared materialism and the pressures of making a living in the United States with late-night discussions over a bottle of vodka at the kitchen table and the normalcy of arriving late for work in the USSR, and contrasted the plight of America's homeless with the Soviet state's provision of housing, jobs, and pensions for everyone. Nostalgia for a cultural life revolving around theater, music, ballet, and stimulating discussions of literature was frequently expressed by countless émigrés to me and among themselves. While these discussions continue, they are now somewhat subdued and altered.[5]

A similar alteration has occurred in the émigrés' memories of the Soviet Union. Although immigrants routinely mentioned perpetual commodity shortages, anti-Semitic remarks, and fear of speaking one's mind, now that return to the USSR presents itself as a possibility, their memories of privation and intimidation are stirred up. As Soviet immigrants talk among themselves, they not only distance their group from the returnees and from the Soviet government, they overtly confirm a collective decision to remain in the United States. Life in America may not always be easy, they continue to acknowledge, but it is better in many ways than that which they had known in the land of their birth. Soviet immigrants are increasingly pointing out to each other that their many fond reminiscences of Russia, particularly those that focus on a stress-free way of life and the privileges of high social status, may not be "facts" at all but simply nostalgia, idealizations of an irretrievable past. A college student responds to her father's desire for his old life:

> Papa is now talking about going back. Mama and I categorically refuse. No way. We are happy here. This is our country, this is our life. Papa— he's one of those people who never should have left. In Russia we lived very well. Papa was a clothes designer. He designed women's coats. Of course, the other side was always the fear [of arrest]—because money was always being exchanged under the table. . . . Now papa is doing what he always hated—sewing, and for somebody else. . . . He thought that as big as he was in Russia he would be bigger in America. He is an idealist with illusions. He never should have left. Now he is thinking about how good our life was, and how that's what he wants. He'll never find that again. He sees too how much my college costs, and drugs, and he doesn't want that. I told him to be realistic, that things have changed

and you can't go back. Let him talk. I'm not going, and my mother isn't going. And he's not going anywhere. Just talking.

With the force of community sentiment behind her, the daughter, certain that her decision to remain in America is right, exposes her father's former social place in the USSR as tenuous and his longing to reclaim it as unrealizable. Once a legitimate vehicle of self-expression, his words are now labelled "just talking," and although his voice may still be audible, his contribution to the conversation is silenced. His daughter and his wife, and the community around them, are making his reality and refuse to allow him to make theirs. Exclusion from the conversation leaves the father, or any other member of the social group for that matter, with a choice: either withdraw from the community and act as a lone deviant, or accept socially agreed upon reality—in this case, adopt the view that one cannot recapture the past, re-join the conversation, and continue in the struggle to make life in America meaningful and satisfying.

As they talk among themselves, individual Soviet immigrants articulate their memories and express their hopes, desires, and dreams. They seek confirmation from each other that these subjective experiences are legitimate and real, and in so doing, each conversation partner gauges, and invariably alters somewhat, his or her perceptions. In the course of conversation, people come to see, in an objectified sense, who they are and how, if they so choose, they can bring their self-images and expectations into line with those of others.

Talk provides individuals with social grounding, a way to work out one's relationship with the broader world, a base that makes possible thoughts, ideas, and action, and a means for reflecting on and evaluating them. While participating in a conversation, one draws upon a historically developed, socially accepted foundation of knowledge, and by using this knowledge to make sense of the world, in expressing one's relationship to this knowledge, people alter its contents if even imperceptibly. It is through conversation, the ability to compare one's reality of here and now with other perhaps overlapping realities, that, for example, a chunk of émigrés' prior knowledge can be relegated to "nostalgia" and a different bundle of knowledge, learned through daily practice in American life, becomes reality in its place.

Talk molds community by themes and schemes and brings subtle groupwide values into stark relief. Rumor and gossip hold the power to channel deviance into acceptable directions (literature, film, music, "just talking") or to force it underground, out of sight. It is no wonder that "no one knew" of anyone's plans to leave for the USSR, although the returnees had long been petitioning the Soviet Embassy for permission to return. These would-be re-emigrants knew that their behavior ran counter to group norms and kept their actions quiet. Through their silence, they removed themselves from the conversation of the community and thereby from group pressure and censure. When they returned to the United States, as did over half by the end of 1987, they claimed that they had outwitted the Soviet government for what they had really wanted to do was visit friends and relatives who had remained behind, not reassume Soviet citizenship. They boasted about the gumption and wits they had used to accomplish these goals, and turned the conversation away from their (supposed) treachery and abnormality to their daring, heroism, wiliness, and loyalty.[6]

Soviet émigrés are geographically scattered, economically differentiated, occupationally diverse, and Americanized to varying degrees. The vast array of ideas and materials that flit across their ethnic boundary is staggering, as people daily confront new things, new ways of doing old things, and new meanings for old ways of doing them, on the streets, at the workplace, in the health club, at school, or on TV. Talk is the means by which all these influences are filtered out, accepted or rejected. Talk is the mortar that shapes and holds together and the sieve that remolds and amends the *bricolage*. As prior knowledge vies with and contours current practice, and as new knowledge emerging from daily life alters or even cancels out prior knowledge, talk is constantly under construction, giving unity and form to thousands of lives. Without these conversations, the otherwise amorphous category, Soviet Jewish immigrants, would remain just that; talk makes them a community.

COMMUNITY AND BEYOND

Throughout the 1970s and into the 1980s, some 100,000 Soviet Jews immigrated to the United States. They came to America to become

Americans, to enjoy a better life than they had known as Soviet citizens. They came to America to stay, to reap the benefits of their talents and expertise in the "free world," to escape the pain of anti-Semitism, and perhaps most important of all, to give their children the opportunity to develop to the fullest.

Already deracinated from a traditional, religiously based, linguistically distinct, geographically bound Jewish community, Soviet Jews arrived in New York as quintessentially modern people. With their values of cosmopolitanism and progress, they had staked everything on knowledge and technology and their professions, and ironic as it seems, on their doubts of an all-encompassing political system that mandates the Truth. They knew, more or less, who they were, having amended and re-invented their Jewish identity during the "century of ambivalence" (Gitelman 1988) prior to the Revolution and then again in the seventy years since. They witnessed the crumbling of their belief in two doctrines—Judaism and Communism—and had become cynical in the wide world. Yet, at the same time, they remained loyal and emotionally expressive toward family and friends. They had learned and knew how to manipulate rules of social behavior—how to present themselves, what was of value, and, usually phrased within the idiom of "science," what was true. What they did not know, at least in the initial stages of life after migration, was how their Soviet-made selves could fit into a different—American—version of reality.

While they were en route and once they arrived at their destination, Soviet Jews, putting into effect their finely honed utilitarianism, looked outward to American institutions—the United States government and "Jewish organizations"—for help settling into the flow of American life. They expected, and usually got, the same paternalistic care that the Soviet state provided for its citizens. Their receipt of financial assistance, English-language classes, health care, job counseling and placement, and housing services, made perfect sense to them—and not only in terms of their lifelong experiences in the USSR: They were indeed political refugees; each family arrived with little if any money with which to get started. Moreover, these newcomers had no home village, not to mention their own synagogue or communal institutions, to provide them with the assistance that other immigrant groups can offer from within. But this absence of a formal social sphere to transplant to America is but a small part of the story. Of much greater importance is that Soviet emigrants came to America with no vision, no intention whatsoever, of creating a community—Russian Jewish, communist, or otherwise. They came to New York as individuals or family groups, as stateless refugees, having forfeited all claims to their native country with the act of emigration. They came not to recreate some image of a hazy past; they came to link their fate with that of the United States, to become Americans.

Yet as they went outside of their migration cohort for guidance and assistance and explored this new world that encourages each person and each group to express its own sense of individuality and truth, these former Soviet Jews discovered quirks, peculiarities, and distasteful qualities in Americans' ideas, language, mannerisms, political reality, and ways of giving assistance that jolted them into a distinct awareness of their differences. Just as important, Americans, including American Jews, let the immigrants know that they *are* different. As a result, while they looked outward, they found themselves pushed inward, not only because they were thrust together with fellow emigrants on their journey through Europe and into New York, but also because the world they had come to join was unlike both the "normal and natural" way of life they had known and the world they had imagined the United States to be.

As they sought and found jobs or schooling in the outside world, they also turned inward, attempting to confirm their findings about America with others they considered to be most like themselves. Through discussions with fellow émigrés, they digested the information they were accumulating. Most important of all, in the course of their conversations Soviet Jewish immigrants developed ways to live with and use the new information, technology, and commodities they daily encountered.

Along the way, individual émigrés discovered a thing or two about themselves, recognizing differences not only between "Russians" and Americans but also within their migration cohort. Throughout migration and resettlement and now as they live out their lives in the midst of a society different from anything previously known or imagined, former Soviet Jews have sought out and sorted out each other. Although they had had no intention of doing so, they came to form a community.

This community, unimagined (cf. Anderson 1983) and unintended as it is, differs sharply in form from traditional communities. It has a few residential clusters and one commercial-residential-social hub, but since most Soviet émigrés live dispersed throughout the New York metropolitan area—to say nothing about settling across the USA, Canada, and Israel—this community is not located in any one tangible place. Even more tellingly, Soviet Jewish immigrants are not united into a compelling structure of formal institutions, nor do they have religious or social organizations directed by the leaders in their midst that they could join (cf. Pattie 1989, who describes the clubs and churches of London's Armenian community). Is there any value in using the word *community* to describe a fragmented "community" removed from a solid tradition as well as a specific on-the-ground place?

In a recent paper, Sherry Ortner (1989) declares that the term *community* as defined and structured in the received wisdom of social science is a "category of unmodernity." Unquestioning use of such a definition automatically precludes finding "community" among the peoples who inhabit the urban sprawl of today's world. Ortner proposes that, instead of accepting this retrospective definition, anthropologists concentrate their efforts on tracing how "community in the sense of locality is transformed into community as a state of mind" (p. 14).

Michael Fischer (1986) urges much the same thing in his discussion of ethnicity. Virtually disregarding utilitarian–interest group theories of ethnic group persistence, he demonstrates that what really seems to matter is that the essence of a historical thread and an ethnic label remain to remind people of their groupwide continuity (or immortality) over the centuries. The label and feeling of commonality persist while, as Fischer shows, the cultural contents attached to the label change dramatically over the generations as people actively remake and reinterpret their ethnic legacy within the contemporary context of their neighborhoods, schools, workplaces, families, national culture. The particular embellishments, lengthenings, shortenings, emendations of that ethnic thread, coupled with its links to the past and its aims for the future, is, I believe, what we can call community, albeit postmodern.

Of course, this kind of community emerges from a different set of structures and processes than the traditional community. Anthony Cohen (1985) points out that in the twentieth century social and geographic holds have broken loose, dispersing peoples and disrupting territorially based, culturally homogeneous groups. In place of those holds, rather than the anticipated rootlessness, anomie, or even homogenized Modern (mass-produced) Man, people have created new communities. This time, however, they are disembedded communities of symbolic affect that get played out socially from time to time in group-specific gathering places (churches, social clubs, restaurants, concert halls, private homes) and talked out over the telephone, face to face, and via newspapers, radio, television, films, and novels.

In much the same vein, Jean-François Lyotard (1984) assures us that postmodernism, in destroying monolithic dogma, or what he calls "the grand Narrative," does not lead to "the dissolution of the social bond and the disintegration of social aggregates into a mass of individual atoms . . ." (p. 15). What he shows instead is that "little narratives" are established, communities of talk where the speakers make, understand, and play the language games that demarcate them from others. These arenas of conversational jousting become the postmodern versions of community.

The postmodern community is a heteroglossic entity derived from talk. Because it is a symbolically constituted, socially constructed arena of debate, argumentation, challenge, enjoyment, and even agreement, it cannot be a place of unitary sameness. It is an entity formed from confrontations with otherness coupled with a historically based idea that some people are more alike than others. Even the groupwide ethnic identity that somehow persists over the centuries does not mandate uniformity, tradition, or unchangingness. Rather it signifies some sort of agreement on origins, hopes, desires, morality, knowledge, sentiment, and sociability—that can be forged only by comparison, experimentation, discussion, and doing.

In the particular case of Soviet Jewish émigrés, I have tried to show how these newcomers to America create an arena for playing out the ongoing struggle between their prior knowledge and values, and a new reality that often challenges and undermines—yet sometimes supports and even enhances—their ability to be fully competent actors in a number of roles. Within this community, through trial and error, comparisons, and conversations, people cultivate a range of theoretical answers to their dilemmas and practical strategies for implementing them. As part of their community, Soviet Jewish immigrants create ways to make the experience of life after migration not only materially comfortable but emotionally meaningful and socially satisfying. This, I am certain, is the reason that people create communities and that group identities persist in the postmodern era.

What kind of future can be predicted for this Soviet émigré community? Is it a fragile entity destined to disappear in a generation? In 1987 I was sorely tempted to say that within thirty years Soviet-Russian Jewish immigrants will have "melted" into the all-embracing, organizationally rooted yet ideologically diverse American Jewish community or into the even broader category of American technocrats. And that remains a distinct possibility.

Militating against this prediction are the remarkable events of the six years of Mikhail Gorbachev's regime. With his policies of *glasnost* and *perestroika* came the decision to allow Soviet citizens to obtain travel passports and tourist visas and visit friends and relatives in the United States. At the same time, Gorbachev reopened the doors of emigration, and hundreds of thousands of Soviet Jews left. By the end of 1991, just before the dismantling of the USSR, over a quarter of a million newcomers had resettled in Israel, and an additional 100,000 had come to the United States, almost half of whom chose to make new homes in New York.[7] Both the Soviet immigrant population of Israel and the American émigré population doubled in the course of four years (1987–1991).[8]

The very new immigrants are arriving to a different world than that of the émigrés of the 1970s. At first glance, these newest newcomers see strong evidence of a "Russian" community, populated by people very much like themselves, where things are as they could have been and should have been in the USSR but were not. It does not take them long, however, to realize that the old friends and relatives they are joining have been removed from Soviet life for over ten years and have changed.

Reunions between these two immigrant cohorts are to a large extent replays of the misunderstandings that resulted from encounters between newly arriving Soviet Jewish refugees and their American Jewish hosts in the 1970s, but, of course, with a twist. The (post) *perestroika* newcomers find old friends and relatives who speak Russian but whose Russian is now sprinkled with strange words and expressions (calques, if not words themselves, from English) and who understand what it means to have lived in and left the Soviet Union, but whose demeanor, dress, eating habits, concerns, and conversations have all been altered in the years spent away from the USSR. Expecting to step into a circle of friendship and conviviality, many new immigrants are surprised to find that their friends of old have become work-motivated, selfish, and not overwhelmingly willing to share their time, their money, or any of the other resources that are necessary for getting nicely established in the United States.

The not-so-new immigrants, after years of Soviet-mandated separation from everything and everyone in the USSR, are shaken by their contacts with a trail of visitors from the Soviet Union and a new, large cohort of refugees. At first eager to see long-lost friends and relatives, they quickly lose their patience with these people, "who look like they're coming from some third world country," with demanding attitudes and outrageous expectations of assistance. While American Jews in the 1970s called newly arriving Soviet refugees "Russians" in reaction to their perception of them as pushy, arrogant, and "not Jewish enough" (Gitelman 1984, 96), veteran immigrants label visitors from Russia *pelesosi* (vacuum cleaners), for, like the appliances, they suck up everything in sight. Not-so-new immigrants fear the demands of newcomers because it is against their ethic of kinship and friendship to refuse, but against their better judgment to comply. They explain their resentment: "They want everything that we have the moment they get here. They do not understand that it took us ten, fifteen years of very hard work to live the way we do."

In reality, however, virtually no veteran immigrants avoid their relatives or refuse them hospitality. A few of my insightful friends take note of the irony that they are repeating the disappointing experience of "welcome" that they received from the American Jewish community years ago. But the encounters of veteran émigrés with people who represent their old selves is jolting in yet another way: it is a moment of reassessment and evaluation of who they were, what they are, and just who it is that they would like to be. Seeing these "real Russians" impels the older émigré cohort to take stock of just how "American" they have become. This split between the "demanding newcomers" and the "hard-working used-to-be-immigrants-now-Americans" has created a new rallying theme in conversations and for refashioning identity in both segments of the émigré community (Markowitz 1990).

Visits from Soviet friends and relatives and trips by émigrés to the USSR, besides the arrival of a new immigrant cohort, have also given rise to a renaissance of Russian language books and periodicals, to say nothing of a whole slew of cultural events. Visiting poets, bards, singers, and drama troupes attract large audiences from among the "American" émigrés, as well as recent arrivals. Perhaps these contacts, should they continue, will eventually create a transnational community (cf. Appadurai 1991), including émigrés in the USA, Russian immigrants in Israel, and citizens of the new Commonwealth of Independent States (CIS) who share a cosmopolitan worldview and sophisticated cynicism, individualistic strivings, and of course, the Russian language.

The Soviet immigrant population of New York has almost doubled since 1987, so that although many of the original residents of Russian-speaking neighborhoods have moved elsewhere, the enclaves are now bursting at the seams. Brighton Beach, it seemed to me in August 1991, is very much what it was in 1985—but more so. In addition to a proliferation of Russian groceries, restaurants, and cafes, there are newcomers standing on the street peddling their old books, shabby teddy bears, used samovars, tins of caviar, and painted souvenirs. One large store displays a sign "We Speak English."

Thus, as might be expected, the Soviet émigré community is moving in a variety of ways. Some émigré and Jewish communal service leaders are making sincere attempts at community outreach and organization. Some synagogues are increasing their recruitment efforts. Wealthy émigrés are hiring newcomers into their businesses and providing then with even faster routes for socioeconomic success than they could have imagined. Russian restaurants are booming—in Manhattan's theater district as well as in Brooklyn. As this book goes to press, the community continues to unfold and redefine itself in several intertwined, countervailing, and complementary directions with continued emigration from Russia and Ukraine and increased opportunities for communication between the USA and the CIS. Although the personnel may change and the sentiments shift, it seems likely that some sort of transnational community will persist into the twenty-first century and beyond. What exactly shall be remains to be seen.

APPENDIX A: THE MECHANICS OF EMIGRATION AND RESETTLEMENT

During the 1970s and 1980s, leaving the Soviet Union was no easy feat. Soviet citizens were rarely able to travel abroad, especially to countries outside the orbit of Soviet influence. With occasional exceptions for elderly people to visit relatives, it was mainly party members and the cultural elite who were granted permission to travel beyond the Soviet border. And they travelled in groups, closely supervised by a tour guide. Emigration, in theory at least, did not exist as an option for Soviet citizens.

In the 1970s, responding to Western pressures to grant human rights, the government of the USSR allowed Jews, ethnic Germans, and Armenians the opportunity to apply to reunite with family members abroad; not everyone who applied to emigrate was granted permission. In 1985 it was estimated that over 300,000 people in the Soviet Union—including "refuseniks," those whose documents had not been processed, and those who had not yet applied for a visa—wished to leave the country.

For those who wanted to leave, the first official step, after making the difficult personal and familial decision, was to arrange for an invitation from a relative in another country; in the case of Soviet Jews, who won the right to emigrate to live in their historic homeland, the letter of invitation had to come from Israel. Finding someone to send an invitation was not problematic because virtually every Soviet Jew had some kind of connection with someone in Israel. Upon receipt of the letter, one then filed an application at OVIR (the Office of Visas and Registration). Because one lost one's citizenship after submitting this application—and often one's job as well—and because one never knew when or if the request to emigrate would be granted, submission of emigration documents was terrifying indeed. Many immigrants, in looking back, are amazed at the courage they found to make this irreparable break; others fondly remember it as an act of defiance; still others say it was not so terrible. All of these people, of course, were ultimately able to leave.

Once permission to emigrate was granted, would-be emigrants had about a month to divest themselves of their property—sell apartments, summer houses, and cars—get documentation to allow for the export of personal items, and take leave of extended family members and friends. Some people were able to ship furniture, china, books, and pianos to the United States (via Austria or Italy); others came with just a few crates and suitcases. Before leaving, many purchased vodka, ballet shoes, cameras, and Russian or Ukrainian folk crafts to sell in the West, for, besides their personal possessions, each emigrant was allowed to take only ninety dollars in cash out of the USSR. At the border, emigrants' baggage and sometimes their persons were searched, and often customs officials strewed people's possessions and broke or tore up items. Delays at the border could mean missed trains and loss of accommodations, so those on their way out usually endured these last humiliations in silence.

Once out of the USSR, the émigrés, now stateless refugees, headed across Czechoslovakia by train to Vienna, where, because of threats from various Arab groups, they encountered machine-gun-armed guards to ensure their safety. Each newly arriving Soviet Jewish émigré met with a representative of the Jewish Agency, *Sokhnut*. Those who wished to resettle in Israel were flown to Tel Aviv the following day. Families who decided to go to the United States spent anywhere from a few days to two weeks in Vienna. Under the auspices of HIAS (Hebrew Immigrant Aid Society), they were housed in hotels and given a stipend by the Jewish Joint Distribution Fund.

From Vienna they were moved to Rome, where they found temporary living quarters while their applications for admission into the United States as stateless refugees were processed. To supplement their small stipends, many families went to the marketplace to sell their vodka, cameras, and souvenirs. Some people led tours for fellow émigrés throughout Italy, and those with English-language skills worked as translators at HIAS. During the height of emigration (1978–80), Soviet emigrants spent four to six months in Rome. (When the number of exit visas sharply dropped after mid-1980, stays decreased to about two months; when emigration began again in earnest during 1988–89, the length of the stay in Rome increased as well.)

Immigrants' impressions of Vienna are universally ecstatic; Italy, too, is remembered with great fondness (see Levkov 1984, 127). Many took full advantage of the opportunity to travel and visit museums, to soak up the wonders of western Europe. They were impressed with Austrian and Italian well-stocked stores and attractive window displays. Immigrants remember their joy at the availability of all sorts of foods, especially the abundance of tropical fruit in the middle of winter. No one mentioned language problems hindering their "Roman holiday." Several people reported that *cuanto costa* ("how much does this cost"), and *grazie* and *prego* ("thank you" and "you're welcome" or "please") were all they needed to know.

In Rome, HIAS representatives interviewed émigrés and asked them where in the United States they wished to live. Those without American friends or kin were sponsored by the Jewish community of the city they selected or were assigned a destination if they stated no preference. The Council of Jewish Federations devised a plan to resettle Soviet Jews throughout the United States in accordance with the proportion of Jews in each region. Thus, New York City, with about 45 percent of the nation's Jewish population, was allotted 45 percent of Soviet émigrés, followed by Los Angeles and then Chicago. Once all documents were processed, émigrés flew to Kennedy Airport in New York, where they were again met by HIAS representatives. Those with destinations other than New York were taken to connecting flights. Émigrés resettling in New York who were not met by friends or family members were taken to temporary living quarters.

Perhaps Edward Limonov (1982) exaggerates for effect his first impressions of his first home in New York, but almost all émigrés relate with horror stories of their initial living accommodations. Like Limonov, many were housed in SROs (single-room occupancy hotels) in midtown Manhattan, where their fellow roomers were transients, welfare families, prostitutes, and cockroaches. The fruit baskets, flowers, furnished apartments, and well-stocked refrigerators that awaited new arrivals in smaller Jewish communities (e.g., Atlanta) were nowhere to be found for new immigrants in New York.

Even those who were taken home by family members were sometimes startled by their first impressions of New York. Lera recalls that the first things she noticed in Brighton Beach were grime and fire escapes: "I was in shock because all the time on Soviet TV when they show reports of poverty in the U.S. they show these brick buildings with metal staircases on the outside. And here it was—my building, my new home, the same. And I thought, did I come to America to live in poverty?"

By 1989 "direct emigration" became possible for those joining family members in the United States. In the 1990s, direct immigration involves a procedure initiated by American relatives, clearance by the U.S. Department of State, an interview at the U.S. Embassy in Moscow, and a one-way ticket from Moscow to New York. Direct immigration is now the only legitimate route for coming as a permanent resident to the United States.

APPENDIX B: PROFILES OF KEY INFORMANTS

BORIS (Borya)—born 1947 in Odessa. Parents Yefim, an Odessa ghetto survivor, and Shura married after World War II, during which Yefim's first family perished. Shura and Yefim emigrated with their daughter, Ludmilla, who is seven years younger than Boris, in 1977. Boris, a professional musician who played on Soviet cruise ships, lost his travel passport and thus his job in 1976 when his parents applied to emigrate. He then played in local Odessa ensembles and became a jeweler until his wife Lera consented to emigrate. Since coming to New York in 1983, Boris, Lera, and their daughter Svetlana (born 1974) have resided in Brighton Beach, Brooklyn. Boris has worked as a jewelry modeler, an independent jeweler, and is presently a self-employed merchandise distributor.

GRIGORY (Grisha)—born 1930 in Kharkov, moved to Kiev with his parents while still very young. Music and art were important components of his family life, and he attended a special music school for talented children. In 1941 Grigory, his mother, and his younger brother left Kiev to spend the war years in the Ural Mountains. His father, a photojournalist, was killed at the front. At age fourteen, Grigory, his mother, and his brother returned to Kiev. He wanted to continue his studies in music but was advised to change fields because, as his teacher said, "It's too late for you to become a pianist," so he studied drawing to become an art teacher. But when Grigory's uncle returned from the war, he came back with an accordion, a gift for his nephew, and Grisha began playing this instrument as a hobby. He decided to switch fields and completed his higher education in music composition. Upon graduation, he played in movie theater orchestras and conducted choral groups. He married in 1955 and had his first composition published in 1958, the same year his daughter was born. He was a successful popular composer until 1977, when he was blacklisted after his paternal cousin emigrated. Grigory, his wife, her mother, and their daughter and son-in-law emigrated in 1980, first settling in Columbus, Ohio, and moving to Brighton Beach after a year. Grigory plays in local restaurants and at Jewish senior citizen centers; his wife works as an accounts clerk, and his daughter and son-in-law work as computer programmers. Grigory is the major care provider for his grandson, who was born in the USA.

IRINA (Ira)—born in 1942 in the Volga region of Central Russia, was raised, attended school, and lived until emigration in Kharkov. Irina never knew her Ukrainian father, who was killed at the front during World War II. Her mother, Raisa, remarried a Jewish man who became Irina's adoptive father. Irina's parents and brother Lyova, who is twelve years younger than she, emigrated in 1975. Irina, her Russian husband Oleg, their nine-year-old son and infant son came to Brooklyn, settling in Brighton Beach, in 1977. She had worked as a cosmetologist in Kharkov; in Brooklyn she works part-time as a hairdresser, and after completing a course at a local community college in 1985, has been working part-time as a travel agent as well.

LARA—born 1964 in Moscow, never knew her father since her parents separated before her birth. Lara's childhood was marked by regularity and security. Private English and ice-skating lessons supplemented her school activities. She emigrated at age fifteen in 1979 with her mother, Nona. She completed high school and community college in Brooklyn while working first in a doctor's office and then in a pharmacy after school. In the fall of 1984 Lara began four-year college but found it too difficult. She left in 1985 to take an intensive secretarial course and then found work as a secretary in a Wall Street firm. Lara and Nona live in Brighton Beach.

LERA—born 1952 in Odessa but spent the first three years of her life in the West Ukraine, where her father was stationed as an army prosecutor. Her parents, who are both lawyers, and she returned to Odessa in 1956, where Lera lived until emigration. She completed the Jurisprudence Faculty of Odessa State University in 1975 and worked as a commercial and labor lawyer until 1983, when she, her husband Boris, and daughter Svetlana left the Soviet Union. Lera's parents initially opposed her emigration, but they joined her in Brighton Beach in 1988. Since arriving in New York, Lera has worked as an interviewer and research assistant on a number of projects and earned an L.L.M. in 1988 from Columbia Law School.

MARINA—born 1950 in Leningrad, the only child of two lawyers. Marina studied music since early childhood, first at a special school for talented children, and then at the Leningrad Conservatory. She worked as an accompanist and vocalist for Len-Koncert (the city's concert booking agent and promoter) after graduation, and then was sent to a special course for show business training in Moscow. Marina married while in her early twenties. Her husband was a successful musician who drank heavily after his nightly performances. Marina wanted to emigrate, but he did not; they divorced and she emigrated with her parents to Brooklyn in 1980. Since then, she has been working as an entertainer at Jewish resorts and community centers and has performed in a number of concerts. In 1982 she married an engineer, also a Soviet Jewish immigrant, but they separated in 1985.

MAXIM—born 1946 in Moscow. Maxim's mother was an actress in the Moscow Yiddish theater, and after secondary school he studied acting and directing. He worked at Mos-Koncert until he decided to emigrate at age thirty-three in 1979. Although he had been an active leader in *Komsomol,* he became involved with Jewish cultural circles and *aliya* (emigration-to-Israel) activists in the 1970s. When he emigrated with his elderly mother, Maxim left behind an ex-wife and his son. During his first months in New York, Maxim tagged baggage and did an assortment of other manual jobs. More recently, he has been chief editor of "Radio Horizons" and a contributor to "Radio Liberty" and the Russian-language and Jewish press. Maxim's teenage son joined him in Brighton Beach in 1988.

NATALYA—born 1938 in Leningrad, survived the siege of Leningrad during World War II with her mother and youngest brother Vlad; their middle brother died. Her mother was a piano teacher at the Conservatory of Music; her father was a photojournalist. Natalya's parents divorced shortly after her birth; her father remarried an actress, and her mother remarried a man who was to become her adoptive father and Vlad's biological father. Her own biological father remained a great friend until his death and, with his wife, exposed Natalya to the world of theater. Natalya completed her higher education at the Institute of Foreign Languages at Leningrad State University, and then taught English and served occasionally as an In-Tourist guide/translator. Natalya never married but had a long-term liaison with a leading actor. After convincing her brother to leave, Natalya emigrated with Vlad and their elderly mother in 1980, following her first cousin Mikhail, who had arrived in New York in 1977, and her two maternal aunts, who came in 1979. Natalya, her mother, her brother, and her aunts live on the same street in Brighton Beach. She works as a secretary in Manhattan and teaches English as a Second Language part-time in the evenings.

NONA—born 1942 and raised in Tbilisi, as her paternal grandfather fled to Georgia after the Civil War, during which he had fought on the side of the

White Army. Both of Nona's grandmothers were Ashkenazi (European) Jews. She completed secondary school and university in Tbilisi, where she received her diploma in Russian language and literature. Nona began publishing her translations (Georgian/Russian, Russian/Georgian) while still a student. In the early 1960s, she moved to Moscow and began working as an editor at a literary publishing firm. She married, divorced, had a child, earned a second diploma in art history, remarried, divorced, and then became ill (a nervous breakdown of sorts) in the late 1970s. Nona and her daughter Lara emigrated in 1979 and settled in Brighton Beach. In Brooklyn, she studied English at a local community college, worked as a sales consultant in an antiques store for two years, and then qualified for SSI.

OLEG—born 1932, an ethnic Russian from Kharkov. Oleg completed his degree in history at the Pedagogical Institute in 1952, whereupon he was assigned to teach in a small village school in the north of Russia. After "surviving" that assignment, he received another one in Moscow, and then, several years later, returned to teach in Kharkov, where he met and married Irina in 1968. For a few years prior to emigration, Oleg worked as a bookstore manager, having quit teaching because of dangers he created for himself after speaking out about inaccuracies in the history curriculum. Since resettling in Brighton Beach in 1977, Oleg has been working as a philatelist and stamp cataloguer for a New York company. He and Irina are very involved in émigré cultural circles. Oleg has become increasingly interested in his Russian Orthodox heritage since emigration. In their small but joyful home Oleg and Irina celebrate all holidays—Jewish, Russian Orthodox, American, and Russian.

PAVEL—born 1948 in Riga, where he grew up, but after completing secondary school he moved to Moscow to work and attend university. He first worked in construction as a skilled laborer, then as an engineer, but he later changed fields and worked as a unit manager and data analyst for Mosfilm (Moscow's film industry). He emigrated from the Soviet Union with his mother and his sister, her husband, and their child in 1979, leaving behind an ex-wife and a daughter. He lives in the Bensonhurst area of Brooklyn near his mother and sister and works for a Wall Street financial investment company as a data programmer and analyst.

REGINA—born 1947 in Leningrad, the youngest of three children, completed Pedagogical Institute and worked as a special education teacher for handicapped children. Regina married Joseph, an engineer, in 1968 and had their child Paul (then named Pavel) in 1970. Joseph initiated their emigration, and they left the Soviet Union at the end of December 1976. They settled in Rego

Park, Queens, in 1977, not wanting to live in a "Russian ghetto." Joseph found a job in his field immediately. Regina worked a few years as a clerk/receptionist until Joseph formed his own business in 1982; she now administers the business with him.

VICTOR—born 1962 in Tbilisi, Georgia, of Ashkenazi parents. Victor's brother is ten years his senior, and he emigrated to Israel with his wife and children in 1979, when Victor was a first-year university student. In 1980, Victor and his parents left the USSR, heading for the United States, at the advice of his brother. Victor loaded crates in Columbus, Ohio, their first destination, and then, after a year, moved with his parents to the Flatbush section of Brooklyn. Since coming to New York, Victor has been working in immigrant businesses.

VLADIMIR (Volodya)—born 1934 in Odessa, ran messages for the Resistance during World War II. Vladimir completed his higher education at Odessa State University in history and then taught history and geography in an Odessa school. He taught only ancient and medieval history "because to teach modern history you must be a member of the party—and I did not want to be in the party—and besides, they keep changing what you have to teach every five years." Vladimir, after much prodding from his wife Sofia, whose brother and family had gone to Toronto a year earlier, emigrated with his wife, ten-year-old daughter, five-year-old son, elderly mother, and parents-in-law in 1977. They came to the United States so that the older family members could get state assistance, which, as they understood the situation, the Canadian government would not have provided. They all settled near each other in Brooklyn. Vladimir worked at various odd jobs when he first arrived, then as a program coordinator for a Russian project at a YM-YWHA, and most recently, as a caseworker for the city of New York. His wife Sofia works as a bookkeeper. His daughter was listed in *Who's Who in American High Schools,* then pursued a course of study in accounting at New York University. She married in 1987 and works as an accountant. After completing eight grades in a Jewish day school, Vladimir's and Sofia's son is attending a special high school for the gifted in New York.

YAKOV (Yasha)—born 1958 in Odessa. He completed secondary school with excellent grades but was failed on his entrance exam to university. This failure caused his parents, both engineers, to apply to emigrate. In 1975, Yakov, then seventeen, his seven-year-old sister, parents, and maternal grandmother arrived in Los Angeles. Less than a year later Yasha moved to New York to attend college, where he resumed his studies in mathematics and physics. He married in 1978, dropped out of college in 1979, and then completed his B.A. in psychology in 1980. In the fall of 1981 Yakov began graduate school in psychology. A few years later he and his wife separated and then divorced. Yakov had been working as a therapist with immigrant youth since beginning graduate school. After earning his doctorate, he has occupied executive positions in Jewish communal service agencies, designing resettlement and mental health programs for Soviet émigrés. Yasha remarried in 1987 and now lives with his wife and child in a suburban town.

NOTES

1. THE NATURE OF THE STUDY

1. See, for example, Aronson et al. 1969; Baron 1964; Ben Ami 1967; Freedman 1984; Gilbert 1984; Gitelman 1971, 1973; Kochan 1972; Levin 1988; Parrish 1981; Pinkus 1988; Schwarz 1972; Smolar 1971; Wiesel 1966.

2. See, for example, the *New York Times Magazine,* December 7, 1980; the *Wall Street Journal,* May 31, 1984; *Newsweek,* August 19, 1985; the *New York Times,* July 6, 1986.

3. Several articles and television spots have been devoted to the transformation of transitional New York City neighborhoods into "Little Odessa" and "Russian Parkway" (e.g., the *New York Times,* December 31, 1978; *New York,* June 1, 1981; *Bay News,* June 7, 1982), the hedonistic character of Russian eating and entertainment patterns (Sokolov 1983, 92–95; *Newsday,* July 17, 1985), and émigrés' successful entry into small businesses (*Forbes,* July 29, 1985; *Staten Island Advance,* October 13, 1986).

4. The ability of Soviets to adapt to American freedom is discussed in almost every article and television program about immigrants from the USSR. ABC-TV documented "success stories" of "Russian" immigrants on Thanksgiving 1984 as part of its *20/20* program. Public television's *Frontline,* "The Russians Are Here," which aired on June 13, 1983, showed not only successful immigrants—a travel agent and a stockbroker—but also an unemployed writer making purchases with food stamps and a disappointed cab driver. The program focused on immigrants' complaints that

America gives "too much freedom," their longing for the camaraderie found within friendship circles in their native cities, and heavy consumption of food and vodka. As part of General Secretary Gorbachev's policy of *glasnost,* this television film was shown throughout the Soviet Union in October 1986. The media also report on the proliferation of the so-called "Russian Mafia," a network of extortionists, counterfeiters, loan sharks, and credit card manipulators, who, on occasion, resort to violence. See, for example, the *New York Times,* February 12, 1983, August 24, 1986; the *New York Daily News,* April 16, 1984; *Jewish Week,* April 27, 1984; the *Miami Herald,* March 31, 1985; the *Christian Science Monitor,* April 15, 1986; *New York Magazine,* November 24, 1986; and the *New York Times,* April 11, 1992.

5. See, for example, Kosmin 1990; Federation of Jewish Philanthropies of New York 1985; Simon and Simon 1982; Gilison 1979; Gitelman 1978. In the mid-1970s, the *Journal of Jewish Communal Studies* issued several articles by Jewish vocational, social service, and religious agencies on the resettlement of Soviet Jewish immigrants.

6. Sylvia Rothchild (1985) published a compilation of Soviet Jewish immigrants' oral histories, Victor Ripp (1984) wrote a "travel book . . . about the third-wave emigration," Roberta Markus (1979) a study of Toronto's Soviet immigrant schoolchildren, and Edgar Goldstein (1979) a clinical psychological analysis of émigrés' adaptation to American life. Most recently, Lydia Rosner (1986) published a study of immigrant crime.

7. Steven J. Gold's *Refugee Communities: A Comparative Field Study* (1992) compares Soviet Jewish and Vietnamese immigrant communities in California.

8. Many of these studies (Tyhurst 1977; Zwingmann and Pfister-Ammende 1973; Richardson 1967) report that immigrants go through three phases— elation, disorientation/depression, adjustment—after uprooting from their native lands.

9. Eisenstadt (1954), and after him Bar-Yosef (1968), view immigrants' task as desocialization and resocialization, resulting in an exchange of old roles and identities for new ones. Other analyses in this vein (for example, Agocs 1981; DeSantis and Benkin 1980; Yuan 1970; Gans 1979; and Gordon 1964) point to the eventual transformation of the immigrant enclave into a diffuse collectivity toward the end of the desocialization-resocialization process.

10. I view human consciousness and freedom as inherently connected but not as one and the same principle. Human consciousness enables people to

transcend the limits of their reality and to imagine opposites or permutations of what is, thus the ability to conceive of pink elephants, Armageddon, and talking coyotes. This ability to imagine alternatives to one's present reality and the desire and ability to carry out these alternatives in the sociopolitical realm distinguish human consciousness from freedom.

11. The circumstances under which Soviet émigrés confront American society certainly differ from those in which, for example, Latin American peasants meet banana companies, African tribesmen confront British administrators, or the "fringe" societies of Europe encountered the spreading capitalist "core."

12. According to Susanne Langer (1951, 290), "Any miscarriage of the symbolic process is an abrogation of our human freedom: the constraint imposed by a foreign language, or a lapse of one's own linguistic ability. . . . But the most disastrous hindrance is disorientation, the failure or destruction of life-symbols and loss or regression of votive acts."

13. Jacqueline Scherer (1972, xii) notes that this is contingent on the nature of the community: "At its best, community provides meaning and purpose to life—but at its worst, community can be a source of tyranny and inhumanity."

14. Campbell (1974, 9) looks to community not as "an organized social group" but as a "social space within which values are shared and the conduct of men and women is evaluated."

15. *Bricolage,* as originally proposed by Lévi-Strauss, may not be an entirely appropriate metaphor for Soviet émigrés' community, because the thoughts and things that compose and subsequently enter Soviet immigrant subculture are not necessarily flotsam and jetsam, haphazardly washed up into their beliefs and lifeways. Lévi-Strauss did not use the term *bricolage* to apply to complex, or "hot," societies. Groups characterized by literacy and a linear view of history strain and pick over the "driftwood" washed onto their shores, discarding some and adding some to the culture. What is tossed out and what is accepted depends on the historically constituted logic of the culture. Barbara Myerhoff (1978, 10) applies Lévi-Strauss's *bricolage* model to the culture of a Jewish senior center. Her use of this concept indicates that she sees no inherent logic determining what materials go into creating this culture, although the result is based on "a few stable, strong symbols and premises." She describes this culture as an amalgam, "impudently eclectic [that is] shifted and stretched to meet individual needs—private, collective, secular and sacred." While I would not go as far as Myerhoff in presenting an individ-

ual needs-based theory of culture, I use the idea of *bricolage* in much the same "heated" sense as she in my analysis of Soviet émigrés' community. I am also indebted to de Certeau's (1984) usage of *bricolage* in explaining the "practice of everyday life" in modern society.

16. This study focuses on Russian-speaking Jews from the heartland of Russia and the Ukraine and only minimally considers Georgian and Bukharan Jews who were able to maintain traditional communities in their home country. Note too that the city of Odessa, where Jews composed about one-quarter of the population, does have predominantly Jewish neighborhoods.

17. Federation of Jewish Philanthropies of New York's survey of Soviet Jewish immigrants (1985, 34) indicates that only 1 percent participated in a Jewish study group in the USSR. An additional 2 percent stated that they had had private Jewish education lessons. This may now be changing as Jewish study groups, schools, and cultural centers have gained semiofficial status during the *glasnost* era. The many small groups that sprang up in the late 1980s and early 1990s are now united in an umbrella organization of Jewish groups, the Va'ad, formed by a congress of representatives from these small groups in December 1989.

18. See, for example, Miner 1965; Simić 1973; Wheatley 1969; Kenny 1962; Stack 1974; Silverman 1984; and the writings of Robert Redfield.

19. There is no reason here to belabor the point that Americans, because of the Soviet Union's enormous size, system of government, and military might, have been fascinated with the so-called "Russian personality."

20. I moved to Brighton Beach with Mark Baskin, who was my husband at the time of fieldwork.

2. HISTORICAL BACKGROUND

1. Whether Byzantine Christians were more or less intolerant of Jews than Roman Catholics or German Lutherans is difficult to assess and certainly not the purpose of this study. What is important to note is Christian Russia's particular way of treating Jews and its long-ranging consequences.

2. Many Jewish immigrants from the Ukraine, where Khmelnitzki is a national hero, unabashedly confessed that they did not know about these mass murders of Jews until they had spent a few years in the United States.

3. Dubnow (1918, 2:373) emphatically claims that "the exodus from Russia was undoubtedly stimulated by the law imposing a fine for evading military

service and by the introduction of the educational percentage norm—two restrictions which threw into bold relief the disproportionate relations between rights and duties in Russian Jewry."

4. The gap between rich and poor among Jews had widened considerably during the latter part of the nineteenth century. The small group of Jewish families who had succeeded in establishing factories, sugar refineries, textile plants, banks, investments in railroad and water transport and in building the related insurance industry accumulated considerable wealth while providing needed products and services for the Russian Empire (see Baron 1964, 106–113; Dijur 1960, 155–182).

5. Dubnow (1920, 3:122–123) notes with irony that the constitution "conferred upon the Jews the highest political privilege—the right of voting for popular representatives—but left them at the same time in a state of civil disenfranchisement."

6. In fact the expulsion order had come from the tsar. The confusion that plagued Russia during those war years, with several competing armies on Russian soil, and the past-in-the-present mode that pervades many immigrants' recountings are illustrated in the above statement. Although Jews were over-represented in the Russian army and remained loyal to the tsar, they were accused of (potential) treachery. A growing awareness among the Russian intelligentsia that these accusations were false and that Jewish equality had to be guaranteed in the reconstruction of Russia's government amounted to naught. "While the majority still entertained hopes that, upon cessation of hostilities, the tsar himself would grant the Jews their well-merited rights, a growing radical minority looked for a revolutionary upheaval as the only means of salvation" (Baron 1964, 200).

7. Baron (1964, 250–251) and Gitelman (1972, 233) note that many artisans pursued their trades underground and engaged in "speculation" to avoid destitution. Thus was the Soviet "second economy" born with the creation of the Soviet state.

8. At the time, Jews constituted an estimated 1.8 to 2 percent of the total population. Their disproportionate representation in higher education and in the professions was to have repercussions in later years.

9. "The failure to implant Yiddish firmly in the trade unions, and hence in the factories, precluded the possibility of identifying Yiddish with the new society and legitimizing it in a predominantly industrial setting. The *Evsektsiia* failed to associate Yiddish with progress, prestige and modernization. In the mind of the Jewish citizen it was linked to the abandoned *shtetl* and a backward, anti-modern culture" (Gitelman 1972, 371). In an

ironic twist of fate, noted by Gitelman (1972, 341), most religious Jews preferred non-Yiddish schools for their children because anti-religious propaganda there was neither as virulent nor specifically anti-Jewish as it was in the schools established by the *Evsektsiia*.

10. Bauer, *The Jewish Problem* ([1843] 1958), and *The Capacity of Today's Jews and Christians to Become Free* (1843), as cited by Marx in McLellan, ed., *Karl Marx: Selected Writings* (1977), 39–62.

11. In his later correspondence with Engels, Marx did concede that as a temporary measure perhaps Poland should be emancipated from Russia and Ireland from Britain because the persistence of nationalistic ties divided workers and diverted them from their common struggle. He never, however, revised his position on the Jewish question.

12. The Russian Socialist Democratic Party was the precursor to the Communist Party of the Soviet Union (CPSU).

13. This caveat later legitimized the inclusion of the Baltic states into the USSR in 1939, the suppression of nationalistic uprisings in the Ukraine, Georgia, Kazakhstan during the 1950s, and most lately it was the legal base for Gorbachev's decision to send Soviet troops to Lithuania in 1990.

14. Immigrants uniformly laughed when I asked them if they or any members of their families moved to or even considered moving to Birobidzhan. Boris looked at me in amazement and said, "We wanted to improve our lives, not make them worse!"

15. Some people told of changing their names long after 1933. With a few rubles and the insistence that the name on the birth certificate was a mistake, Dovid became Dmitri, and Motel-Pinkhus was changed to Mark.

16. At birth, children are assigned the nationality of their mothers. Children of mixed marriages, at age sixteen, are given the option of selecting the nationality of either parent. Children whose parents are both Jews (or Latvians, or Uzbeks, etc.) cannot change their nationality designation.

17. Those who had followed Bukharin's admonition to "enrich themselves" under the New Economic Plan (NEP). Many immigrants draw strong parallels between the fate of NEP-men and what lies in store for the followers of Gorbachev's economic initiatives as part of *perestroika*.

18. Estimates greatly vary. The Soviet Union has never recorded specifically Jewish losses. Yad Vashem in Jerusalem, Israel, continues to research and document the extent of the Holocaust in the Soviet Union.

19. Walter Zenner (1977) points to lachrymosity, or the shedding of tears, as a unifying sentiment among Jews. Jews create group solidarity through the retelling of their sad history.

20. The passive voice is purposefully used here to underscore the ambiguity surrounding these actions. No one, nor any organization (e.g., KGB), has ever taken responsibility for Mikhoels's death; the official story is that he was run over in a motor vehicle accident.

21. Lysenko's plan to cultivate oranges in Siberia and to completely centralize agriculture without offering alternatives in the event of a crop failure are the most notable. Lera recalls a conversation on a train from the West Ukraine to Odessa in the early 1950s:

> This time, as we were riding, a peasant woman came into our compartment with several children. All of them—I remember this—looked terrible, frightening. So skinny, gaunt, so pale and pasty. And my father, just like this, greeted her, asking *Kak dela?* [How are things?] And she told how on her *kolkhoz* people were starving to death—that there was no food—that according to the central plan they had to send out all of their produce for centralized distribution. They didn't have enough to feed their animals, and without that, they had absolutely no meat or eggs for themselves. There was starvation during that time, very bad starvation. . . . There was a general famine; some of these agricultural policies failed terribly, and there were no contingency plans. One year everyone was directed to plant corn instead of wheat, and when the corn failed in some areas, there was absolutely nothing, no bread, no animals. You've heard of Lysenko and some of his theories? They were implemented, and people died.

22. Soviet Jews created a joke in response to official ignoring of Jewish nationality: "A performance will be given by the musical ensemble Friendship Between Nations, which includes the following performers: Ivanov (Russian), Kazachenko (Ukrainian), Dumbadze (Georgian), Rabinovich (accordian)" (Ben Ami 1967, 154). Yevgeny Yevtushenko's poem, "Babi Yar," calls serious attention to this oversight. Although all Soviet citizens suffered during the Second World War, Yevtushenko, a Ukrainian non-Jew, proclaims that the special tragedy that befell Jews at the hands of the Nazis must be noted.

23. *Judaism Without Embellishment* was a libelous account of Jewish "religious practices" that includes among them swindling and black-marketeering, and a Jewish "morality" that is based on hypocrisy and bribery. It is illustrated with caricatures of long-nosed, traditionally dressed Jews reminiscent of Nazi propaganda. The book was published by the Ukrainian Academy of Sciences (see Shapiro 1969, 476–479; also Katz 1972, 323–324).

24. Acquisition of a cooperative apartment, when it occurred, is mentioned without fail in informants' life histories. Many families acquired theirs during the Khrushchev years; others a little later under the Kosygin-Brezhnev regime.

25. Although 1967 is usually given as the year in which Jews began to apply to emigrate, some had applied and even left earlier. From May 15, 1948, to the end of 1951, only four old women and one invalid man were allowed to leave the Soviet Union for Israel. Between May 1948 and May 1952, however, almost 300,000 Jews from Poland, Rumania, Hungary, Czechoslovakia, and Bulgaria arrived in Israel (Schechtman 1969, 437). In the late 1950s, Golda Meir, then Israel's Foreign Minister, disclosed that she had received 9,236 requests from Russian Jews to rejoin their relatives (Schechtman 1969, 437). At the same time, around 200,000 former Polish citizens who had fled eastward to Russia in 1939 were allowed to repatriate to Poland, and many of the 15,000 Jews among them found their way to Israel (Zaslavsky and Brym 1983, 33). In 1965, with Kosygin as Prime Minister, exit visas on the average of fifty to sixty a month were granted to elderly Jews from newly annexed regions. In 1966, 2,700 Soviet-born Jews, including young people, were permitted to leave the USSR for Israel (Schechtman 1969, 439).

26. Zaslavsky and Brym (1983, 107–109) explain this new episode of anti-Jewish discrimination in terms of a growing multi-ethnic middle class and a decrease in need for white-collar specialists. To ensure proportionate representation of all nations and nationalities in university enrollment and in the professions, those who were over-represented (Jews, Armenians, Georgians) had to be limited to their percentage of the total population.

27. Never, of course, did Jews occupy 90 percent of these positions. This over-inflated sense of Jews' contributions is mentioned over and over again by immigrants and will be treated further in chapter 5.

28. Of course, not all Soviet Jews left their homeland in the 1970s; only about 17 percent emigrated. Zaslavsky and Brym (1983, 113–115) identify two other responses to the discriminatory policy of the Soviet state: The "assimilatory ideology," nothing new to Russian Jews, asserts that the Jews have in fact assimilated, and that the Jewish nationality designation in their passports will be eliminated in the near future. The second response, the "pragmatic complex" or "ideology of professional superiority," is founded on the belief that the regime does not want to lose its "good," loyal, hardworking Jewish intelligentsia, and therefore conditions for Jews are bound to improve.

29. An informant who arrived in Israel in 1972 and then came with his family to the United States six years later describes his disappointment with Israel: "It was because Israel is a Jewish state that I was sure life there would be much better for us. I guess I had unreal expectations, but I thought it would be a perfect society. One day my eighty-some-year-old grandmother was just walking along, and two young boys pulled her gold earrings right from her ears and her gold necklace off from her neck. They weren't Arabs, they were Jews. I always have Israel to go back to, to visit, but I don't want to live there anymore. America is a wonderful country." It must be noted, however, that secondary migration of Soviet Jews from Israel to the United States and other destinations is only about 9 percent.

30. The direct translation is not "cousin," but "sister." The Russian words *brat* and *sestra* are used to include cousins, on both the mother's and father's side, as well as one's immediate brother and sister.

31. Émigrés are very much worried about the Jewish groups that have gained semiofficial status in the USSR. Concerned that after *perestroika* (restructuring) will come *perestrelka* (reshooting), they are certain that the first candidates for execution will be Russia's traditional scapegoats, the Jews. They point to the rise of nationalistic organizations like *Pamyat* as proof of these fears.

3. COMMUNITY AS SOCIAL RELATIONS

1. See Appendix A, "The Mechanics of Emigration and Resettlement," for a description of the USSR to New York migration process.

2. In the eighty-two-year period, 1897–1979, Jews have radically changed their native language. In 1897, 97 percent claimed Yiddish as their mother tongue; in the 1979 census, 84 percent claimed Russian, while 97 percent reported first- or second-language fluency in Russian.

3. The question of the "Jewish race" and its distinguishing physical characteristics is an old one. Certainly mandatory wearing of distinctive garb in the Middle Ages, and more recently under the Third Reich, speaks to the difficulty of identifying Jews from among Christians on the basis of appearance. Russian Jews do speak of a "Jewish type"—curly-haired, long-nosed, stooped-shouldered, and either dark-complected or red-headed.

4. "Radio Horizons," an hour-long Russian language radio program, is broadcast six nights a week in New York City. Sponsored by Chamah, an organization within the network of the Lubavitcher Hasidim, it presents

ten to fifteen minutes of news (international, national, and local), stories about great Jewish leaders, messages about upcoming holidays and Jewish religious life, interviews with prominent members of the immigrant community, excerpts from Hebrew and Yiddish songs, and many, many commercial and personal announcements.

5. Although Americans voted in overwhelming support of Reagan in 1984, New York City's out-borough population, especially those in the Jewish neighborhoods of Brooklyn and Queens, where most Soviet émigrés live, tends to be Democrat. Thus, those with whom immigrants have most face-to-face contact are people with more liberal political leanings than they themselves.

6. In the USSR, the usual public facial expression is a cold, tight-lipped, emotionless "Soviet face." Shop clerks, bureaucrats, and other public servants greet clients with a scowl, as these relationships are adversarial. Smiles are reserved for the people one knows and cares about (see Smith 1976; Shipler 1984; Shlapentokh 1989).

7. These special schools are limited to very few students of the urban elite and are no more representative of foreign-language learning in the USSR than the Bronx High School of Science is representative of science instruction in American schools. Indeed, people who studied a foreign language during their school years (grades 5–10) usually exhibit very little active knowledge of that language.

8. Howells and Galperin (1984) take this one step further, claiming that Soviet Jews' primary identification in the USSR is with the concept of Soviet Man. They discuss immigrants' attitudes toward America in terms of their membership in the pseudo-species *Homo Sovieticus,* which implies a steadfast belief in the superiority of this group.

9. As Kurt Lewin (1948, 186) points out, Jews have a long tradition of establishing intragroup differences and of despising those outside of their subgroup. He attributes this process of division and opposition to Jews' self-hate. American Jews have rejected ensuing waves of immigrants out of fear that the acceptance they obtained by their own good behavior will be threatened by the arrival of loud, pushy, primitive, obnoxious greenhorns. "Jewish paranoia" may also account for NYANA's rush to find any job for any immigrant. Keeping Jews off welfare roles, it is reasoned, makes America receptive to Jewish immigrants and helps prevent anti-Semitism.

10. These proclamations are based not only upon immigrants' personal observations and experiences but may also reflect internalization of the ethnic hierarchy they have learned from Americans.

11. The phrase "snows of yester year" is from "Ballade des dames du temps jadis," by François Villon.

12. In Russian restaurants and in the course of daily life in Brighton Beach it is difficult to distinguish Muscovites from Odessans. Women seem equally made up and showy in their stylish clothes. Leather pants look the same on men from Odessa and from Moscow. See chapter 4 for further discussion on this theme.

13. And, indeed, Maxim proved to be right. The Russocentric status hierarchy has little relevance for Central Asians, who have established their own "urban villages" with formal religious organizations. It is more important for Russian-speaking Jews to distinguish themselves from the Easterners than for the Easterners to challenge their place in this social hierarchy.

14. One might argue that these so-called spiritual things were high-status commodities and that not all self-dubbed intelligentsia were far removed from materialistic strivings.

15. Of course, the size of these samples is not large enough to warrant generalization. An attempt was made to be representative of the population by selecting informants who represent a variety of residential patterns: Of seven Odessans, five are from Brighton Beach, while two live outside; of seven Muscovites, two are from Brighton Beach, three from Bensonhurst/Flatbush, and two from outside; of six Leningraders, three are from Brighton Beach, one from Rego Park, and two from outside; of three Kievans/Kharkovites, two live in Brighton Beach, and one in Forest Hills.

16. The Russian language distinguishes among three categories of friends: *drug*—close, intimate friend; *priatel*—friend; *znakomy*—acquaintance. The first two words were used by Boris.

17. This friendship subsequently broke up in 1988, as one couple made a much more rapid economic ascent than the other. Almost three years later, after the second couple had attained a higher standard of living, the wives reconciled, and the relationship between these two families consists once again of frequent telephone and in-person visits.

18. These factors are: previous friendship in the USSR (37% of the sample); shared migration cohort (3%); common acquaintances (17%); common interests (19%); same neighborhood (11%); and "other" (11%), which includes chance encounters.

19. Later in the conversation, this girl explained that to her, here in America, "Russian" means Jewish immigrants from the USSR like herself and her parents.

20. There are some exceptions to this rule, particularly those immigrants who are having difficulties letting go of their past and adjusting to America; as discussed above, they find themselves increasingly isolated. Émigrés in immigrant neighborhoods find anonymity a near impossibility. It must be stressed that research for this study occurred during 1984–85, five to six years after the height of emigration, allowing time for friendships and acquaintances to form.

21. Only once did an immigrant speak with some nostalgia about communal apartment life: "We all got along so well, it was like one big family. And on Sunday mornings we would put together a big table in the corridor and all sixteen of us would have breakfast together."

22. Unlike English, which distinguishes *building* or *apartment building* from *house,* and *house* from *home,* Russian-speakers use the word *dom* to mean home—be it house or apartment building. Reports of gossip often begin with, "*V nashem dome govoryat . . .*" (In our home they are saying . . .).

23. A new neighbor who is white and American would be asked about being Jewish, and, if an immigrant, where he or she is from in the USSR. Asian, black, and Puerto Rican neighbors are not questioned because Soviet immigrants identify them immediately by their physical and linguistic characteristics.

24. This figure is based on a survey of the shops along Brighton Beach Avenue that I took in 1984–85.

25. Haggling is the rule at peasant markets and commission shops in the Soviet Union. The state does not determine prices in these institutions. This buying behavior often carries over in America to small, privately owned shops, to outdoor flea markets, and even to the sweets and toys offered for sale at yearly Purim bazaars in synagogues and Jewish community centers.

26. Some Soviet immigrants who live in Staten Island and on Long Island own businesses in Brooklyn that cater to a predominantly "Russian" clientele. Others, who live in Brooklyn, may own businesses or work in concerns that are part of mainstream America.

4. THE MORAL COMMUNITY

1. The term "total system" is used to describe the Soviet Union because it is more accurate and less emotionally charged than the much-debated designation, "totalitarian system." What is meant here follows from Marcel

Mauss's (1967, 1) definition of total social phenomena in which "all kinds of institutions find simultaneous expression: religious, legal, moral, and economic. In addition, the phenomena have their aesthetic aspect and they reveal morphological types." The Soviet system is considered a total system because it provides its citizenry with its economic, political, social, moral, cultural, and legal arenas of interaction. It is, theoretically at least, a complete social whole, not just a political institution. Activities that do occur outside this system take place "underground," and they are either not recognized as real or prosecuted as illegal by the Soviet state. Please note that the ethnographic present of this study is the USSR of the 1970s, although subsequent interviews with post-1987 immigrants reveal that not very much has changed despite *glasnost* and *perestroika*.

2. Indeed, Gorbachev relaxed his anti-alcohol measures when sugar disappeared from stores (as it was used to brew homemade spirits) as well as toothpaste and other commodities containing alcohol.

3. This is, at the very least, folk wisdom. Counselors at resettlement agencies in the United States have commented (personal communications) on what they see as disturbing drinking behavior. Future research in both the USA and the USSR would be helpful in assessing the veracity of this folk wisdom.

4. They are also jealously guarded and sometimes overly protected to the detriment of the friendship. Hurt that I was spending more time with Lera than with her, Nona called me to say that I was exercising poor judgment in my selection of friends. When I insisted that Lera is a lovely person, Nona interrupted to assert, "If you lie with shit, you will smell like shit." Maxim had similar lectures from her.

5. Immigrants explain that in America, where people can buy whatever they wish, it is better to give money than a shirt or a sweater that might not exactly suit the recipient. What is not discussed is that party-givers often use their gifts to defray the costs of their celebrations and that most Russian restaurants in 1985 charged about twenty-five dollars per person.

6. Specifically from 1956 onward, when Stalin's reign of terror was unmasked and finally put to an end.

7. Immediately prior to this speech, the speaker was complaining about having to pay a large amount of money in federal, state, and local income taxes. "Ha!" his companion chided him after his plea for Americans to give and be humane, "Where is your humanity? What are you willing to give? Here you are complaining about taxes, about giving back to this country what it gives to you."

8. The literal translation of the phrase *kultura povedeniia* is "culture of behavior," which means the rules and practices of (socially correct) behavior. Because the phrase is awkward, an alternate phrase, "cultured behavior," is here used in its place.

9. This helps to explain the emphasis immigrants place on language when determining one's position in the status hierarchy and their high degree of self-consciousness in speaking accented English.

10. Perhaps because it was used during the French Revolution, which ultimately failed, the Russian revolutionary leadership did not adopt the term "citizen" (*grazhdanin/grazhdanka*). "Comrade" implies an ethos of friendship and mutual assistance and has no connection to other (failed) social movements. Interestingly, prisoners, labor camp detainees, and would-be emigrants are addressed as Citizen, a legal status, not Comrade, a social status.

11. Russian Jewish men are frequently named Mikhail (Misha), Yefim (Fima), Dmitri (Dima), Grigory (Grisha), Aleksandr (Sasha), Vladimir (Volodya), Boris (Borya), and Mark (Marek). Women often have the following names: Lina, Lena, Ludmila (Mila), Luba, Inna, Evgenia (Zhenya, Zhanna), Dina, Irina, Svetlana, Ella, Marina (Masha), and Alexandra (Sanya, Shura, Sasha).

12. During feudalism, the nobility referred to their serfs and servants by this form of address; it can be found in the great novels of the nineteenth century. The *-ka* designation kept them always in the status of children and denied them equality with their masters. Informants have related that men who are drunkards or ne'er-do-wells are referred to throughout their lives by the *-ka* form of their first name, which indicates society's scorn for those who have refused to accept the responsibilities of adulthood. Casual use of this form of the name subtly signals that one thinks its possessor is without *kulturnost,* is unworthy of respect.

13. In the Soviet Union, veterans of World War II receive special privileges, such as first place in lines and other entitlements. In America, this sometimes leads to tragicomic moments of cross-cultural misunderstanding, as men in their sixties push their way up to the front of lines or try to get special privileges from social service agencies, announcing that they are veterans.

14. The Russian word *kultura* translates as "culture," but its meaning is specifically tied to the concept of high culture.

15. Their own lack of openmindedness in this regard is noteworthy, but this seems to be a pan-European cultural given. See the analysis of French geography by Pierre Bourdieu (1984, 105).

16. Soviet Jews tell a joke about the widely used Russian phrase *zhidovskaya morda,* a pejorative that translates literally as "kike mug" as opposed to the polite term, *evreiskoye litso* ("Jewish face"): One day a man was on a bus, and some Russian came over to him and started yelling, "*Zhidovskaya morda!* Get off this bus! Go to Israel!" The man looked up from the book he was reading and replied, "Exucse me, Comrade. I am not a Jew. I just happen to have an intelligent face." See also Rothchild (1985, 49–50) for an explanation of *zhidovskaya morda* through oral history.

17. In Israel during the 1970s and 80s, the *Sokhnut* (Jewish Agency) allocated funds to new immigrant authors from the USSR to assist them in publishing their previously suppressed works. Russian-language publications in Israel are second only to Hebrew; English follows as third.

18. Ilya Oblomov is the title character of Ivan Goncharev's 1858 novel *Oblomov,* who represents the tired, physically alive but morally dead Russian nobility. Although inspired in his youth by noble ideas and every so often throughout his life by plans to revive his estate and provide a road to his village and education for the peasantry, he cannot awaken from his malaise. Incapable of action, he lies about in bed in a peaceful kind of living death.

19. The furnishings of the apartment alone immediately speak to fellow immigrants about the *intelligentny* character of its inhabitants. Among many former Soviet Jews, chrome, brass, and mirrors are preferred; velour, or better yet, (white) leather sofas and armchairs, and prominent television and stereo equipment furnish the living room, speaking to *meshchanstvo.*

5. COMMUNITY AS HISTORY AND DESTINY

1. Bernhard Goetz, a young white man, turned himself in to the Concord, New Hampshire, police on December 31, 1984, after having shot four black youths in a near-deserted New York City subway car. He claimed self-defense in justification of his actions.

2. Boris, a tall, broad-shouldered man, after much prodding explains, "In Russia we don't have so many Mediterranean peoples, Italians, and so on. Maybe here and there a Georgian, an Armenian, but even so—they always knew I was Jewish."

3. The closer Jews became in appearance, language, occupation, and life-style to their non-Jewish European neighbors, the more the Gentile world looked for factors to explain how Jews differ from them. Sander Gilman's (1986) analysis is the most comprehensive and thought provoking to date; Kurt Lewin's (1948) essay touches these points as well. Jewish blood, un-like language, beliefs, and lifestyle, cannot be changed. It indelibly marks the Jew as genetically different, and worse.

The notion of the *Übermensch,* derived from Nietsche and applied by the Nazis to legitimize their conquest of Europe, has implicit in it its opposite, the *Untermensch.* The application of genetic principles and the notion of blood to these philosophical constructs created a reality in which certain humans came to be regarded as subhuman, and, using the language of science, contact with such subhumans was deemed polluting. Thus, the Jew, the Nazis' quintessential *Untermensch* could pollute even the most pure Aryan and forever deprive him or her of superhuman status. It is interesting to consider why the superior blood of the *Übermensch* does not have the power to conquer the inferiority of Jewish blood, but here is not the place for such an inquiry (see Douglas 1979 for an analysis of the concepts of pollution and taboo). According to Soviet law, however, chil-dren of mixed-nationality parents may choose whichever nationality they prefer; thus neither Jewish nor Russian "blood" is stronger or more pollut-ing than others.

4. This very attitude, Lewin (1948) points out, gets Jews into even deeper trouble with anti-Semites who view them as overly pushy, aggressive, and sneaky for working their way to the top.

5. Quoting Samuel Breidner, headmaster of the new Liberal Jewish Day School, in *Jewish Week,* August 23, 1985.

6. *Haftarah* is a Hebrew term meaning "conclusion" applied to the portion from the Prophets read on Sabbaths and festivals immediately after the reading of the Torah. The *Haftarah* section, preceded and followed by special benedictions, usually relates to the Torah portion. The child cele-brating his Bar Mitzvah chants the *Haftarah* portion when he is called to the Torah; he usually does not read from the Torah itself.

7. The Federation of Jewish Philanthropies of New York's (1985, 11) survey reveals that 68 percent of their Soviet Jewish immigrant interviewees pos-sess an active understanding of Yiddish, and 43 percent speak the lan-guage. This finding was recently duplicated (Kosmin 1990, 19): in a six-city survey, 43 percent of those interviewed from the 1979 immigrant cohort claim to speak Yiddish. These data are quite noteworthy because they

point to the continuing importance of a distinctive Jewish identity within the family setting among Jews in the USSR.

8. In the Passover service (*seder*) a role is assigned to the youngest member of the gathering to ask the Four Questions that inspire the retelling of the flight from Egypt.

9. According to Jewish law, all people born of Jewish mothers are Jews. To be a good and righteous Jew, one must live according to the Law of Moses and perform the deeds (the 613 *mitzvot*) and rituals this law commands.

10. A major difference between Hasidim and other Orthodox Jews is that the former have leaders (*rebbes*) who take an active role in each member's life, e.g., the Lubavitcher Rebbe either personally arranges or at the very least gives his approval to marriage matches made between persons in his community. Members of the Agudath Israel movement are traditional Orthodox Jews whose dress is slightly less conservative than the Hasidim (men in both movements wear full beards, but Agudath men are not confined to wearing only white shirts and black suits), and no spiritual/lay leader is the ultimate authority in their lives.

11. In Europe, circumcision is not at all widespread; with few exceptions only Jews and Muslims are circumcised.

12. An unintended consequence is the denial of a "good" Jewish identity to "non-Jewish" boys who had endured insults in the Soviet Union. These boys who had always considered themselves Jewish, and were considered Jewish in their native country, are now told that they are, in fact, not Jews because of intermarriage a generation or two ago.

13. These Jewish circumcisions are performed in hospitals or outpatient clinics. The patient is given a local anesthetic, and the operation takes place quickly and privately, witnessed only by a rabbi, parents, and godparents.

14. At the height of immigration (1979–80), Jewish schools were swamped with requests for enrollment of Russian-speaking youngsters. One solution to this problem was to establish special groups for immigrant children within preexisting schools; another was to establish whole schools for Russian Jewish children. These schools were hastily conceived, and staff at the Board of Jewish Education, in personal interviews, conceded that they are educationally inferior to "mainstream" Jewish day schools. A parent related that after visiting one such school she was determined to enroll her child in public school, "These conditions I never imagined still exist in the present century!" Many immigrant parents' dream is to enroll their child in a "modern" yeshiva, like Brooklyn's Yeshiva of Flatbush, which has strin-

gent admissions criteria, a strong general studies curriculum, and very limited scholarship monies, or, better still, a "non-religious" yeshiva, which does not exist.

15. Svetlana became Bat Mitzvah at age twelve in a Russian restaurant, with a minimum of Jewish religious instruction.

16. According to informants, Bar/Bat Mitzvahs are virtually nonexistent in the USSR (also Rozenblum 1982, 97–99).

17. See note 6, above.

18. "Assimilated" Jews, including those who have converted to Christianity, look with fear and revulsion at more traditional Jews because they dread being associated with the backwardness, clannishness, and darkness that the *shtetl* Jew embodies to them. German Jews, by adopting German in favor of Yiddish, seeking new occupations, modernizing their appearance, and identifying with the German state, distanced themselves from their East European counterparts. As Gilman (1986) points out throughout his book, the "Polish, Oriental Jew" becomes the embodiment of the "bad," anachronistic Jew. German Jews were very surprised that they were included in Hitler's annihilation program; they believed that only inferior Polish and Russian Jews would be the Nazis' target.

19. Spiro's (1981, 193) observation on the inhabitants of Kiryat Yedidim fits the case of Soviet émigrés, "They have, in short, an intense need to love and an intense need to hate; and what is more, they abhor uncertainty and cannot tolerate ambivalence."

20. The present tense is used here not only to reflect the ethnographic present of 1984–86 but also because in 1990 and even in 1991 many émigrés believe that "*Rossiya bez tsara—ne mozhet byt*" (A Russia without a tsar can never be). They strongly doubt that the dissolution of Soviet communism will lead to a free and democratic commonwealth of (former) Soviet republics and fear an imminent bloodbath.

21. These two proposals are also widely debated among American government leaders, in the media, and among American citizens. It would be foolhardy to suggest that the solutions immigrants propose to America's problems derive solely from their Soviet experiences, for they also reflect prevalent American attitudes.

22. One informant supplied an alternate interpretation of Soviet immigrants' strong support of President Reagan. She suggested that they were for Reagan precisely because he was president and that it would not matter

much whether the president were Mondale, Carter, Ford, or Nixon. "They are used to supporting whoever happens to be in power."

23. Soviet Jewish immigrants were far from alone in their support of Goetz's actions. The *New York Times* front-page story of January 1, 1985, reported that "a special telephone line that police set up to receive tips to lead them to a suspect instead attracted hundreds of callers who expressed support for the gunman's actions. Some people offered to help pay legal expenses and others suggested he run for mayor."

6. THE RHYTHM OF DAILY LIFE

1. The works of Bronislaw Malinowski, Ruth Benedict, Margaret Mead, Clyde and Florence Kluckhohn, and George Murdock, more recently followed by Rosaldo and Lamphere (1974), Reiter (1975), Ortner and Whitehead (1981), Murphy and Murphy (1985), and Ginsburg and Tsing (1990) are most noteworthy.

2. The Russian Orthodox wedding ceremony included a ritualistic handing down of the father's whip to the bridegroom (see Atkinson 1977, 7, citing M. F. Vladimirskii-Budanov, *Obzor istorii russkogo prava* [Kiev, 1886], p. 91, and V. I. Sergeevich, *Leksii po istorii russkogo prava* [1890], p. 564). This symbol of man's dominance over woman was often put into practice when husbands were displeased with their wives.

3. One of the first scenes of the film shows women arriving at work, opening their purses and taking out combs and makeup. They then apply green eyeshadow, rouge, black eyeliner, and lipstick, and comb and tease their hair. This scene produced howls of laughter among the twenty or so immigrants who were viewing the film. "You see, Franushka," Irina, the evening's hostess said to me, "it is hard to break these habits that we learned when we were twenty years old. I have a very hard time going out onto the street without any eye makeup or lipstick."

4. Here the traditional Jewish practice of women working so that the man may study has been reversed. In the *shtetl,* nonetheless, most men's primary role was that of provider, and then after the Revolution, when religious study was outlawed as a form of parasitism, Jewish men worked to support themselves and their families. In America, as will be discussed later, man's role as economic provider reaches new proportions.

5. It is noteworthy that while abortion is mentioned as a cause of women's physical problems, Mr. Lasky does not explicitly mention menstruation-

linked illnesses commonly discussed in American media, such as stomach cramps or pre-menstrual syndrome.

6. Only once did I hear a logical, structural opposite to this term. At a performance of *Porgy and Bess,* Irina turned to me to give her opinion of Bess's illness upon her return to Catfish Row: "*Oni perefakalis,*" she said, meaning "they over-fucked." But this word is not native Russian. It is a good example of the linguistic syncretism that occurs among immigrants, as it incorporates an Anglo-Saxon root word with a Russian prefix and verb ending.

7. Official Soviet ideology takes a puritanical view toward sex. Pornography and erotic art, films, and literature are all banned. The Soviet codex of law prohibits male homosexuality, and informants have told of men sentenced to five years' imprisonment for their sexual misconduct. The codex does not even mention female homosexuality (although informants report that it does exist); the very idea of lesbianism in a culture that worships mother-hood is so abhorrent that it is beyond the imagination of lawmakers (see Gray 1990, 95–96).

8. Immigrants frequently contrasted Ferraro with Jeane Kirkpatrick, calling the latter a strong, forceful leader as opposed to Ferraro, whom they perceived as weak. Of course, much of this perception derives from Fer-raro's affiliation with Walter Mondale and the Democratic party and Kirk-patrick's association with the tough Reagan administration stance on for-eign affairs. Immigrants deny that they are in principle against women in high office; they do insist, however, that women in politics be strong and forceful. A woman who cannot even control her husband enough to know the extent of his business dealings has no business seeking control of an entire country.

9. Soviet émigrés like to say, "The Soviet Union is composed of fourteen republics—and Georgia," to note that life in this Caucasian republic is different from Soviet life everywhere else. Georgians pride themselves on their independence and their ability to thwart the Soviet system while using aspects of it to further their own ends. The man quoted, a Georgian Jewish restaurateur, tells of his father's restaurant in Tbilisi: "No, of course he isn't the official owner. You know that everything in the Soviet Union is state-owned. He was the director—but he was like the owner. To fulfill the plan [meet the government's quota] is very easy, and then everything else went back into building up the restaurant and into our family. Like there is capitalism in New York, there is capitalism in Georgia."

10. Jewish men are considered desirable husbands by Russian women as well as Jewish women because they are reputed to neither drink nor beat (*ne piyut i ne biyut*) and to be good providers (see Ben Ami 1967, 144; Gray 1990, 56).

11. On the other hand, one man, who is certainly not alone, relates that, until he decided to get married, in his mid-thirties, he had no problem whatsoever finding girlfriends and lovers in the USA. In fact, he reports that his social and sex life was much more active in New York than in his native Ukrainian city.

12. *Dallas* and *Dynasty* are immensely popular among émigrés (see Aksyonov 1989, 142).

13. Soviet pedagogy courses instruct teachers on both *vospitaniye*, "upbringing," and *obrazovaniye*, "education," of children.

14. Oral contraceptives are rare and unrefined in the USSR. Other birth control devices are almost unheard of. Premature withdrawal, rhythm, and abortion are virtually the only birth control methods in the USSR.

15. The Federation of Jewish Philanthropies (1985, 13) indicates that 30 percent of its New York–based sample left the Soviet Union for their "children's future."

16. I am indebted to Misha Galperin with whom I spent several hours in conversation during fieldwork, for sharing his perspective, developed as a psychometrist and psychologist, on the Russian Jewish émigré family. He views the embedded immigrant family in a negative light and believes that children in such families suffer dire consequences. His doctoral research (1988) demonstrates that teenagers from enmeshed families with high achievement orientation suffer internally, especially from depression, while those from families with low achievement orientations display their disturbances through overtly antisocial acts.

Agreeing in principle that this phenomenon of enmeshment typifies Soviet Jewish immigrant families and influences children's (and parents') personality development and social skills, I do not believe it necessarily results in maladaptive, bewildered, suffering, or aggressive individuals (cf. Hulewat 1981). In the text I delineate differences in embedded family types that derive from the extent of the parents' ability to serve as examples and live up to the ideals they set for their children.

17. Many single mothers, of course, have worked very hard not only at reestablishing themselves in their new country but also in providing a warm and

supportive home environment for their children. I by no means wish to imply that all or even most single mothers reverse roles with their daughters.

18. A common practice in Brighton Beach (and elsewhere) is for shopkeepers to hire part-time clerks without processing federal, state, or city tax forms for them. The clerks are paid in cash and have no record of working in these establishments.

19. Certainly these role reversals are not as simple and conflict-free as this may imply. Some children do indeed express anger and confusion over a new environment and distorted family roles through antisocial behavior and school truancy (Steinfirst 1980, 11–13). As Galperin's study (1988) shows, more research should be done on this very troubling subject.

20. Parents often transfer their children from yeshiva to public school at the end of eighth or ninth grade, especially if their children gain admission to a special public high school program or one of the specialized New York City high schools. They fear that their children's secular education will suffer in yeshiva and believe that by the time they are teenagers their moral character is basically formed. There are other families, although far fewer, who enroll their children in yeshiva, or even in military boarding schools, after encountering behavioral problems while their children attended public schools.

21. Markus (1979, 62) notes that "the offspring of these immigrants, prior to departure from the Soviet Union, lived a secure and orderly existence." A pilot study that I recently conducted in Chicago of young adult women who had come to the United States in the late 1970s as teenagers confirms this finding. See Markowitz 1991 for the interpretations these (now grown) children give to their family dynamics, both before and after immigration.

22. Some older children have told me of forging their parents' signatures on report cards when their school performance was poor. While this is certainly not unknown to Americans, émigré children do this to protect their parents from aggravation rather than to screen themselves from punishment.

23. After two or three years in America, immigrant children usually prefer English to Russian and use English almost exclusively with their age-mates. It is not uncommon for a parent to address a child in Russian and the child to respond in English.

24. During fieldwork I was often used as an example to immigrant children. Parents would say, "Look, she's spent so many thousands of dollars in college to learn our language! Why are you just throwing it away?" or,

more frequently, "Aren't you ashamed of yourself—she's American and speaks our language better than you do!"

25. These are the children I met; none of the parents with whom I am acquainted, save one, has had psychological counseling or psychiatric care. I do not have data from school guidance offices or juvenile officers attesting to overtly rebellious acts, but my hunch is that the automobile-parts thieves, drug dealers, etc., are rare in the immigrant youth population. This does, however, remain an empirical question.

26. Soviet émigrés speak quite freely about the salaries they earn, and freely ask others about their earnings. It may take more than several years to understand what a "good wage" is for a particular job and to learn that money matters are secret—confined to the private domain.

27. A group of Soviet immigrants who are veterans of World War II waged an unsuccessful campaign for pensions from the U.S. military, claiming that since the Red Army and American forces fought together as allies, they ought to receive the same benefits as American veterans.

28. Several elderly immigrants have complained that when they first arrived in America they had absolutely nothing to do. Shopping for food and other consumer items in the USSR used to take them hours, and their victorious finds earned them applause from grateful family members. Here, "You can buy everything in fifteen minutes, and there's still the whole day."

29. Some funeral homes supplement their newspaper advertisements by painting huge signs on building facades, visible as one steps onto the Brighton Beach subway platform, to announce their service to the Russian-speaking Jewish public. Many also distribute Jewish calendars, printed in Russian, during the High Holy Days.

7. THE ELUSIVE SHAPES OF COMMUNITY

1. The only exception noted in the literature is Israeli emigrants. Moshe Shokeid (1988) explains their lack of organizations by a number of factors, most important of which is their desire for invisibility deriving from the stigma of having emigrated and their own refusal to admit that their emigration is permanent.

2. Annelise Orleck (1987, 296) contends that Soviet émigrés fail to form organizations due to their lack of organizational experience. However, as I have demonstrated elsewhere (Markowitz 1992), the "non-organizations" of Hebrew study circles, Jewish history and culture seminars, dissemination

of *samizdat* (underground publications), to say nothing of experience in the Soviet second economy, provides (former) Soviet citizens with the organizational skills to become successful American business people (see Kestin 1985) and organizers of voluntary associations.

3. Michel de Certeau (1984) describes an analogous diversionary tactic in the West, *la perruque,* "work disguised as work for his employer. . . . In the very places where the machine he must serve reigns supreme, he cunningly takes pleasure in finding a way to create gratuitous pleasures" (p. 25).

4. The Federation of Jewish Philanthropies' (1985, 37) survey indicates very low rates of involvement with cultural-service organizations, ranging from a high of 4 percent to a low of 2 percent of its sample 233 émigrés. Although more than one-third belong to a YM-YWHA or Jewish community center, this high rate of membership reflects involvement with sports and exercise much more than with cultural or community service activities.

5. In 1989, however, with a new cohort of several thousands of Soviet Jewish refugees arriving in the United States, the local "powers that be" relented, and a successful dinner was held in Brighton Beach's National Restaurant to raise funds for the resettlement of new immigrants from the USSR in both the United States and Israel. This event was repeated in 1990.

6. By "anarchistic community" I do not mean to imply that it is a "chaotic political condition of lack of order" (Zadrozny 1959, 33). The "anarchy" that underlies this community more closely resembles Krishan Kumar's definition in *The Social Science Encyclopedia* (Kuper and Kuper 1985, 24): "Anarchy is a political philosophy which holds that societies can and should exist without rulers. Anarchists believe that this will not, as is commonly supposed, lead to chaos . . . but on the contrary to an increase in social order. Anarchists see the state as the decisive source of corruption and disorder in the body politic."

7. "Russian" here includes both popular Soviet-Russian songs and those composed by émigrés. It covers as well Odessa thieves' songs, Russian-Gypsy music, and popular melodies from the Caucasian and Central Asian republics. The term "Russian" is here used in the sense of the (old) Russian empire not in the national or ethnic sense of the word.

8. A performance in 1984 by a most popular Russian-Gypsy singer elicited grumbling complaints from the audience, and people even walked out before the evening was over. The audience expected the same Dmitri they had seen years ago in the USSR; instead, he was quite an old man and was

unable to perform with the intensity he once had. Concerts of minor singers who are trying to incorporate American material into their repertoire also evoke negative criticism. Some people comment that it is too sad for them to go to these concerts any more; others simply state that they are a waste of time.

9. Published by Boris Vetrov in *Novoye Russkoye Slovo* on February 13, 1985. This English version is my translation.

10. This is a Russian tradition that Jews have, to no small extent, incorporated into their mourning traditions as well. Muscovites in the know tell me that a jigger of vodka and a crust of brown bread are still placed on Vysotsky's dressingroom table in the Taganka Theater to honor his memory.

11. Lermontov and Pushkin died in their thirties from wounds they suffered in duels. Vysotsky died from cardiac arrest at age forty, but folk wisdom says he drank himself to death.

8. A POSTMODERN COMMUNITY

1. An émigré journalist who covered the story of the returnees for *Novoye Russkoye Slovo* interprets this anger and bitterness as a "Soviet syndrome," a response not unlike the slurs of traitor that were hurled at them as would-be emigrants when they were leaving the Soviet Union.

2. Irving Howe (1976, 58) explains that Jews characteristically come to America as permanent immigrants: "While only two thirds of the total number of immigrants to the United States in the years between 1908 and 1924 were to remain here permanently, 94.8 percent of the Jews remained permanently. In the crucial year of 1908, only 2 percent of the Jewish immigrants returned to the old country."

3. The journalist who reported on re-immigration for *Novoye Russkoye Slovo* confirms that among the 145 returnees many are not Jewish, several are from the Causcasus, and many are in mixed marriages (exact numbers were not known).

4. One family of four decided to repatriate to the USSR and then returned to the United States in a matter of days. Newspaper accounts report that when ordered to throw down their American passports in a dramatic gesture upon arrival in Moscow, they realized just what their American freedom meant and came home to Jersey City. The family head refused to speak to me in March 1987, relaying a message through her boss: "I already

gave one interview, and they quoted me wrong, and I do not want to talk to anyone again."

5. More recently, in June 1991 at a birthday party in Chicago some émigrés were talking about an acquaintance or relative who does not wish to leave the USSR because of its stimulating intellectual life. These not-so-new immigrants laughed and asked each other, "What does intellectual life matter if you can't find food to eat, clothes to wear, and have anti-Semites all around you?"

6. By mid-1987 it became increasingly simple for former Soviet citizens to obtain tourist visas to visit the USSR. By 1988, Soviet citizens with friends and relatives abroad were permitted to cross the border and visit them. Most important of all, emigration accelerated from a mere trickle to a new wave.

7. In the 1990s New York receives about 43 percent of Soviet Jewish refugees coming to the United States.

8. According to the 1990 HIAS (Hebrew Immigrant Aid Society) *Annual Reports,* 85,323 Soviet Jews arrived in the United States from 1987 through 1990. An additional 30,000 were expected for 1991. Statistics from the Soviet Jewish Research Bureau indicate that during the same years 198,169 Soviet Jews arrived in Israel. As of April 30, 1991, another 50,146 emigrants from the USSR made Israel their new home.

BIBLIOGRAPHY

Abramsky, C. 1972. "The Biro-Bidzhan Project, 1927–1959." In *The Jews in Soviet Russia Since 1917*, 2d ed., ed. L. Kochan, 62–75. London: Oxford University Press.

Agocs, C. 1981. "Ethnic Settlement in a Metropolitan Area: A Typology of Communities." *Ethnicity* 8: 127–148.

Ainsztein, R. 1972. "Soviet Jewry in the Second World War." In *The Jews in Soviet Russia Since 1917*, 2d ed., ed. L. Kochan, 269–287. London: Oxford University Press.

Aksyonov, V. 1989. *In Search of Melancholy Baby*. New York: Vintage Books.

Anderson, B. 1983. *Imagined Communities: Reflections on the Origin and Spread of Nationalism*. London: Verso Editions.

Appadurai, A. 1991. "Global Ethnoscapes: Notes and Queries for a Transnational Anthropology." In *Recapturing Anthropology: Working in the Present*, ed. R. G. Fox, 191–210. Santa Fe: School of American Research Press.

Aronson, G. 1969. "The Jewish Question During the Stalin Era." In *Russian Jewry 1917–1967*, ed. G. Aronson et al., 171–208. New York: Thomas Yoseloff.

Aronson, G., J. Frumkin, A. Goldweiser, and Joseph Lewitan, eds. 1969. *Russian Jewry, 1917–1967*. New York: Thomas Yoseloff.

Atkinson, D. 1977. "Society and the Sexes in the Russian Past." In *Women in Russia*, ed. D. Atkinson, A. Dallin, and G. W. Lapidus, 3–38. Stanford: Stanford University Press.

Atwood, L. 1990. *The New Soviet Man and Woman: Sex Role Socialization in the U.S.S.R.* Bloomington: University of Indiana Press.

Bakhtin, M. 1981. "Discourse in the Novel." In *The Dialogic Imagination: Four Essays by M. M. Bakhtin,* ed. M. Holmquist, 259–422. Austin: University of Texas Press.

Baron, S. W. 1964. *The Russian Jew Under Tsars and Soviets.* New York: Macmillan.

Barth, F. 1969. *Ethnic Groups and Boundaries.* Boston: Little, Brown.

Bar-Yosef, R. W. 1968. "Desocialization and Resocialization: The Adjustment Process of Immigrants." *International Migration Review* 2(6): 27–45.

Bauer, B. 1843. *The Capacity of Today's Jews and Christians to Become Free.* Zurich. As cited in Marx 1977.

Bauer, B. 1958. *The Jewish Problem.* Cincinnati: Hebrew Union College, Jewish Institute of Religion.

Bauer, O. 1909. *The National Question and Social Democracy.* N.p.: Serp Publishing House. As cited in Stalin 1975.

Bauer, R., A. Inkeles, and C. Kluckhohn. 1960. *How the Soviet System Works.* New York: Vintage Books.

Beals, R. 1951. "Urbanism, Urbanization and Acculturation." *American Anthropologist* 53: 1–9.

Ben Ami. 1967. *Between Hammer and Sickle.* Philadelphia: Jewish Publication Society of America.

Berger, P., B. Berger, and H. Kellner. 1974. *The Homeless Mind.* New York: Vintage Books.

Berger, P., and T. Luckmann. 1967. *The Social Construction of Reality.* Garden City, N.Y.: Anchor Books.

Blu, K. I. 1980. *The Lumbee Problem: The Making of an American Indian People.* Cambridge: Cambridge University Press.

Boswell, T. D., and J. R. Curtis. 1983. *The Cuban-American Experience: Culture, Image, and Perspectives.* Totowa, N.J.: Rowman and Allandad.

Bourdieu, P. 1977. *Outline of a Theory of Practice.* Cambridge: Cambridge University Press.

Bourdieu, P. 1984. *Distinction: A Social Critique of the Judgement of Taste.* Cambridge: Harvard University Press.

Breton, R. 1964. "Institutional Completeness of Ethnic Communities and the Personal Relations of Immigrants." *American Journal of Sociology* 70: 193–205.

Brodsky, B. 1983. "Social Work and the Soviet Immigrant." *Migration Today* 10(1): 15–20.

Brokhin, Y. 1975. *Hustling on Gorky Street.* New York: Dial Press.

Bronfenbrenner, U. 1972. *Two Worlds of Childhood, U.S. and U.S.S.R.* 2d ed. New York: Simon and Schuster.

Brownmiller, S. 1984. *Femininity*. New York: Simon and Schuster.

Brym, R. J. 1985. "The Changing Rate of Jewish Emigration from the USSR: Some Lessons from the 1970s." *Soviet Jewish Affairs* 15(2): 23–35.

Campbell, J. K. 1974. *Honour, Family and Patronage*. New York: Oxford University Press.

Clements, B. E. 1979. *Bolshevik Feminist: The Life of Alexandra Kollontai*. Bloomington: Indiana University Press.

Cohen, A. P. 1985. *The Symbolic Construction of Community*. London: Tavistock.

Conquest, R. 1968. *The Great Terror*. New York: Macmillan.

Daniels, R. 1983. "On the Comparative Study of Immigrant and Ethnic Groups in the New World." *Comparative Studies in Society and History* 25(2):401–404.

de Certeau, M. 1984. *The Practice of Everyday Life*. Berkeley: University of California Press.

DeSantis, G., and R. Benkin. 1980. "Ethnicity Without Community." *Ethnicity* 7: 137–143.

Dewey, J. 1929. *The Public and Its Problems*. New York: Holt and Sons.

Dewey, J. 1930. *Individualism Old and New*. New York: Minton, Balch.

DiFrancisco, W., and Z. Gitelman. 1984. "Soviet Political Culture and 'Covert Participation' in Policy Implementation." *American Political Science Review* 78(3): 603–621.

Dijur, I. M. 1960. "Evrei v ekonomicheskoi zhizni v Rossii." In *Kniga o russkom evreistve ot 1860-x godov do 1917,* 155–182. New York: Union of Russian Jews.

Dostoyevsky, F. M. 1973. *The Brothers Karamazov,* trans. C. Garnett. New York: Random House.

Douglas, M. 1979. *Purity and Danger*. London: Routledge and Kegan Paul.

Dublin, R. A. 1977. "Some Observations on Resettling Soviet Jews." *Journal of Jewish Communal Service* (Spring): 278–281.

Dubnow, S. M. 1916–1920. *The History of the Jews in Russia and Poland from the Earliest Times until the Present Day*. 3 vols. Philadelphia: Jewish Publication Society.

Dundes, A., ed. 1991. *The Blood Libel Legend*. Madison: University of Wisconsin Press.

Dunham, V. S. 1976. *In Stalin's Time: Middle-Class Values in Soviet Fiction*. New York: Cambridge University Press.

Dunnigan, T. 1982. "Segmentary Kinship in an Urban Society: The Hmong of St. Paul–Minneapolis." *Anthropological Quarterly* 55(3): 126–134.

Dunnigan, T., and D. P. Olney. 1985. "Hmong." In *Refugees in the United States,* ed. David W. Haines, 111–126. Westport, Conn.: Greenwood Press.

Durkheim, E. 1951. *Suicide*. New York: Free Press.

Durkheim, E. 1964. *The Division of Labor in Society*. Glencoe, Ill.: Free Press.

Ebihara, M. 1985. "Khmer." In *Refugees in the United States*, ed. David W. Haines, 127–148. Westport, Conn.: Greenwood Press.

Eisenstadt, S. N. 1954. *The Absorption of Immigrants*. London: Routledge and Kegan Paul.

Encyclopedia Judaica. 1971. Jerusalem: Macmillan.

Erikson, K. T. 1976. *Everything in Its Path*. New York: Simon and Schuster.

Ettinger, S. 1972. "The Jews in Russia at the Outbreak of the Revolution." In *The Jews in Soviet Russia Since 1917*, 2d ed., ed. L. Kochan, 14–28. London: Oxford University Press, 1972.

Fain, B., and M. F. Verbit. 1984. *Jewishness in the Soviet Union*. Jerusalem: Jerusalem Center for Public Affairs.

Fallers, L., ed. 1967. *Immigrants and Associations*. The Hague: Mouton.

Farnsworth, B. B. 1977. "Bolshevik Alternatives and the Soviet Family." In *Women in Russia*, ed. D. Atkinson, A. Dallin and G. Lapidus, 139–165. Stanford: Stanford University Press.

Federation of Jewish Philanthropies of New York. 1984. *The Jewish Population of Greater New York: A Profile*. New York: Federation of Jewish Philanthropies.

Federation of Jewish Philanthropies of New York. 1985. *Jewish Identification and Affiliation Among Soviet Jewish Immigrants in New York—A Needs Assessment and Planning Study*. New York: Federation of Jewish Philanthropies.

Fischer, C. S. 1982. *To Dwell Among Friends: Personal Networks in Town and City*. Chicago: University of Chicago Press.

Fischer, M. M. J. 1986. "Ethnicity and the Post-Modern Arts of Memory." In *Writing Culture: The Poetics and Politics of Ethnography*, ed. J. Clifford and G. E. Marcus, 194–233. Berkeley: University of California Press.

Fisher, M. 1978. "Creating Ethnic Identity: Asian Indians in the New York City Area." *Urban Anthropology* 7(3): 271–285.

Fisher, M. 1980. "Indian Ethnic Identity: The Role of Associations in the New York Indian Population." In *The New Ethnics: Asian Indians in the United States*, ed. P. Saran and E. Eames, 172–192. New York: Praeger.

Formanovskaya, N. I. 1982. *Vy Skazali Zdrastvyte!* Moscow: Izdatel'stvo "Znanie."

Freedman, R. O., ed. 1984. *Soviet Jewry in the Decisive Decade, 1971–80*. Durham: Duke University Press.

Galperin, M. D. 1988. "Soviet Jewish Émigré Adolescents' Adjustment to the United States: Comparisons with American Norms and Inter-Relationships of Parent- and Self-Reported Adolescent Psychopathology and Social Adjustment with Family Environment Factors, Parent Attitudes, and Demographics." Ph.D. diss., New York University.

Gans, H. 1962. *The Urban Villagers*. New York: Free Press.

Gans, H. 1979. "Symbolic Ethnicity: The Future of Ethnic Groups and Cultures in America." *Ethnic and Racial Studies* 2: 1–20.

Geertz, C. 1963. "The Integrative Revolution: Primordial Sentiments and Civil Politics in the New States." In *Old Societies and New States,* ed. C. Geertz, 105–157. Glencoe, Ill.: Free Press.

Geertz, C. 1973a. "The Impact of the Concept of Culture on the Concept of Man." In *The Interpretation of Cultures,* C. Geertz, 33–54. New York: Basic Books.

Geertz, C. 1973b. "Religion as a Cultural System." In *The Interpretation of Cultures,* C. Geertz, 87–125. New York: Basic Books.

Giddens, A. 1984. *The Constitution of Society*. Berkeley: University of California Press.

Gilbert, M. 1976. *The Jews of Russia: Their History in Maps and Photographs*. London: National Council for Soviet Jewry of the United Kingdom and Ireland.

Gilbert, M. 1984. *The Jews of Hope: The Plight of Soviet Jewry Today*. New York: Viking.

Gilboa, Y. 1982. *A Language Silenced: The Suppression of Hebrew Literature and Culture in the Soviet Union*. New York: Herzl Press.

Gilison, J. M. 1979. *Summary Report of the Survey of Soviet Jewish Emigres in Baltimore*. Baltimore: Baltimore Hebrew College, Center for the Study of Soviet Emigration and Resettlement.

Gilman, S. L. 1986. *Jewish Self-Hatred*. Baltimore: Johns Hopkins University Press.

Ginsburg, F., and A. L. Tsing, eds. 1990. *Uncertain Terms: Negotiating Gender in American Culture*. Boston: Beacon Press.

Gitelman, Z. 1971. *The Jewish Religion in the USSR*. New York: Synagogue Council of America.

Gitelman, Z. 1972. *Jewish Nationality and Soviet Politics: The Jewish Sections of the CPSU, 1917–1930*. Princeton: Princeton University Press.

Gitelman, Z. 1973. *Assimilation, Acculturation and National Consciousness Among Soviet Jews*. New York: Synagogue Council of America.

Gitelman, Z. 1978. "Soviet Immigrants and American Absorption Efforts: A Case Study in Detroit." *Journal of Jewish Communal Service* 55(1): 11–28.

Gitelman, Z. 1982. "Soviet Immigrant Resettlement in the United States." *Soviet Jewish Affairs* 12(2): 3–18.

Gitelman, Z. 1984. "Soviet-Jewish Immigrants to the United States: Profile,

Problems, Prospects." In *Soviet Jewry in the Decisive Decade, 1971–80*, ed. R. O. Freedman, 89–98. Durham: Duke University Press.

Gitelman, Z. 1988. *A Century of Ambivalence*. New York: Schocken Press.

Gluckman, M. 1963. "Gossip and Scandal." *Current Anthropology* 4: 307–315.

Gold, S. J. 1985. "Refugee Communities: Soviet Jews and Vietnamese in the San Francisco Bay Area." Ph.D. diss., University of California, Berkeley.

Gold, S. J. 1987. "Dealing with Frustration: A Study of Interaction Between Resettlement Staff and Refugees." In *People in Upheaval*, ed. S. Morgan and E. Colson, 108–128. New York: Center for Migration Studies.

Gold, S. J. 1992. *Refugee Communities: A Comparative Field Study*. Newberry Park, Calif.: Sage Publications.

Goldberg, B. Z. 1961. *The Jewish Problem in the Soviet Union: Analysis and Solution*. New York: Crown Publishers.

Goldstein, A. 1969. "The Fate of the Jews in German-Occupied Soviet Russia." In *Russian Jewry 1917–1967*, ed. G. Aronson et al., 88–122. New York: Thomas Yoseloff.

Goldstein, E. 1979. "Psychological Adaptations of Soviet Immigrants." *American Journal of Psychoanalysis* 39(3): 257–263.

Goncharev, I. A. 1953. *Oblomov*, trans. N. Duddington. London: J. M. Dent and Sons.

Gordon, M. M. 1964. *Assimilation in American Life*. New York: Oxford University Press.

Gray, F. D. P. 1990. *Soviet Women: Walking the Tightrope*. New York: Doubleday.

Greenberg, L. 1976. *The Jews in Russia: The Struggle for Emancipation*. 2 vols. New York: Schocken Press.

Grubel, H. B., and A. D. Scott. 1967. "Determinants of Migration: The Highly Skilled." *International Migration* 9(1–2): 5–35.

Haines, D. W. 1985. "Refugees and the Refugee Problem." In *Refugees in the United States*, ed. D. W. Haines, 3–16. Westport, Conn.: Greenwood Press.

Hannerz, U. 1969. *Soulside*. New York: Columbia University Press.

Hannerz, U. 1986. "Theory in Anthropology: Small Is Beautiful? The Problem of Complex Cultures." *Comparative Studies of Society and History* 28: 362–367.

Hawks, I. K. 1977. "The New Immigrant: A Study of the Vocational Adjustment of Soviet Jews." *Journal of Jewish Communal Service* (December): 161–165.

Holmes, C. 1991. "The Ritual Murder Association in Britain." In *The Blood Libel Legend*, ed. A. Dundes, 99–134. Madison: University of Wisconsin Press.

Howe, I. 1976. *World of Our Fathers*. New York: Simon and Schuster.

Howells, P., and M. Galperin. 1984. "Pseudo-speciation and the Soviet Jewish Immigrants." Paper presented at the Erik Erikson Conference of the Soviet-American Relationship, Esalen Institute, California, 1984.

Hubbs, J. 1988. *Mother Russia: The Feminine Myth in Russian Culture*. Bloomington: Indiana University Press.

Hulewat, P. 1981. "Dynamics of the Soviet Jewish Family: Its Impact on Clinical Practice for the Jewish Family Agency." *Journal of Jewish Communal Service* 58:53–60.

Iankova, Z. A. 1978. *Sovietskaia Zhenshchina*. Moscow: Izdatel'stvo politichesko: literatury.

Indochinese Refugee Action Center. 1981. *The Indochinese Mutual Assistance Associations: Characteristics, Composition, Capacity Building Needs, and Future Directions*. Washington, D.C.: Indochinese Refugee Center.

Inkeles, A., and R. A. Bauer. 1959. *The Soviet Citizen*. Cambridge: Harvard University Press.

Jackson, R. M. 1977. "Social Structure and Process in Friendship Choice." In *Networks and Places: Social Relations in the Urban Setting*, ed. C. S. Fischer, 59–78. New York: Free Press.

Jacobs, D. N., and E. F. Paul, eds. 1981. *Studies of the Third Wave: Recent Migrations of Soviet Jews to the United States*. Boulder: Westview Press.

Jacobson, D. 1973. *Itinerant Townsmen: Friendship and Social Order in Urban Uganda*. Menlo Park, Calif.: Cummings Publishing.

Katz, Z. 1972. "After the Six-Day War." In *The Jews in Soviet Russia Since 1917*, 2d ed., ed. L. Kochan, 321–336. London: Oxford University Press.

Kenny, M. 1962. *A Spanish Tapestry: Town and Country in Castile*. Bloomington: Indiana University Press.

Kestin, H. 1985. "Making Cheese From Snow." *Forbes,* July 29: 90–95.

Keyes, C. F. 1981. "The Dialectics of Ethnic Change." In *Ethnic Change,* ed. C. F. Keyes, 3–320. Seattle: University of Washington Press.

Kim, I. 1981. *New Urban Immigrants: The Korean Community in New York*. Princeton: Princeton University Press.

Kliger, H. 1985. "Communication and Ethnic Community: The Case of Landsmanshaftn." Ph.D. diss., University of Pennsylvania.

Kochan, L., ed. 1972. *The Jews in Soviet Russia Since 1917,* 2d ed. London: Oxford University Press.

Koenig, R. 1968. *The Community,* trans. E. Fitzgerald. London: Routledge and Kegan Paul.

Kon, I. C., ed. 1983. *Slovar' po Etike*. Moscow: Politizdat.

Korey, W. 1968. "The Legal Position of the Jewish Community of the Soviet Union." In *Ethnic Minorities in the Soviet Union,* ed. E. Goldhagen, 315–350. New York: Praeger.

Kosmin, B. 1990. *The Class of 1979: The "Acculturation" of Jewish Immigrants from the Soviet Union*. New York: Council of Jewish Federations.

Kuper, A., and J. Kuper, eds. 1985. *The Social Science Encyclopedia*. London: Routledge and Kegan Paul.

Kurganoff, I. A. 1971. *Women in the U.S.S.R.* London, Ont.: S.B.O.N.R. Publishing House.

Langer, S. K. 1951. *Philosophy in a New Key*. 2d ed. Cambridge: Harvard University Press.

Langmuir, G. I. 1991. "Thomas of Monmouth: Detector of Ritual Murder." In *The Blood Libel Legend,* ed. A. Dundes, 3–40. Madison: University of Wisconsin Press.

Lattimore, B. G., Jr. 1974. *The Assimilation of German Expellees into the West German Polity and Society Since 1945*. The Hague: Martinus Nijhoff.

Lenin, V. I. 1951. *Critical Remarks on the National Question* (originally published 1913). Moscow: Foreign Languages Publishing House.

Lestchinsky, J. 1960. "Evreiskoe naselenie rossii i evreiskii trud." In *Kniga o russkom evreistve ot 1860x godov do revolutzii 1917,* 183–206. New York: Union of Russian Jews.

Levin, N. 1988. *The Jews in the Soviet Union Since 1917: Paradox of Survival*. 2 vols. New York: New York University Press.

Lévi-Strauss, C. 1970. *The Savage Mind*. Chicago: University of Chicago Press.

Levkov, I. I. 1984. "Adaptation and Acculturation of Soviet Jews in the United States: A Preliminary Analysis." In *Soviet Jewry in the Decisive Decade, 1971–80,* ed. R. O. Freedman, 109–143. Durham: Duke University Press.

Lewin, K. 1948. "Self-Hatred Among Jews." In *Resolving Social Conflicts,* K. Lewin, 186–200. New York: Harper and Brothers.

Liegle, L. 1975. *The Family's Role in Soviet Education,* trans. S. Hecker. New York: Springer.

Limonov, E. 1982. *Eto Ia—Edichka*. 2d ed. New York: Index.

Lvavi, J. 1971. "Jewish Agricultural Settlement in the USSR." *Soviet Jewish Affairs* 1(June): 91–100.

Lyotard, J.-F. 1984. *The Postmodern Condition: A Report on Knowledge,* trans. G. Bennington and B. Massumi. Minneapolis: University of Minnesota Press.

McClellan, D., ed. 1977. *Karl Marx: Selected Writings*. Oxford: Oxford University Press.

Maine, H. J. S. 1906. *Ancient Law*. New York: Henry Holt.

Makarenko, A.S. 1967. *The Collective Family: A Handbook for Russian Parents* (originally published as *A Book for Parents,* 1937), trans. R. Daglish. Garden City, N.Y.: Anchor Books.

Marcuse, H. 1966. *Eros and Civilization*. Boston: Beacon Press.

Markowitz, F. 1986. "Soviet Jews Coming of Age in America." Paper presented at the annual meetings of the American Anthropological Association, Philadephia.

Markowitz, F. 1988a. "Jewish in the USSR, Russian in the USA." In *Persistence and Flexibility: Anthropological Studies of American Jewry,* ed. W. P. Zenner, 79–95. Albany: SUNY Press.

Markowitz, F. 1988b. "Rituals as Keys to Soviet Immigrants' Jewish Identity." In *Between Two Worlds: Ethnographic Essays on American Jewry,* ed. J. Kugelmass, 128–147. Ithaca: Cornell University Press.

Markowitz, F. 1990. "Responding to Events from Afar: Soviet Jewish Refugees Reassess Their Identity." Paper presented at the annual meetings of the American Anthropological Association, New Orleans.

Markowitz, F. 1991a. "The Not Lost Generation: Family Dynamics and Ethnic Identity Among Soviet Adolescent Immigrants of the 1970s." Paper presented at the Wilstein Institute for Jewish Policy Studies Conference, Soviet Jewish Acculturation—Beyond Resettlement, Palo Alto, California.

Markowitz, F. 1991b. "Striving for Femininity: Soviet Un-Feminism." Paper presented at the annual meetings of the American Anthropological Association, Chicago.

Markowitz, F. 1992. "Community Without Organizations." *City and Society* (December).

Markus, R. L. 1979. *Adaptation: A Case Study of Soviet Jewish Immigrant Children in Toronto, 1970–1978.* Toronto: Permanent Press.

Martynova, E. I. 1983. *Formirovanie Dukhovnogo Mira Sovietskoi Zhenshchiny.* Krasoiarsk: Krasnoiarskoe knizhnoe izdatel'stvo.

Marx, K. 1975. *A World Without Jews* (reprint and translation of the 1843 essays, "On the Jewish Question"). New York: Philosophical Library.

Mauss, M. 1967. *The Gift,* trans. I. Cunnison. New York: W. W. Norton.

Mead, G. H. 1962. *Mind, Self and Society.* Chicago: University of Chicago Press.

Mead, M. 1955. *Soviet Attitudes Toward Authority.* New York: William Morrow.

Mehnert, K. 1961. *The Anatomy of Soviet Man.* London: Weidenfeld and Nicolson.

Menashe, L. 1985. "The New Wave From Russia." *New York Times Magazine* (May 5): 58–73ff.

Merry, S. E. 1981. *Urban Danger: Life in a Neighborhood of Strangers.* Philadelphia: Temple University Press.

Miller, W. W. 1961. *Russians as People.* New York: E. P. Dutton.

Miner, H. 1965. *The Primitive City of Timbuktoo.* New York: Anchor Books.

Molière, J. B. P. 1978. *Tartuffe* (originally published in 1669), in *Four Comedies,* trans. R. Wilbur, 301–470. New York: Harcourt Brace Jovanovich.

Monteo, D. 1979. *Vietnamese Americans: Patterns of Resettlement and Socio-economic Adaptation in the United States*. Boulder: Westview.

Murphy, Y., and R. Murphy. 1985. *Women of the Forest*. 2d ed. New York: Columbia University Press.

Myerhoff, B. 1975. "Organization and Ecstacy: Deliberate and Accidental Communitas among Huichol Indians and American Youth." In *Symbol and Politics in Communal Ideology,* ed. S. F. Moore and Barbara G. Myerhoff, 33–67. Ithaca: Cornell University Press.

Myerhoff, B. 1978. *Number Our Days*. New York: Simon and Schuster.

Nisbet, R. 1969. *Quest for Community*. 2d ed. New York: Oxford University Press.

Noonan, L. 1988. "Russians Go Republican." *Jewish Journal* (November 18–24): 31.

Nove, A., and J. A. Newth. 1972. "The Jewish Population: Demographic Trends and Occupational Patterns." In *The Jews in the Soviet Union Since 1917,* 2d ed., ed. L. Kochan, 125–158. London: Oxford University Press.

Orleck, A. 1987. "The Soviet Jews: Life in Brighton Beach, Brooklyn." In *New Immigrants in New York,* ed. N. Foner, 273–304. New York: Columbia University Press.

Ortner, S. B. 1978. *Sherpas Through Their Rituals*. Cambridge: Cambridge University Press.

Ortner, S. B. 1989. "Categories of Un-Modernity: Community." Paper presented at the annual meetings of the American Anthropological Association, Washington, D.C.

Ortner, S., and H. Whitehead, eds. 1981. *Sexual Meanings*. Cambridge: Cambridge University Press.

Pannish, P. 1981. *Exit Visa: The Emigration of the Soviet Jews*. New York: Coward, McCann and Geoghegan.

Pattie, S. P. 1989. "Faith in History: Armenians Rebuilding Community in Cyprus and London." Ph.D. diss., University of Michigan.

Pearson, L. 1990. *Children of Glasnost: Growing Up Soviet*. Seattle: University of Washington Press.

Pedraza-Bailey, S. 1985. *Political and Economic Migrants in America: Cubans and Mexicans*. Austin: University of Texas Press.

Peterson, W. 1964. *The Politics of Population*. Garden City, N.Y.: Doubleday.

Pinkus, Benjamin. 1988. *The Jews of the Soviet Union*. Cambridge: Cambridge University Press.

Pipes, R. 1961. "The Historical Evolution of the Russian Intelligentsia." In *The Russian Intelligentsia,* ed. R. Pipes, 47–62. New York: Columbia University Press.

Pisarowicz, J. A., and V. Tosher. 1982. "Vietnamese Refugee Resettlement:

Denver, Colorado, 1975–1977." In *Involuntary Migration and Resettlement,* 69–81. Boulder: Westview.

Portes, A., and R. L. Bach. 1985. *Latin Journey: Cuban and Mexican Immigrants in the United States.* Berkeley: University of California Press.

Rappaport, E. A. 1991. "The Ritual Murder Accusation: The Persistence of Doubt and the Repetition Compulsion." In *The Blood Libel Legend,* ed. A. Dundes, 304–335. Madison: University of Wisconsin Press.

Redfield, R. 1973. *The Little Community.* Chicago: University of Chicago Press.

Reichlin, I. 1983. "Russian Neighbors: News or Nuisance?" M.A. thesis, Columbia University, School of Journalism.

Reiter, R. R., ed. 1975. *Toward an Anthropology of Women.* New York: Monthly Review Press.

Richardson, A. 1967. "A Theory and a Method for the Psychological Study of Assimilation." *International Migration Review* 2(4): 3–30.

Richmond, A. H. 1974. *Aspects of the Absorption and Adaptation of Immigrants.* Ottawa: Canadian Immigration and Population Study.

Richmond, A. H. 1981. "Immigrant Adaptation in a Post Industrial Society." In *Global Trends in Migration,* ed. M. Kritz, C. Keely, and S. Tomasi, 298–319. New York: Center for Migration Studies.

Riesman, David. 1950. *The Lonely Crowd.* New Haven: Yale University Press.

Ripp, V. 1984. *From Moscow to Main Street: Among the Russian Émigrés.* Boston: Little, Brown.

Rogg, E. 1971. "The Influence of a Strong Refugee Community on the Economic Adjustment of Its Members." *International Migration Review* 5(4): 474–481.

Rosaldo, M. Z., and L. Lamphere, eds. 1974. *Women, Culture, and Society.* Stanford: Stanford University Press.

Rosenham, M. S. 1977. "Images of Male and Female in Children's Readers." In *Women in Russia,* ed. D. Atkinson, A. Dallin, and G. W. Lapidus, 293–305. Stanford: Stanford University Press.

Rosner, L. S. 1986. *The Soviet Way of Crime.* South Hadley, Mass.: Bergin and Garvey.

Rothchild, S. 1985. *A Special Legacy: An Oral History of Soviet Jewish Emigres in the United States.* New York: Simon and Schuster.

Rozenblum, S.-A. 1982. *Etre Juif en U.R.S.S.* Paris: Collection de la R.P.S.

Rubin, B. S. 1975. "The Soviet Refugee: Challenge to the American Community Resettlement System." *Journal of Jewish Communal Service* (December): 195–201.

Rydanova, I. I. 1982. *Semia i Mir Prekrasnogo.* Minsk: Narodnaia Asveta.

Schechtman, J. 1969. "Soviet Russia, Zionism and Israel." In *Russian Jewry 1917–1967,* ed. G. Aronson et al., 406–443. New York: Thomas Yoseloff.

Scherer, J. 1972. *Contemporary Community: Sociological Illusion or Reality?* London: Tavistock.

Schneider, D. 1980. *American Kinship: A Cultural Account.* 2d ed. Chicago: University of Chicago Press.

Schwarz, S. M. 1972. *The Jews in the Soviet Union.* 2d ed. New York: Arno Press.

Shanin, T. 1972. *The Awkward Class: Political Sociology of Peasantry in a Developing Society: Russia 1910–1925.* Oxford: Clarendon Press.

Shapiro, L. 1969. "Russian Jewry After Stalin." In *Russian Jewry 1917–1967,* ed. G. Aronson et al., 444–502. New York: Thomas Yoseloff.

Shils, E. 1957. "Primordial, Personal, Sacred and Civil Ties." *British Journal of Sociology* (June): 130–145.

Shipler, D. K. 1984. *Russia: Broken Idols, Solemn Dreams.* New York: Penguin Books.

Shlapentokh, V. 1984. *Love, Marriage and Friendship in the Soviet Union: Ideals and Practices.* New York: Praeger.

Shlapentokh, V. 1989. *Public and Private Life of the Soviet People.* New York: Oxford University Press.

Shokeid, M. 1988. *Children of Circumstances.* Ithaca: Cornell University Press.

Silberman, C. E. 1985. *A Certain People: American Jews and Their Lives Today.* New York: Summit Books.

Silverman, S. 1984. "Toward an Anthropology of Urbanism: The View from the Village (Italy)." In *Culture and Community in Europe,* ed. O. Lynch, 13–35. Delhi: Hindustan Publishing.

Simić, A. 1973. *The Peasant Urbanites.* New York: Seminar Press.

Simmel, G. 1950a. "The Metropolis and Mental Life." In *The Sociology of Georg Simmel,* ed. K. H. Wolff, 409–424. Glencoe, Ill.: Free Press.

Simmel, G. 1950b. "The Stranger." In *The Sociology of Georg Simmel,* ed. K. H. Wolff, 402–408. Glencoe, Ill.: Free Press.

Simmel, G. 1978. *The Philosophy of Money.* London: Routledge and Kegan Paul.

Simon, R. J. 1983. "The Jewish Identity of Soviet Immigrant Parents and Children." In *Culture, Ethnicity, and Identity,* ed. W. McCreedy, 327–339. New York: Academic Press.

Simon, R. J., ed. 1985. *New Lives: The Adjustment of Soviet Jewish Immigrants in the United States and Israel.* Lexington: Lexington Books.

Simon, R. J., and M. Brooks. 1983. "Soviet Jewish Immigrants' Adjustment in Four United States Cities." *Journal of Jewish Communal Service* (Fall): 56–64.

Simon, R. J., L. Shelley, and P. Schneiderman. 1986. "The Social and Economic Adjustment of Soviet Jewish Women in the United States." In *International Migration: The Female Experience*, ed. R. J. Simon and C. B. Brettell, 76–94. Totowa, N.J.: Rowman and Allanheld.

Simon, R. J., and J. L. Simon. 1982. *The Soviet Jews' Adjustment to the United States*. New York: Council of Jewish Federations.

Smith, H. 1976. *The Russians*. New York: Ballantine Books.

Smolar, B. 1971. *Soviet Jewry Today and Tomorrow*. New York: Macmillan.

Sokolov, R. 1983. "Tashkent on the Subway." *Natural History* (May): 92–96.

Spicer, E. H. 1980. *The Yaquis: A Cultural History*. Tucson: University of Arizona Press.

Spiro, M. 1981. *Kibbutz*, augmented ed. Cambridge: Harvard University Press.

Srole, L., and A. K. Fischer. 1978. *Mental Health in the Metropolis: The Midtown Manhattan Study*. New York: New York University Press.

Stack, C. B. 1974. *All Our Kin: Strategies for Survival in a Black Community*. New York: Harper and Row.

Stalin, J. 1975. *Marxism and the National-Colonial Question* (originally published 1913). San Francisco: Proletarian Publishers.

Steinfirst, J. F. 1980. "The New Russian Jewish Immigrant: Acculturation, Sociological and Mental Health Issues." Paper presented at the American Association of Psychiatric Services for Children annual meeting, New Orleans.

Suttles, G. 1972. *The Social Construction of Communities*. Chicago: University of Chicago Press.

Toennies, F. 1957. *Community and Society*, trans. and ed. C. Loomis, 247–259. East Lansing: Michigan State University Press.

Turner, V. 1969. *The Ritual Process: Structure and Anti-Structure*. Chicago: Aldine.

Tyhurst, L. 1977. "Psychosocial First Aid for Refugees: An Essay in Social Psychiatry." *Mental Health and Society* 4: 319–343.

Tyler, S. A. 1986. "Post-Modern Ethnography: From Document of the Occult to Occult Document." In *Writing Culture: The Poetics and Politics of Ethnography*, ed. J. Clifford and G. E. Marcus, 122–140. Berkeley: University of California Press.

United States Bureau of the Census. 1980. *Census of Population and Housing, 1980 United States*. Washington, D.C.: Bureau of the Census.

Van Esterick, J. L. 1985. "Lao." In *Refugees in the United States*, ed. D. W. Haines, 146–166. Westport, Conn.: Greenwood Press.

Weber, M. 1958. *The City*, trans. and ed. D. Martindale and G. Neuwirth. Glencoe, Ill.: Free Press.

Weinryb, B. 1972. "Antisemitism in Soviet Russia." In *The Jews in Soviet Russia Since 1917,* 2d ed., ed. L. Kochan, 288–330. London: Oxford University Press.

Wellman, B. 1979. "The Community Question: The Intimate Network of East Yorkers." *American Journal of Sociology* 84(5): 1201–1231.

Wheatley, P. 1969. *The City as Symbol.* An Inaugural Lecture Delivered at University College, London 20 Nov. 1967. London: H. K. Lewis.

Wiesel, E. 1966. *The Jews of Silence.* New York: Holt, Rinehart and Winston.

Wireman, P. 1984. *Urban Neighborhoods, Networks, and Families.* Lexington: Lexington Books.

Wirth, L. 1938. "Urbanism as a Way of Life." *American Journal of Sociology* 44: 1–24.

Yee, L. 1982. "Interpersonal Interactions Among Foreign- and American-Born Chinese." In *Ethnicity and Interpersonal Interaction: A Cross-Cultural Study,* ed. D. Y. H. Wu, 237–253. Singapore: Maruzen Asia.

Yuan, D. Y. 1970. "Voluntary Segregation: A Study of New York Chinatown." In *Minority Responses: Comparative Views of Research in Subordination,* ed. M. Kurokawa, 134–144. New York: Random House.

Zadrozny, J. T. 1959. *Dictionary of Social Sciences.* Washington, D.C.: Public Affairs Press.

Zaslavsky, V., and R. J. Brym. 1983. *Soviet-Jewish Emigration and Soviet Nationality Policy.* New York: St. Martin's Press.

Zborowski, M., and E. Herzog. 1952. *Life Is With People.* New York: International Universities Press.

Zenner, W. P. 1977. "Lachrymosity: A Cultural Reinforcement of Minority Status." *Ethnicity* 4: 156–166.

Zwingmann, C., and M. Pfister-Ammende. 1973. *Uprooting and After.* New York: Springer Verlag.